NEET (UG)

Handwritten Notes

Biology

ENRICHED WITH

Memory Tricks • NEET Synapse

NEET (UG)

Handwritten Notes

Biology

ENRICHED WITH

Memory Tricks • NEET Synapse

Dr. Archi Maheshwari

BDS

ARIHANT PRAKASHAN (Series), MEERUT

卐 Administrative & Production Offices

Regd. Office

'Ramchhaya' 4577/15, Agarwal Road, Darya Ganj, New Delhi -110002
Tele: 011- 47630600, 43518550

卐 Head Office

Kalindi, TP Nagar, Meerut (UP) - 250002
Tel: 0121-7156203, 7156204

卐 Sales & Support Offices

Agra, Ahmedabad, Bengaluru, Bareilly, Chennai, Delhi, Guwahati, Hyderabad, Jaipur, Jhansi, Kolkata, Lucknow, Nagpur & Pune.

卐 **PRICE** ₹385.00

卐 **PO No. :** TXT-59-T069523-2-26

Published by Arihant Publications (India) Ltd.

For further information about the books published by Arihant, log on to www.arihantbooks.com or e-mail at info@arihantbooks.com

Follow us on   

Preface...

A Word for Aspiring NEET Scholars

First of all, congratulations on starting one of the most challenging and rewarding journeys of your life—the preparation for **NEET (National Eligibility cum Entrance Test)**. The path ahead may seem difficult, but remember, it is also full of chances for learning and personal growth..

These **handwritten notes** have been crafted with the aim to guide you through the vast and intricate landscape of Biology, one of the most fundamental and most important subjects in the NEET syllabus. As someone who has been through the rigorous grind of NEET before, I understand the importance of clarity, simplicity, and conceptual depth when it comes to mastering Biology. This is exactly what I've tried to bring into these notes.

The notes are designed to help you develop a deep understanding of core concepts, which is crucial for tackling the application-based questions often found in NEET.   I have tried a different approach with dividing each topic into digestible segments that you can easily comprehend and retain.

The Features like **NEET Synapse**, will help you build a strong foundation while keeping the subject engaging.

Remember, success in NEET is not about rote learning or memorising facts. It's about developing a clear understanding and applying it in innovative ways. These notes are not just a tool to help you study; they are meant to be a companion in your journey, designed to build your problem-solving skills and foster a deeper connection with the subject.

I encourage you to go through these notes with patience, consistency and an open mind. Don't hesitate to revisit any topic as many times as necessary. Believe in yourself, stay focused, and keep pushing forward. With the right approach, hard work, and these notes in hand, you are well on your way to achieving your NEET goals.

Best wishes for your preparation. May you achieve all the success you aim for!

Dr. Archi Maheshwari
BDS

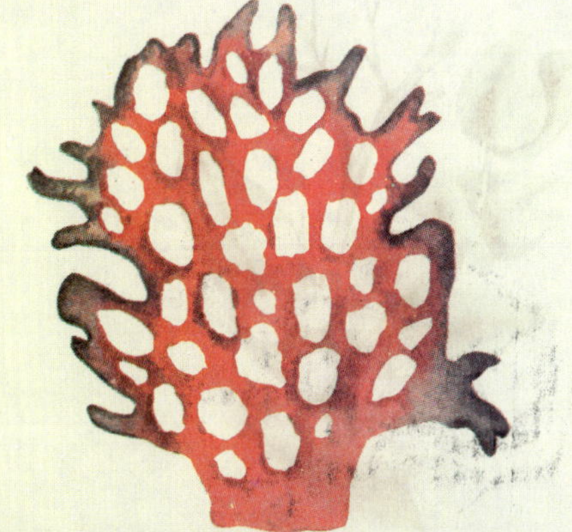

Key Features

Memory Tricks

Special trick or Mnemonics to memorise concept easily

- Reproduction-
  - Vegetative - fragmentation
  - Asexual - zoospores formed in zoosporangia
  - Sexual - isogamous, anisogamous & oogamous.
- Examples - (Memory trick) CCSUV
  - Chara, Chlamydomonas, Spirogyra, Ulothrix, Volvox.

Phaeophyceae

- Habitat - mostly marine; cold water dwelling except Sargassum
- Thallus - immobile & multicellular.
  - simple branched filamentous - Ectocarpus
  - profusely branched (Kelps) - Macrocystis (largest)
- Cell wall - cellulose, pectose, algin (gelatinous coating)

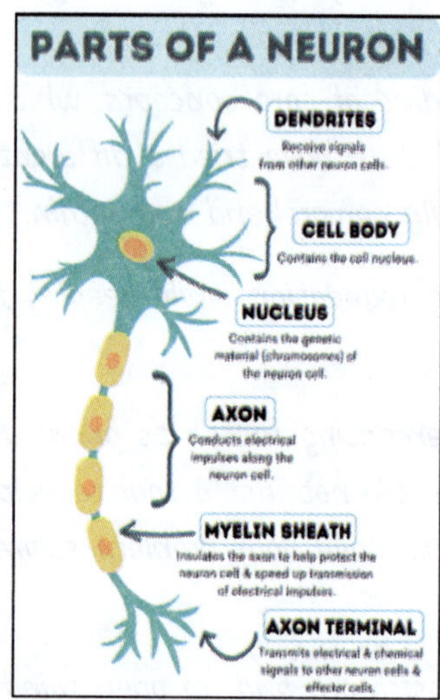

Detailed Diagram

Detailed diagram with merged theory for in depth conceptual understanding.

NEET Synapse

Specialised Tips & conceptual Info most Important from NEET preparation prospective

NEET SYNAPSE

Characteristic features do not define a living organism. For eg - movement. Some living organisms may not carry out any movement (in case of injury etc), yet they are considered living because metabolism (defining feature) is active.

Contents

1. The Living World	1-5
2. Biological Classification	6-16
3. Plant Kingdom	17-27
4. Animal Kingdom	28-42
5. Morphology of Flowering Plants	43-56
6. Anatomy of Flowering Plants	57-63
7. Structural Organisation in Animals	64-75
8. Cell : The Unit of Life	76-86
9. Biomolecules	87-102
10. Cell Cycle and Cell Division	103-110
11. Photosynthesis	111-122
12. Respiration in Plants	123-130
13. Plant Growth and Development	131-141
14. Breathing and Exchange of Gases	142-149
15. Body Fluids and Circulation	150-159
16. Excretory Products and their Elimination	160-168
17. Locomotion and Movement	169-180
18. Neual Control and Coordination	181-189

19. *Chemical Coordination and Integration*	190-200
20. *Sexual Reproduction in Flowering Plants*	201-214
21. *Human Reproduction*	215-233
22. *Reproductive Health*	234-241
23. *Principle of Inheritance and Variations*	242-258
24. *Molecular Basis of Inheritance*	259-274
25. *Evolution*	275-287
26. *Human Health and Diseases*	288-299
27. *Microbes in Human Welfare*	300-304
28. *Biotechnology : Principles & Processes*	305-312
29. *Biotechnology and its Applications*	313-320
30. *Organisms and Population*	321-327
31. *Ecosystem*	328-333
32. *Biodiversity and Conservation*	334-339

1. The Living World

- Living organisms are found everywhere on earth.
- Habitats of living organisms include -
  - Fresh water lakes
  - Deciduous forests
  - Deserts
  - Deep oceans
  - Cold mountains
  - Hot springs

  (Deep oceans, Cold mountains, Hot springs } Extreme living conditions)

Defining features of living organisms

- Features exhibited by all organisms without exception.

Metabolism Cata + Ana Breakdown Make up	Sum total of all chemical reactions in body CATABOLISM → ← ANABOLISM
Cellular organisation	All living beings are made up of cells - either single or aggregates.
Response to stimulus.	This is called consciousness. All organisms respond to their surroundings. Eg. Photosynthesis is affected by intensity & duration of light.

NEET SYNAPSE

Self consciousness is a characteristic feature of humans. It means awareness of self.
When a person is in coma, he/she is not self conscious but metabolism is going on, hence he/she is considered alive.

Characteristic features of living organisms

- These features are generally exhibited by living organisms.

  Eg. Growth, reproduction, respiration, excretion etc.

NEET SYNAPSE

Characteristic features do not define a living organism. For eg - movement. Some living organisms may not carry out any movement (in case of injury etc.), yet they are considered living because metabolism (defining feature) is active.

GROWTH

Intrinsic / Internal growth

- Takes place in living organisms
- Involves cell enlargment & cell division.

Growth in animal (Definite)

Growth in plants (Indefinite)

Extrinsic / External growth

- Occurs in non living systems.
- Involves accretion (accumulation of materials on surface)

Growth of sand dunes (accretion)

Growth of stones (accretion)

- In unicellular organisms ➡ cell division = reproduction

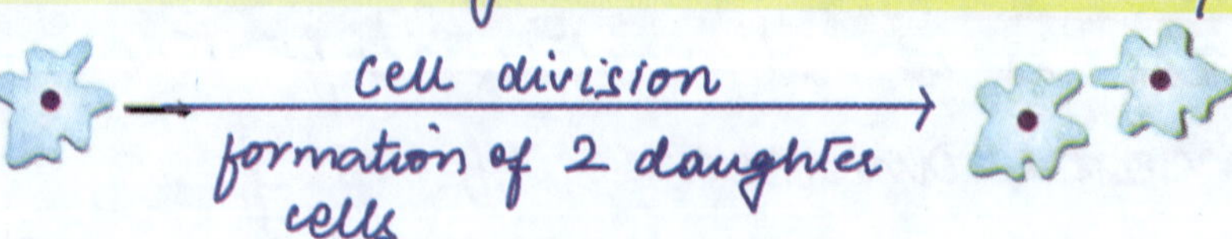

REPRODUCTION

- When parents give rise to offsprings, it is called reproduction (to produce again)
- There are 2 types of reproduction –

Asexual reproduction	Sexual reproduction
- Single parent gives rise to progeny	- Two parents give rise to progeny
- Progeny is identical to parents.	- Progeny is similar to both parents
- Offsprings are called clones	- Fusion of gametes takes place

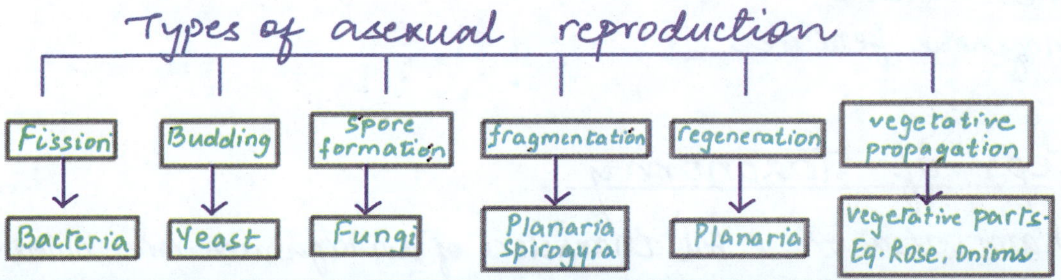

NEET SYNAPSE

Reproduction is necessary to prevent a species from extinction. It is not necessary for survival of an individual

- Mule = Female horse (mare) × male donkey
  - ↳ sterile - cannot produce offsprings.
  - ↳ no reproduction, yet living

∴ Reproduction is not a defining feature of living organisms.

DIVERSITY IN THE LIVING WORLD

- Biodiversity (Bios - living ; Diversity - variety)
- Variety of living organisms on earth
- Includes organisms like animals, plants, fungi, bacteria etc.
- About 1·7 - 1·8 million species are known to exist on earth.

TAXONOMY

(Taxis - arrangement ; nomos - law)

- Taxonomy includes identification, nomenclature and classification of organisms.

Basis of taxonomy

a) Morphological features — External appearance of an organism
b) Anatomical features — Internal structure of the body.
c) Physiological features — Functions carried out by different organs
d) Genetic traits — Study of inherited traits
e) Phylogenetic features — Evolutionary relationships.

Steps of Taxonomy

1. **Characterisation** - All characters of an organism are noted.
2. **Identification** - To identify similarities & dissimilarities with already identified organisms.
3. **Classification** - Arrangement of organisms on the basis of their features as mentioned in basis of taxonomy.
4. **Nomenclature** - It is the process of naming organisms.

Problem
↓
- known by multiple names in different regions → makes identification difficult.
- Eg: Vernacular / regional names.

potato 'aalu' batata.

Solution
- Single, standardised name, that makes identification easy throughout the world.

Solanum tuberosum

(standardised name)
Scientific name
Universal - remain same throughout the world.

- The organisations that provide scientific names are

  ICBN - International code of Botanical Nomenclature
  ICZN - International code of Zoological Nomenclature
  ICVN - International code of Viral Nomenclature
  ICNB - International code of Nomenclature of Bacteria.

BINOMIAL SYSTEM OF NOMENCLATURE

- Given by Carolus Linnaeus
- According to this system, the scientific name of organism consists of two (bi) parts. (Nomial - names)

Generic name	Specific epithet
• First part	• Second part
• Represents genus	• Represents species

Epithet describes the features of species

RULES OF BINOMIAL NOMENCLATURE

- Generic name starts with capital letter.
- Species name starts with small letter.
- All names are derived from Latin language
- All names are written in Italics if printed, and if handwritten, they are underlined
- Name of author is written after species name as an abbreviation and is not underlined

Eg. Pisum sativum Linn
Genus Species Scientist name

2. Biological Classification

- Categorisation and organisation of living organisms into groups & sub groups is called biological classification.

- **Aristotle's classification** – First scientific classification
  - ↳ Plants — Based on morphological characters — Herbs, Shrubs, Trees
  - ↳ Animals — Based on presence or absence of RBCs — Anaima (without RBC), Enaima (with RBC)

- **Two Kingdom classification** Carolus Linnaeus
  - Plantae (cell wall +nt) Bacteria, fungi, chrysophytes, ferns, gymnosperms, angiosperms.
  - Animalia (cell wall -nt) Protozoans, insects & other invertebrates; vertebrates

Drawbacks – System did not distinguish between
- Prokaryotes & eukaryotes – bacteria & fungi kept together
- Unicellular & multicellular – Chlamydomonas, Spirogyra & algae
- Autotrophic & heterotrophic – plants & fungi kept together.

- **Three Kingdom classification** Ernst Haeckel

  Plantae Animalia Protista

  – Algae, fungi, protozoa, bacteria

- **Four Kingdom classification** Copeland

  Plantae Animalia Protista Monera (bacteria)

- **Five Kingdom Classification** — R.H. Whittaker

Plantae Animalia Fungi Protista Monera

- **Six Kingdom Classification** — Carl Woese — **Three Domain Classification**

Archaea → ① Archaea

Bacteria → ② Bacteria

Eukarya → ③ Plantae, ④ Animalia, ⑤ Fungi, ⑥ Protista

NEET SYNAPSE

Three domain classification was based on rRNA sequences (16S rRNA genes).

FIVE KINGDOM CLASSIFICATION

- Criteria for classification
  - Complexity of cell structure - prokaryotic / eukaryotic
  - Complexity of body structure - unicellular / multicellular
  - Mode of nutrition - autotrophic / heterotrophic
  - Reproduction - Asexual / Sexual
  - Phylogenetic (evolutionary) relationships

Characteristics	Monera	Protista	Fungi	Plantae	Animalia
Cell Type	Unicellular, Prokaryotic.	Unicellular, Eukaryotic.	Multicellular, Non-green and Eukaryotic.	Multicellular, Eukaryotic.	Multicellular, Eukaryotic.
Nucleus	Absent	Present	Present	Present	Present
Body Organisation	Cellular Level of Organisation	Cellular Level of Organisation	Multicellular with loose tissue.	Tissue Level & Organ Level.	Tissue, organ and organ system
Mode of Nutrition	Auto (or) Heterotrophic	Auto (or) Heterotrophic	Saprophytic, Parasitic some time symbiotic	Autotrophic	Heterotrophic
Example	Bacteria and Blue green algae	Spirogyra and Chlamydomonas	Rhizopus and Agaricus	Herb, Shrub and Trees.	Fish, Frog, Crocodile, Birds and human being.

multicellular eukaryotes

Plantae (auto) Fungi (hetero) Animalia (hetero)

Protista (auto + hetero) — unicellular eukaryotes

Monera (auto + hetero) — unicellular prokaryotes

Drawbacks

- No place for acellular virus or viroids and lichens
- Some algae kept under protista. eg: Chlamydomonas

KINGDOM MONERA

- Main members - bacteria ; most abundant organisms
- Ubiquitous / Cosmopolitan / Omnipresent - present everywhere
- Mode of nutrition

Autotrophic
- Chemosynthetic — Eg. Purple sulphur bacteria
- Photosynthetic — Eg. Cyanobacteria

Heterotrophic
- Parasitic — obtain nutrition from host body
- Saprophytic — obtain nutrition from dead & decaying bodies.
- Symbiotic — Bacteria & other organism in mutually beneficial relationship

Classification based on shape

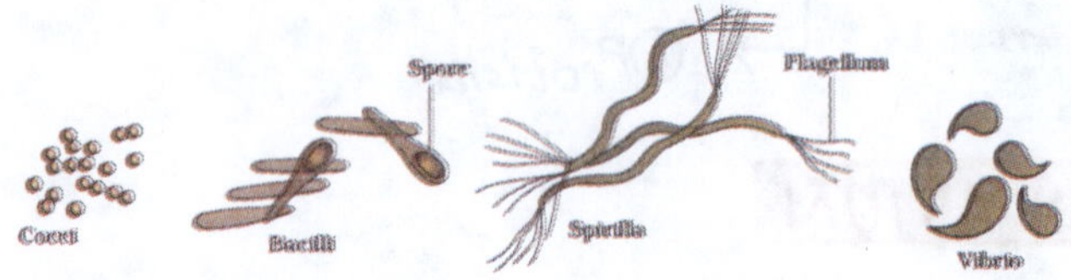

Classification based on features

Archaebacteria
- Most primitive
- Extremophiles - due to cell wall composition.
- Halophiles - saline enviroment
- Acidophiles - acidic conditions
- Thermophiles - high temperature
- Methanogens - release methane in the gut of ruminant animals.

Eubacteria
- True bacteria
- Cell wall made of peptidoglycan
- If motile - flagellum present.
- Gram +ve - stained with gram stain
- Gram -ve - not stained with gram stain
- Aerobic - grow in presence of O_2
- Anaerobic - grow in absence of O_2

Reproduction in bacteria

- Asexual - Binary fission → (Method of reproduction in most bacteria)

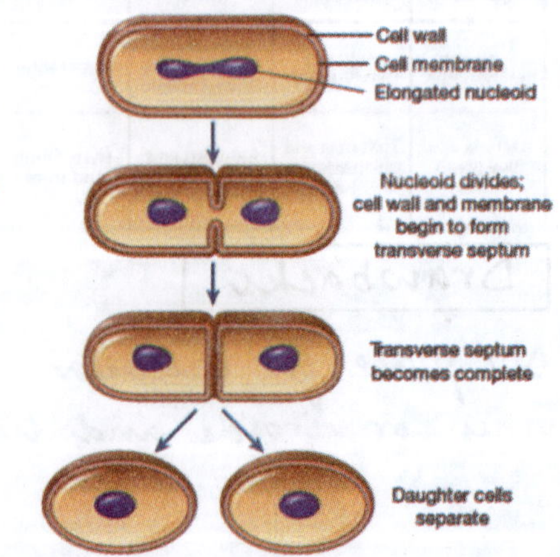

- Sexual
  - Conjugation
  - Transformation
  - Transduction

Cyanobacteria

- Also called blue green algae
- Unicellular - Spirulina
- Filamentous - Nostoc
- Colonial - Anabaena
- Photosynthetic autotrophs
- Reproduce asexually
- Heterocysts are present
  ↳ N_2 fixation takes place here

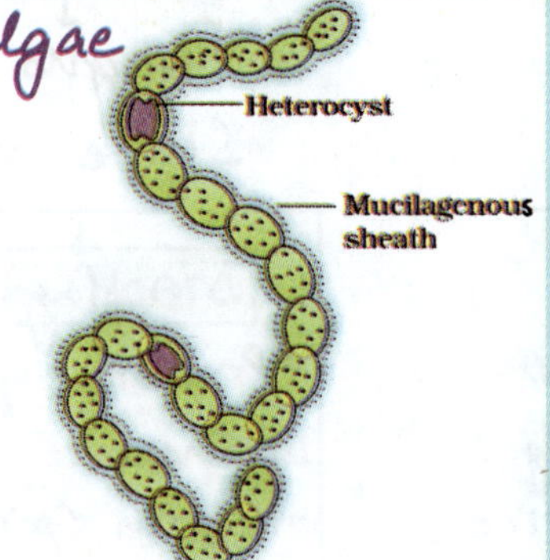

Nostoc

Heterocyst
- responsible for fixing atmospheric nitrogen.
- Lacks photosynthetic apparatus

Mucilagenous sheath
- responsible for protection and delaying dessication.

Mycoplasma

- PPLO - Pleuro Pneumonia like organisms
- Lack cell wall - no rigid shape - called
- Smallest organisms - 0.2 - 0.3 μm
- Can survive without oxygen
- Pathogenic to animals & plants.
- Also called Jokers of plant kingdom

NEET SYNAPSE

Cyanobacteria are
- Abundantly found in paddy fields
- Form Symbiotic association with roots of Cycas

KINGDOM PROTISTA

- Members are unicellular & eukaryotic
- Habitat - mostly aquatic
- Possess well defined nucleus & membrane bound organelles.
- Locomotion through - flagella, cilia, pseudopodia
- Reproduction - asexual & sexual
- Modes of nutrition -
  - Holophytic - by photosynthesis - Diatoms, dinoflagellates, euglenoids.
  - Holozoic - ingestion of solid food particles with internal digestion
    Eg: Amoeba & Paramoecium
  - Saprophytic - feeding on dead & decaying matter. Eg: Slime moulds
  - Parasitic - obtain nutrition from another organism (host).
    Eg: Plasmodium, Trypanosoma

Classification of Protists

– Protista is considered as a heterogenous kingdom

- Plant like
- Fungus like – Slime moulds
- Animal like – Protozoa

Chrysophytes

- Diatoms & Desmids
- Desmids - golden algae
- Freshwater & marine
- Microscopic - phytoplankton
- Float on water surface
- Diatoms are indestructible
- Cell wall contains silica
  - Two overlapping halves that fit together like two lids of soap box
- Diatomaceous earth - silicious shells that pile up under the sea.
- Diatomaceous earth uses -
  - Filters in brewing industry
  - Sugarcane refineries
  - Polishing of metals
  - Filtration of oils & syrups.
- Reproduction - asexual & sexual
- Chief producers of ocean - significant contribution to global photosynthesis

Dinoflagellates

- Presence of 2 flagella
  1-transverse, 1-longitudinal → help in spinning motion
- Mostly marine
- Microscopic
- Can appear yellow, green, brown, blue.
- Cell wall made of plates of cellulose.
- Groove is present in between plates - it lodges transverse flagellum
- Some dinoflagellates are bioluminiscent - emit light; Eg. Noctiluca, Gonyaulax

Red tide - Gonyaulax multiply rapidly & cover the surface of sea, making sea water appear red

Red sea - is red because of overgrowth of algae called Trichodesmium

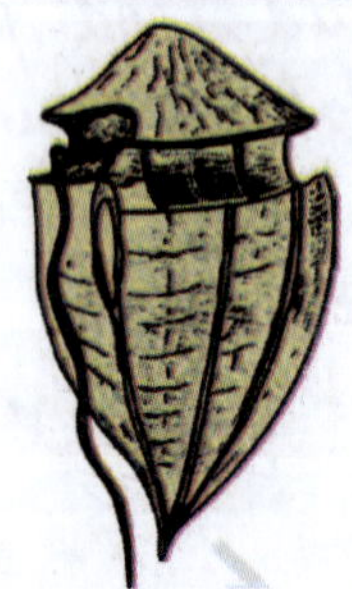

Euglenoids

- Link b/w plants & animals
- Mostly freshwater
- Cell wall absent.
- Pellicle surrounds cell.
  - made of lipoprotein
  - flexible
  - protects cell membrane
  - provides support to cell
- Presence of 2 flagella
  1-long ; 1-short
- Flagella help in locomotion
- Contractile vacuole is present - helps in excretion & osmoregulation
- Nutrition - Mixotrophic - autotrophic + heterotrophic
  Eg. Euglena with Holozoic as well as Saprophytic nutrition
- Reproduction - Longitudinal binary fission - Euglena

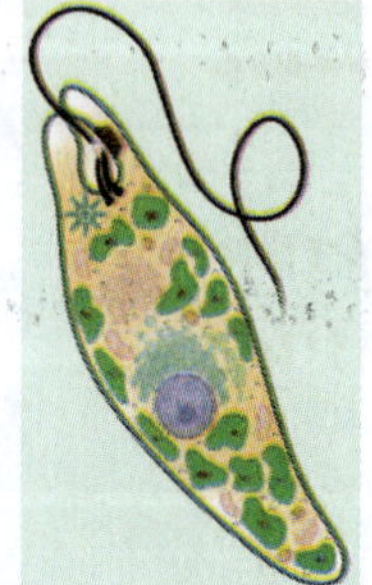

Slime moulds

- Habitat - warm & moist places
- Fungus like protists
- Saprophytic nutrition
- Plasmodium - aggregation formed during favourable conditions.
- It grows and spreads several feet appearing multinucleate
- During unfavourable conditions - it gives out fruiting bodies.
- They bear spores at tips
  Spores have a cell wall → resistant to adverse conditions → survive for many years
- Dispersal of spores takes place through air currents.

Protozoa

- Animal like protists
- Proto - first ; zoa - animals
- Motile due to presence of locomotory structures - cilia, flagella etc.
- Nutrition - holozoic / parasitic
- Classification of protozoans
- Amoeboid - marine, freshwater, terrestrial
  (Amoeba) - possess pseudopodia
  - marine forms have silica shells
- Flagellated - parasitic or free living
  (Trypanosoma) - possess flagella
- Ciliated - - possess cilia
  (Paramoecium) - gullet for ingestion
- Sporozoans - all endoparasites
  (Plasmodium) infectious stage - spore

KINGDOM FUNGI

- All members are eukaryotic, heterotrophic & non vascular
- Cosmopolitan ; Mostly terrestrial, few forms aquatic
- Bodies are haploid (n) and thalloid (thallus like)
- Thallus → Unicellular → Yeast.
  → Filamentous → most fungi
- Mycelium makes up thallus. Hyphae make up mycelium.
- Hyphae - long filamentous thread like structures.

↳ Septate - contain cross walls & are uninucleate
Eg. Ascomycetes

↳ Aseptate - no cross walls → hence continuous & multinucleate (coenocytic)
Eg. Phycomycetes

- Cell walls made of chitin

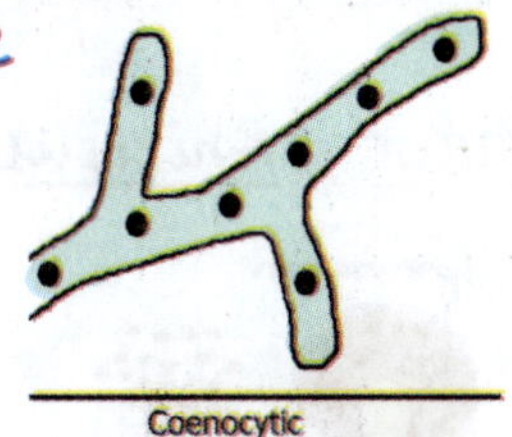
Coenocytic

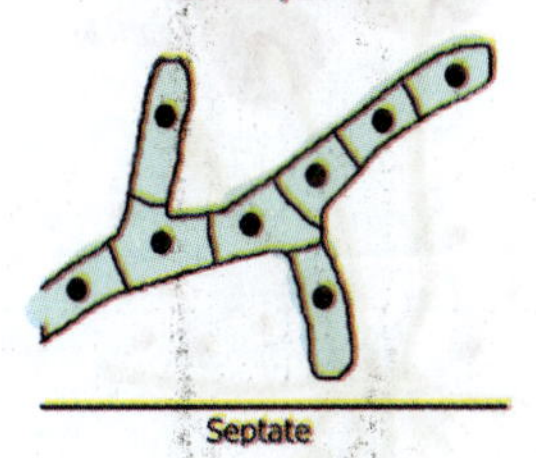
Septate

NEET SYNAPSE

Saprophytic organisms secrete digestive enzymes on the dead organic matter which break it down into absorbable substances.

Nutrition in Fungi

Saprophytic
- Grow on dead & decaying organic matter and absorb nutrients.
- Eg. Penicillium

Parasitic
- They grow in or on a living host and absorb nutrients
- Eg. Albugo

Symbiotic
- Some fungi live in mutually beneficial relationships with other organisms.
- Lichens - algae + fungi
  Mycorrhiza - fungi + roots of higher plants.

Reproduction in Fungi

Vegetative reproduction

- **Fragmentation**
  Mycelium breaks into fragments → Each fragment grows into independent mycelium
  Eg. Mucor, Rhizopus
- **Fission**
  Vegetative cell splits into two daughter cells through amitosis
  Eg. Yeast
- **Budding**
  Small buds arise from parent body → buds detach and grow into new organisms
  Eg. Yeast, Ustilago

Asexual reproduction

- **Sporangiospores**
  Thin walled
  Uni / Multinucleated
  Non motile
  Also called aplanospores
  Eg. Mucor, Rhizopus
- **Zoospores**
  Thin walled
  Uninucleated
  Motile - flagellated
  Endogenous; formed in zoosporangia
  Eg. Mucor, Rhizopus
- **Conidia**
  Thin walled
  Non- motile
  Arranged in chains
  Exogenous; present freely on tips
  Eg. Aspergillus

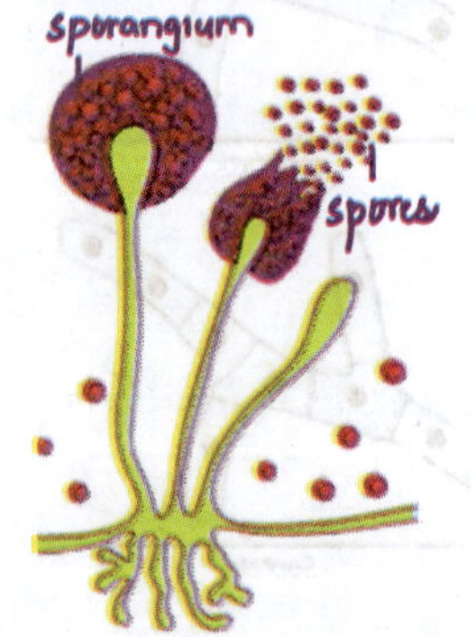

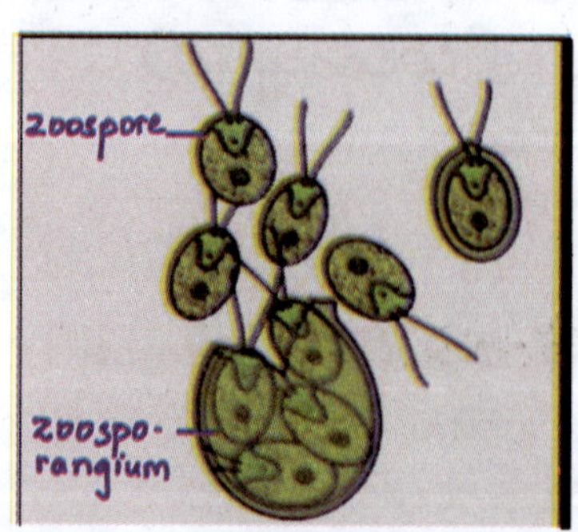

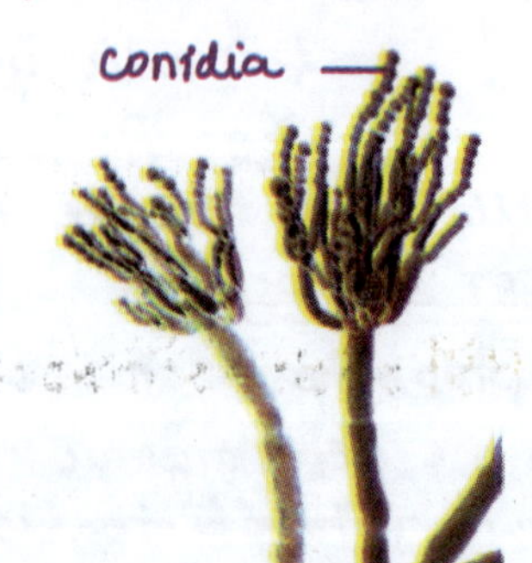

Sexual reproduction

- Involves fusion of gametes or two compatible nuclei
- Nuclei belong to two different strains / parents.
- Stages of sexual reproduction

① Plasmogamy
- first stage
- fusion of protoplast of two cells
- Single cell possesses two nuclei

② Karyogamy
- 2 haploid nuclei fuse to form diploid zygote
Dikaryotic stage - n+n
intervening stage
two nuclei per cell

③ Zygotic meiosis
Meiosis takes place in diploid zygote to form haploid spores.

- Types of gametic fusions

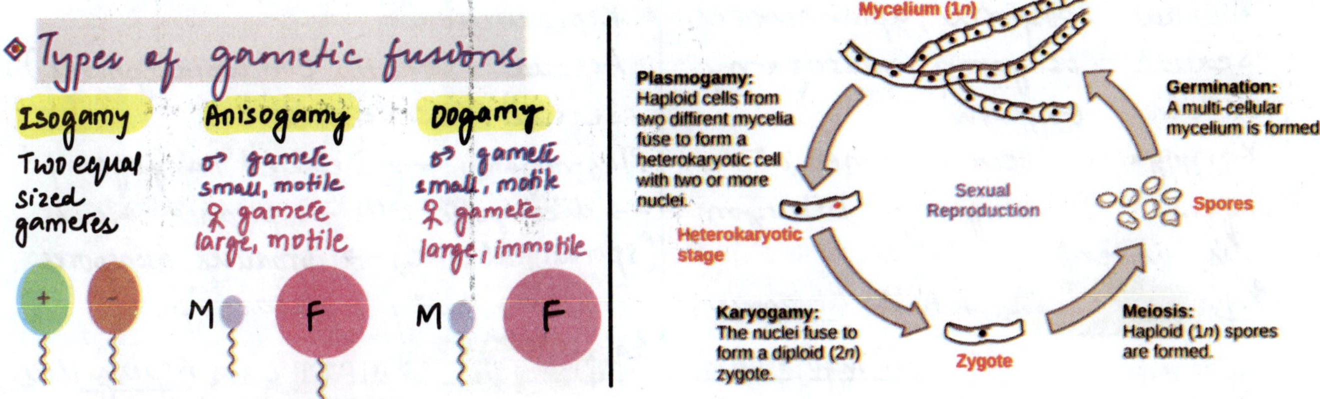

- Sexual spores

- In fungi, sexual reproduction takes place through sexual spores. They are borne on fruiting bodies.

① Oospores - found in oogonium (female structure)

② Zygospores - produced by fusion of entire gametangia

③ Ascospores - endogenous spores. Present in clusters of four or eight

④ Basidiospores - exogenous spores. Produced on basidium.

Classification of Fungi

- Phycomycetes — lower fungi
- Ascomycetes — sac fungi
- Basidiomycetes — club fungi
- Deuteromycetes — Fungi imperfecti

Phycomycetes

- Habitat - obligate parasite/saprophyte
  - terrestrial and aquatic
- Mycelium - aseptate, branched coenocytic hyphae
- Reproduction -
  Asexual - zoospores, aplanospores
  Sexual - isogamy, anisogamy, oogamy.
  Karyogamy occurs immediately after plasmogamy. Dikaryon is absent.

Eg: Memory trick RAM Rhizopus, Albugo, Mucor

Basidiomycetes

- Habitat - soil, logs, tree branches
  - parasitic
- Mycelium - branched, septate
  - motile structures absent
  - dikaryotic
- Reproduction
  Asexual - spores not formed
  Vegetative - fragmentation
  Sexual - dikaryon forms basidium
  → basidiospores form on basidium
  ↳ exogenous (4 spores)
  → Fruiting bodies - basidiocarp

Eg: Memory trick BAPU Ustilago, Agaricus, Puccinia

Ascomycetes

- Yeast is unicellular
- Habitat - saprophytic, parasitic
- Thallus - branched, septate hyphae
  Mycelium is monokaryotic
- Dikaryotic mycelium lasts for short duration
- Reproduction -
  Asexual - conidia (on conidiophores)
  Sexual - ascospores
  Plasmogamy → Delayed karyogamy → dikaryotic cells → produce ascus (sporangial sac) → produces ascospores.
  Fruiting body - ascocarp.

Eg: Memory trick MPTY CAN Aspergillus, Claviceps Penicillium, Neurospora Morels & truffles (edible), Yeast

Deuteromycetes

- Habitat - decomposers of litter
- Mycelium - septate, highy branched
- Sexual stages of members is not known.
- Members are actually ascomycetes or basidiomycetes whose sexual stage is absent or unknown.
  ∴ Reproduction - only asexual
  - conidia

Eg. Memory trick CAT Colletotrichum, Alternaria, Trichoderma

KINGDOM PLANTAE

- All organisms- multicellular, photosynthetic
- Cell wall- cellulose- provides rigidity & support
- Plastids - chloroplast, chromoplast, leucoplast
- Partially heterotrophic- insectivorous plants - eg. Venus fly trap.
  ↳ Carnivorous plants- digest insects to obtain nutrition.
- Alternation of generations - diploid sporophyte → haploid gametophyte
- Include algae, bryophytes, pteridophytes, gymnosperms, angiosperms

KINGDOM ANIMALIA

- Multicellular, eukaryotic, heterotrophic
- Mode of nutrition - holozoic; stored food- glycogen & fats.
- Growth- definite; sensory & motor neuromechanisms present.
- Exhibit locomotion unlike plants.
- Reproduction- mostly sexual.

ACELLULAR ORGANISMS

VIRUSES

- Ultramicroscopic & infectious
- Have inert crystalline structure outside the host body
- Multiply only in specific host using its machinery → causing damage.
- Connecting link between living & non living - cannot survive on their own (obligate parasites)
- Structure - Nucleoprotein
  - Nucleic acid (DNA/RNA) - genetic material
  - Protein (Capsid) ↓ made of capsomeres

No virus contains both RNA & DNA

Based on Tobacco Mosaic Disease study

- Ivanovsky - coined term virus
  ↳ virus smaller than bacteria
- Beijerinck - 'contagium vivum fluidum'
- Stanley - crystallised virus, crystals mostly contained proteins

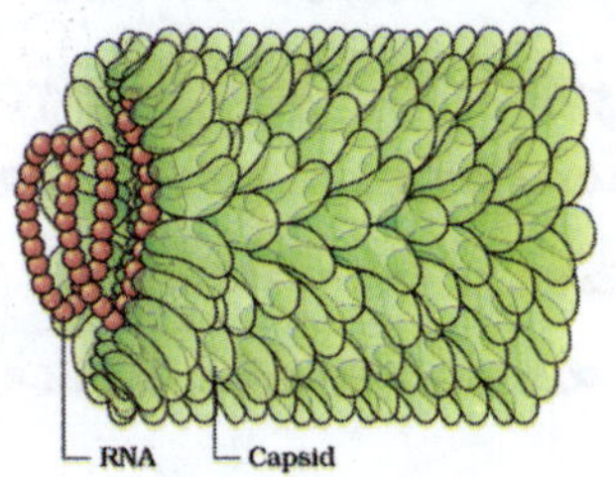

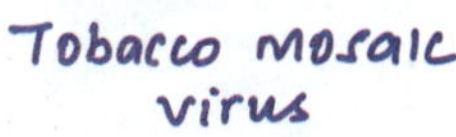
Tobacco mosaic virus

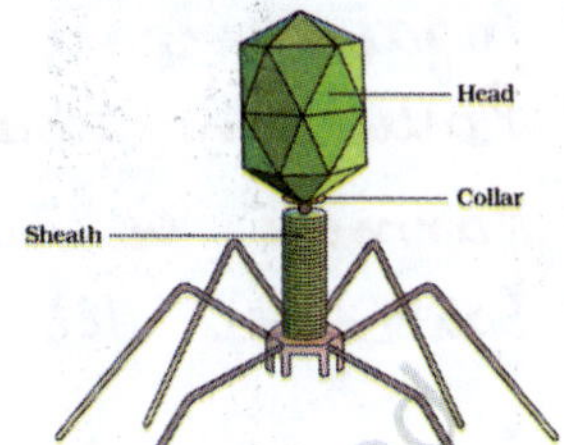

Bacteriophage

- Diseases caused by viruses

In animals – mumps, measles, AIDS, herpes, chicken pox, small pox, influenza, polio etc.

In plants – Mosaic disease, leaf rolling & curling, yellowing and vein clearing, dwarfing and stunted growth.

VIROIDS

- Discovered by T.O. Diener
- Smaller than viruses & are infectious.
- Composed of genetic material only – ss RNA (circular)
- Lack protein coat ; molecular weight low.
- Cause potato spindle tuber disease – reduced growth of tubers.

PRIONS

- Abnormally folded proteins
- Cause neurological diseases in humans & animals
- Mad cow disease / BSE (Bovine Spongiform Encephalopathy)
- Creutzfeldt - Jacob disease in humans

NEET SYNAPSE

Virus	Viroid	Prions
Genetic material + Protein	Genetic material only	Protein only

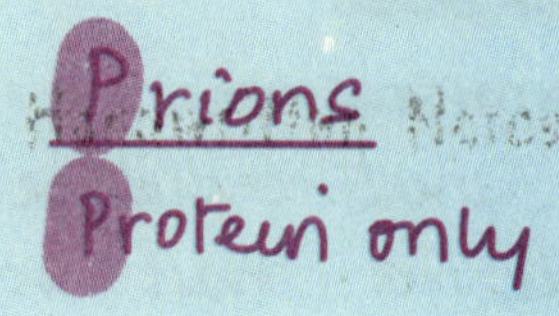

LICHENS

- Symbiotic association between algae & fungi
- Phycobiont (algae - autotrophic) + Mycobiont (fungi - heterotrophic)
- Algae prepare food ; fungi provide shelter & absorb nutrients.
- Pollution indicators - grow only in least polluted areas
- Farmers of nature - pioneer species in succession.
- Source of litmus - acid base indicator.

3. Plant Kingdom

SYSTEMS OF CLASSIFICATION

Artificial System

- Proposed by Carolus Linnaeus
- Basis of classification
  - Vegetative characters
  - Androecium structure (no. of stamens)
- Also called sexual system of classification.
- Rejected because vegetative characters can be easily affected by environment

Natural System

- Proposed by Bentham & Hooker
- Basis of classification
  - Morphology
  - Anatomy
  - Ultrastructure
  - Embryology
  - Phytochemistry

Phylogenetic system

- Proposed by Engler & Prantl
- Basis of classification
  - Morphological characters
  - Evolutionary relationships
- Explains organisms in one taxonomic category.

Taxonomy

- Numerical taxonomy
  Numbers assigned to characters
- Cytotaxonomy
  Chromosome no., structure, behaviour
- Chemotaxonomy
  chemical constituents of plants.

Present classification

Cryptogamae

- Crypto - Hidden; Gamae - marriage
- Reproduce by forming spores.
- Reproductive organs are hidden
- Require water for fertilisation
- Lack a well developed vascular system.

Thallophyta, Bryophyta, Pteridophyta

Phanerogamae

- Phanero- visible; gamae - marriage
- Reproduce by forming seeds
- Reproductive organs are visible
- Water not required for fertilisation
- Possess a well developed vascular system.

Gymnosperms, Angiosperms

THALLOPHYTA / ALGAE

- Habitat - Aquatic - freshwater & marine
  Terrestrial - moist surfaces ; in association like lichens & on animal bodies
- Plant body - Thalloid
  - Unicellular - Chlamydomonas
  - Colonial - Volvox
  - Filamentous - Spirogyra
- Cell wall - contains mainly cellulose
- Reproduction
  - Vegetative reproduction - Fragmentation - Ulothrix
  - Asexual reproduction - Spores

Spores
- motile - Flagellated - zoospore - Chlamydomonas
- non motile - Non flagellated - aplanospores - Ulothrix

- Sexual reproduction

Fusion of gametes (n) ⟶ zygote (2n) ⟶ no embryo

Fertilisation external - requires water

Fusion of gametes is of 3 types

Isogamy -
- Both gametes similar in size & motile

Eg - Ulothrix

2 equal sized gametes

Anisogamy -
- Both gametes dissimilar in size.

Eg. Eudorina , Chlamydomonas

small gamete (male) — large gamete (female)

Oogamy
- Female gamete larger and non motile
- Male gamete - small & motile

Eg Volvox , Fucus

small mobile gamete (male) — large immobile gamete (female)

Classification of Algae

- Chlorophyceae (Green algae)
- Phaeophyceae (Brown algae)
- Rhodophyceae (Red algae)

Chlorophyceae

- Habitat - mostly freshwater, few marine
- Thallus - unicellular, colonial & filamentous.
- Cell wall - inner layer - cellulose ; outer layer - pectose
- Pigments - Chl a, b (maximum), carotenes, xanthophylls
- Food reserve - pyrenoids (storage bodies)
  - ↳ located in chloroplasts
  - ↳ protein centre surrounded by starch layers.
  - some forms have oil droplets as food reserve.
- Reproduction -
  - Vegetative - fragmentation
  - Asexual - zoospores formed in zoosporangia
  - Sexual - isogamous, anisogamous & oogamous.
- Examples - Memory trick CCSUV
  - Chara, Chlamydomonas, Spirogyra, Ulothrix, Volvox.

Phaeophyceae

- Habitat - mostly marine; cold water dwelling except Sargassum
- Thallus - immobile & multicellular.
  - simple branched filamentous - Ectocarpus
  - profusely branched (Kelps) - Macrocystis (largest)
- Cell wall - cellulose, pectose, algin (gelatinous coating)
- Pigments - chl a, b, carotenes, xanthophylls, fucoxanthin.
- Food reserve - laminarin & mannitol
- Reproduction -
  - Vegetative - fragmentation - Sargassum
  - Asexual - zoospores - biflagellate
  - Sexual - isogamous, anisogamous & oogamous

> **NEET SYNAPSE**
> Oogonia are unicellular in all brown algae

- Examples - Memory trick SELFDM
  - Sargassum, Ectocarpus, Laminaria, Fucus, Dictyota, Macrocystis

Rhodophyceae

- Habitat - mostly marine ; on surface as well as deep oceans.
- Thallus - multicellular, filamentous, feathery, ribbon like.
- Cell wall - cellulose, pectin, hydrocolloids like agar & carageen
- Pigments - Chl a, d , phycoerythrin (main) & phycocyanin (blue)
- Food reserve - Floridean starch - similar to glycogen & amylopectin
- Reproduction-
  - Vegetative - fragmentation
  - Asexual - non motile spores
  - Sexual - oogamous - non motile gametes.
- Examples - Memory trick PPGG
  Polysiphonia, Porphyra, Gracilaria, Gelidium

Classes	Common Name	Major Pigments	Stored Food	Cell Wall	Flagellar Number and Position of Insertions	Habitat
Chlorophyceae	Green algae	Chlorophyll *a, b*	Starch	Cellulose	2-8, equal, apical	Fresh water, brackish water, salt water
Phaeophyceae	Brown algae	Chlorophyll *a, c,* fucoxanthin	Mannitol, laminarin	Cellulose and algin	2, unequal, lateral	Fresh water (rare) brackish water, salt water
Rhodophyceae	Red algae	Chlorophyll *a, d,* phycoerythrin	Floridean starch	Cellulose, pectin and poly sulphate esters	Absent	Fresh water (some), brackish water, salt water (most)

NEET SYNAPSE
Hydrocolloids are substances that can hold large amount of water, hence are used as thickening agents.

Economic importance of algae

- Fix half of the total CO_2 on earth
- Major producers through Photosynthesis.
- Hydrocolloids - carrageen (red algae) ; algin (brown algae)
  Agar (Gelidium) - used in ice creams & jellies making
  (Gracilaria) - used as nutrient medium in labs.
- Food supplements
  - Chlorella (protein rich) - used by space travellers.
  - Porphyra, Laminaria & Sargassum are edible
  - Fucus, Laminaria - rich source of iodine

BRYOPHYTA

- Habitat - terrestrial → moist & shady places / sciophytes
  Some forms are aquatic, saprophytic or epiphytic.
- Amphibians of the plant kingdom.
- Require water for fertilisation
- Plant body - more differentiated than algae; non vascular
  Root like, stem like & leaf like structures are present
- Alternation of generations
  Gametophyte - haploid, dominant, green & independent
  Sporophyte - diploid, dependent on gametophyte.
- Reproduction -

NEET SYNAPSE - Rhizoids are gametophytic while true roots are sporophytic

Vegetative - fragmentation, budding & gemmae.
Gemmae - asexual reproductive bodies.
Sexual - fusion of gametes - oogamous.

Sex organs - surrounded by jacketed sterile cells
→ ♂ Antheridium → antherozoids (male gametes) (flagellated, motile)
→ ♀ Archegonium → single egg (female gamete)

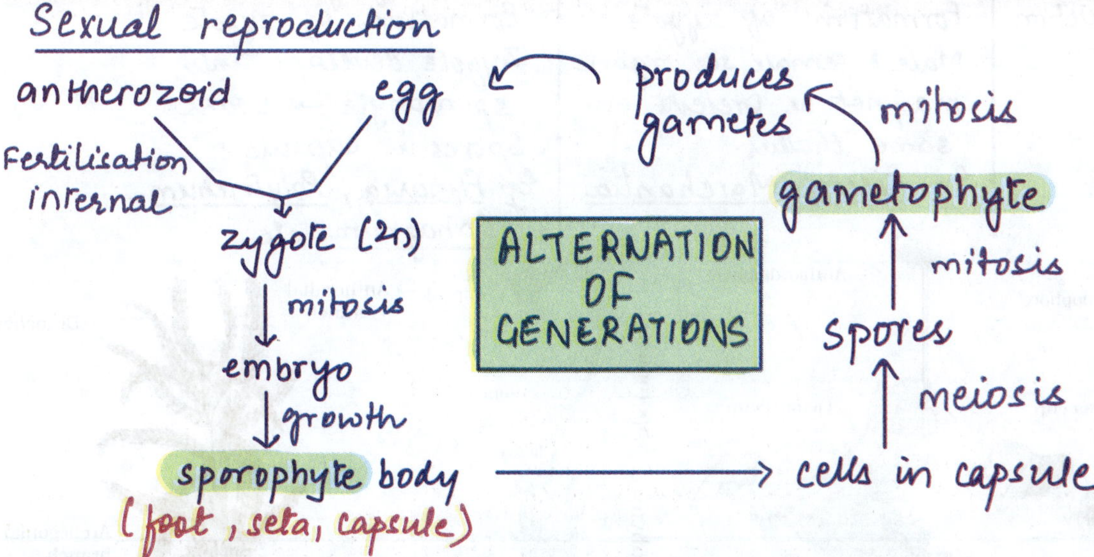

Trick - GPS - Gametophyte, parasitic sporophyte

Classification of Bryophyta

	Liverworts	Mosses
◆ Habitat	• Marshy ground, moist soil, banks of streams etc.	• Forests, wetlands, other damp areas.
◆ Plant body	• Thalloid. Undifferentiated dorsiventral thallus; appressed to substrate Dichotomous branching. - division of apical meristem into two axes 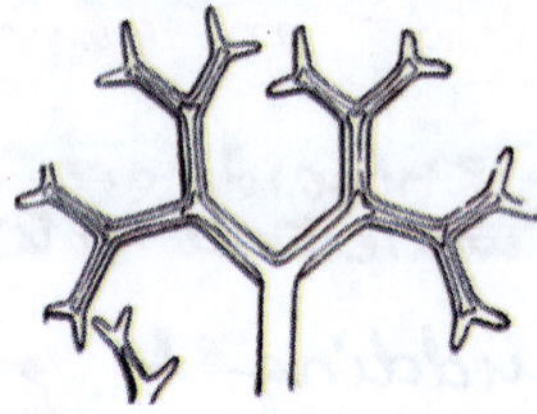	• Gametophyte has sub stages ① Protonema stage - Green, branched & creeping - Develops from spore ② Leafy stage - Develops from parts other than spores. - Starts from a lateral bud - Leaves are upright & spirally arranged & attach to soil with rhizoids.
◆ Asexual reproduction	• Fragmentation; • gemmae - develop in gemma cups present on thalli Gemmae develop into new individuals	• Fragmentation • Budding in secondary protonema Mosses are advanced bryophytes - leafy stems with rhizoids.
◆ Sexual reproduction	• Fusion of gametes Formation of zygote Male & female sex organs may not be present on same thallus. Eg. Riccia, Marchantia	Fusion of gametes Formation of zygote Zygote develops into sporophyte → bears Spores in capsule. Eg. Funaria, Polytrichum, Sphagnum etc.

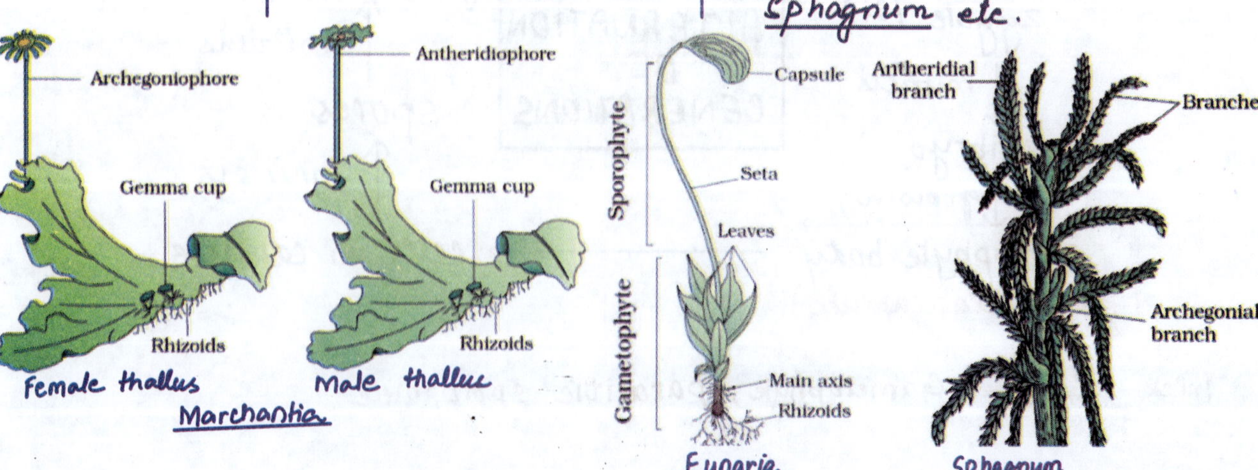

Economic importance of Bryophytes

- Source of food - fodder for animals.
- Sphagnum - constituent of peat (used as fuel)
  - constituent of ethyl alcohol, paraffin etc.
  - used as covering of live plant & animal parts during transportation as it retains moisture.
- Prevent soil erosion, act as binders.

> **NEET SYNAPSE**
> Pteridophytes lack xylem vessels. Phloem lacks companion cells.

PTERIDOPHYTA

- Seedless vascular plants.
- Reptiles of the plant kingdom.
- Habitat - wet, moist, shady places.
- Plant body - main body sporophyte - dominant phase.
  - Body differentiated into root, stem & leaves
- Vascular tissue - primitive xylem & phloem present.
- Sporophyte → Macrophyllous - bear large leaves Eg. Ferns
  → Microphyllous - bear smaller leaves Eg. Selaginella
- Reproduction - Asexual - through spores
  Sexual - fusion of male & female gametes

Sex organs → ♂ Antheridium (jacketed) ⟶ multiciliated sperms
→ ♀ Archegonium (flask shaped) ⟶ sperms enter to fertilise egg.

Body structure

Sporophyte (plant body)
↓
Sporophyll (spore bearing leaf)
↓
Sporangia (vessel of spores)
↓
Spores

Sporophyte is the dominant phase of life that bears special leaves called sporophylls which bear vessels called sporangia which bear spores.

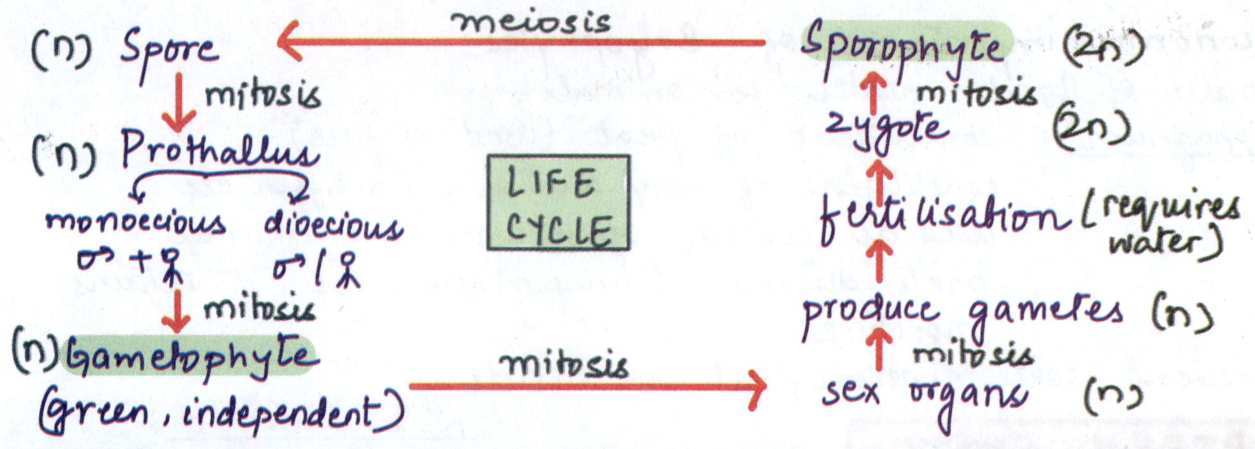

Classification of pteridophytes, based on types of spores

① Homosporous - all spores similar; released from sporophyte. All spores form bisexual gametophyte

② Heterosporous - 2 different spores - male & female

↓

Selaginella, Salvinia

- male spores (microspores) → released from sporophyte → form male gametophyte outside sporophyte.
- Female spores (megaspores) → retained on sporophyte → spores form female gametophyte while still present on the body of sporophyte → female gamete formed on gametophyte (still attached to sporophyte) → fertilisation occurs → zygote forms and develops into young sporophyte & then gets detached.

SEED HABIT

- Ability of a plant to form seeds.
- Heterospory paved way for seed habit.
- Retaining of female gametophyte on the sporophyte body gave rise to seed habit

Classification of Pteridophyta

- **Psilopsida**
  - Homosporous
  - Psilotum
- **Lycopsida**
  - Club moss
  - Lycopodium
- **Sphenopsida**
  - Homosporous
  - Equisetum
- **Pteropsida**
  - Fronds +nt
  - Pteris, Dryopteris, Adiantum.

Economic importance of Pteridophytes

- Marsilea - used as food by tribal people
- Equisetum - used for polishing metals
- Dryopteris - source of antihelminthic drug
- Adiantum, Pteris - Ornamental plants
- Azolla - used as biofertiliser
- Selaginella - prevent soil erosion
- Anabaena - nitrogen fixation

> **NEET SYNAPSE**
> Pinus seeds cannot germinate in the absence of 'mycorrhizae'

GYMNOSPERMS

- Gymno - naked ; sperma - seeds
- All members perennial and woody
- Ginkgo biloba - only surviving species of Ginkgos.
- Sequoia - tall tree species.
- Habitat - temperate regions
- Plant body - main body - sporophytic
  - well differentiated into true roots, stem & leaves.
- Root system - well developed with tap root system.
  - Coralloid roots - Cycas - symbiotic association with nitrogen fixing cyanobacteria
  - Mycorrhiza - Pinus - symbiotic association with fungi
- Stem
  - → branched - Pinus, Cedrus
  - → unbranched - Cycas
- Leaves - adapted to reduce water loss.

Adaptations - pinnately compound, needle like, thick cuticle, sunken stomata

- Spore formation - heterosporous [microspores / megaspores]
- Strobili / Cones - sporophylls are arranged spirally forming cones.
  Male strobili - made of microsporophylls containing microsporangia
  Female strobili - made of megasporophylls containing megasporangia
- Male or female cones may be present on same tree (Pinus) or different trees (Cycas)
- Pollen grains - male gametophyte ; reduced & haploid.
- Ovules / Megasporangium

Sporophyte → (bears) Megasporophyll → (bears) Megasporangium → (bears) Nucellus tissue → (differentiation) Megaspore mother cell → (meiosis) megaspore → (mitosis) Female gametophyte → (mitosis) Female gamete → (+ male gamete) Fertilisation → (fusion) zygote → (mitosis) sporophyte

- Female sex organ - Archegonium - contains single egg
  - venter canal cell
- Female gametophyte remains inside megasporangia

- Pollination - landing of pollen grains on opening of ovule (present on megasporophylls)
- Fertilisation - siphonogamy (formation of pollen tube)

Pollen tube discharges male gamete at the mouth of archegonium
↓
Fusion of male & female gametes
↓
Diploid zygote is formed
↓
Grows to form embryo.

Post fertilisation
Ovule → Seed

Economic importance of Gymnosperms

- Source of food, timber, paper etc.
- Pine cones are used as oranmental pieces
- Pinus and Cycas have edible seeds.
- Ephedra is source of ephedrine (component of cough syrups)

ANGIOSPERMS

- Flowering plants.
- Pollen grains & ovules are formed in a flower and not naked like gymnosperms
- After fertilisation –
  - Ovary ⟶ Fruit
  - Ovule ⟶ Seed
- Classification – based on the number of cotyledons (seed leaf)
  - Monocotyledons – 1 cotyledon
  - Dicotyledons – 2 cotyledons.
- Smallest angiosperm – Wolffia
- Economic importance –
  - provide food, fodder, fuels, medicines etc.

4. Animal Kingdom

BASIS OF CLASSIFICATION

- **Levels of body organisation**
  - Cellular – Porifera
  - Tissue – Cnidaria, Ctenophora
  - Organ – Platyhelminthes
  - Organ system – Aschelminthes to Chordates

- **Complexity of organ systems**

Digestive system

Incomplete – only one opening present
Cnidaria, Ctenophora, Platyhelminthes

Complete – 2 openings are present – mouth & anus.
Aschelminthes to chordates

Circulatory system

Open – blood flows in open spaces called sinuses
– Organs bathe in blood
Arthropods, Molluscs, Echinoderms, Hemichordates

Closed – blood flows in vessels
Annelida & Chordata

- **Body Symmetry**

Asymmetrical
Body does not show symmetry
Porifers are assymetrical

Radial
Body divisible into 2 equal halves in any plane.

Bilateral
Body divisible into 2 equal halves in 1 plane only

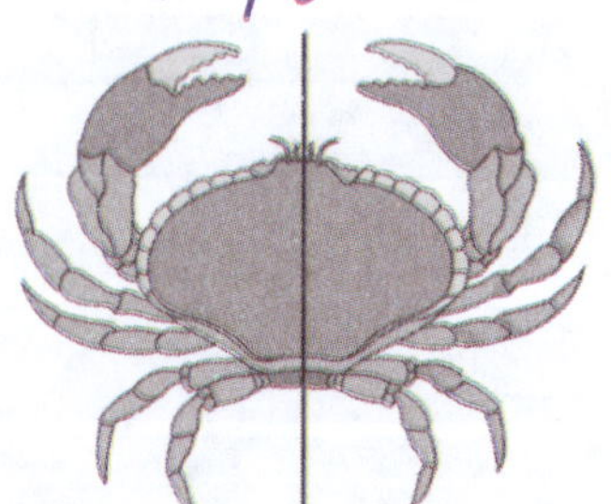

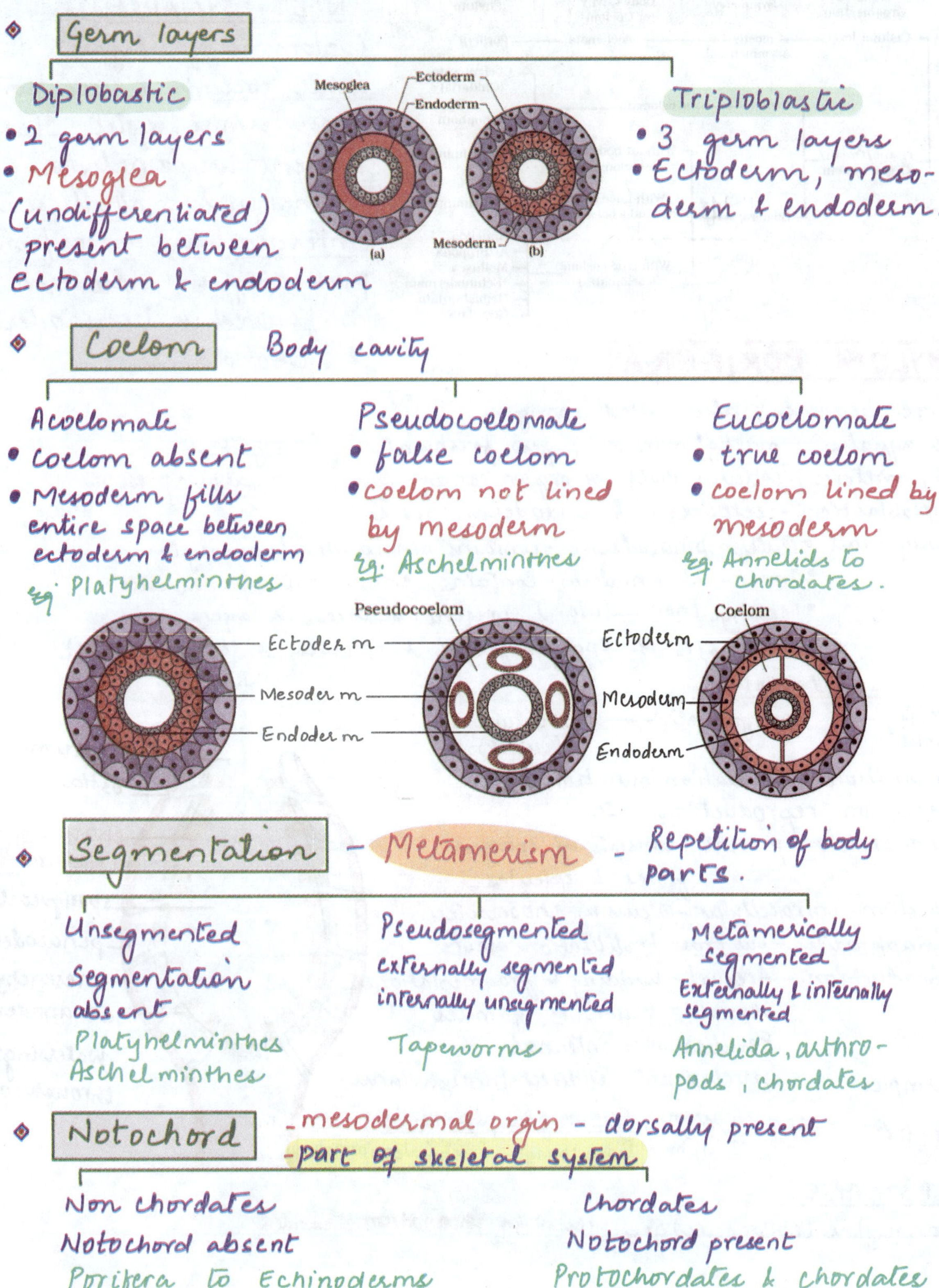
Germ layers
Diploblastic
• 2 germ layers
• Mesoglea (undifferentiated) present between ectoderm & endoderm
Mesoglea
Ectoderm
Endoderm
Mesoderm
(a)
(b)
Triploblastic
• 3 germ layers
• Ectoderm, mesoderm & endoderm.
Coelom Body cavity
Acoelomate
• coelom absent
• Mesoderm fills entire space between ectoderm & endoderm
eg. Platyhelminthes
Pseudocoelomate
• false coelom
• coelom not lined by mesoderm
eg. Aschelminthes
Eucoelomate
• true coelom
• coelom lined by mesoderm
eg. Annelids to chordates.
Ectoderm
Mesoderm
Endoderm
Pseudocoelom
Coelom
Ectoderm
Mesoderm
Endoderm
Segmentation – Metamerism – Repetition of body parts.
Unsegmented
Segmentation absent
Platyhelminthes
Aschelminthes
Pseudosegmented
externally segmented internally unsegmented
Tapeworms
Metamerically segmented
Externally & internally segmented
Annelida, arthropods, chordates
Notochord – mesodermal orgin – dorsally present
– part of skeletal system
Non chordates
Notochord absent
Porifera to Echinoderms
Chordates
Notochord present
Protochordates & chordates

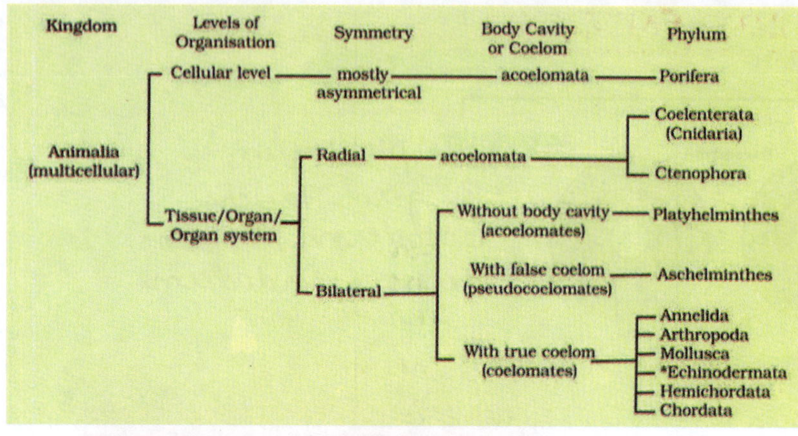

NEET SYNAPSE

Coelom is of 2 types -
Schizocoelom - arises from mesodermal split. It is present in Annelida, Arthropoda, Mollusca
Enterocoelom - arises from pocketing in mesoderm. It is found in Echinoderms & Chordates

PHYLUM PORIFERA

- Pore bearers ; also called sponges
- All aquatic ; mostly marine ; few freshwater (Spongilla)
- Asymmetric ; cellular level of organisation - division of labour present
- Diploblastic - ectoderm & endoderm present
- Body wall
  - Outer - pinacoderm - contains pinacocytes & porocytes.
  - Inner - choanoderm - contains choanocytes (collar cells)
  - Mesohyl (non cellular) present between 2 layers.
    - ↳ consists of spongin fibres & spicules (skeletal structure)
- Water canal system
  - Ostia (inlet) ⟶ spongocoel ⟶ osculum (outlet)
  - Respiration, circulation, nutrition, excretion reproduction etc.
- Endoskeleton present - consists of spongin fibres & spicules.
- Digestion - intracellular - occurs in choanocytes
- Hermaphrodites - but cross fertilisation occurs.
- Reproduction - Asexual - budding & fragmentation
  - Sexual - fusion of gametes
  - Fertilisation - internal
  - Development - indirect through larva
- Examples

Memory trick - SES - Sycon, Euspongia, Spongilla
Scypha, Bath sponge, Freshwater sponge.

osculum
ostia
choanocytes (flagellated cells)
spongocoel
pinacoderm
mesenchyme
choanoderm
Water ingressing through ostia

NEET SYNAPSE

Choanocytes (collar cells) are present in choanoderm & canals

PHYLUM CNIDARIA / COELENTERATA

- Cnidaria - needle like cells - cnidocytes / cnidoblasts present.
- Mostly marine, few freshwater eg Hydra
- Radially symmetrical
- Sessile (attached to substrate) or free living
- Tissue level organisation
- Diploblastic

NEET SYNAPSE
Coelenterates & zooxanthelle (algae) share symbiotic relationship

- Cnidoblast / cnidocyte / stinging cells contain nematocyst
  ↳ Function - food capture, defence, locomotion.
  ↳ Release hypnotoxin through needle to ward off enemies or for capturing prey
- Coelenteron - gastrovascular cavity - opens through single opening (mouth as well as anus)
- Hypostome - present below mouth - helps in anchoring the animal to a substrate.
- Digestion - first extracellular ; then intracellular
- Exoskeleton present in some coelenterates eg. corals.
- Metagenesis - alternation of life forms eg. Obelia
  Polyp & Medusa - both are diploid

Polyp	Medusa
sessile	free swimming
cylindrical	Umbrella shaped
Asexual reproduction	Sexual reproduction.
Adamsia	Aurelia

- Examples -
  - Physalia - Portugese men of war
  - Adamsia - Sea anemone
  - Pennatula - Sea pen
  - Gorgonia - Sea fan
  - Meandrina - Brain coral
  - Aurelia - Jelly fish
  - Hydra - Freshwater polyp
  - Obelia - sea fur

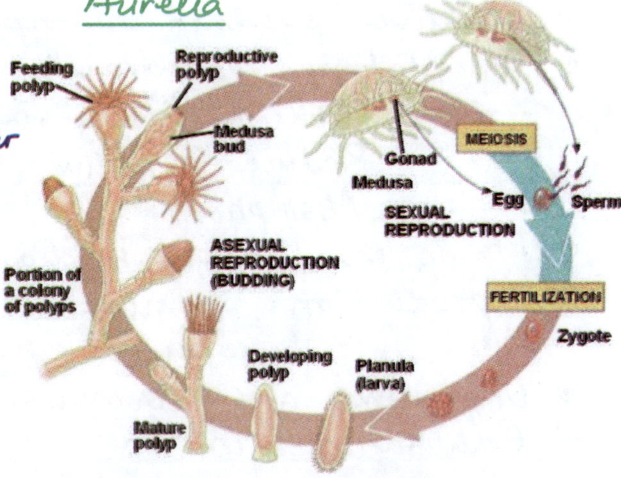

Life cycle of Obelia

PHYLUM CTENOPHORA

- Cteno - comb ; phore - bearing
- Also called comb jellies / sea walnuts / sea gooseberries.
- Radial symmetry, diploblastic, tissue level of organisation
- Eight rows of ciliated comb plates present.
- 2 tentacles present - one on each side
- Exclusively marine
- Digestive system - incomplete; digestion - extra + intracellular
- Bioluminescence - emit light.
- Reproduction - sexual ; Fertilisation - external
  Organisms - Hermaphrodite; Development - indirect
- Larva - Cydippid larva
- Example - Pleurobrachia and Ctenoplana.

PHYLUM PLATYHELMINTHES

- Platy - flat ; helminth - worm → Flatworms.
- Dorsoventrally flat
- Members are free living and parasitic.
- Parasitic forms live inside host body.
- Bilaterally symmetrical
- Triploblastic but acoelomate
- Organ level of organisation
- Digestive system - incomplete
- Adaptations for paracitism -
  Hooks & suckers to cling on to host's body
  Reduced digestive system
  Absorption of nutrients from body surface.
- Flame cells / protonephridia - excretion & osmoregulation.
- Reproduction - Asexual - Planaria - Transverse binary fission.
  Sexual - fusion of male & female gametes.
- Organisms are hermaphrodite / monoecious.
- Fertilisation - internal ; development - indirect.
  Planaria - regeneration well marked.
- Examples - Taenia - Tapeworm   Fasciola - Liver fluke
  Schistosoma - Blood fluke

NEET SYNAPSE
Platyhelminthes is the first phylum to exhibit cephalisation

PHYLUM ASCHELMINTHES

- Ascos- sac ; helminthes → Sac like worms
- Also called roundworms- round in cross section
- Organisms may be free living or parasitic
- Triploblastic with pseudocoelom
- Organ system level of organisation
- Complete digestive system - two openings present
- Muscular pharynx present - helps in sucking
- Renette cells - excretion & osmoregulation
- Reproduction- asexual reproduction absent
  - Sexual reproduction takes place.
- Sexes are separate - dioecious.
- Sexual dimorphism is present - sex of organism can be identified by morphological features. Females are longer than males.
- Fertilisation- internal ; Development - indirect / direct
- Examples - Ascaris - roundworm
  Wuchereria - filarial worm
  Ancylostoma - hook worm.

NEET SYNAPSE
Aschelminthes is the first phylum to exhibit sexual dimorphism

PHYLUM ANNELIDA

- Annuli- rings → ring like structures present on body.
- Organ system level of organisation
- Circulatory system- closed ; Digestive system - complete.
- Bilateral symmetry
- Triploblastic with true coelom - eucoelomate.
- Metamerism - inner body segmented into compartments.
- locomotion- alternate contraction of muscles of body wall.
  ↳ longitudinal & circular muscles contract alternatively.
- Chitinous setae - help in locomotion.
- Parapodia - present in Nereis , help in swimming
- Excretion and osmoregulation - nephridia.
- Nervous system - double ventral solid nerve cord.
  paired ganglia present ;
  connected by connectives & commissures.

- Reproduction - sexual
- Hermaphrodites - earthworm & leech
  Dioecious - Nereis - aquatic & burrowing
- Oviparous; fertilisation - external.
  (aquatic - water; terrestrial - cocoon)
- Examples - Pheretima (Earthworm)
  Hirudinaria (Leech)
  Nereis - aquatic annelid

NEET SYNAPSE

Leech secretes 'Hirudin' - an anticoagulant & is therefore used for therapy in cases of superficial blood clotting.

PHYLUM ARTHROPODA

- Arthro - jointed; poda - legs. → Jointed appendages.
- Largest phylum. - over 2/3 of identified species are arthropods
- Cosmopolitan in distribution
- Triploblastic, eucoelomate, bilaterally symmetrical.
- Metamerically segmented
- Exoskeleton made of chitin - polymer of N-acetyl glucosamine.
- Chitinous plates present over the body are called sclerites.
- Body divided into head, thorax & abdomen
- Digestive tract complete. Digestion - extracellular
- Circulatory system - open - blood flows in sinuses.
- Blood is called haemolymph - white in colour.
- Blood does not contain respiratory pigment.
- Gas exchange through general body surface or through specialised respiratory structures.
  ↳ Gills - prawn ; Trachae - cockroach
  Book gills - scorpion ; Book lungs - crab
- Excretory structures - Coxal / Green glands - arachnids
  Malpighian tubules - insects.
- Sensory organs - statocyst - balancing organs
- Antennae or sensory hair - tactile & chemoreceptive organs
  Compound eyes & simple eyes - vision
- Dioecious organisms; sexual dimorphism well marked.
- Fertilisation - internal; development - direct or indirect
- Animals oviparous or ovoviviparous.
- Examples - Gregarious pest - Locust; Living fossil - Limulus
  Economically important insects - Memory trick: LAB Laccifer, Apis, Bombyx
  Vectors - Anopheles, Culex, Aedes

PHYLUM MOLLUSCA

> **NEET SYNAPSE**
> In *Pila*, bilaterally symmetry is lost in adulthood due to Torsion (twisting)

- Mollusc - soft bodied animal
- Second largest phylum
- Triploblastic eucoelomate, bilaterally symmetrical.
- Body unsegmented ; divisible into -
  - Head - bears mouth, eyes, tentacles
  - Visceral hump - digestive tract & visceral organs
  - Foot - large muscular part.
    modified for crawling, burrowing, food capture & swimming
- Mantle - soft spongy layer - covers visceral hump
  ↳ secretes shell of calcium carbonate - protects and supports the soft tissues.
- Mantle cavity - space between mantle & visceral mass
- True coelom reduced to cavities called haemocoel.
- Digestive tract complete ; digestion - extracellular
- Radula - rasping organ - minute chitinous teeth.
- Ctenidia - feather like gills for gaseous exchange
  In terrestrial forms - gas exchange occurs through pulmonary sacs or diffusion through body surface.
- Excretion - metanephridia (sac like kidneys) or through gills.
- Sense organs - sensory tentacles located in head
  - Statocyst - present in foot
  - Osphradium - testing nature of water
  - Eyes - present in head.
- Dioecious animals
- Fertilisation - external or internal
- Oviparous. Development - direct or indirect
- Examples - Pila (Apple snail), Pinctada (Pearl oyster)

Memory trick: **CLAP PODS**

- Sepia (Cuttle fish)
- Octopus (Devil fish)
- Aplysia (Sea hare)
- Chaetopleura (Chiton)
- Loligo (squid)
- Dentalium (Tusk shell)

PHYLUM ECHINODERMATA

- Echino - spiny ; dermata - skin ; spiny skinned animals
- Exclusively marine , non parasitic
- Habitat - usually sea bottom , free swimming & sessile
- Body - polymorphic , lacks distinct head.
- Triploblastic, coelomate, unsegmented, organ system level.
- Symmetry - adult - radial
  larva - bilateral
- Mesodermal endoskeleton - calcareous plates / ossicles.
- Body covered with epidermis - bears spines.
- Water vascular system - characteristic feature.
- Tube feet present - help in locomotion, capture of food, respiration, excretion.
- Ammonotelic ; special excretory organs absent ; Gills help in excretion
- Sexes are separate ; sexual dimorphism absent.
- Fertilisation - external ; Development - indirect.
- Examples -
  Antedon (sea lily)
  Asterias (starfish)
  Cucumaria (sea cucumber)
  Ophiura (brittle star)
  Echinus (sea urchin)

Memory trick
Ant
Ate
Cucumber
Of (Oph)
Echinus

NEET SYNAPSE
Echinoderms have the ability to regenerate after autotomy

PHYLUM HEMICHORDATA

- Hemi - half ; chordata - cord bearing
- Lack notochord ; Possess stomochord (rudimentary notochord)
- Exclusively marine
- Worm like animals, also called tongue worms.
- Bilaterally symmetrical, triploblastic, coelomates.
- Body - unsegmented - divisible into 3 regions
  Proboscis - anteriormost, also called protostome.
  Collar - muscular middle region; contains stomochord
  Trunk - lower most part.

- Digestive system - complete
- Respiration - through gills.
- Excretion - through proboscis gland
- Circulatory system - open type ; Heart - dorsal
  - ↳ Blood lacks respiratory pigment.
- Reproduction - sexual ; sexes separate
- Fertilisation - external
  Development - mostly indirect.
- Examples - Balanoglossus
  Saccoglossus.

> **NEET SYNAPSE**
> Notochord is found only in chordates while nerve cord is found in chordates as well as non-chordates

PHYLUM CHORDATA

FUNDAMENTAL CHARACTERISTICS

- **Notochord**
  - Mesodermally derived
  - Rod like structure
  - Present dorsally - below nerve cord & above alimentary canal

> Notochord -
> - May persist throughout life
>   - Cephalochordates, cyclostomes & some fishes
> - May be replaced partially or completely by vertebral column
>   - Most chordates

- **Nerve cord**
  - Hollow, dorsal, ganglionated
  - Forms brain & spinal cord
  - Spinal cord enclosed within vertebral column.
- **Gill slits**
  - Paired narrow openings.
  - Present on lateral side of pharynx ; hence also called pharyngeal clefts
  - Present only in embryonic life in terrestrial chordates

Other features

- Post anal tail
- Closed circulatory system
- Ventral heart
- Bilaterally symmetrical
- Triploblastic
- Eucoelomate
- Organ system level of organisation
- Metamerically segmented
- Complete digestive system
- Central nervous system - single, hollow, dorsal

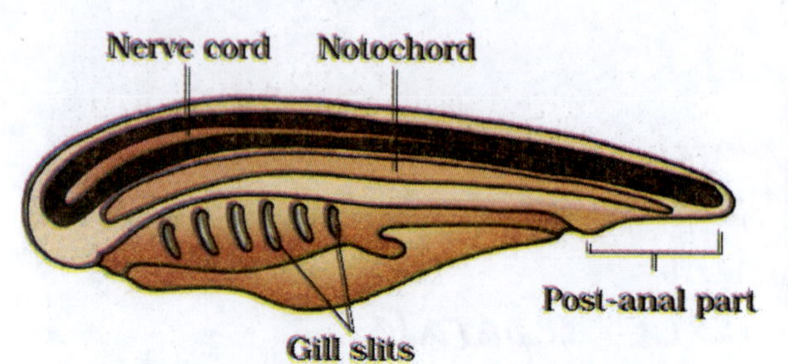

Characteristics of chordates

Phylum Chordata

- Group : Acraniata or Protochordata (Lower Chordates)
  - Subphylum : Urochordata
  - Subphylum : Cephalochordata
- Group : Craniata or Euchordata (Higher Chordates)
  - Subphylum Vertebrata
    - Division : Agnatha (Jaw less)
      - 1. Ostracodermi
      - 2. Cyclostomata
    - Division Gnathostomata (Jaw present)
      - Superclass Pisces
        - 3. Placodermi
        - 4. Chondrichthyes
        - 5. Osteichthyes
      - Superclass Tetrapoda
        - 6. Amphibia
        - 7. Reptilia
        - 8. Aves
        - 9. Mammalia

SUBPHYLUM

UROCHORDATA

- Also called tunicates
- Larval tail has notochord
- Exclusively marine
- Filter feeders.
- Notochord lost in adult stages.
- Example Ascidia, Salpa, Doliolum

CEPHALOCHORDATA

- Small, fish like
- Notochord extends from head to tail & persits throughout life.
- Exclusively marine
- Example - Branchiostoma (Amphioxus or Lancelet)

VERTEBRATA

- Characterised by presence of vertebral column.
- Notochord present only in embryonic stage.
- Ventral heart ; closed circulation.
- Excretion & osmoregulation - through kidneys.
- Presence of paired appendages - fins / limbs.
- Cephalisation present - distinct head
- Exoskeleton protects skin
- Exoskeleton can be made of hair, scales, feathers.
- All vertebrates are chordates, but all chordates are not vertebrates

Class Cyclostomata

- Cyclo - circular ; stomata - mouth
- Body - elongated - eel like , scales absent.
- Paired fins present. ; cartilaginous endoskeleton.
- Mouth - ventral & circular
- Marine habitat but migrate to freshwater for spawning

NEET SYNAPSE: Anadromous - migrate from marine to freshwater for spawing - laying eggs

- May be parasitic - feed on host species.
- May be scavengers - feed on dead fishes.
- 6 - 15 pairs of gills present
- Heart is two chambered ; circulation is closed.
- Example - Petromyzon (lamprey)
  Myxine (hagfish)

Class Chondricthyes - cartilaginous fish.

- Chondro - cartilage ; icthyes - fish
- Mostly marine & predaceous.
- Endoskeleton - cartilaginous.
- Teeth are modified Placoid scales - backwardly directed
- Poikilotherms - cold blooded.
- Operculum / gill cover - absent
- Mouth ventral , powerful jaws present.
- Paired fins present.
- Caudal fin - heterocercal - asymmetrical
- Air bladder absent. They swim constantly to avoid sinking
- Heart - 2 chambered - 1 auricle , 1 ventricle
- Notochord is persistent throughout life.
- Torpedo (electric ray) - have electric organs
- Trygon (sting ray) - have poison sting
- Sexes are separate. Sexual dimorphism present.
- Males possess claspers - copulatory organ.
- Fertilisation internal ; development - direct.
- Examples - Carcharodon (great white shark), Scoliodon (dog fish)
  Pristis (saw fish), Torpedo , Trygon

Class Osteichthyes

> **NEET SYNAPSE**
> Male seahorses carry out parental care in their brood pouch.

- Osteon - bony ; ichthyes - fishes
- Marine & freshwater; streamlined body
- Endoskeleton made of bones
- Notochord replaced by bony vertebral column.
- Cycloid, ctenoid, ganoid scales
- Mouth - terminal ; cloaca - absent
- Four pairs of gills - covered by operculum
- Air bladder / swim bladder present - provides buoyancy.
- Heart - 2 chambered
- Lateral line system well marked
- Poikilotherms (cold blooded)
- Sexes separate. Claspers absent
- Fertilisation - external ; Oviparity present
- Development - direct
- Examples -
  - Exocoetus (flying fish), Hippocampus (sea horse) } Marine
  - Labeo, Catla, Clarias } Freshwater
  - Betta (fighting fish), Pterophyllum (angel fish) } Aquarium

Class Amphibia

- Amphi - dual ; bios - life
- Aquatic as well as terrestrial habitat
- Tetrapods - 2 pairs of limbs ; pentadactyl limbs.
- Poikilotherms - cold blooded
- Body divisible into head & trunk
- Skin moist - rich in glands - mucus & poison glands
- Alimentary canal & urogenital duct - open in cloaca.
- Respiration - larva - gills ; adult - skin, lungs & mouth.
- Heart - 3 chambered - 2 auricles & 1 ventricle
  Mixed blood flows through heart.

- Eyes have eyelids
- Ear represented by tympanum.
- Sexes separate. Sexual dimorphism present.
- Male has copulatory organ
- Fertilisation - external ; exception - Salamander.
- Development indirect ; larva - tadpole.
- Larva becomes adult by metamorphosis.
- Metamorphosis requires thyroxine.
- Examples - Bufo (toad), Rana (frog),
  Hyla (tree frog), Salamandra (Salamander)
  Ichthyophis (limbless amphibian)

Class Reptilia

- Repere or reptum - to crawl or creep.
- True terrestrial animals.
- Horny scales / scutes (epidermal origin)
- Internal fertilisation
- Leathery shell around egg
- Poikilotherms - cold blooded
- Skin - rough & dry - without glands
  ↳ periodically shed off - called moulting or skin cast.
- Tympanum represents ear.
- Heart - usually 3 chambered - 2 auricles ; 1 ventricle
- Exception - Crocodile - 4 chambered - 2 auricles + 2 ventricles
- Sexes separate, development - direct.
- Examples - Chelone (turtle), Testudo (tortoise)
  Chameleon (tree lizard), Calotes (garden lizard)
  Hemidactylus (wall lizard)
  Crocodilus (crocodile), Alligator
  Poisonous snakes - Naja (Cobra)
  Vipera (Viper)
  Bangarus (krait)

> **NEET SYNAPSE**
>
> Fish scales - Mesodermal in origin

- Limbs may or may not be present

Class Aves

- Glorified reptiles - possess advanced reptilian characters.
- Homeotherms - warm blooded. (Endotherms)
- Oviparous, bipedal, feather covered.
- Forelimbs modified into wings.
- Hindlimbs adapted for walking, perching, swimming.
- Epidermal exoskeleton - feathers, scales, claws, beaks.
- Skin - dry - lacks glands. Oil glands present at base of tail
- Bony endoskeleton present.
- Bones are pneumatic (hollow) - reduces weight for flying
- Respiration - through lungs - Air sacs assist respiration.
- Alimentary canal has special structures - crop & gizzard.
  Crop - stores food; Gizzard - muscular - crushes food.
- Heart - 4 chambered - 2 auricles & 2 ventricles.
- Sexes separate; sexual dimorphism present.
- Fertilisation - internal; development - direct.
- Examples - Corvus (crow), Columba (pigeon)
  Psittacula (parrot), Pavo (peacock)
  Struthio (ostrich), Aptenodytes (penguin)
  Neophron (vulture)

Memory trick

SCAN P_2C

Class Mammalia

- Presence of mammary glands (modified sweat glands)
- Homeotherms / Endotherms - warm blooded
- Exoskeleton - made of hair (protective & maintains temperature)
- Sebaceous glands present - secrete oily substance (on skin)
- External ears or pinna present.
- Two pairs of limbs present, pentadactyl limbs
- Whales & dolphins - flippers present.
- Heterodont - different types of teeth present.
- Heart - 4 chambered; 2 auricles & 2 ventricles.
- Sexes separate. Fertilisation - internal. Development - direct
- Viviparous. Exception { Ornithorhynchus (duck billed platypus)
- Oviparous ← { Echidna (spiny ant eater)
- Examples - Macropus (kangroo), Pteropus (flying fox)
  Camelus, Macaca (Monkey), Canis, Felis,
  Balaenoptera (whale), Delphinus (Dolphin)

5. Morphology of Flowering Plants

- Flowering plant
  - Vegetative parts - root, stem, leaves
  - Reproductive parts - Flowers fruits.
- Two major organ systems
  - Root system - includes underground parts
  - Shoot system - includes aerial parts - stem, leaves, flowers, fruits etc.

THE ROOT

- Underground; non green, positively geotropic
- Lacks nodes, leaves, buds; give out lateral branches.
- Main functions - absorption of water & minerals.
  - anchorage of plants
- Types of root systems -

Tap roots	Fibrous roots	Adventitious roots
• Primary root formed by elongation of radicle • Primary root gives out lateral branches called secondary & tertiary branches. • All dicots have tap roots	• Primary root is short lived and is replaced by fibrous roots. • Arise from base of stem • Monocots like wheat, maize etc.	• Arise from parts other than radicle • Can be underground, aerial or subaerial. • Grass, Monstera, banyan tree, sugarcane

Regions of root

- Root cap - thimble like, covers root
  - protection of root apex.
  - facilitates root penetration
- Meristematic zone - Active cell division - Cells are small & thin walled
- Zone of elongation - responsible for growth of root in length.
- Zone of maturation - cell mature. Formation of root hair takes place.

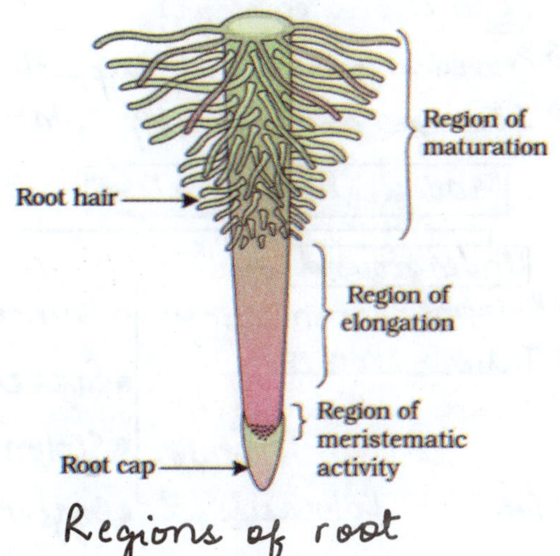

Regions of root

5. Morphology of Flowering Plants

Modifications of root

- Food storage / fleshy roots ; example- radish, carrot , turnip etc.
- Respiratory roots / pneumatophores - found in plants of swampy / marshy regions. Roots are aerial - above ground. Ex. Rhizophora Halophytes possess pneumatophores.
- Supporting roots - adventitious roots
  - Prop roots - develop from branches , grow vertically downwards. Eg. banyan.
  - Stilt roots - develop from nodes of stem near soil. - provide support , help in better anchorage. Eg. Sugarcane

THE STEM

- Develops from plumule of embryo , forms main plant axis
- Negatively geotropic - grows above ground.
- Characterised by presence of nodes and internodes
- Nodes - leaves arise from them
- Internodes - region between 2 nodes
- Stem bears buds - young & immature shoots.
  - Terminal: Present at tip of stem
  - Lateral: Present on side of stem.
- Stem appears green when the plant is young & becomes brown or woody in later stages.

NEET SYNAPSE
Internodes are reduced in plants with exhibiting Rosette habit

Functions of stem

- Provides mechanical support
- Transportation of water, minerals & food
- Storage of food - Eg. potato
- Vegetative propagation Eg. Rose

Modifications of stem

Underground
- Rhizome - Banana, Ginger
- Tuber - Potato
  Axillary buds are found in eyes of potato.
- Corm - Colocasia

Sub aerial
- Runner - lawn grass, strawberry
- Sucker - Pineapple, Chrysanthemum
- Stolon - Jasmine , peppermint
- Offset - water hyacinth

Aerial
- Tendrils - vines cucumber , gourds
- Thorns - rose
- Phylloclades - Eg. Opuntia

THE LEAF

- Green, flatenned, lateral structure present on stem.
- Develops from nodes; bears axillary buds.
- Axillary bud develops into branch
- Leaves are main organs of photosynthesis

Parts of leaf

Leaf base / Hypopodium

- Attaches leaf to branch.
- Stipule - lateral leaf like structures on either side of leaf
  ↳ may or may not be present
- Pulvinus - thickening present at base of leaf
  - present in leguminous plants.
- Sheath - leaf base becomes broad & covers the whole node
  - present in monocots like wheat.

NEET SYNAPSE
Veins provide rigidity to leaf blade

Petiole / Mesopodium

- Stalk of leaf that joins lamina with branch.
- Long, thin, flexible. Holds the blade for light exposure.
- Allow leaf to flutter in wind - bring fresh air to leaf surface.

Lamina / Epipodium

- Also called leaf blade. Green - carries out photosynthesis
- Possesses veins & veinlets - channels for food & water transport.
- Midrib - most prominent vein present in middle
- Shape, margin, apex, extent of incision varies in different leaves.

Venation

Reticulate

- Veins form a network
- Main vein divides into veinlets
- Characteristic feature of dicots.
- Eg. Peepal, mango etc.

Parallel

- Veins are parallely arranged
- Main vein does not divide into veinlets
- Characteristic feature of monocots.
- Eg. Rice, banana, wheat

Types of leaves

Simple leaf

- Lamina is not divided
- leaf bears axillary bud
- Leaf may be incised but incisions do not touch midrib
- Eg. mango, guava etc.

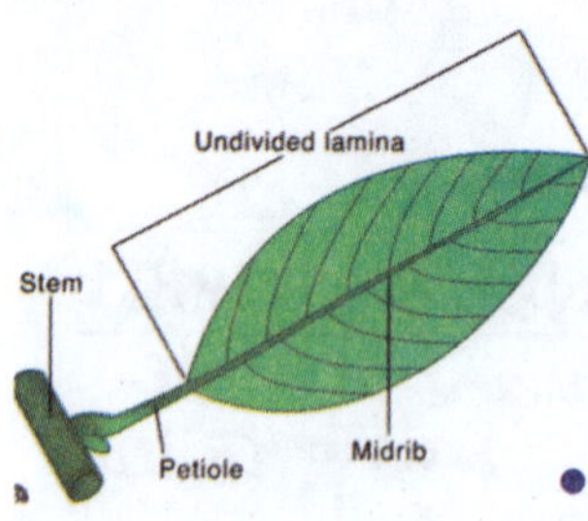

Compound leaf

- Lamina is completely incised upto midrib
- Distinct segments called leaflets are formed
- Axillary bud present at axil of petiole but not on axil of leaflets

Pinnately compound

- Leaflets present laterally on rachis

Eg. Neem

Palmately compound

- Leaflets appear palm like.

Eg. Silk cotton.

Phyllotaxy

- Arrangement of leaves on branches.

Alternate

- Single leaf present at each node
Leaves arranged alternatively

Eg. Hibiscus, mustard, sunflower

Opposite

- Two leaves borne on each node, opposite to each other.

Eg. Calotropis
Guava

Whorled

- More than 2 leaves borne on a single node, in a whorled manner.

Eg. Alstonia

Modifications of leaf

Leaf tendrils

Coiled structures
Help in climbing
Coil around support
Eg. Pea

Leaf spines

Adaptation for desert plants
Reduces surface area, thereby transpiration
Eg. cactus

Fleshy leaves

Store food, onion & garlic

NEET SYNAPSE
Bulb of onion is modified stem, but edible parts are fleshy leaves.

Carnivorous leaves

Trap insects to fulfill nitrogen requirements
Eg. Venus fly trap
Pitcher plant

Phyllodes

Petiole enlarged and modified for photosynthesis.
Eg. Acacia

THE INFLORESCENCE

- Flower is a modified shoot.
- Shoot apical meristem changes to floral meristem.
- Axis gets condensed - internodes do not elongate.
- Floral appendages are produced at nodes, instead of leaves.
- When a shoot tip transforms into a flower, it is always solitary.
- Arrangement of flowers on floral axis
- Pedicel - stalk like, attaches flower to peduncle
- Bract - green leaf like structures providing protection to buds.
- Solitary terminal flower - single flower found on terminal part of branch.
- Solitary axillary flower - single flower present in the axil of leaf.

Types of Inflorescence

Racemose

- Floral axis grows continuously
- Flowers arise acropetally
- Younger flowers towards apex
- Older flowers towards base

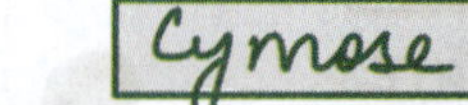

- Peduncle terminates into a solitary flower
- Flowers arise basipetally.
- Younger flowers arise at base
- Older flowers at apex.

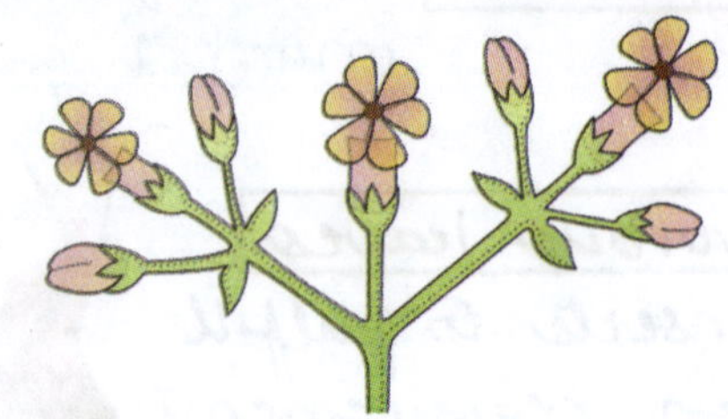

> NEET SYNAPSE
> Racemose inflorescence is also called Indefinite inflorescence

THE FLOWER

- Reproductive part of plant.
- Receptacle / thalamus – the rounded part of stalk on which the parts of flower are attached.
  - ↳ It is a part of stem & not of flower.

Whorls of a flower

Accessory whorls

Calyx

- Outermost whorl
- Made of sepals (green- leaf like)
- Protects flowers in bud stage
- Polysepalous – sepals free
- Gamosepalous - sepals fused

Corolla

- Present inside calyx
- Made of petals (colourful)
- Polypetalous - petals free
- Gamopetalous - petals fused

Essential whorls

Androecium

- Present inner to corolla
- Made up of stamens

Gynoecium

- Innermost whorl
- Made up of carpels

◈ **Perianth**

- Sepals and petals cannot be differentiated
- Units are called tepals • Eg. Lily

NEET SYNAPSE
Tepals can be
sepaloid - green
Petaloid - colourful

◈ **Aestivation**

- Arrangement of sepals and petals on thalamus

Types of aestivation

- Petals & sepals close to each other
- No overlap

Eg. Calotropis

Valvate

- One petal external
- One petal internal
- Remaining partially external or internal

Imbricate Eg. Cassia, gulmohar

- Regular overlapping
- Margin of one petal overlaps next one

Eg. Hibiscus, cotton, ladyfinger

Twisted

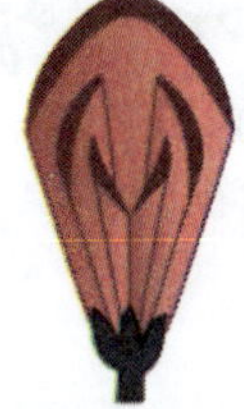

- Posterior petal (standard) overlaps two smaller lateral petals (wings)
- Wings overlap two anterior petals (keel)

Vexillary Eg. Pea and bean

Characteristic of Papilionaceae

Androecium

◈ Represents male reproductive part. Unit - Stamen.
◈ Each stamen = filament (stalk like) + anther (bag like)
◈ Angiospermic anther - mostly dithecous (two lobes)
◈ Each lobe has two chambers - pollen sacs.
◈ Pollen sacs contain pollen grains (male gametophyte)
◈ Staminode - sterile anther.
◈ Types of stamens on the basis of adhesion

- Epipetalous - stamens fused with petals. Eg. Brinjal
- Epiphyllous - stamens fused with tepals. Eg. Lily

- Types of stamens on the basis of fusion
- Polyandrous - stamens are free Eg. Lotus
- Adelphous - Filaments fused; anthers free
  - Monoadelphous - filaments fuse to form single group; China rose
  - Diadelphous - filaments fuse to form two groups; Pea
  - Polyadelphous - filaments fuse to form more than two groups; Citrus (lemon)
- Types of stamens on the basis of length of filaments
- Didynamous - 2 short ; 2 long Eg. Ocimum, Salvia
- Tetradynamous - 4 inner - long ; 2 outer - short Eg. Brassicaceae

Gynoecium

- Innermost whorl; represents female part of flower.
- Units are called carpels.
- Each carpel = ovary (swollen base) + style (stalk) + stigma (receptive)
- Types based on cohesion of carpels -
- Apocarpous - carpels are free. Eg. lotus, rose etc.
- Syncarpous - carpels are fused. Eg. mustard, tomato etc.

Placentation

- Arrangement of ovules inside ovary.
- Placenta - Tissue with which ovules attach to ovary.
- Types of placentation
- Marginal - placenta forms ridge along ventral suture of unilocular ovary (single chamber)
  - Ovules are borne on this ridge.
  - Eg. Pea
- Axile - multilocular ovary (multicarpellary syncarpous)
  - placenta is axial; ovules attached to axis.
  - Eg - China rose, tomato, lemon.

Memory trick: Lemon & Tom got axile in China

- Parietal - unilocular & syncarpous ovary.
  - placenta present towards inner side
  - ovules develop on inner side of ovary.
  - Formation of false septum makes ovary look 2 chambered
  - Eg. Mustard and Argemone

Memory trick: Argemone's party must be false

Party - parietal
Must - Mustard

- **Free central** – unilocular ovary
  – placenta bearing ovules arises from central axis
  Eg. Dianthus, primrose etc.
  Memory trick: FREE DP

- **Basal** – unilocular ovary
  – placenta present at base, contains single large ovule
  Eg. Sunflower, marigold etc.
  Memory trick: Mary's sunflowers are Beautiful (B – Basal)

Types of flower

Based on reproductive parts

- Bisexual – carpels + stamen
- Unisexual – carpels / stamen
  (pistillate) (staminate)

Based on presence of whorls

- Complete – All 4 whorls present
- Incomplete – One or more whorls absent

Based on floral symmetry

- Actinomorphic – radially symmetrical
  Eg: Mustard, datura, chilli
- Zygomorphic – bilaterally symmetrical
  Eg: Gulmohar, bean, Cassia
- Assymetric – No symmetry
  Eg- Canna

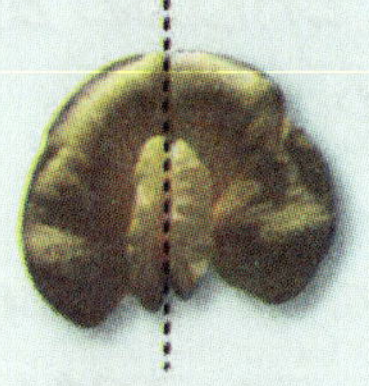

a. Actinomorphic b. Zygomorphic c. Asymmetric

Floral symmetry

Based on position of parts

- Hypogynous – Gynoecium at top Superior ovary
  Mustard, china rose, brinjal

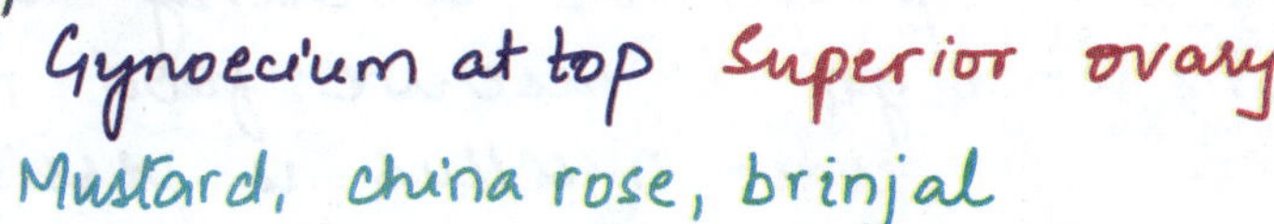

- Perigynous – Gynoecium at same level as other parts
  plum, rose, peach

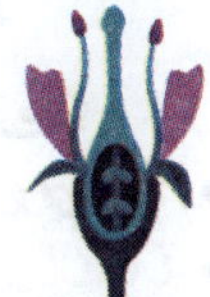

- Epigynous – Gynoecium below other floral parts
  Inferior ovary
  ray florets of sunflower, Guava, cucumber

Based on presence or absence of bract

Bracteate - Bract present around sepals

Ebracteate - Bract absent

Based on floral appendages

Trimerous - 3 or multiples of 3

Tetramerous - 4 or multiples of 4

Pentamerous - 5 or multiples of 5

FRUIT

- Ovary transforms into fruit after fertilisation.
- Parthenocarpic fruit - formed from ovary without fertilisation
- Pericarp - fruit wall
  - Epicarp - outer layer
  - Mesocarp - middle layer
  - Endocarp - innermost layer

NEET SYNAPSE

In dry fruits, the pericarp is thin & undifferentiated

Drupe or Stone fruit

- Fleshy, single seeded fruit
- Seeds enclosed in stony endocarp.
- Develop from monocarpellary superior ovary
- Single ovule develops into seed.
- Mango - mesocarp fleshy, edible
- Coconut - mesocarp fibrous

Epicarp
Mesocarp
Seed
Endocarp

SEED

- Ovule transforms into seed after fertilisation.
- Seed coat - protective covering of seed.
- Contains embryo & reserve food material.
- Perispermic seeds - nucellus is persistent Eg. black pepper.
- Formation of seed completes the process of reproduction.
- Parts of seed

Embryo

- Plumule
- epicotyl
- cotyledon
- Hypocotyl
- Radicle

Endosperm

- Nutritive tissue for embryo development
- May or may not be consumed by growing embryo.
- Rich in nutrients

Seed coat

- made of 2 layers
- testa (outer)
- tegmen (inner)
- Micropyle - small hole through which water enters
- Hilum - point of attachment of seed with stalk.

Types of Seeds

Based on numbers of cotyledons

Dicotyledonous
Two cotyledons present
Eg. pea, gram, mango etc.

Monocotyledonous
Single cotyledon.
Cotyledon called scutellum
Eg. rice, wheat, maize.

Based on presence or absence of endosperm

- Endospermic
- Albuminous
- Seeds store food in endosperm
  Eg. Castor, zeamays etc.

- Non endospermic
- Ex- albuminous
- Seeds lack endosperm.
- Endosperm completely consumed during embryonic development.
  Eg. pea, beans, orchids

MAIZE

Endosperm - food reserve for growing embryo
Scutellum - single cotyledon
Coleoptile - covering of plumule
Plumule - future shoot
Radicle - future root
Coleorhiza - covering of radicle

NEET SYNAPSE
Aleurone layer
- proteinaceous
- outer covering of endosperm.

In cereals, like maize, the seed coat is fused with the fruit wall

SOME IMPORTANT FAMILIES

- Malvaceae
- Cruciferae / Brassicaceae
- Leguminosae / Fabaceae
- Compositae / Asteraceae
- Gramineae / Poaceae

Malvaceae

1 2 3 4 5 6 7 8

$Br \oplus ⚥ Epi_{3-9} K_{5 \text{ or } (5)} \widehat{C_5 A_{(\infty)}} \underline{G}_{(2-\infty)}$

1. Bracteate
2. Actinomorphic
3. Bisexual
4. Epicalyx (formed by bracteoles)

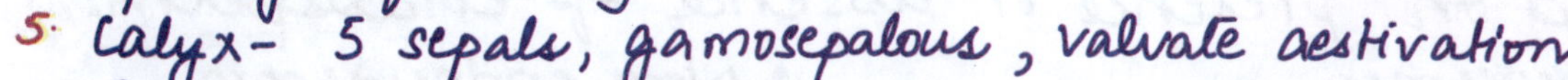

5. Calyx - 5 sepals, gamosepalous, valvate aestivation
6. Corolla - 5, polypetalous, twisted aestivation
7. Androecium - Numerous stamens, $\widehat{C\ A}$ - epipetalous, monoadelphous
8. Gynoecium - superior ovary ($\underline{G}$), syncarpous, axile placentation.

Eg: Ladyfinger, cotton, Hibiscus (china rose)

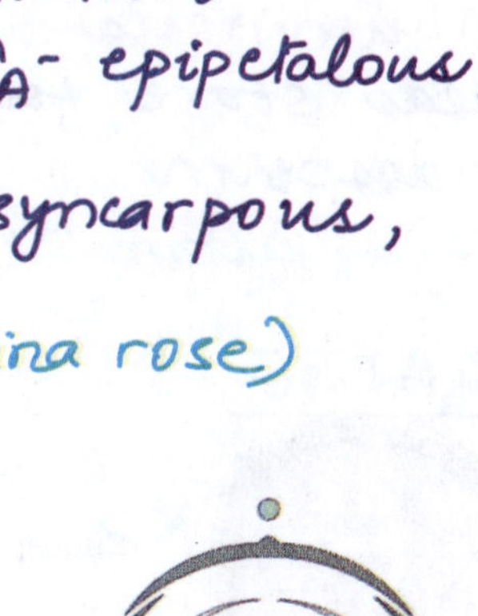

Cruciferae / Brassicaceae

1 2 3 4 5 6 7

$Ebr \oplus ⚥ K_{2+2} C_4 A_{2+4} \underline{G}_{(2)}$

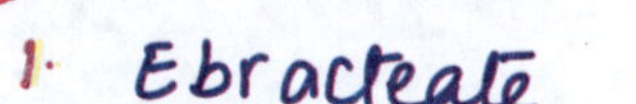

1. Ebracteate
2. Actinomorphic
3. Bisexual
4. Calyx - 4, polysepalous in 2 whorls, imbricate aestivation.
5. Corolla - 4, polypetalous - cruciform.
6. Androecium - Six stamens - arranged in two whorls of 2 & 4 stamens
7. Gynoecium - Bicarpellary, syncarpous $\underline{G}$ - superior ovary. parietal placentation.

Eg: Mustard, cauliflower, Iberis (ornamental) Lepidium (asthma medicines)

Leguminosae | Fabaceae.

1 2 3 4 5 6 7

Br % ⚥ $K_{(5)}$ $C_{1+2+(2)}$ $A_{(9)+1}$ $\underline{G}_1$

1. Bracteate
2. Zygomorphic
3. Bisexual
4. Sepals- gamosepalous - 5 sepals ; imbricate
5. Corolla- 5 , gamopetalous , papilionaceous vexillary aestivation.
6. Androecium - Ten, diadelphous
7. Gynoecium - Monocarpellary , superior ovary ($\underline{G}_1$) marginal placentation.

Eg. Leguminous plants- pea, beans, grams. soyabean, groundnut

Compositae | Asteraceae (sunflower family)

Ray florets

Br % ⚥ K_{pappus} $C_{(3-5)}$ A_0 $\overline{G}_{(2)}$

1 2 3 4 5 6 7

1. Bracteate
2. Zygomorphic
3. Bisexual | unisexual
4. Calyx- Pappus - ring of fine hair persistent.
5. Corolla- 5 petals, gamopetalous.
6. Androecium- absent
7. Gynoecium- bicarpellary, syncarpous , inferior ovary , unilocular, basal placentation.

Ray floret

Disc florets

Br ⊕ ⚥ K(pappus) $\widehat{C_{(5)}\,A_{(5)}}$ $\overline{G}_{(2)}$

Bracteate , actinomorphic , bisexual .
Calyx- pappus
Corolla- 5 petals , gamopetalous
Androecium - 5 stamens $\widehat{C\;A}$- epipetalous
Gynoecium - inferior ovary, unilocular bicarpellary syncarpous, basal placentation.

Disc floret

Gramineae/ Poaceae

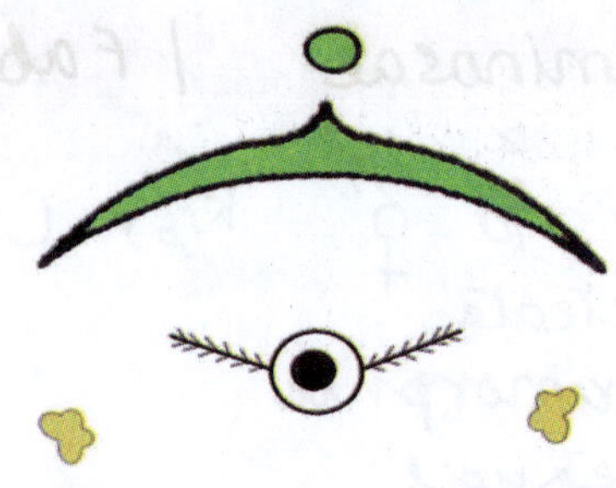

1 2 3 4 5 6

Br % ⚥ P_2 A_{3-6} $\underline{G}_1$

1. Bracteate
2. Zygomorphic - bilateral symmetry.
3. Bisexual
4. Perianth - reduced to 2 scales called lodicules.
5. Androecium - stamens - 3-6, polyadelphous.
6. Gynoecium - unilocular, superior ovary. Monocarpellary, basal placentation.

Eg. Jowar, wheat, rice, maize, sugarcane etc.

6. Anatomy of Flowering Plants

- **Plant anatomy** - study of structure & arrangement of tissues and their organisation in the plant body.

THE TISSUE SYSTEMS

Epidermal | Ground | Vascular

Epidermal Tissue System

- Forms outer covering of whole plant body.
- Contacts the external environment directly
- Functions - provide mechanical support to plants
  Absorption, secretion, gaseous exchange, protection
- Components of epidermal tissue system are

Epidermis -

- outermost covering, single layered.
- contains elongated, compactly arranged cells.
- Cells are parenchymatous with large vaculole & small amount of cytoplasm lining the wall.
- Cuticle - thick waxy layer covering epidermis
  ↳ prevents loss of water.

NEET SYNAPSE - root epidermis lacks cuticle as primary function of root is water absorption & cuticle repels water.

Stomata

- Minute openings on epidermis of leaves.
- Regulate transpiration & exchange of gases.

- Guard cells - part of stoma, contain chloroplasts.
  - surround stomatal pore
  - Kidney bean shaped in dicots
  - Dumbbell shaped in monocots
- Subsidiary cells - 4-8 in numbers
  - surround guard cells

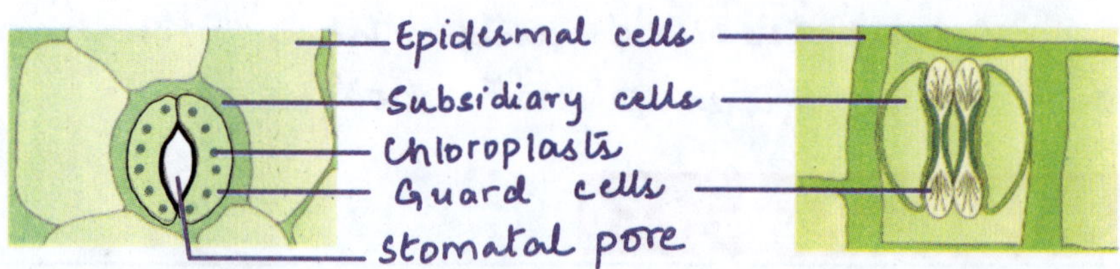

NEET SYNAPSE

- Guard cells regulate the opening and closing of stomatal pores.
- Outer wall of guard cells is thin, inner wall is thick

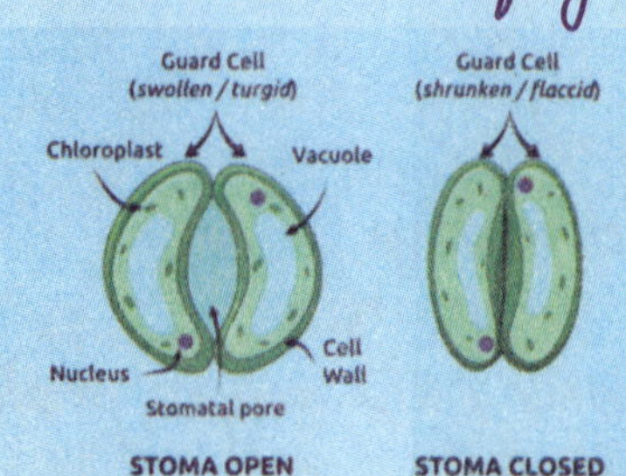

- When guard cell swell up due to inflow of ions & water, the walls are pulled towards outside, thereby opening the stomatal pore.
- When guard cells become flaccid, the stomatal pore closes.

Stomatal apparatus = stomatal aperture + guard cells + subsidiary cells.

Epidermal outgrowths

- Trichomes - epidermal hair of stem
  - can be unicellular or multicellular.
  - prevent water loss due to transpiration
- Root hair - tubular, unbranched outgrowths usually unicellular.
  - increase absorptive surface area of roots.

Ground Tissue System

- Also called fundamental tissue system.
- Makes up main bulk of plant body; largest tissue system.
- Includes all tissues except epidermis & vascular bundles.
- Contains parenchyma, collenchyma & sclerenchyma
- Usually includes cortex, pericycle, pith & medullary rays in primary stems & roots.
- In leaves, it consits only of mesophyll cells containing chloroplasts

NEET SYNAPSE

Epidermis - outermost layer in roots, stem & leaves.
Hypodermis - present beneath epidermis; only in roots & stem
Endodermis - specialised layer found in roots - controls movement of water & nutrients into vascular system.

Vascular Tissue system

- Consists of vascular bundles
- Vascular bundle = xylem + phloem
- Open vascular bundle - found in dicot stem & roots cambium present between xylem & phloem.
  - ↳ thin strip of meristematic tissue
  - ↳ involved in secondary growth.
- Closed vascular bundle - found in monocot stem & roots.
  - ↳ lacks cambium, hence secondary growth absent.
- Radial bundles - xylem & phloem present on different radii.
  - present in roots
- Conjoint bundles - xylem & phloem situated on same radius.
  - present in stem & leaves.

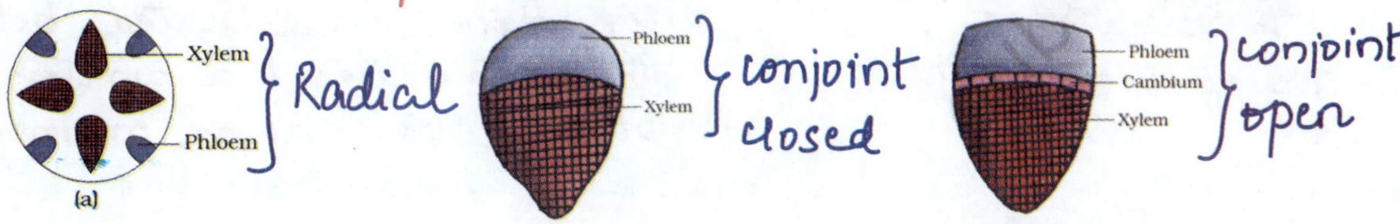

ANATOMY OF DICOT & MONOCOT PLANTS

ANATOMY OF ROOT

Dicot Root

- Epiblema - outermost layer, gives rise to unicellular root hair
- Cortex - consists of multiple layers of parenchymatous cells.

Endodermis - innermost layer of cortex.
cells are tightly packed
Cells possess thickenings of suberin & form a band called Casparian strips - they are impermeable to water.

Pericycle - present below endodermis
made of parenchymatous cells
gives rise to vascular cambium & lateral roots during secondary growth.

Pith - small or inconspicuous.

- Vascular bundles - radial,
usually 2-4 xylem & phloem patches present
xylem exarch protoxylem towards periphery

STELE - All tissues inner to the endoderm including pericycle, vascular bundles & pith.

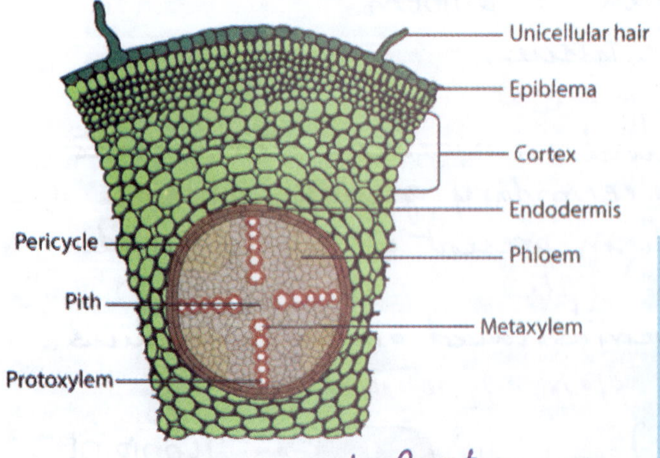

T.S. of Dicot Root

Parenchymatous cells present between xylem & phloem constitute conjuctive tissue.

NEET SYNAPSE

During secondary growth, cambium ring originates from conjunctive tissue located below phloem bundles & a portion of pericycle tissue above protoxylem.

Monocot Root

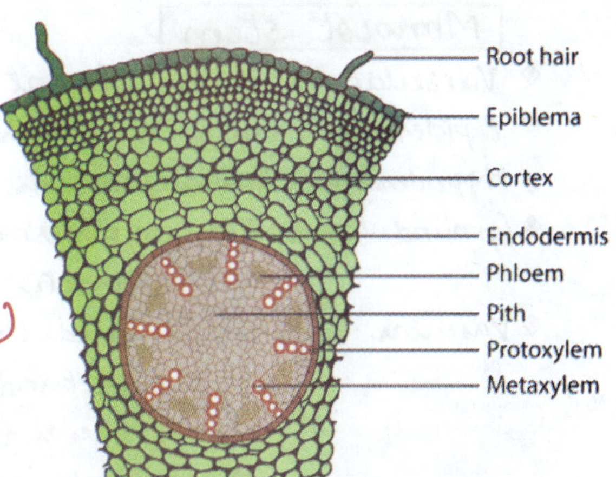

- Tissues similar to dicot root- including epidermis, cortex, endodermis, pericycle, vascular bundles and pith
- xylem- polyarch (more than 6)
- Pith - large & conspicuous
- Secondary growth absent.

ANATOMY OF STEM

Dicot Stem

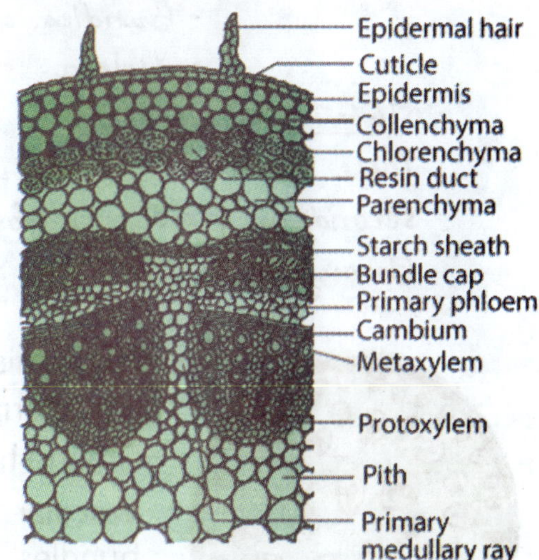

- Epidermis - outermost protective layer. covered by cuticle may bear trichomes & few stomata.
- Hypodermis - 3-4 layers of collenchymatous cells. Provides mechanical strength to stem in early stages.
- Cortex - made of parenchymatous cells
- Endodermis - single, innermost layer of cortex made of barrel shaped cells without intercellular spaces cells bear starch grains, hence also called starch sheath. Casparian strips absent

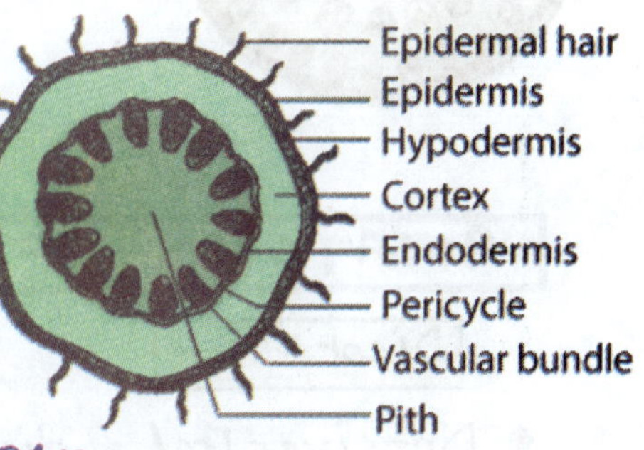

- Pericycle - multilayered, present between endodermis & vascular bundl
- Vascular bundles - conjoint, collateral, open arranged in a ring, definite in number. Xylem endarch (protoxylem towards middle)
- Medullary rays - present between vascular bundles. help in radial conduction of food & water.
- Pith - present in centre, contains parenchymatous cells with large intercellular spaces.

Monocot stem

- Vascular cambium absent, no secondary growth.
- Epidermis - outermost layer, hair absent
- Hypodermis - below epidermis, made of sclerenchymatous cells.
- Ground tissue - below hypodermis, made of parenchymatous cells. Not differentiated into cortex, endodermis, pericycle & pith.
- Vascular bundles - scattered throughout ground tissue.
  Peripheral bundles - numerous & small than at the centre.
  Bundle sheath - surrounds each vascular bundle.
  ↳ sclerenchymatous.
  - Bundles are conjoint, collateral & closed.
  - Xylem endarch; phloem parenchyma absent

NEET SYNAPSE

There is little increase in diameter with age in monocot stems as secondary growth is absent. Primary vascular tissue remains functional throughout the life of plant.

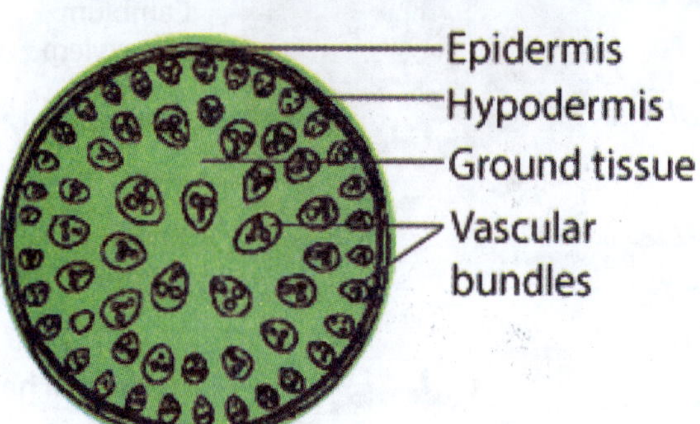

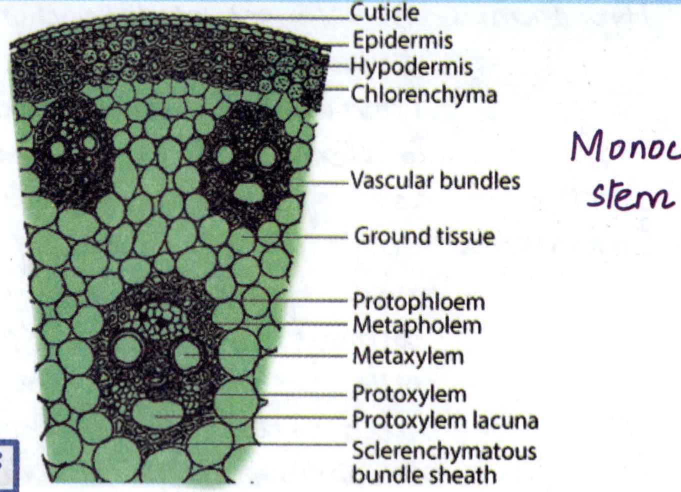

Monocot stem

ANATOMY OF LEAF

Dicot leaf

- Dorsiventral - distinct upper (adaxial) & lower (abaxial) surfaces due to unequal illumination.
- Epidermis - outermost layer. - lined by cuticle
  Upper epidermis - single layer of parenchymatous cells.
  Lower epidermis - has more stomata than adaxial.
- Mesophyll - ground tissue present between adaxial & abaxial epidermis.

Mesophyll differentiated into

- Palisade parenchyma - elongated tightly packed cells.
  - perpendicular to adaxial epidermis
  - cells possess chloroplasts, carry out photosynthesis actively.
- Spongy parenchyma - present below palisade parenchyma
  - cells spherical/oval in shape
  - Cells irregularly arranged with large air spaces

◆ Vascular bundles
- found in veins & midrib of leaf.
- dicots exhibit reticulate venation.
- Vascular bundles are conjoint, collateral & closed.
- Bundle sheath cells - surround each vascular bundle.

Monocot leaf

◆ Isobilateral - no distinction between upper & lower surfaces

◆ Epidermis
- made of single layer of cells.
- Cells possess stomata.
- Bulliform cells present

NEET SYNAPSE

Bulliform cells are responsible for inward curling of leaves in monocots. During dry conditions, loss of water from vacuoles induce bulliform cells to fold the two leaf edges towards each other, resulting in leaf curl.

◆ Mesophyll -
not differentiated into palisade & spongy parenchyma
- cells are spherical & irregularly arranged.

Vascular bundles - conjoint & closed.
- uniform size due to parallel venation, except in main veins.
- Bundle sheath - surrounds each vascular bundle
- Vascular bundles are scattered throughout the space.

7. Structural Organisation in Animals

COCKROACH

- Belong to class Insecta of phylum Arthropoda
- Nocturnal (active at night), omnivorous, cursorial (fast runners)
- Size - 1/4 - 3 inches (0.6-7.6 cm)
- Habitat - warm & damp places, availability of food.

MORPHOLOGY

- Common species Periplaneta americana
- Size - 34 - 53 mm long.
- Bilaterally symmetrical, segmented.
- Body divisible into head, thorax and abdomen.
- Body covered with chitinous exoskeleton.
- Sclerites - hardened plates covering the body
  Tergites - dorsal sclerites
  Sternites - ventral sclerites
  Pleurites - lateral sclerites
  Arthroidal membrane - thin, flexible articular membrane joining the sclerites.

HEAD

- Hypognathous (facing downwards), anteriorly located
- Triangular in shape
- Formed by the fusion of 6 embryonic segments.
- Flexible neck allows movement of head in all directions.
- Bears a pair of antennae, compound eyes & simple eyes.

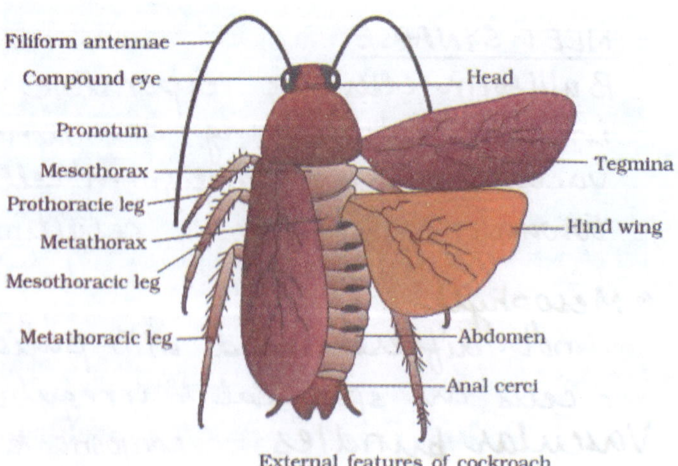

External features of cockroach

- **Antennae** - Sensory in nature; possess tactile, olfactory & thermal receptors.
- **Mouth parts** - biting & chewing type
  ↳ Labrum - upper lip
  Maxilla - paired
  Mandible - paired
  Labium - lower lip
  Hypopharynx - Tongue like.

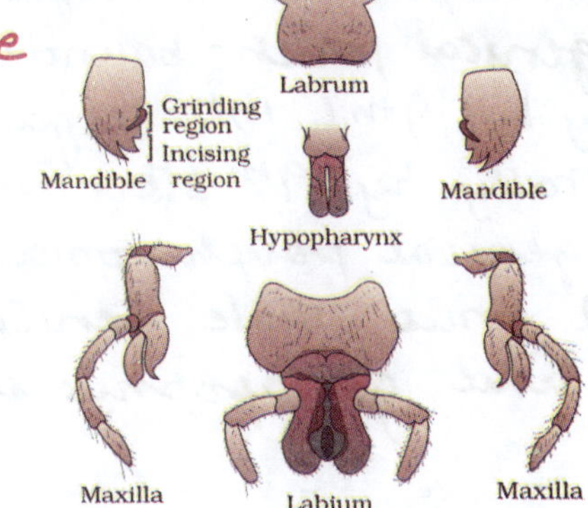

THORAX

- Consists of prothorax, mesothorax and metathorax
- Prothorax - gives rise to a pair of legs
  ↳ extends to form neck → connects head with thorax

The tergite of prothorax is very large. It covers the neck which connects thorax to head.

- Mesothorax - gives rise to forewings & a pair of legs
  - forewings are thick, opaque, leathery also called elytra or tegmina - not used for flying.

- Metathorax - gives rise to hindwings & a pair of legs
  - hindwings are transparent, membranous and are used for flying.

NEET SYNAPSE - Total number of legs in cockroach is 6. Hence it is called hexapoda. It is a characteristic feature of animals belonging to class Insecta.

ABDOMEN

- Number of segments in embryo = 11
- Number of segments in adults (both ♂ & ♀) = 10

- Sexual dimorphism is present -
- Males | Females

Males	Females
• Abdomen has 9 sternites	• Abdomen has 7 sternites.
• Anal styles present in 9th segment.	• 7th sternum - boat shaped
• Male genital pouch - bounded dorsally by 9th & 10th terga & ventrally by 9th sternum	• 7th + 8th + 9th sterna = brood pouch / genital pouch.
• Male genital pouch contains dorsal anus, male genital pore and gonapophysis.	• Anterior part of brood pouch contains female gonopore, spermathecal pores & collateral glands.

Both sexes bear anal cerci on the 10th segment.

ANATOMY

DIGESTIVE SYSTEM

- Consists of alimentary canal + digestive glands.
- Alimentary canal is 5-6 long. Extends from mouth to anus. It consists of -

NEET SYNAPSE
A pair of salivary glands are present on each side of oesophagus & crop.

Foregut

- Lined by thick chitinous cuticle
- Mouth → Pharynx → Oesophagus → Crop → Gizzard

Crop - largest part of foregut
- stores food

Gizzard - also called proventriculus
- muscular, thick walled chamber
- Contain 6 chitinous teeth that crush & grind food.

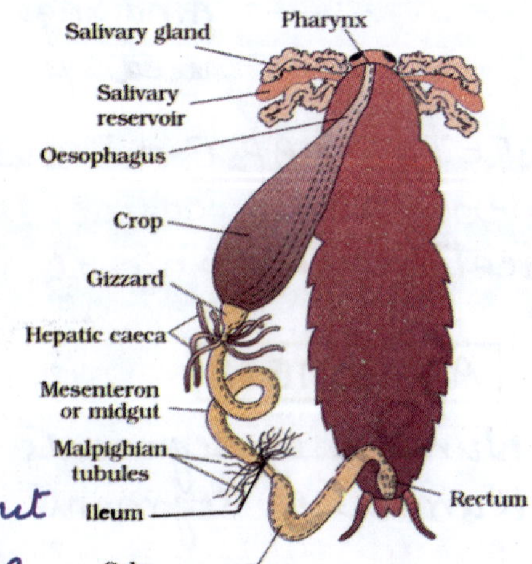

Midgut

- Lined with glandular epithelium.
- Hepatic / Gastric caeca - 6-8 in number
  ↳ present at junction of foregut & midgut
- Malpighian tubules - 100-150 thread like, yellow coloured tubules. They perform excretion. They are present at the junction of midgut and hindgut

Hindgut

- Divided into ileum, colon & rectum.
- Rectum opens through anus.

NEET SYNAPSE
Rectum has 6 papillae that assist in water conservation from faecal matter

RESPIRATORY SYSTEM

- Trachae are present for respiration.
- Spiracles - 10 pairs, present on lateral side of body.
  ↳ 2 pairs thoracic ; 8 pairs abdominal.
  ↳ receive air from outside & pass to trachae.

Sphincters - guard the opening of spiracles.

- Each trachea divides into tracheoles
- Tracheoles - carry out diffusion for air exchange
  ↳ supply oxygen to all body parts.

CIRCULATORY SYSTEM

- Open circulatory system, blood (haemolymph) flows in haemocoel. Visceral organs bathe in haemolymph.
- Haemolymph - rich in trehalose
  - contains blood cells called haemocytes
  - lacks respiratory pigment; hence white in colour.
- Heart - elongated ; has 13 chambers.
  - Inhalant openings (through which blood enters heart) are called ostia - guarded by valves.
- Blood from heart is pumped into sinuses anteriorly.
- Pumping action brought about by contraction & relaxation of alary muscles.
- Alary muscles - 12 pairs present.
- Blood flows unidirectionally in heart from posterior to anterior end.

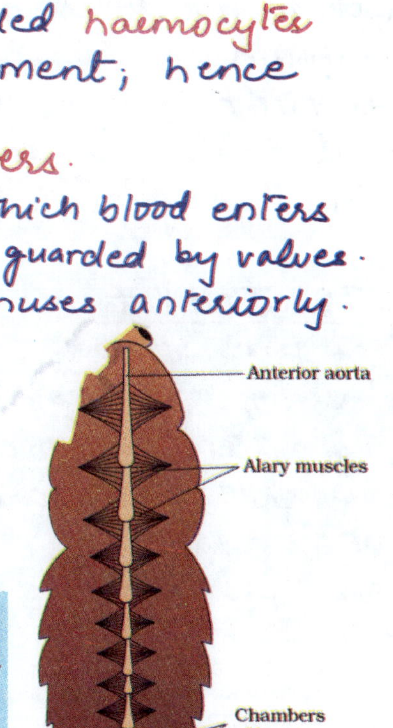

NEET SYNAPSE
Hoemocoel of cockroach is divided by dorsal & ventral diaphragms into 3 sinuses - pericardial sinus, perivisceral sinus & perineural sinus

EXCRETORY SYSTEM

- Cockroach is uricotelic (excretes uric acid)
- Excretory organs – Malpighian tubules, fat body, nephrocytes & uricose gland (mushroom glands) – in males only.
- Malpighian tubules are main organs of excretion.
  - ↳ lined by glandular & ciliated cells.
  - ↳ absorb nitrogenous wastes & convert them into uric acid – excreted through hind gut.

NERVOUS SYSTEM

Central Nervous System

- Supra oesophageal ganglion
  - situated above oesophagus
  - supply to eyes & antennae
- Sub oesophageal ganglion
  - lies below oesophagus
  - Main motor centre
  - Supply to mandibles, maxillae & labium.
  - Gives rise to ventral nerve cord.
- Ventral nerve cord – solid double, ganglionated.

Peripheral Nervous System

- Consists of nerves given out by CNS.
- Cephalic ganglion – eyes, antennae & other parts of head.
- Thoracic ganglion – wings & legs innervation.
- Abdominal ganglia – 5 in numbers – supply musculature of body.

Last abdominal ganglion – supply to reproductive organs.

NEET SYNAPSE

Ventral part of body contains most part of nervous system. Therefore even if head of cockroach is cut, it can still survive upto 1 week.

Nervous system of cockroach →

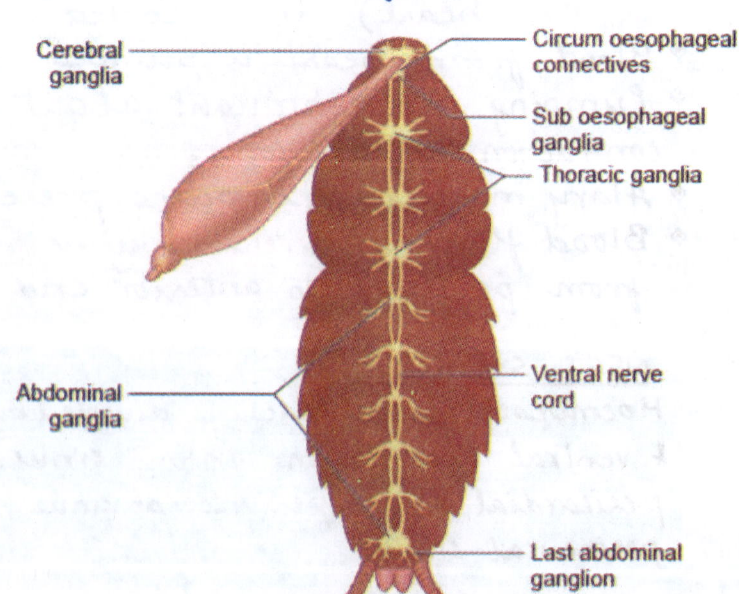

SENSE ORGANS

- Compound eyes (1 pair) - units of photoreception.
  Each compound eye contains 2000 - 2500 Ommatidia
  Each ommatidium has its own lens, thus several images of an object are formed.
  Images have less resolution (blurred) } lead to
  Sensitivity to light is high. } Mosaic vision
  Such an arrangement favours nocturnal vision.
- Tactile receptors - (sensitive to touch) - help in search of food.
  ↳ Antennae & bristles on body
- Chemoreceptors - perceive taste (gustatory)
  ↳ tips of maxillary & labial palps, labium & hypopharynx.
- Auditory receptors - perceive sound vibrations.
  ↳ antennae & anal cerci.

NEET SYNAPSE
Spermatophore ensures survival of sperms until it is deposited in female.

REPRODUCTIVE SYSTEM

Male Reproductive System

- Testes - paired; 4th - 6th abdominal segments.
- Vas deferens - paired; connect testes to ejaculatory ducts.
- Mushroom gland - 6th - 7th abdominal segment.
  - its secretion nourishes sperms.
- Ejaculatory duct - paired. Present between 9th - 10th sterna.
  - open into genital pouch through genital pore.
- Seminal vesicles - numerous sacs
  - store sperms.

Spermatophore - mass of glued sperms of seminal vesicle.
- Discharged during copulation.
- Phallic or Conglobate gland - Secretes outer layer of spermatophore
- External genitalia - Gonapophysis Contains 3 chitinous structures called phallomeres.

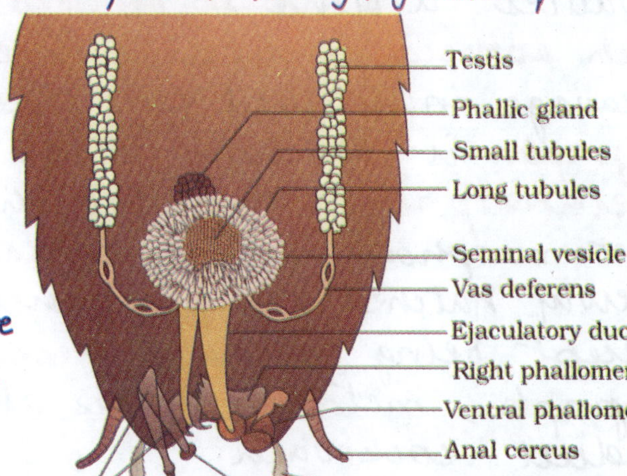

FEMALE REPRODUCTIVE SYSTEM

- Ovaries - paired ; 2nd to 6th segment.
- ↳ Each ovary consists of 8 ovarian tubules / ovarioles. Ova develop in ovarian tubules.
- Oviducts and Vagina - ovarioles unite to form oviduct. Oviducts combine to form vagina
- Spermatheca / Seminal receptacle - present in 6th segment.
  ↳ opens into genital pouch on 9th segment.
- Collaterial Gland - paired, branched tubular glands.
  - secrete oothecal covering.
- Genital pouch -

large boat shaped.

↳ anterior part - brood pouch.

↳ posterior part - Oothecal chamber (fertilisation occurs here)

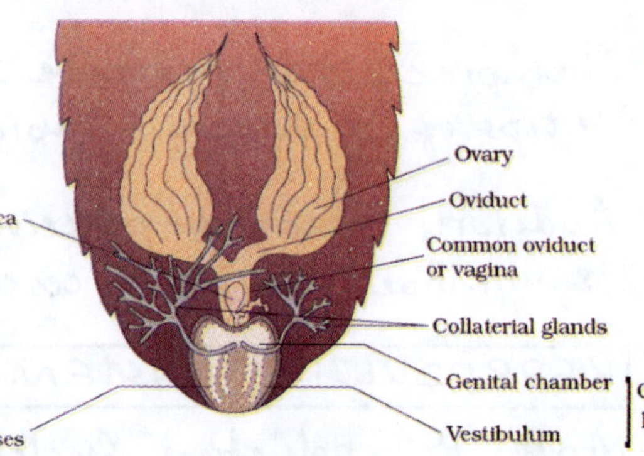

LIFE CYCLE OF COCKROACH

- Spermatozoa enter spermatheca
- Spermateca stores sperms
- Fertilisation takes place in genital pouch.
- On an average, female cockroach produces around 10 oothecae.
  Each ootheca contains 14-16 fertilised eggs.
- Cleavage in fertilised eggs takes place
- Nymph is hatching stage.
- Metamorphosis occurs through various nymphal stages.
- Metamorphosis is paurometabolous.
- Newly hatched nymphs possess all adult characteristics except being sexually immature & without wings
- Nymph metamorphosis about 13 times to become adult cockroach.
- Only adult cockroaches have wings. A stage prior to adult has wing pads.

FROG

- Belongs to Class Amphibia of Phylum Chordata.
- Poikilotherm (cold blooded)
- Habitat - freshwater areas; moist terrestrial areas.
- Common Indian frog - Rana tigrina
- Frogs undergo aestivation (summer sleep) & hibernation.
- Exhibit camouflage (match with surroundings)

MORPHOLOGY

- Skin - smooth, moist, slimy, devoid of scales.
- Colour - greenish yellow with dark spots.
- Ventral surface has pale yellow colour.
- Body consists of head and trunk (neck & tail absent)

Head - triangular in shape.
- Tip bears nostrils.
- A pair of eyes present (upper eyelid immovable, lower eyelid slightly movable)
- Nictitating membrane - transparent fold near lower eyelid
  - ↳ protects eyes from water.
  - ↳ keeps eyeballs moist when on land.
- Eardrum or tympanum - receives sound waves.

Trunk - bears a pair of forelimbs - each with 4 digits
a pair of hindlimbs - each with 5 digits

- Exhibits sexual dimorphism - male develops nuptial pad in the first digit of forelimb for mating.
  Males also have vocal sacs (for producing mating calls).

ANATOMY

DIGESTIVE SYSTEM

- Short alimentary canal as they are carnivorous.
  Consists of buccal cavity, pharynx, oesophagus, stomach, intestines, rectum, and cloaca.

NEET SYNAPSE
Frog leaps on land by elongated hindlimbs.
It swims in water by using webbed feet.

- Tongue- bilobed, captures insects for food.
- Digestive glands- Liver (secretes bile) + pancreas (pancreatic juice)
- Bile stored in gall bladder.
- Stomach secretes gastric juice. (HCl + digestive enzymes)
- Chyme (partially digested food) moves to duodenum.
- Digestive juices also reach duodenum.
- Intestinal wall bears microvilli (absorption of food)
- Undigested food goes to rectum + removed through cloaca.

RESPIRATORY SYSTEM

- Can utilise free as well as dissolved oxygen.
- Modes of respiration in frog-
- Cutaneous - through skin by diffusion.
- Buccopharyngeal - occurs by mouth + pharynx lining.
- Pulmonary - through lungs, a pair present in thoracic cavity.
- During aestivation & hibernation - cutaneous respiration.
- Diffusion is the method of gas exchange in all modes.

CIRCULATORY SYSTEM

- Closed circulatory system - blood flows in vessels.
- Circulatory system includes heart, blood vessels, blood.
- Heart - 3 chambered (2 atria, 1 ventricle)
  ↳ surrounded by pericardium.

  Conus arteriosus

  Sinus venosus - receives blood from vena cava.
  ↳ opens into right auricle.
- Mixed blood flows throughout body.
- Blood = Plasma + WBC, RBC & platelets.
  - Transports nutrients, gases & water.
  - Heart pumps blood into blood vessels.

NEET SYNAPSE

Erythrocytes of frogs are nucleated & biconvex.

Erythrocytes of humans are enucleated & biconcave

EXCRETORY SYSTEM

- Frogs are ureotelic (excrete urea)
- Consists of kidneys } paired, ureters } paired; urinary bladder } unpaired, cloaca } unpaired.
- Kidneys are bean shaped – present posteriorly on either side of vertebral column.
- Nephrons – structural & functional units of kidneys.
  ↳ also called uriniferous tubules.
- Flow of urine –
  Kidneys → ureters → urinary bladder → cloaca.
- Males – urinogenital ducts – ureters – pass out urine as well as semen.
  ↳ excretory + reproductive system = urinogenital system.
- Females – passage of ova & urine is different.
  – oviduct & ureter open into cloaca.

NERVOUS SYSTEM

Central Nervous System

- Consists of brain & spinal cord.
- Cranium – bony structure – encloses brain.

Brain

↳ Forebrain – olfactory lobes, cerebrum, diencephalon.
↳ Midbrain – optic lobes & crura cerebri
↳ Hindbrain – cerebellum & medulla oblongata.

Spinal cord – enclosed by vertebral column.
– extends from medulla oblongata through foramen magnum.

Peripheral Nervous System

- Consists of 10 pairs of cranial nerves and 10 pairs of spinal nerves.

Autonomous Nervous System

- Controls involuntary activities of internal organs.
- Consists of – Sympathetic nerves
  – Parasympathetic nerves.

SENSE ORGANS

- Tactile receptors - sensory papillae
- Gustatory receptors - taste buds.
- Olfactory receptors - nasal epithelium, Jacobson's organ
- Vision - eyes
- Auditory receptors - tympanum (represents external ears)
  Ear is the organ of hearing as well as equilibrium (balance)
- Eyes & internal ears are well organised, others are cellular aggregates.

ENDOCRINE SYSTEM

- Hormones bring about chemical coordination.
- Main glands - pituitary, thyroid, parathyroid, pineal, thymus, adrenal, gonads.

REPRODUCTIVE SYSTEM

Male Reproductive system

- Testes - paired, produce spermatozoa.
  Testes are attached to kidneys by mesorchium.
- Vasa efferentia - 10-12 - arise from testes.
  ↳ enter kidneys on either side & open into Bidder's canal.
- Bidder's canal present longitudinally in the kidney.
  Sperms enter urinogenital duct from Bidder's canal.
- Cloaca - receives sperms from urinogenital duct.
  ↳ common passage for sperms, urine & faecal matter.

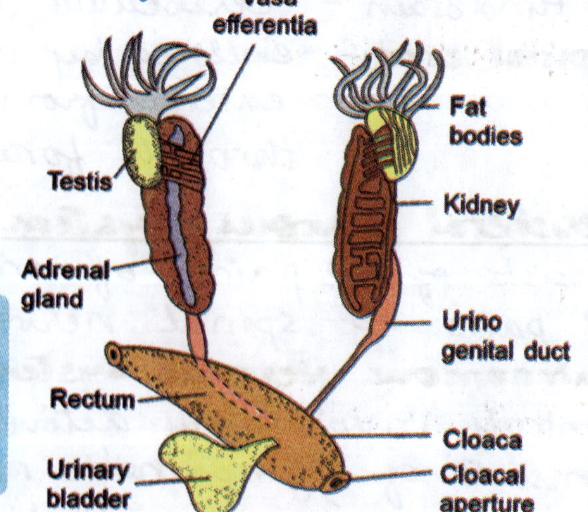

Flow of sperms
Testes → Vasa efferentia → Bidder's canal → urinogenital duct → cloaca

Female reproductive system

- Ovaries - paired, situated near kidneys.
  - ↳ Attached to abdominal wall by mesovarium.
- Oviducts - paired, coiled tubes.
  - ↳ Receive ova from ovaries
- Ovisacs - broad, posterior ends of oviducts.
  - ↳ temporarily stores ova.
  - ↳ open into cloaca.

A mature female frog can lay upto 2500 - 3000 ova at a time.

Spawn - mass of eggs laid by female frog

FERTILISATION AND DEVELOPMENT

- Breeding occurs during rainy season.
- Male grasps female from the back using copulatory pads. This process is called amplexus.
- Female releses eggs in water & male discharges sperms over eggs - Fertilisation is external.
- Zygote becomes larva in about 2 weeks. Larvae are called tadpoles. Tadpole undergoes metamorphosis to become adult. Metamorphosis is controlled by thyroxine hormone.

NEET SYNAPSE

Tadpole has characteristics like fishes. It is aquatic. It lacks legs. They have gills for respiration (branchial respiration)

8. Cell: The Unit of Life

- All living organisms are made up of cells.
- Organisms → Unicellular – exist independently
  → Multicellular – exhibit division of labour.

Hall of Fame

Robert Hooke – discovered cell in dead cork sections.
Antonie van Leeuwenhoek – first to observe animal cell
Schleiden and Schwann – gave cell theory
Rudolf Virchow – Omnis cellula-e-cellula
Singer & Nicolson – Fluid mosaic model of cell membrane
Robert Brown – Discovered nucleus
Camillo Golgi – Discovered Golgi apparatus
Palade – Discovered Ribosomes

① Cell theory

- All living organisms are made up of cells.
- All cells arise from pre existing cells.

② Exceptions to cell theory

- Viruses (not made of cells)
- RBCs, sieve tube cells

③ Drawbacks of cell theory

- Did not explain how new cells are formed.

DIFFERENT TYPES OF CELLS

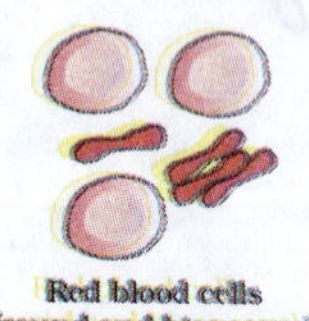
Red blood cells (round and biconcave)

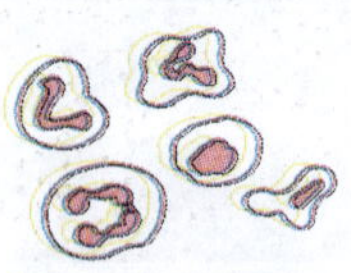
White blood cells (amoeboid)

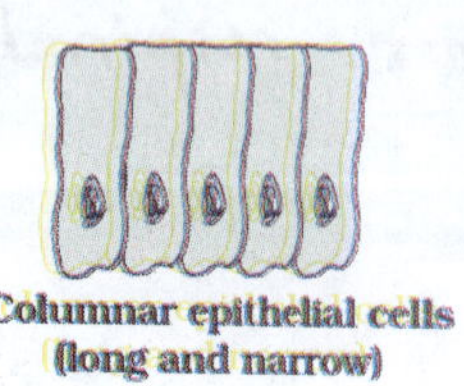
Columnar epithelial cells (long and narrow)

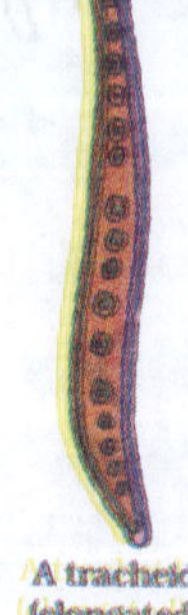
A tracheid (elongated)

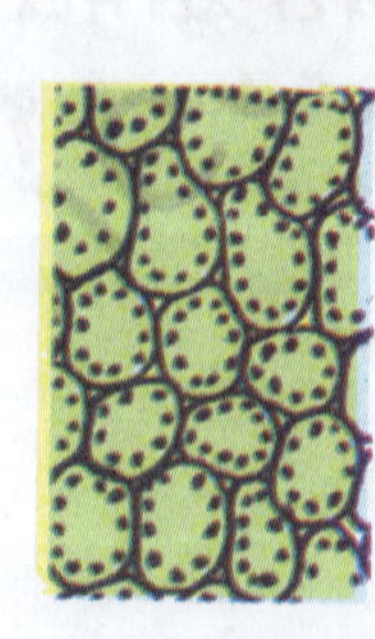
Mesophyll cells (round and oval)

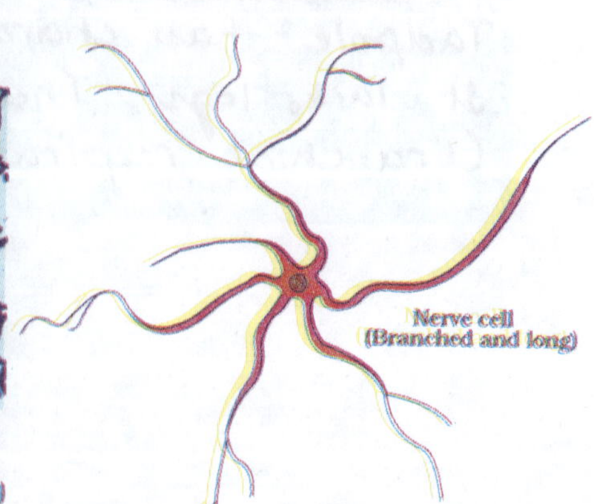
Nerve cell (Branched and long)

SIZE OF CELLS

- Smallest cell - Mycoplasma (0.3 µm)
- Largest cell - Ostrich egg (6 inches)
- Longest cell - Neuron
- Bacterial cell - 3-5 µm
- Human RBC - 7.0 µm (diameter)
- Factors affecting size of cell -
  - N/C ratio
  - Surface : Volume ratio
  - Metabolism

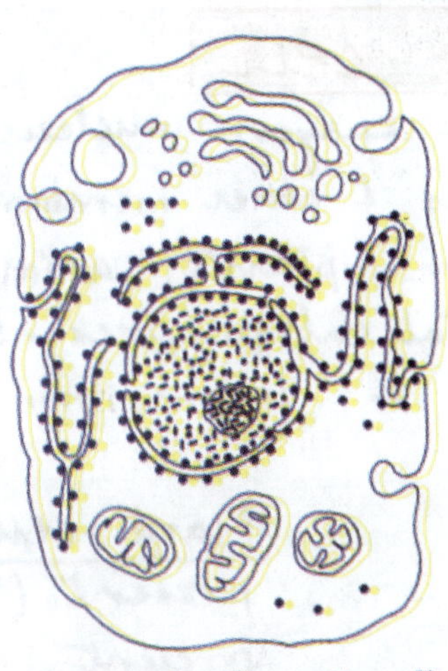

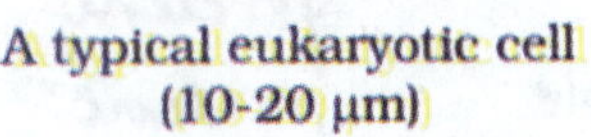

A typical eukaryotic cell (10-20 µm)

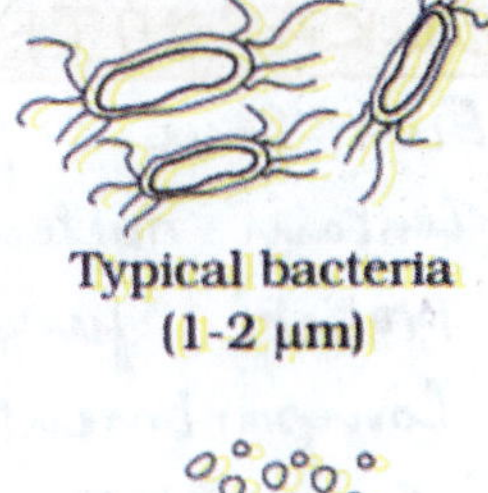

Typical bacteria (1-2 µm)

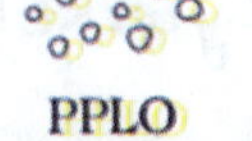

PPLO (about 0.1 µm)

Viruses (0.02-0.2 µm)

PROKARYOTIC CELL

(Pro - Primitive ; Karyon - nucleus)

Cell Envelope - Glycocalyx, Cell wall, Cell membrane

- Glycocalyx:
  - Capsule - thick & tough
  - Slimy layer - sticky & slimy

Plasmid - extra chromosomal DNA - provides specific traits to bacteria.

Basal body

Hook

Flagellum - help in movement

Inclusion bodies

Ribosomes 70S

conjugation ← Pili (Sexual reproduction)

Chromatophores - Pigment containing membranous invaginations - present in cyanobacteria

Fimbrae - help in attachment with substrate

Nucleoid ↓ circular DNA present freely in cytoplasm

Mesosome

- Membranous invagination
- Help in
  - formation of cell wall
  - replication of DNA
  - respiration to produce ATP
  - increasing surface area of plasma membrane
  - secreting glycocalyx

NEET SYNAPSE

Gas vacuoles are considered as inclusion bodies

EUKARYOTIC CELL

Eu- True ; Karyon- nucleus

- Contain nucleus & other membrane bound cell organelles.
- Protist, fungi, plants, animals contain eukaryotic cell.(s)
- Compartmentalisation present
- Cytoskeleton & locomotory structures present.

Features	Plant cell	Animal Cell
Cell wall	present (cellulose)	absent
Chloroplast	present	absent
Central vacuole	present	absent
Centriole	absent	present

Cell Wall

- Plant cell - cellulose
- Fungi - chitin
- Layers -

	Middle lamella	Primary cell wall	Secondary cell wall
location	• Outermost	• Younger plants	• inner to primary
composition	• Ca & Mg pectate	• cellulose	• cellulose, suberin, lignin - rigidity
	• Cementing layer	• First formed wall	

- Plasmodesmata - cytoplasmic connections in plant cells.
- Patterns of growth - Intussusception: deposition in form of grains; Apposition: deposition in form of thin plates.

NEET SYNAPSE
Cell walls have pits- regions where secondary cell wall is absent.

- **Functions**
  - Maintains shape of cell
  - Protects the cell
  - Provides mechanical support
  - Forms protoplasmic connections
  - Helps in cell adhesion
  - Prevents entry of undesirable macromolecules.

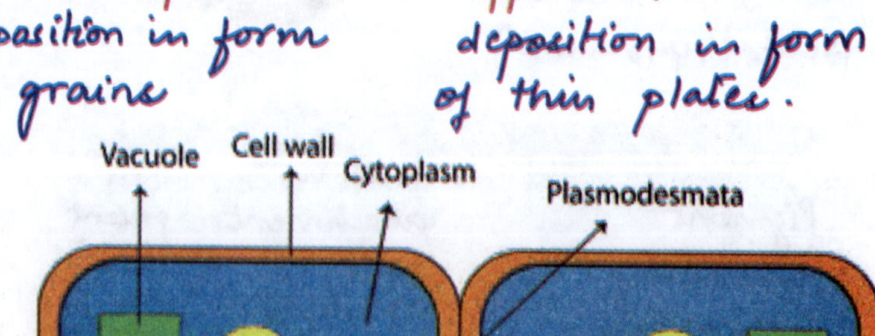

Plant cells connected by plasmodesmata.

Cell Membrane / Plasma membrane / Plasmalemma

- Thin & elastic
- Selectively permeable
- Made up of lipids & protein
  - Concentration of lipids & protein can vary
  - Eg: RBC - 52% lipids ; 40% protein ; 8% carbohydrates
    Myelinated neuron - 80% lipids ; 20% protein

NEET SYNAPSE
Human RBC membrane has glycoproteins called Antigens.

- **Lipids**
  - Mainly phospholipids

PO_4^{3-}
Polar head (Hydrophilic) Towards aqueous medium
Non polar tails (Hydrophobic) Away from aqueous medium
→ Amphipathic molecule

- **Proteins**

Peripheral (30%)	Integral (70%)
• outer surface	• embedded
• extrinsic	• intrinsic / Tunnel
• Function	• Function
- cell recognition - cell interaction	- transfer substances across cell membrane

Fluid Mosaic Model

- Singer & Nicolson
- Icebergs of proteins in sea of phospholipids.
- Quasi fluid nature - due to unsaturated fatty acids
- Phospholipid bilayer with
- proteins & sterols embedded
- Intrinsic proteins perform side to side motion.

Glycoprotein - acts as antigen
Hydrophilic heads of phospholipid molecules
Phospholipid bilayer
Glycolipid
Integral protein
Hydrophobic tails of phospholipid molecules
Cholesterol
Intrinsic protein molecule passing through phospholipid membrane
Extrinsic protein present at the surface

Functions of Plasma Membrane

- Cell growth & cell division - by allowing change in surface area & volume.
- Formation of intercellular junctions. - communication with other cells.
- Cell recognition & cell adhesion - due to antigens.
- Secretion - of hormones, proteins, glandular secretions etc.
- Transport

Passive	Active	Bulk
• High conc → low conc • Along the conc. gradient • No energy spent METHODS • Simple diffusion movement of non-polar substances • Osmosis movement of water • Facilitated diffusion movement of polar substances across membrane with the help of carrier proteins. Eg. Entry of glucose into cells using GLUT-4	• low conc → high conc • Against the conc. gradient • Energy required METHODS • Primary active transport Eg. Na^+-K^+ pump using ATPase complex • Secondary active transport Eg. glucose transport in E.coli	• outside → inside • inside → outside from one cell to another. METHODS • Endocytosis → into the cell - Pinocytosis - cell drinking - Phagocytosis - cell eating • Exocytosis → out of cell → Transports materials outside the cell.

Protoplasm

(Proto - first ; plasm - fluid)

- Fluid part of the cell
- Colourless & viscous.
- Components

cytoplasm → present between cell membrane & nucleus

nucleoplasm → protoplasm of nucleus

NEET SYNAPSE

Protoplasm	Protoplast
- living content of the cell excluding cell wall.	- a cell in which cell wall has been removed leaving plasma membrane & contents intact

CELL ORGANELLES

- Non membrane bound – Ribasome
- Membrane bound
  - → single – Golgi, ER, lysosome, peroxisome etc.
  - → double – Mitochondria, chloroplast, nucleus etc.

Mitochondria

- Powerhouse of the cell – produces ATP during cellular respiration
- Semi autonomous – replicate by binary fission, contain DNA & ribosomes
- Size – 0.2 – 1.0 um in diameter & 1.0 – 4.1 um in length
- Number – differs depending upon activity of cell.
  active cells – more mitochondria.
- Structure.

Matrix – Ground substance where oxidative phosphorylation occurs

Cristae
density indicates intensity of respiration in cell

Outer membrane
Phospholipids & cholesterol
Smooth & straight

DNA
naked & circular

Inter membrane space – 40-70 A°

Oxysome | $F_0 F_1$ particle
F_1 – contains ATPase
– synthesis of ATP
F_0 – embeds in inner mitochondrial membrane

Inner membrane
semi-permeable folded to form cristae

Ribosome – 70S
(resemble prokaryotic ribosomes)

NEET SYNAPSE – Mitochondria are also called cell within a cell

---

Plastids

- Present in plant cells
- Double membrane bound

Leucoplast	Chromoplast	Chloroplast
• lack pigment, store food • Amyloplast starch • Elaioplast lipid • Aleuroplast Protein	• red, orange, yellow • also carry out lipid synthesis • Pigments – carotenes xanthophylls etc	• green • chlorophyll is present • involved in photosynthesis.

Chloroplast

- Kitchen of cell
- Double membrane - outer & inner - both freely permeable
- Main site of photosynthesis
- Stroma- ground substance - enclosed by inner membrane.
- Semi - autonoumous cell organelle
- space between outer and inner membrane - intermembrane space.

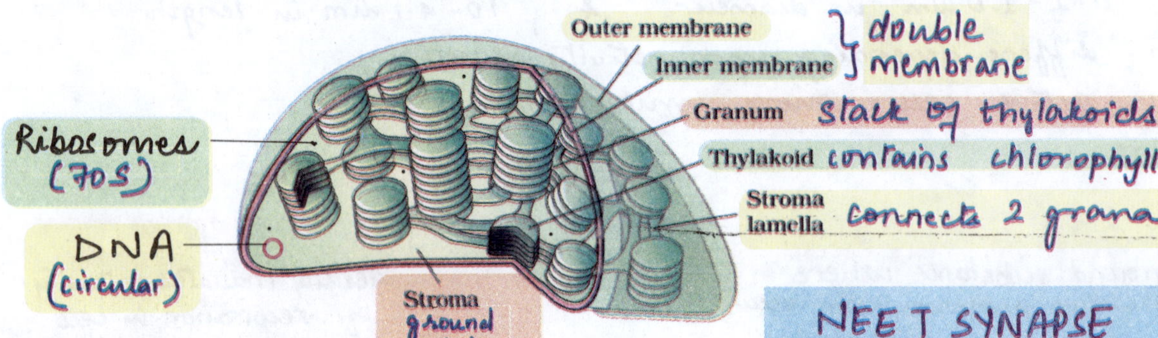

Chloroplasts help in maintaining gaseous balance in atmosphere by taking in CO_2 & releasing O_2

NEET SYNAPSE
Change in colour in tomatoes and chillies from green to red is due to replacement of chlorophyll by lycopene

Ribosomes

- Site of protein synthesis
- Also called Palade particles
- Positively charged
- RNA - protein complexes
- Can be attached to ER or free.
- Size measured in Svedberg units (S)
- Prokaryotes - 70S ; Eukaryotes - 80S
- Mitochondria & chloroplast - 70S
- Monosomes - occur individually
- Polysomes / Polyribosomes
  ribosomes complexed with mRNA

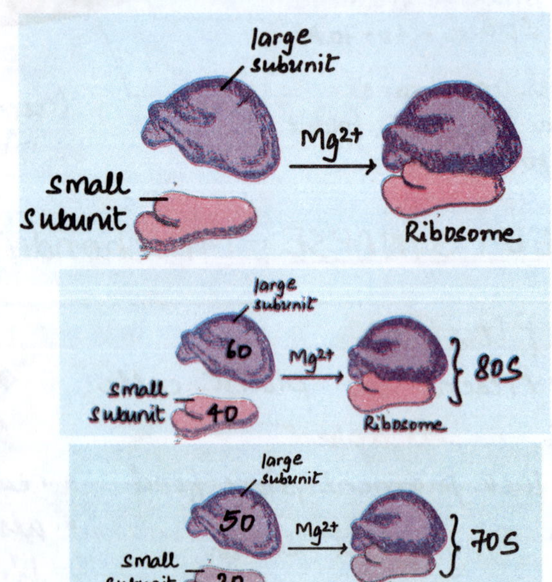

Endomembrane system

Nuclear envelope continuous with ER (SER & RER are in continuation)

↓

Substances produced by ER move to golgi via transport vesicle

↓

Golgi carries out packaging & modification of substances

↓

Golgi pinches off vesicles; they can become lysosomes/vacuoles

↓

Lysosome fuses with another vesicle for digestion.

vesicle can secrete its secretion outside the cell

Endoplasmic Reticulum

- Divides cell into compartments
- Component of cytoskeleton
- Extend from nucleus to plasma membrane
- Thickness of ER membrane = 50 Å
- Forms - cisternae; tubules; vesicles
- RER - originates from nuclear membrane.
  - Forms 2/3 of total ER
  - Site for protein synthesis
- SER - originates from RER
  - Site for cholesterol & lipid synthesis

Golgi Apparatus

- Also call dictyosomes
- Structure
  - Cisternae - flattened sac like
  - Tubules - connect cisternae
  - Vesicles - round; secretory
- Forming face - cis face
- Maturing face - trans face
- Functions
  - Storage, packaging, secretion
  - Formation of glycolipids & glycoproteins
  - Zymogen granules originate from golgi & fuse with plasmalemma.
- Absent in RBC of humans & sieve tubes of plants.

Lysosomes

- Small & spherical
- Contain acid hydrolases
- Also called suicidal bags
- Functions
  - Hydrolysis of carbohydrates, lipids & proteins – at acidic pH
  - Autophagy & heterophagy
  - Removal of ageing & dead cells.

1° lysosome – inactive hydrolases
2° lysosome – 1° lysosome + phagosome
3° lysosome – Residual bodies (contain undigested materials)

Autophagic vacuole – 1° lysosome + degenerated cell

Vacuoles

- Store ions, sugars, amino acids, proteins, carbohydrates.
- Tonoplast – membrane of vacuole
- Active transport through tonoplast takes place → increases concentration of ions in vacuole
- Vacuole contains cell sap → increases osmotic pressure → keeps plant cell turgid
- Responsible for cell enlargement during growth.
- Store tannins, alkaloids, toxins – to avoid predation
- Store pigments to provide colour to plant parts.

Centrosomes

- Absent in plant cells
- Composed of ⊥ centrioles
- Centriole has 9+0 arrangement
- Centrosome forms spindle fibres during cell division
- Centrioles form basal bodies.
- Centrioles help in formation of cilia & flagella

NEET SYNAPSE

9 + 0
peripheral tubules | central tubule

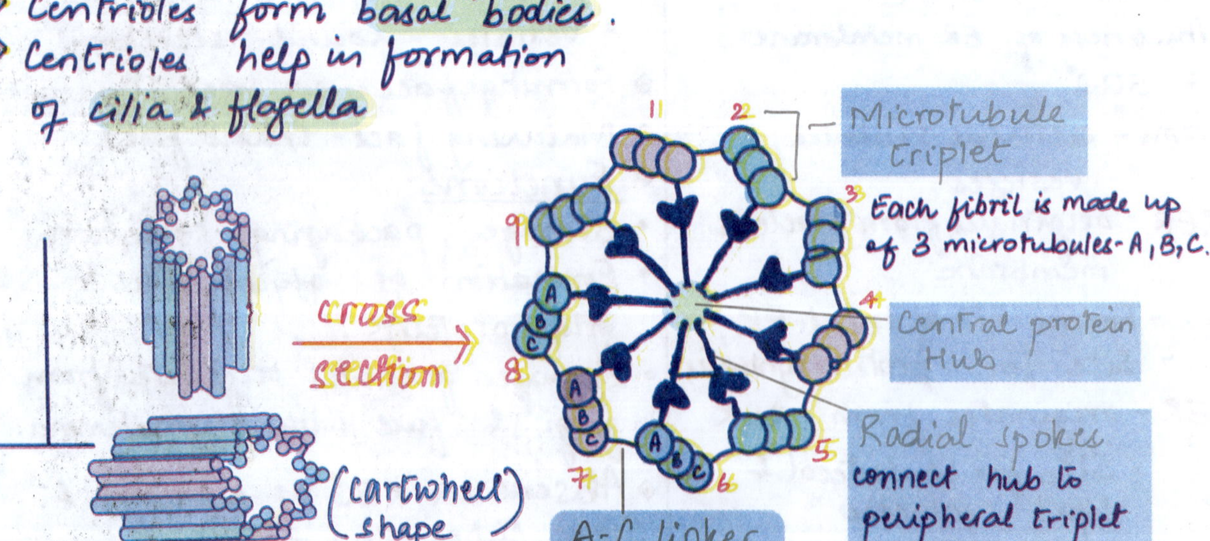

Cilia and Flagella

- Thread like outgrowths
- Cilia - short & numerous
- Flagella - long & few
- Structure

Basal body, hook, filament

Axoneme

↳ 9+2 arrangement [9 peripheral doublets + 2 central singlet]

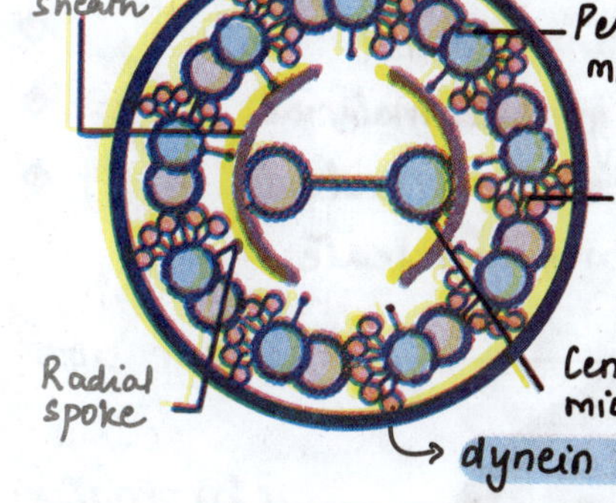

- Function
  - Locomotion & movement
  - Movement & food capture in protozoa
  - Movement of ova in fallopian tube
  - Creation of water current - eg sponges
  - Locomotion of gametes

NEET SYNAPSE
Basal body - 9+0
Filament - 9+2

Cytoskeleton

- Criss cross network present in eukaryotic cells.
- Maintains shape of cell
- Anchor cell organelles at fixed locations.
- Made up of -
  - Microtubules
    - hollow & unbranched
    - made of 13 protofilaments of tubulin proteins
    - spindle fibres, centriole etc.
  - Microfilaments
    - solid & unbranched
    - contain actin protein
  - Intermediate filaments

Microbodies

- Small, single membrane bound organelles.
- Peroxisomes

Found mainly in mesophyll cells of C_3 plants.
Site of breakdown of H_2O_2
Involved in photorespiration

- Glyoxysomes

Help in β oxidation of fatty acids
Help in glyoxylate cycle.

- Sphaerosomes

Synthesis & storage of lipids

Nucleus

- Largest component of cell
- Double membrane bound
- Encloses DNA - genetic material
- Usually 1 per cell - uninucleate
- Can be >1 - multinucleate
- Stores genetic information
- Controller of cell
- Nucleolus - site of rRNA synthesis

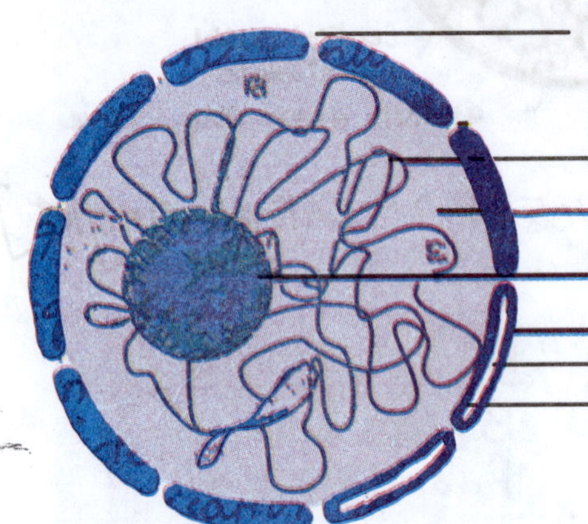

NEET SYNAPSE
opening of nuclear pores is guarded by annuli

Chromosome

- Thread like structure
- Formed during cell division
- Studied during metaphase - thickest & shortest
- Parts of chromosome
  - Chromatid - 2 identical structures present in chromosome
  - Centromere - primary constriction
  - Kinetochore - present over centromere spindle fibres attach here during cell division
  - Telomere - terminal part of chromosome
  - Secondary constriction (NDR) narrow region other than centromere
    NDR - Nucleolar Organiser Region
  - Satellite - part of chromosome beyond secondary constriction

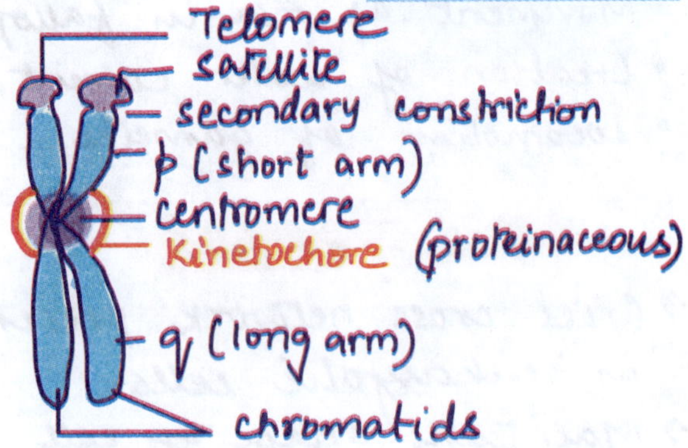

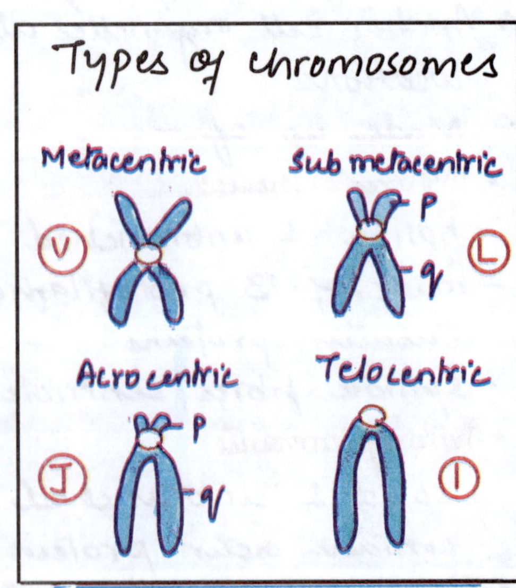

9. Biomolecules

CHEMICAL ANALYSIS OF A LIVING TISSUE

- Living tissues contain abundant amounts of C, H, O.
- Molecules present within the cells are called biomolecules.

How to analyse chemical composition of a living tissue?

Living tissue + CCl_3COOH (Trichloracetic acid)
↓
Grind together using mortar & pestle
↓
Filter through cheese cloth
↓
One fraction is filtered (Filtrate)
Another fraction remains in cheesecloth (Retentate)

NEET SYNAPSE

Filtrate → contains trichloracetic acid + products dissolved in it. Hence called acid soluble pool.

Retentate - contents that do not dissolve in acid, and remain in filter cloth. Hence called acid insoluble pool.

Biomolecules

Biomacromolecules

- Large molecules
- Mol wt >1000 Da (<10000 Da)
- Include proteins, nucleic acids, polysaccharides, lipids etc.
- Found in acid insoluble pool.

Biomicromolecules

- Small molecules
- Mol wt - 18-800 Da
- Include monosaccharides, amino acids, nucleotides
- Found in acid soluble pool.

NEET SYNAPSE
Lipids are not strictly macromolecules.
Their mol. wt. is <800 Da, but they form aggregates which do not dissolve in acid ∴ remain in acid insoluble pool.

Composition of living system

Organic + inorganic
↓ Compounds ↓ Elements

Wet weight – weight of living tissue
Dry weight – weight when water evaporates
Ash – contains only inorganic elements
– organic substances burn and are released as CO_2.

Elemental analysis

Element	% Weight of Earth's crust	% Weight of Human body
Hydrogen (H)	0.14	0.5
Carbon (C)	0.03	18.5
Oxygen (O)	46.6	65.0
Nitrogen (N)	very little	3.3
Sulphur (S)	0.03	0.3
Sodium (Na)	2.8	0.2
Calcium (Ca)	3.6	1.5
Magnesium (Mg)	2.1	0.1
Silicon (Si)	27.7	negligible

METABOLITES

Primary metabolites
- Part of normal metabolic pathways
- Their functions are known Eg amino acids, sugars,
- fats, nucleotides etc.

Secondary metabolites
- Formed by alteration of primary metabolites.
- Functions are not known
- Include pigments, flavinoids, alkaloids etc

Common secondary metabolites

Pigments	Carotenoids, Anthocyanins, etc.
Alkaloids	Morphine, Codeine, etc.
Terpenoides	Monoterpenes, Diterpenes etc.
Essential oils	Lemon grass oil, etc.
Toxins	Abrin, Ricin
Lectins	Concanavalin A
Drugs	Vinblastin, curcumin, etc.
Polymeric Substances	Rubber, gums, cellulose

AMINO ACIDS

- Contain C, H, O, N, S.
- Also called substituted methanes
- Monomers of proteins.
- Structure – Each amino acid has
  Free carboxyl group, Free amino group, R – side chain } attached to α carbon atom.
- R group is variable
- -COOH gives acidic character
- $-NH_2$ gives basic character

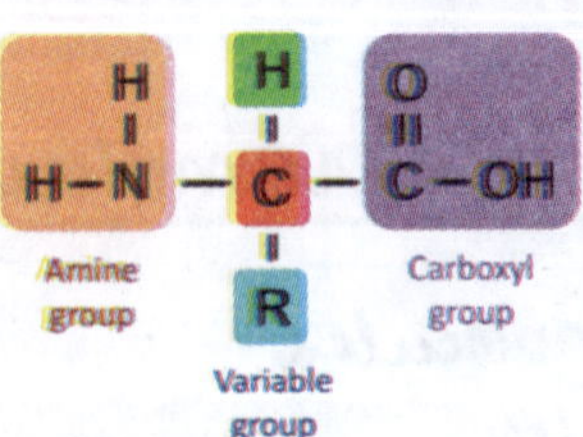

NEET SYNAPSE
Glycine is the simplest amino acid.

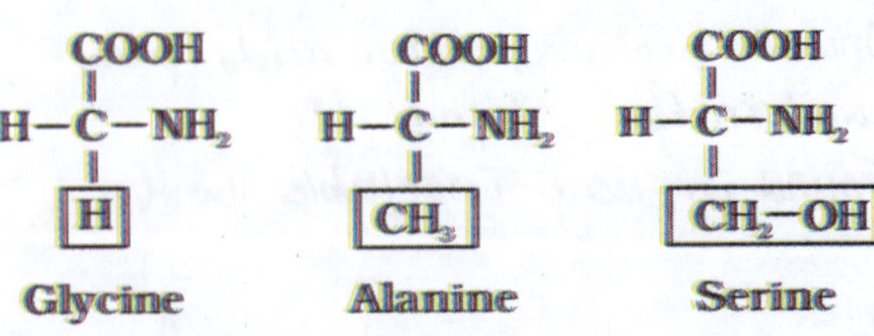

Zwitter ion and Isoelectric Point

- Amino acids are amphoteric in nature (act as both acids & bases)
- They behave differently in solutions of different pH.
- Neutral solution - amino acid exists as zwitter ion.
- Zwitter ion - molecule containing positive & negative ionic group.
- Isoelectric point - pH at which amino acid exists as zwitter ion, i.e. it is electrically neutral.
- Acidic solution - amino group (NH_2) picks up H^+ ions and becomes NH_3^+ - positively charged.
- Basic solution - amino acid donates H^+ ions and becomes negatively charged.

Amino acid ⇌ Zwitterion form

Classification of amino acids

Based on synthesis

- Essential amino acids - cannot be synthesised in the body, hence must be taken in diet.
- Non essential amino acids - can be synthesised in the body, hence not required to be taken in diet.
- Semi essential amino acids - partially synthesised by body but not in sufficient quantity. Arginine & Histidine.

Based on nature

- Neutral - 1 NH_2 group + 1 -COOH group
  Eg. Glycine, alanine, valine, leucine etc.
- Acidic — More - COOH groups than NH_2 groups
  Eg - Glutamic acid, Aspartic acid
- Basic — More $-NH_2$ groups than -COOH groups.
  Eg - Lysine, arginine & histidine.

NEET SYNAPSE
Tryptophan is the precursor of melatonin and serotonin.

Based on side chain

- Sulphur containing - Cysteine, methionine
- Alcoholic - Threonine, serine
- Aromatic - Phenylalanine, tryptophan, tyrosine
- Heterocyclic - Histidine, proline, tryptophan.

LIPIDS

- Made up of C, H, O; general formula $C_nH_{2n}O_2$
- Lipids are not polymers.
- Hydrophobic ; insoluble in water ; soluble in non-polar solvents.
- Lipids can be either fatty acid or glycerol or both.

Fatty acids

- Long chain hydrocarbons - 1 -COOH group attached to R group.
- R-group can be $-CH_3$, $-C_2H_5$ or higher.
- Chain can be 1-19 C long
- They are simplest constituents of lipids.
- Fatty acids can be
- Saturated
  - Only single bonds in hydrocarbon chain, no double bonds.
  - Solid at room temperature
  - No effect of hydrogenation
  - Eg. Palmitic acid (16C)
    Stearic acid (18C)
    Arachidic acid (20C)

Unsaturated
  - Possess one or more double bonds in the hydrocarbon chain.
  - Liquid at room temperature.
  - Hydrogenation converts them into saturated fats.
  - Eg. Oleic acid (18C) - 1 double bond
    Linoleic acid (18C) - 2 double bond
    Linolenic acid (18C) - 3 double bond
    Arachidonic acid (20C) - 4 double bond

NEET SYNAPSE
Omega 3 and Omega 6 fatty acids play crucial role in brain and heart health.

Classification of lipids

Simple lipids

- Esters of fatty acids with alcohol. (mainly glycerol)

(i) Fats and oils

- Esters of higher fatty acids with glycerol (trihydroxy propane)
- Also known as triglycerides.
- Fats act as reserve food material,
  - form insulation coats in mammals
  - act as shock absorbers when present around visceral organs
- Oils have low melting point, ∴ remain liquid at room temp.

Eg. gingelly oil.

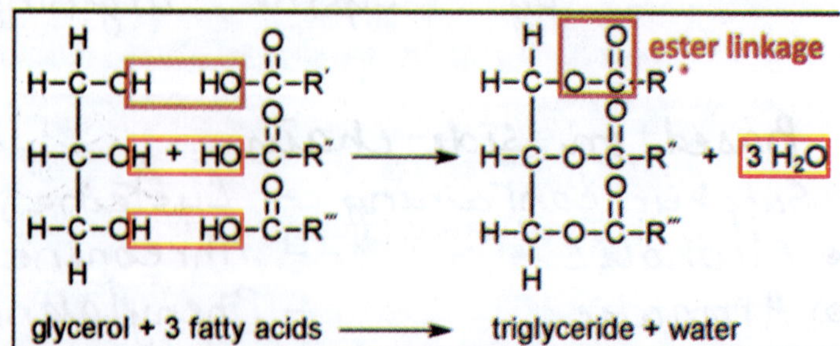

(ii) Waxes

- Esters of fatty acids with long chain monohydric alcohols.
- Waxes protect (earwax), lubricate and provide flexibility to hair and skin.
- Waxes also make the body water resistant.

Compound lipids

- Esters of fatty acids with alcohol + some other substance.

(i) Phospholipids

- 2 fatty acids + 1 glycerol + Phosphoric acid
- Glycerol has 3 hydroxyl groups (OH)
  2 -OH are attached to 2 fatty acid chains
  Third -OH is attached to phosphoric acid.
- Common phospholipids – lecithin & cephalin

Phosphate
Glycerol
Saturated fatty acid
Unsaturated fatty acid

Phospholipid structure

Phospholipid (Lecithin)

cephalin

- Lecithin contains choline
- It lines the alveoli
- Cephalin contains ethanolamine
- It is present in the brain

(ii) Glycolipids

- They contain fatty acid, alcohol (sphingosine) and a sugar.
- They are present in myelin sheath of nerve fibres.
- Eg. Cerebrosides and gangliosides.

Derived lipids

- They are obtained from simple and compound lipids.

Sterols

- Do not contain fatty acids.
- Have lipid like properties
- Cholesterol – most common
  ↳ Precursor of steroid hormones.

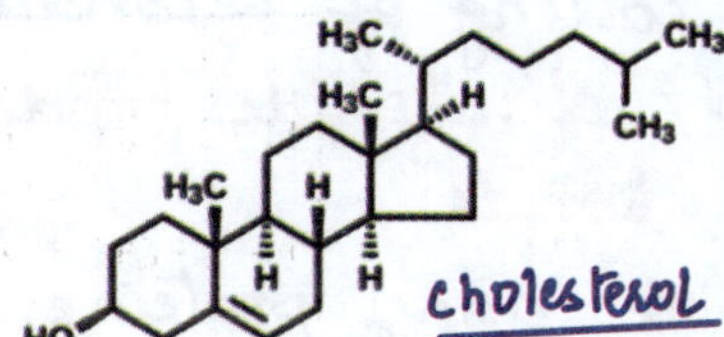

cholesterol

NEET SYNAPSE
Diosgenin (sterol) used for manufacturing anti-fertility pills.

PROTEINS

- Heteropolymers of amino acids
  ↳ 20 different types of amino acids form proteins.
- Polypeptide- amino acids linked in a linear chain with peptide bonds.

Table 9.5 Some Proteins and their Functions

Protein	Functions
Collagen	Intercellular ground substance
Trypsin	Enzyme
Insulin	Hormone
Antibody	Fights infectious agents
Receptor	Sensory reception (smell, taste, hormone, etc.)
GLUT-4	Enables glucose transport into cells

- Functions of proteins
  - Enzymatic - pepsin, trypsin etc.
  - Hormonal- insulin, prolactin etc.
  - Transport - haemoglobin, albumin etc.
  - Storage - casein, ferritin etc.
  - Contractile- actin myosin etc.
  - Structural - collagen, keratin etc.
  - Protective - immunoglobulin etc.

Structural levels of proteins

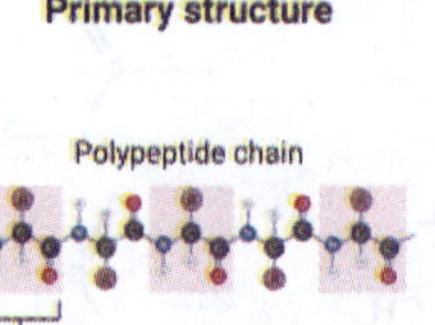

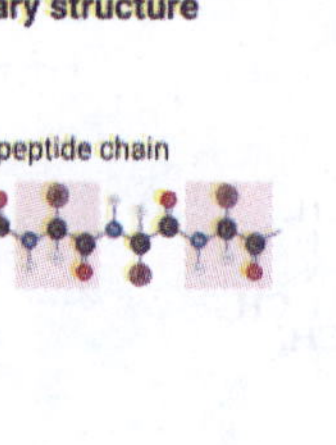

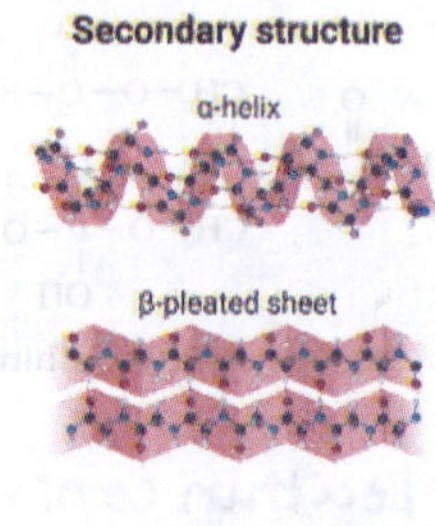

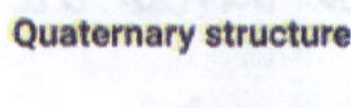

Primary structure

- Linear sequence of amino acids.
- Determine N-terminal & C-terminal
- Contains peptide bonds.

Secondary structure

- Primary str folds to form secondary str.
- Types of secondary structure
  - α- helix - spiral str., right handed coiling
  - β- pleated- amino acids packed together to form sheets.
- Stabilised by Hydrogen bonds.

Tertiary structure

- 3-D woollen ball like structure.
- Formed by further coiling of secondary structure.
- Stabilised by H-bond, disulphide bonds, ionic, covalent, peptide and hydrophobic bonds.
- Determines activity of many proteins.

NEET SYNAPSE
Enzymes are formed in tertiary str

Quaternary structure

- Formed by joining of two or more polypeptide chains.
- Each polypeptide is in tertiary structure.
- Eg. Haemoglobin ($2\alpha + 2\beta$ chains)

Classification of Proteins

Simple	Compound	Derived
• made up of amino acids only Eg. Collagen- most abundant protein in animal world RuBisCO- most abundant protein in biosphere.	• Protein + Non protein part part Eg. Nucleoprotein Glycoprotein Lipoprotein	• Obtained by hydrolysis of proteins. Eg. Peptones, polypeptides, peptides, amino acids

CARBOHYDRATES

- Also called saccharides (sugars)
- Molecular formula $C_nH_{2n}O_n$.
- Main soure of energy for the body.

NEET SYNAPSE

Carbohydrates are also referred to as polyhydroxy ketones or aldehydes.

Classification of Carbohydrates

On the basis of reducing properties

Reducing

- Possess free aldehyde or keto group
- Reduce cupric (Cu^{2+}) ions to cuprous (Cu^+) ions.
- All monosaccharides, some disaccharides like maltose, lactose etc.

Non reducing

- Do not Possess free aldehyde or keto group
- Cannot Reduce cupric (Cu^{2+}) ions to cuprous (Cu^+) ions.
- Eg. Sucrose, all polysaccharides.

On the basis of hydrolysis

Monosaccharides	Oligosaccharides	Polysaccharides
• Mono - single • Simplest carbohydrates • Can't be hydrolysed further • Functional group - Aldehyde (aldo sugar) Ketone (Keto sugar) • They are soluble in water.	• Oligo- few • Consist of 2-9 monosaccharide units • Glycosidic bonds present • Are crystalline, sweet in taste. • Soluble in water • Formed by condensation	• Poly- many • >9 monosaccharides • Can have linear or branched pattern • Insoluble in water, • do not taste sweet • Glycosidic bonds present.

Monosaccharides

C_3 - Triose - Glyceraldehyde
C_4 - Tetrose - Erythrose
C_5 - Pentose - Ribose, Deoxyribose
C_6 - Hexose - Glucose, Fructose
C_7 - Heptoses - Glucoheptose

Disaccharides

- Sucrose - cane sugar
  Glucose + Fructose
- Lactose - milk sugar
  Glucose + Galactose
- Maltose - malt sugar
  Glucose + Glucose.

Polysaccharides

Homopolysaccharides

- Formed by polymerisation of only one type of monosaccharide unit
- Example - starch, glycogen, cellulose, insulin.

Heteropolysaccharides

- Formed by polymerisation of two or more type of monosaccharide unit
- Example peptidoglycan

NEET SYNAPSE - Right end of polysaccharide chain is reducing end and the left end is non-reducing end.

Starch

- Major food reserve in plants
- Polymer of glucose
- Gives blue colour with iodine as it holds iodine in its helical structure.
- Consits of amylose & amylopectin
  - Amylose - unbranched
    → made up of 200-500 glucose units
    → Has α-1,4 linkages
  - Amylopectin - branched
    → made up of 2000-20000 glucose units
    → Has α-1,4 & α-1,6 linkages.

α-1,4-Glycosidic bond

CH_2OH CH_2OH O H H H α 1 4 α OH HO OH H OH H OH H OH O H_2O H OH

α-1,6-Glycosidic bond

CH_2OH O H H α 1 OH H O H OH 6 CH_2 CH_2OH H α 1 4 α OH H OH H O H_2O H OH

- Glycosidic bond is formed by dehydration (one H_2O molecule is released)
- It is a non-reducing sugar.
- Branching always takes place at C_6.

Glycogen

- Reserve food material of animals - also called animal starch.
- More extensively branched than amylopectin.
- Contains about 5000-15000 glucose units.
- It is a non-reducing sugar.
- Gives violet colour with iodine.

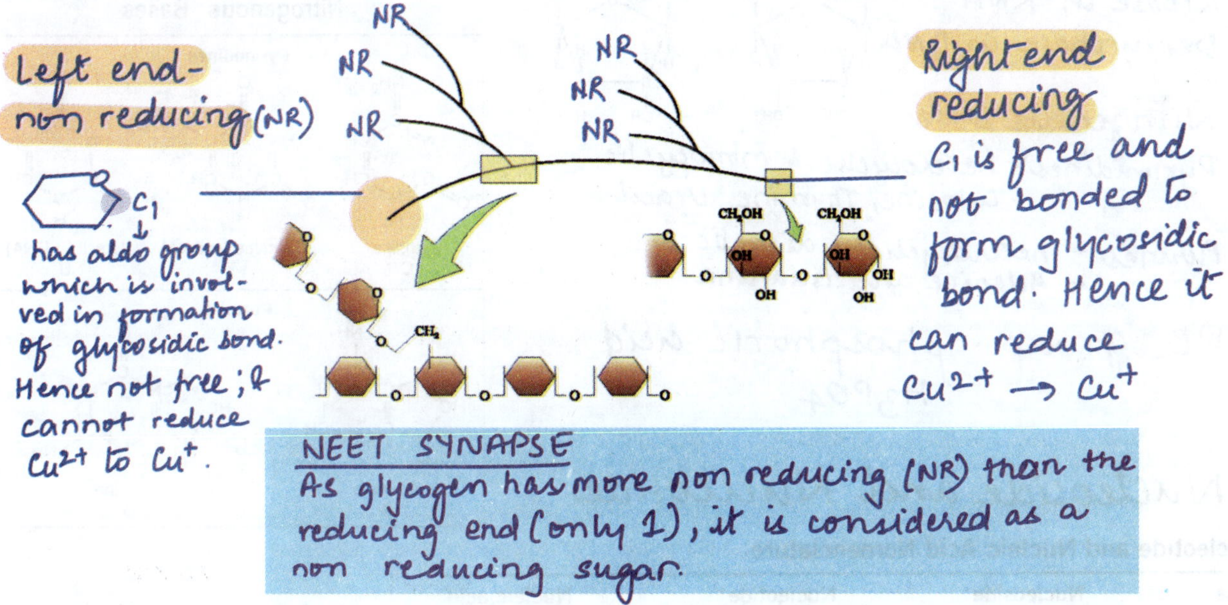

NEET SYNAPSE
As glycogen has more non reducing (NR) than the reducing end (only 1), it is considered as a non reducing sugar.

Cellulose

- Polymer of β-D glucose; contains β-1,4 & β-1,6 linkages.
- Main structural component of plant cell wall.
- Does not have complex helices, hence can't hold iodine
- Found abundantly in paper and cotton fibres.

Inulin

- Polymer of fructose; cannot be metabolised by humans.
- 30-35 fructose units join by β-2,1 glycosidic linkages.
- It is an unbranched chain

Chitin

- Polymer of NAG (N-Acetyl Glucosamine)
- Found in exoskeleton of arthropods and cell wall of Fungi.

NUCLEIC ACIDS

- Make up genetic material of all living organisms
- Most important nucleic acids – DNA & RNA
- They are polymers of nucleotides.
- Each nucleotide contains –
  Pentose sugar + Nitrogenous base + PO_4

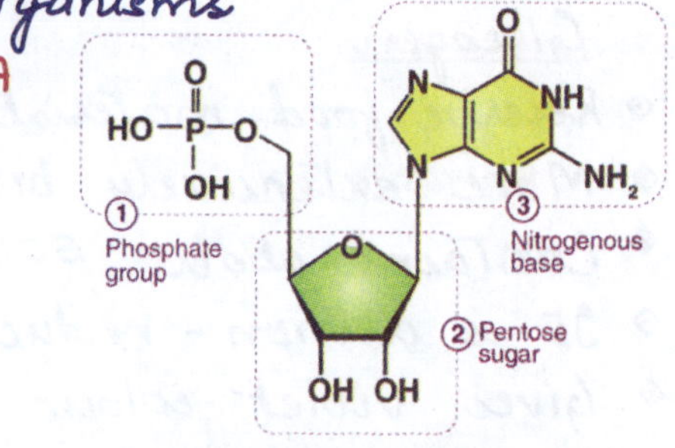

- Pentose sugar
  Ribose in RNA
  Deoxyribose in DNA

Ribose | Deoxyribose

Nitrogenous Bases

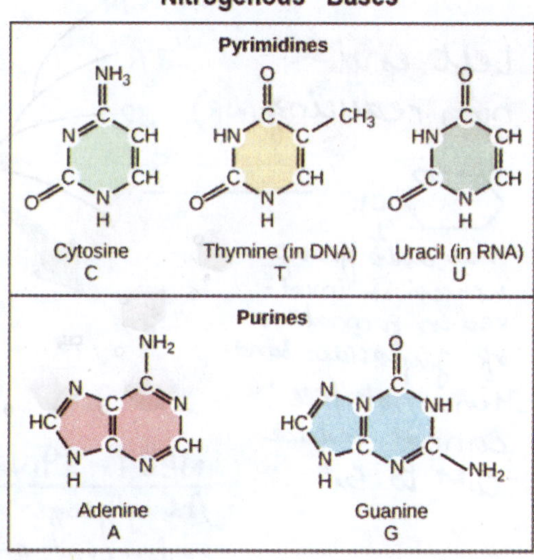

- Nitrogenous bases
  Pyrimidines – heterocyclic & monocyclic
  – Cytosine, Thymine, Uracil

  Purines – heterocyclic & dicyclic
  – Adenine and Guanine

- PO_4 group – phosphoric acid
  H_3PO_4

- Nucleoside and Nucleotide

Nucleotide and Nucleic Acid Nomenclature

Base	Nucleoside*	Nucleotide*	Nucleic acid
Purines			
Adenine	Adenosine	Adenylate (AMP)	RNA
	Deoxyadenosine	Deoxyadenylate	DNA
Guanine	Guanosine	Guanylate (GMP)	RNA
	Deoxyguanosine	Deoxyguanylate	DNA
Pyrimidines			
Cytosine	Cytidine	Cytidylate (CMP)	RNA
	Deoxycytidine	Deoxycytidylate	DNA
Thymine	Thymidine or deoxythymidine	Thymidylate or deoxythymidylate (TMP)	DNA
Uracil	Uridine	Uridylate	RNA

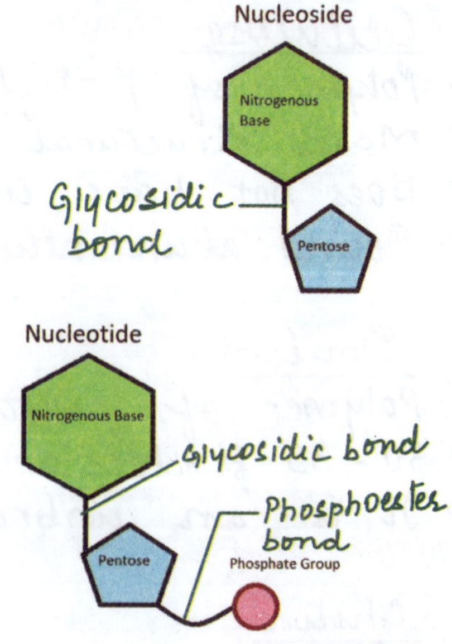

DNA – deoxyribo poly nucleotides

RNA – ribo poly nucleotide
(ribo → ribose, poly → many, nucleotide → nucleotides)

NEET SYNAPSE

N_2 base is joined at 1'C of pentose sugar by one of its N-atoms.

DNA (Deoxyribonucleic acid) – deoxyribopolynucleotide

- Main genetic material of living beings.
- Eukaryotes – DNA associated with histone proteins
- Prokaryotes – DNA not associated with proteins.
- Structure of DNA –
  - Double helical model given by Watson & Crick.
  - DNA consists of two helically coiled antiparallel strands
  - Sugar phosphate backbone – Alternating molecules of sugar & phosphate Linked with phosphodiester linkage
  - Phosphate is attached to C_5 of pentose sugar present one side and C_3 of pentose sugar present on other side.

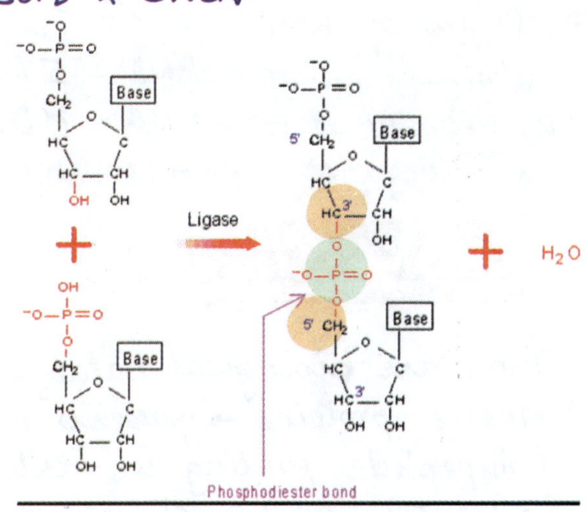

PENTOSE SUGAR IN DNA – DEOXYRIBOSE

- The two strands form a right handed helix. – B DNA.

> **NEET SYNAPSE**
> Z-DNA has left handed helix

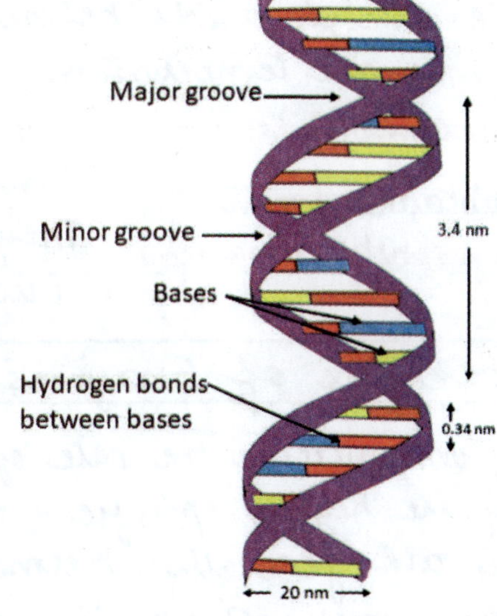

- The two strands are joined by Hydrogen bonds.
- A & T have 2 hydrogen bonds (A=T)
  C & G have 3 hydrogen bonds (C≡G)
- DNA has uniform thickness throughout its length – 2 nm
- Length of pitch – 3.4 nm
- 1 pitch (turn) has 10 base pairs
- Distance between 2 base pairs = 0.34 nm

> **NEET SYNAPSE**
> Chargaff's rule – A always bonds with T, C always bonds with G ∴ A = T, C = G

RNA (Ribonucleic acid) - ribopolynucleotide

- Found predominantly in cytoplasm
- Genetic material in some viruses - Reoviruses.
- Structure of RNA
  Mostly single stranded (Retroviruses have dsRNA)
  Single RNA strand is folded upon itself.
- Types of RNA
  (i) Messenger or mRNA - 5% of total cellular RNA
  (ii) Ribosomal or rRNA - 80% of total cellular RNA
  (iii) Transfer or tRNA (soluble RNA) - 10-15% of total cellular RNA

ENZYMES

- They are biological catalysts → Alter the rate of chemical reaction.
- Mostly proteins → possess primary, secondary & tertiary structure.
- Polypeptide folding in tertiary structure -
  - creates a 3D structure with pockets / crevices.
  - Pockets act as 'active sites' → allow binding of substrate.
- Some nucleic acids behave as enzymes, called ribozymes.
- Enzymes are temperature specific.
- Thermostable enzymes - obtained from organisms residing in high temperature zones like thermal springs.
  ↓ obtained from Thermophilic organisms. - They remain active even at high temperatures. (upto 80-90°C)

Properties of Enzymes

- They only increase the rate of reaction, do not get consumed in reaction.
- They are highly specific - they catalyse a specific reaction.
- They are generally thermolabile (temp specific) → 25°C - 35°C
- They work at specific pH.
- Turnover number - Number of substrate molecules converted into product per unit time (second).

NEET SYNAPSE

Fastest enzyme - carbonic anhydrase (10^6/sec)
Slowest enzyme - Lysozyme.

Enzyme	vs. Inorganic catalyst
Organic- generally proteins	Small simple molecules - eg. Ni
Occur in living systems	Do not occur in living systems.
Thermolabile	Efficient even at high temp.

Mechanism of enzyme action

- Each enzyme (E) has active site where substrate (S) binds

E + S ⟶ E-S complex (highly reactive & short lived - transient)

↓

E + P ⟵ E-P complex (Enzyme product complex)

product is released ; Substrate is converted into product

Example- when surose (S) binds with sucrase (E), it releases glucose & fructose (P).

DIGESTIVE ENZYMES

Substrate (Sucrose) | Active site | Enzyme (Sucrase) | H_2O | Enzyme-substrate complex | Enzyme-products complex | Products (Glucose) (Fructose) | Products are released

Lock and Key hypothesis

- Lock - enzyme
- Keyhole - active site
- Key - substrate

• Only a specific key can fit in keyhole of lock

• Only a specific substrate can bind to the active site of an enzyme

(a) Key (substrate) | Lock (enzyme) | Substrate | Active site | Enzyme

(b) Lock-Key Complex | Enzyme-Substrate Complex

Induced fit hypothesis

- Shape of active site & substrate is not complementary - it is induced to assume complementary shape.
- Active site contains two groups-
  - Buttressing group - support group
  - Catalytic group - catalyses reaction

Induced Fit Model

Substrate | Active Site | Enzyme | Enzyme adjust its shape | Enzyme-Substrate Complex | Enzyme-Product Complex | Products | Enzyme

- Substrate binds to buttressing group ⟶ conformational change in active site ⟶ reaction occurs.

How do enzymes bring about such high rate of chemical conversions?

Concept of activation energy

- The energy required for a reation to proceed (S ⟶ P)
- Enzymes reduce the activation energy, hence increase the rate of reaction.
- Substrate has certain energy
  - It has to cross various transition stages to convert into product.
  - Transition stages are unstable.

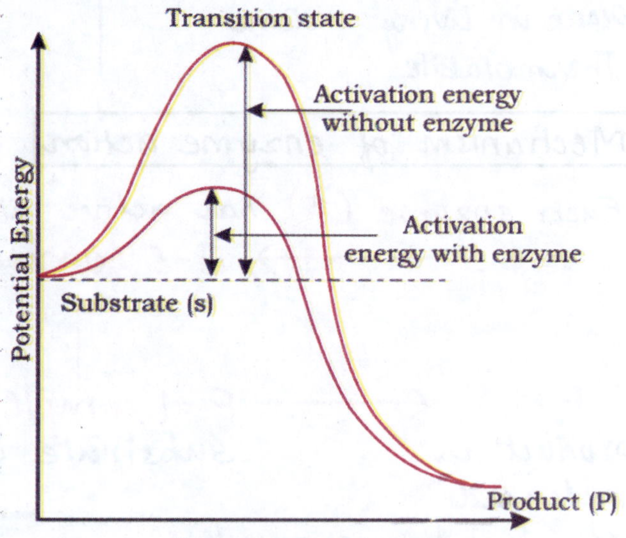

NEET SYNAPSE

P has lower energy than S, it means S lost energy → heat released → Exothermic reaction

P has higher energy than S, it means S gained energy → heat absorbed → Endothermic reaction.

Higher activation energy is required in an uncatalysed reaction.

Factors affecting enzyme activity

1. Temperature

Optimum temperature - high activity
High temperature - denaturation
Low temperature [preservation, inactivity

2. pH

Optimum pH - max. activity
High pH } denaturation.
Low pH }

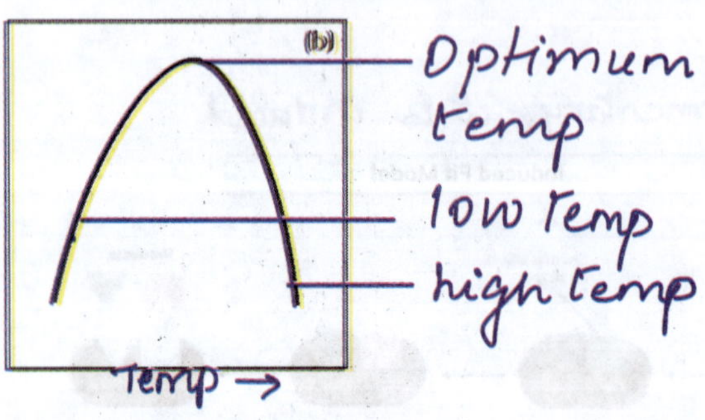

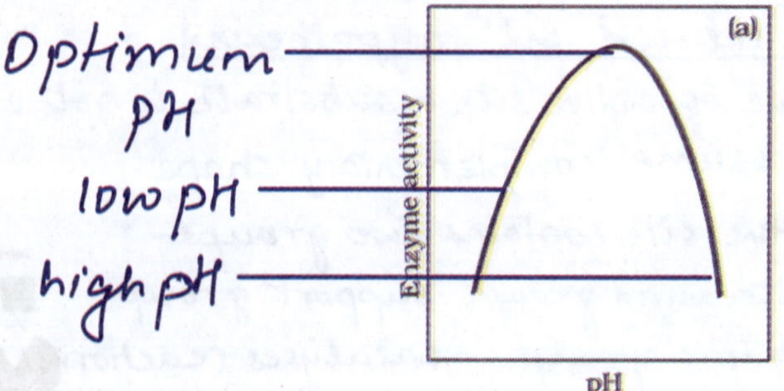

3. Substrate concentration.

- Initial ↑ in subs. conc →

↓

Filling of active sites

↓

↑ in rate of chemical reaction

↓

Vmax – maximum velocity achieved

↓

Saturation of active sites by substrate molecules

↓

Any further increase in substrate has no effect on reaction velocity

↓

Plateau stage

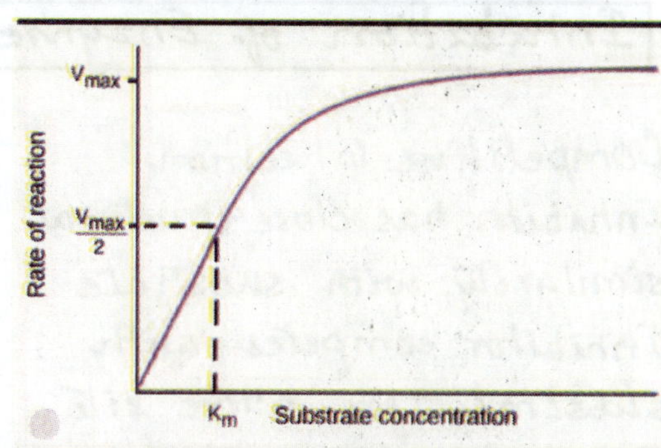

Km – Michaelis-Menten constant

Km – substrate conc. at which reaction reaches half of its maximum velocity.

NEET SYNAPSE

Enzyme conc. also affects its action. More enzyme molecules → faster rx^n

4. Product concentration

- Accumulation of product usually slows down the chemical reaction.

Classification and Nomenclature of Enzymes

- Class I – Oxidoreductases S reduced + S' oxidised ⟶ S oxidised + S' reduced.
  Catalyse oxidation reduction reactions.
- Class II – Transferases S - G + S' ⟶ S + S' - G
  Catalyse transfer of functional groups
- Class III – Hydrolases
  Catalyse breakdown of molecules in the presence of water.
- Class IV – Lyases
  Catalyse removal of groups leaving a double bond. X–C–C–Y (X, Y attached to adjacent C) ⟶ X - Y + C = C
- Class V – Isomerases
  Catalyse rearrangement of molecular structure.
- Class VI – Ligases
  Catalyse joining of molecules.

Inhibition of Enzyme Action

Competitive inhibition

- Inhibitor has close structural similarity with substrate
- Inhibitor competes with substrate for active site
- Inhibitor binds to the active site and stops the reaction from occuring.
- EI (Enzyme Inhibitor) complex is formed; ES complex is inhibited.
- Effect can be reversed by increasing substrate concentration.
- Vmax remains constant. Km increases
- Eg. Inhibition of succinic dehydrogenase by malonate.

Non-competitive inhibition

- Inhibitor binds at a site other than the active site
- Inhibitor brings about conformational change in the enzyme which affects substrate binding.
- Both EI and ES complexes are formed.
- Effect cannot be reversed by increasing substrate concentration.
- Vmax is lowered. Km is unchanged.
- Eg: Inhibition of cytochrome oxidase by cyanide.

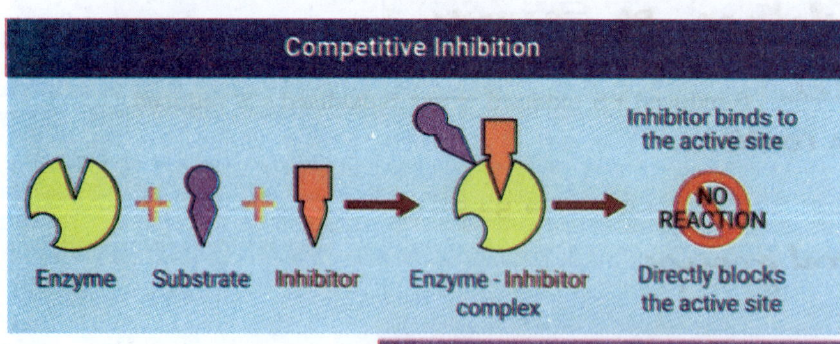

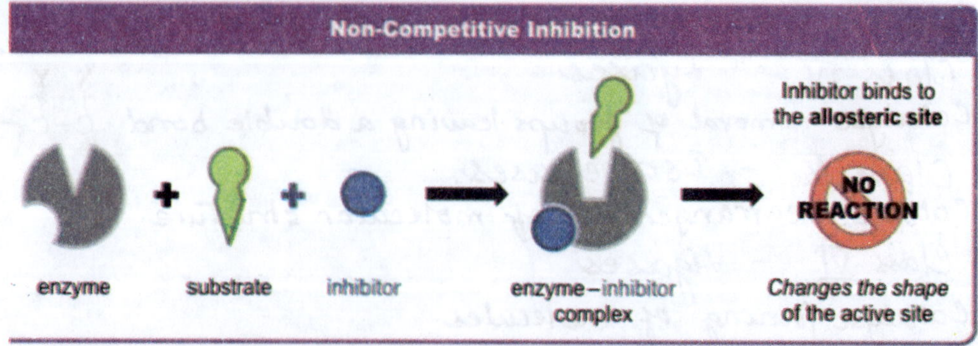

10. Cell Cycle and Cell Division

- Cell division is required for growth, repair & reproduction.
- Cell cycle – sequential repetition of dividing & non-dividing phases of a cell.
  - ↳ It includes – duplication of genome
    - – synthesis of other cellular components.
    - – division of cell into 2 daughter cells.
- Duration of cell cycle varies from cell to cell & from organism to organism.
  - E. coli divides in 20 min
  - Human cells – generally divide in 24 hrs.

NEET SYNAPSE

In humans, out of 24 hrs [Interphase – 23 hrs
Dividing phase – 1 hr.

- Generation time – Period between 2 successive cell divisions in a cell.

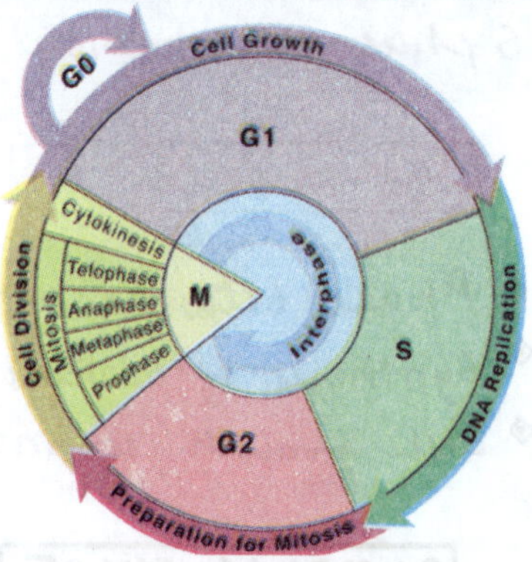

Cell growth (cytoplasmic increase) is a continuous process but DNA replication occurs only once.

PHASES OF CELL CYCLE

INTERPHASE

- Also known as preparatory phase
- It is a long resting phase or non dividing phase
- Lasts for more than 95% of total duration of cell cycle.
- Intense cytogenic activities take place during this phase.
- Interphase is subdivided into 3 phases –

(i) G_1 phase (First gap/growth phase)
(ii) S phase (Synthesis phase)
(iii) G_2 phase (Second gap/growth phase)

G_1 phase

- Cell grows in size - acquires nutrients from the environment.
- Synthesis of RNA, ribosomes, proteins, lipids etc.
- No change in DNA content
- Metabolic rate of cell is high
- After G phase, a cell can enter one of the following-
  → S phase or → G_0 phase

S- phase

- Synthesis phase
- DNA synthesis takes place (in nucleus)
- DNA content doubles (2C→4C)
- No change in chromosome number
- Ploidy level remains same
- Duplication of centrioles takes place in cytoplasm of animal cells.
- Synthesis of proteins & cell growth occurs.

G_0 phase

- Quiescent phase
- Extension of G_1 phase
- Cells do not exhibit division
- May divide ocassionally to replace injured or dead cells.
- Cells are metabolically active
- Cells can differentiate.

Eg - heart & nerve cells in humans

NEET SYNAPSE

S phase in haploid cell → DNA content - 1C → 3C

G_2-phase

- Phase between DNA synthesis and next division.
- Synthesis of proteins (required for cell division) takes place.
- Cell growth continues.

DIVIDING PHASE

- Can be mitosis or meiosis
- In humans - mitosis takes place in somatic cells (diploid)
  meiosis takes place in germ cells (form gametes)
- In male honeybee - mitosis takes place in germ cells (haploid)

NEET SYNAPSE

In plants - mitosis takes place in haploid spore and leads to the formation of gametophyte

Dividing phase includes
Karyokinesis - nuclear division
Cytokinesis - cytoplasmic division.

MITOSIS

- Also called equational division
- No. of chromosomes in daughter cells is same as that of parent cell.

Phases of Karyokinesis

Prophase

- Chromatin —condensation→ chromosomes
- Each chromosome has 2 chromatids
- Chromatids are joined at centromere.
- Centrioles move towards opposite poles
- Formation of asters & spindle fibres
- Mitotic apparatus → asters + spindle + centrioles
- Nucleoli disappear, nuclear envelope broken down.

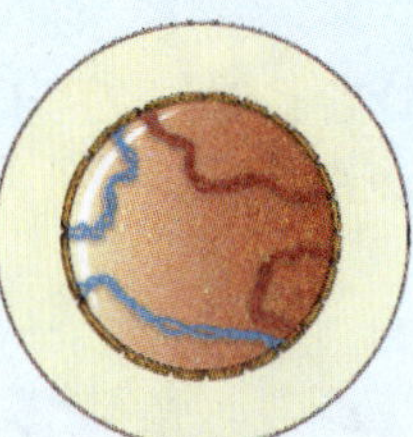

Early Prophase

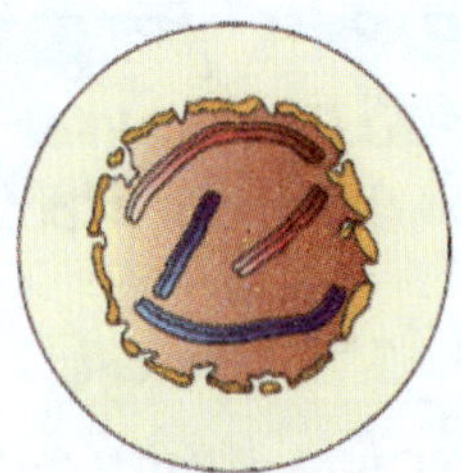

Late Prophase

Metaphase

- Chromosomes are thickest & shortest.
- Best phase to study chromosomes.
- Complete disintegration of nuclear envelope
- Chromosomes completely condensed.
- Spindle fibres attach to kinetochore.
- Chromosomes align at equator forming equitorial plate/metaphasic plate.

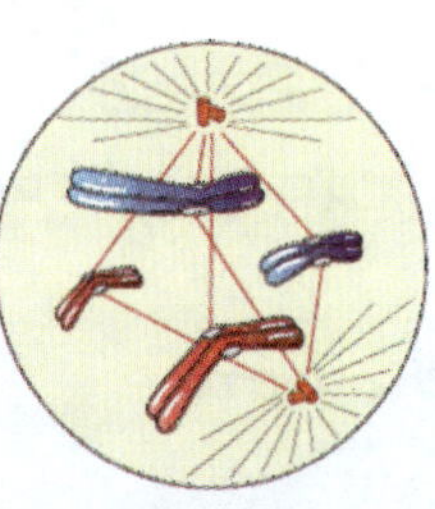

Transition to Metaphase

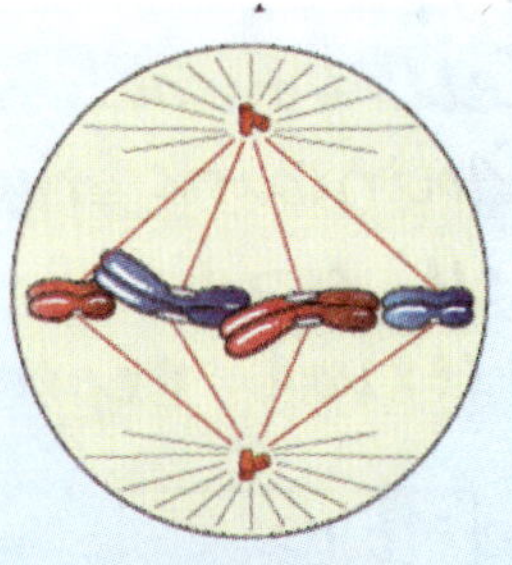

Metaphase

Anaphase

- Chromosomes start moving towards opposite poles.
- Centromeres split & chromatids are separated.
- While moving, centromere leads and arms follow.

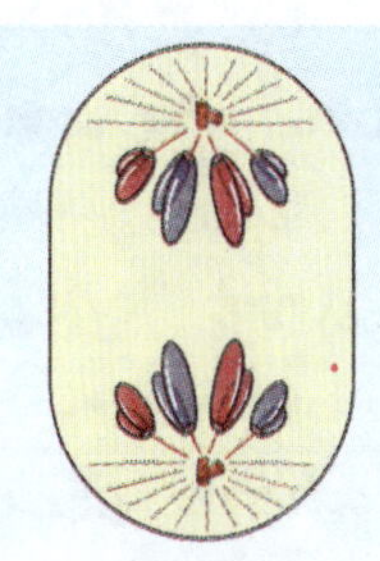

Anaphase

Telophase

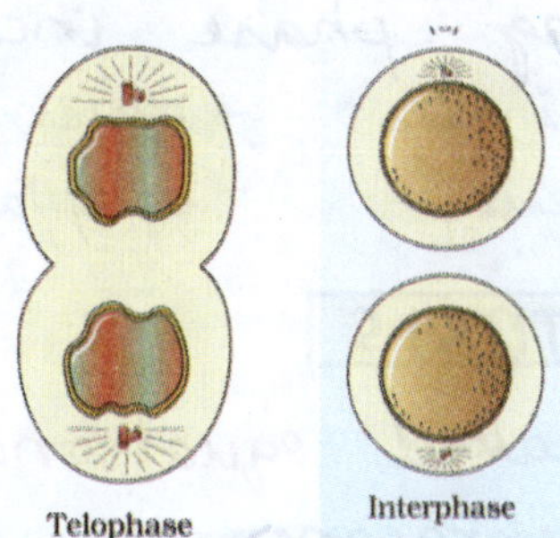

- Last phase of karyokinesis.
- Spindle fibres disintegrate
- Formation of nuclear envelope starts.
- Cell organelles reappear.
- Formation of cleavage furrow takes place

> **NEET SYNAPSE**
> In some organisms, karyokinesis is not followed by cytokinesis. This leads to multinucleate condition called syncitium. Eg skeletal muscle fibre

Cytokinesis

- Division of cytoplasm.
- Furrow is formed
  - ↳ It moves from cell membrane to centre
  - ↳ Centripetal division.

> **NEET SYNAPSE**
> In plants, separation of daughter cells takes place by formation of cell plate or Phragmoplast. They exhibit centrifugal division.

Significance of Mitosis

- Cell formation causes 'growth'
- Maintains nuclear-cytoplasmic ratio
- Cell repair
- Asexual reproduction

MEIOSIS

- Also called reductional division
- Number of chromosomes becomes half in daughter nuclei compared to the parent nuclei.
- Occurs in germ cells during gamete formation.
- Involves two successive nuclear divisions - Meiosis I and Meiosis II.
- The period between Meiosis I & Meiosis II is called interkinesis.
- DNA replication occurs only once

MEIOSIS - I

- True reductional division
- It is further divided into stages

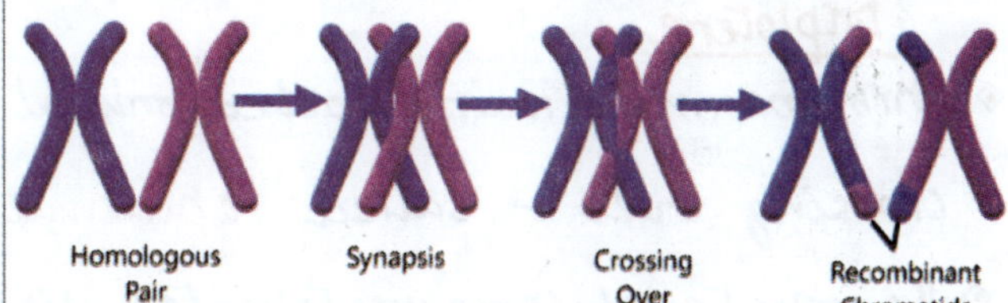

Prophase I

- Longest phase of meiosis.
- Further divided into five substages

Leptotene

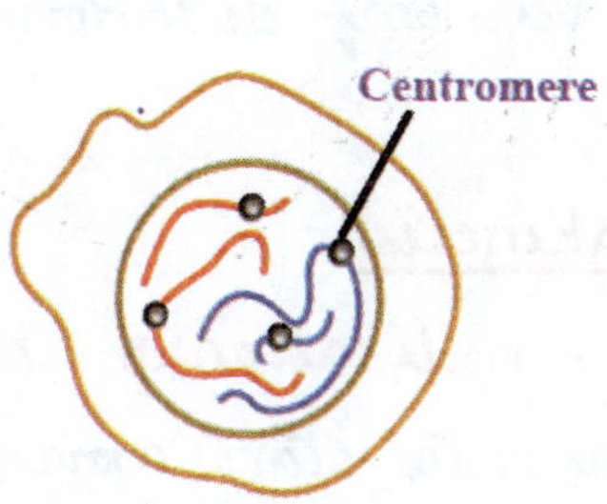

Leptotene

- Chromosomes shorten & become visible
- Chromomeres are seen on chromosomes

Zygotene

- Homologous chromosomes pair up.
- Pairing is called synapsis
- Chromosomes are held by synaptonemal complex.
- Pair of homologous chromosomes is called bivalent.
- Each chromosome contains 2 chromatids - thus together all four chromatids (in a pair) is called tetrad.
- Each chromosome contains a centromere where chromatids are attached; hence 2 centromeres in a pair.

Pachytene

- Longest stage of Prophase I
- Recombination nodule is formed.
- Non sister chromatids of homologous chromosomes exchange segments - called crossing over / recombination.
- Recombination - carried out by enzyme recombinase.
- End of pachytene -
  - recombination completed
  - homologous chromosomes remain attached at the site of crossing over.

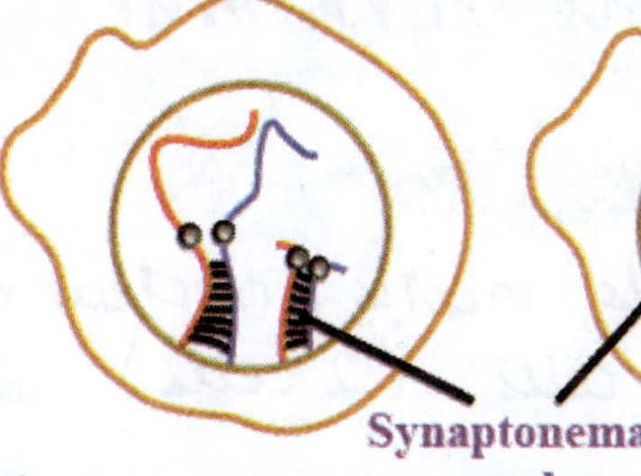
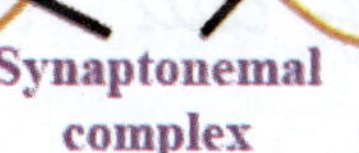

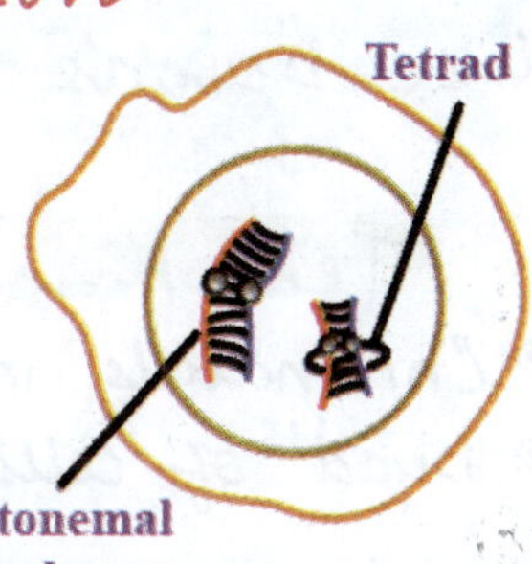

Zygotene Pachytene

Diplotene

- Chromosomes remain attached only at sites of
- crossing over – called chiasma
- In oocytes of some vertebrates, diplotene lasts for very long duration – dictyotene stage.

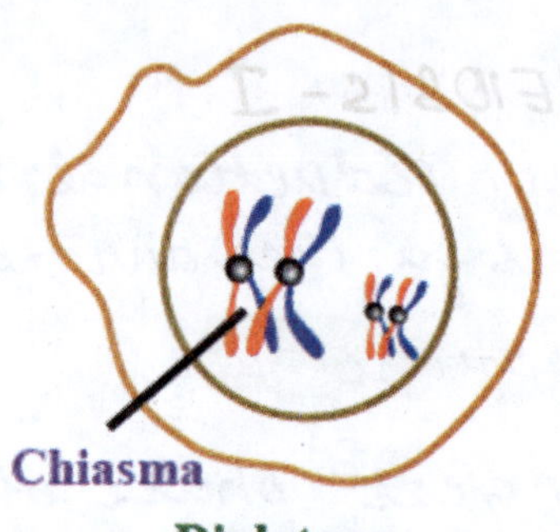

Diplotene

Diakinesis

- Terminalisation of chiasmata occurs. Chiasmata start moving towards terminals.
- Nucleolus disappears, nuclear membrane disintegrates completely.

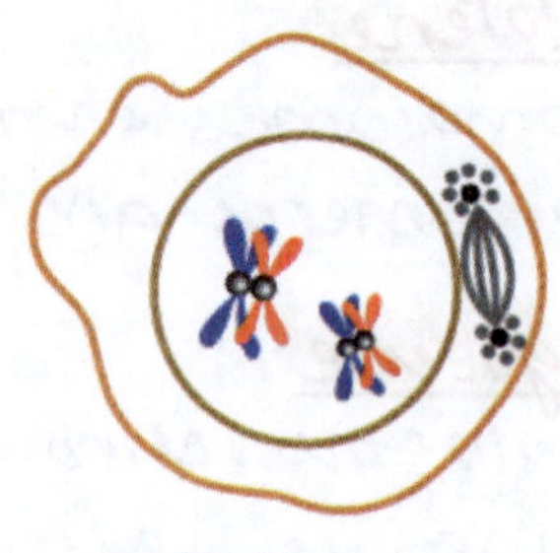
Diakinesis

Metaphase I

- Homologous chromosomes align at metaphasic plate.
- 2 metaphasic plates are formed.
- Spindle fibres attach at kinetochore

Anaphase I

- Disjunction – Movement of homologous chromosomes towards opposite poles

NEET SYNAPSE
Failure of disjunction leads to chromosomal abnormilities like Down's syndrome

Telophase I

- Chromatids uncoils, nuclear membrane reforms.
- Dyad of cells (2 cells) is observed.

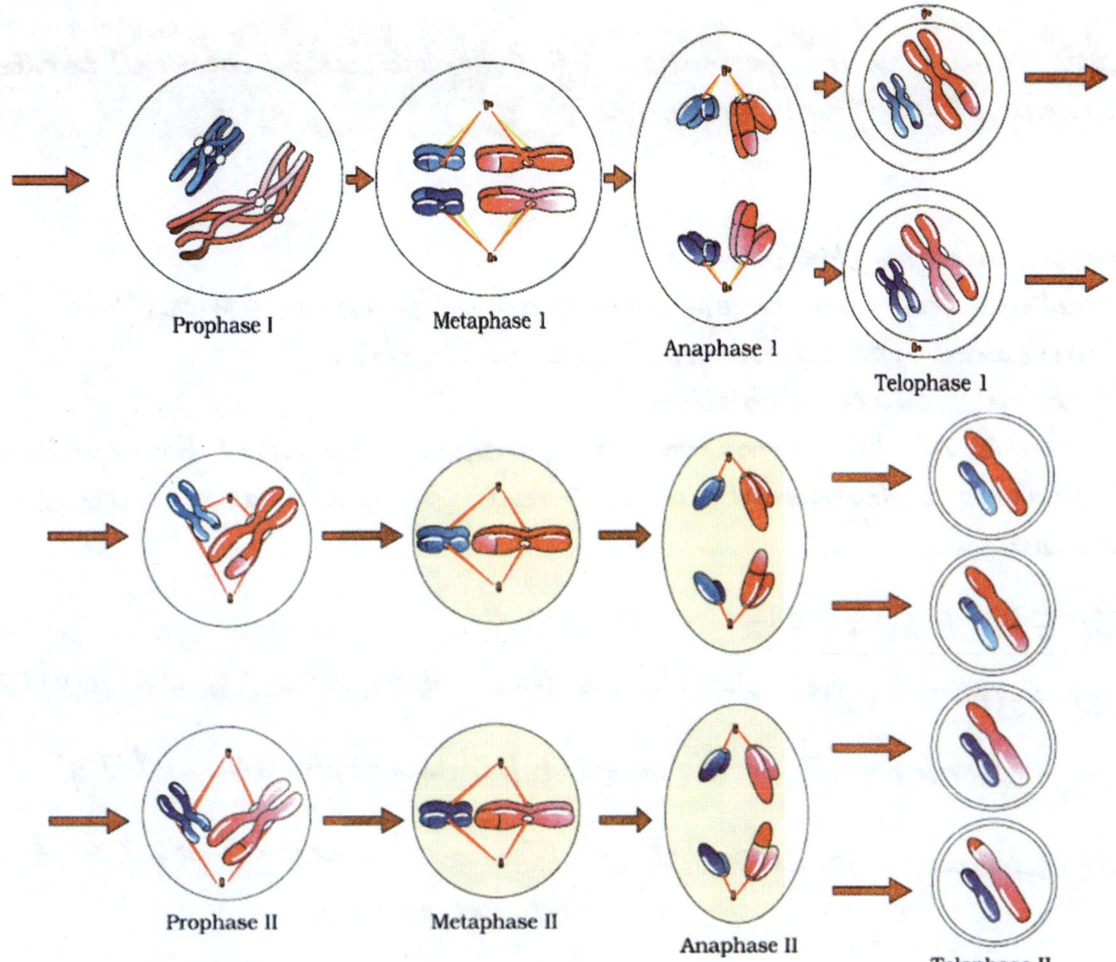

MEIOSIS - II

- It is equational division - like mitosis

Prophase II

- Each chromosome (having 2 chromatids) condenses & becomes visible
- Centrosomes start moving to opposite poles.

Nuclear envelope dissolves.

Metaphase II

- Chromosomes align at equitorial / metaphasic plate.

Anaphase II

- Sister chromatids of each chromosome separate and move towards opposite poles.

Telophase II

- Chromosomes arrive at opposite poles of cell
- Nuclear envelope is formed.
- Spindle fibres disappear.

Meiosis results in the formation of 4 haploid cells – each cell contains a unique set of chromosomes.

Significance of Meiosis.

- It restores the number of chromosomes in each generation.
- It increases variation due to recombination.
- Variations cause evolution.
- It results in the formation of gametes – essential for reproduction
- It leads to independent assortment of maternal & paternal chromosomes.

NEET SYNAPSE

Checkpoints = they decide further progression of cell division.

1. G_2 checkpoint – Present b/w G_2–M boundary
2. Metaphase checkpoint – Metaphase-anaphase boundary.
3. G_1 checkpoint – At G_1-S boundary.

11. Photosynthesis

- Plants, phytoplanktons, cyanobacteria carry out photosynthesis (PS)
- Photo - light ; synthesis - formation.
- $$6 CO_2 + 12 H_2O \xrightarrow[Chl]{\text{sunlight}} C_6H_{12}O_6 + 6 H_2O + 6 O_2$$

EARLY EXPERIMENTS

- **To demonstrate the role of chlorophyll in Photosynthesis**

Variegated leaf experiment

green part containing chlorophyll

staining with iodine

Part containing chlorophyll turned blue after staining with Iodine indicating the presence of starch

- **To demonstrate CO_2 is necessary for Photosynthesis**

Moll's half leaf experiment

- Leaf - half exposed to air
- Other half dipped in container containing KOH
- Starch formation not seen in dipped part
- Conclusion - PS did not take place in it because KOH absorbs CO_2

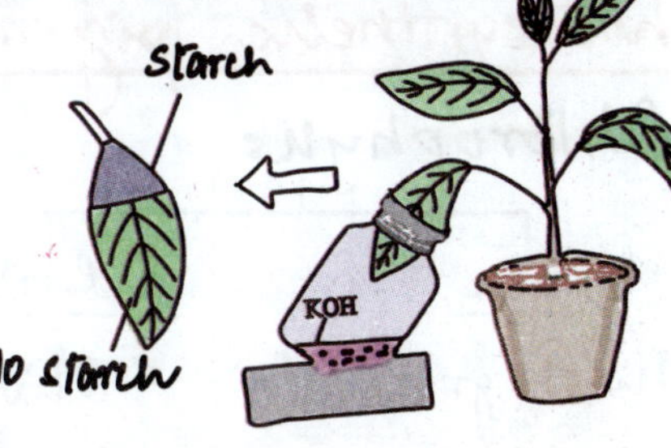

Hall of Fame

- Joseph Priestley - conducted bell jar experiment with mouse, candle & mint plant → Proved that plants can purify atmosphere by taking up CO_2 & releasing O_2
- Jan Ingenhouse - Sunlight necessary for Photosynthesis & only done by green parts of plants
- Julius von Sachs - Final product of Photosynthesis is starch (saccharide)
- Engelmann - experimented on Cladophora. He split light using prism and found aerobic bacteria gathered near blue & red region
- Van Niel - Some bacteria use H_2S & reduce CO_2.

Site for Photosynthesis

- Mesophyll cells of leaves have large number of chloroplasts.

Thylakoid
- contains lumen & chlorophyll
- has a double membrane
- site of light reaction

Outer membrane freely permeable due to porins

Inter membrane space

Chlorophyll
- present in thylakoid
- Absorbs sunlight during light reaction

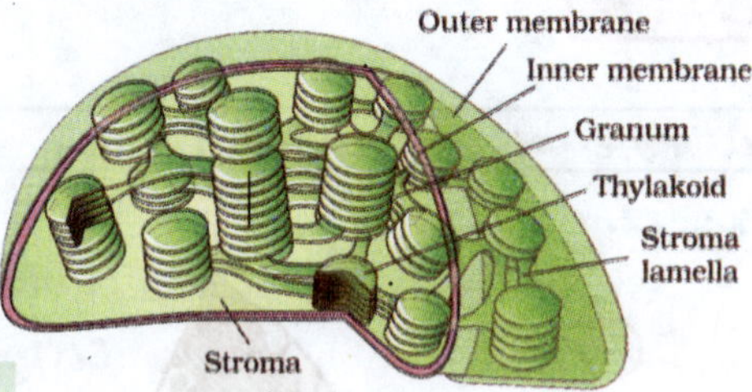

Inner membrane Not freely permeable

Granum
- stack of thylakoids
- Increase surface area for PS

Stroma site of dark reaction

Stroma lamellae connects adjacent grana. PS I is present here

Photosynthetic pigments

- **Chlorophylls**

Chl a	Chl b
• Bluish green	• Olive green
• found in all green plants	• Found mainly in algae & higher plants
• Primary pigment of PS	

- **Carotenoids**
  - Yellow, brown & orange
  - Absorb light in blue-violet region
    - Carotenes (orange)
    - Xanthophylls (yellow)
    - Phycobilins (blue & red)

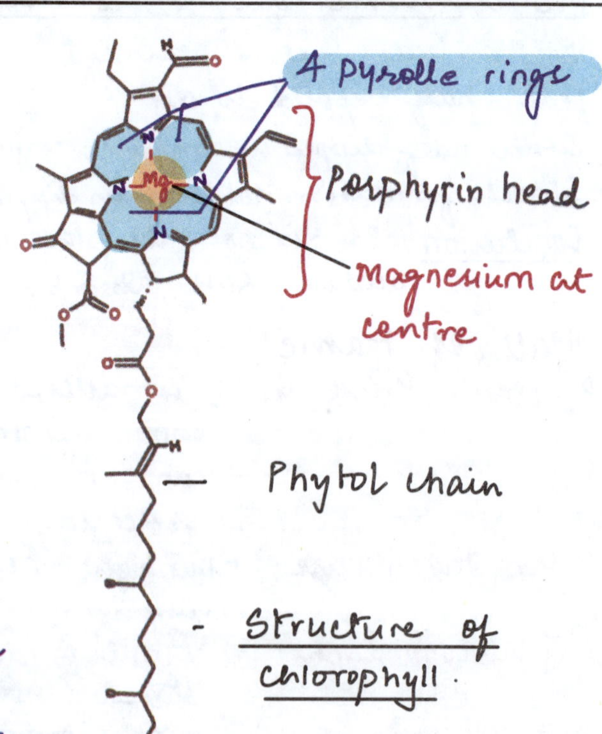

Absorption spectrum

Visible part of light is called Photosynthetically Active Radiation (PAR)

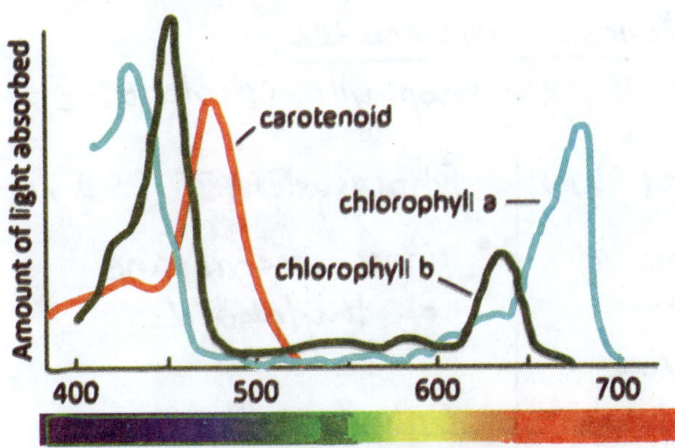

Chla - blue violet & red region
Chlb - red blue region
Green light is not absorbed; it is reflected.

Action spectrum

Rate of photosynthesis at different wavelengths.

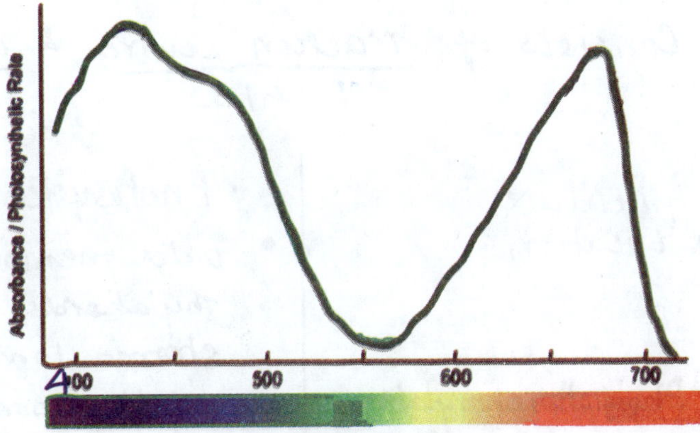

Rate of PS maximum in absorption spectrum of Chla - ∴ it is the chief pigment of PS.

NEET SYNAPSE

Red Drop | Emerson effect
At wavelength beyond 700 nm - rate of PS drops significantly.

Process of Photosynthesis

Light reaction
Photochemical phase

- Occurs in presence of light
- Site - thylakoids & stroma lamellae
- Light energy converted into chemical energy
- End products - ATP ; NADPH

Dark reaction
Biosynthetic phase

- Can occur in presence or absence of light
- Site - stroma
- Utilises products of light
- reaction
- End product - glucose

LIGHT REACTION

Light harvesting complexes or photosystems

- Consists of reaction centre (Chl a) & antenna molecules (Chl b, xanthophylls, carotenoids).

Feature	Photosystem I (PS I)	Photosystem II (PS II)
• Location	• outer membrane of thylakoids + stroma lamellae	• inner membrane of thylakoids.
• Photophosphorylation	• cyclic + non cyclic	• Only non-cyclic
• Reaction centre	• P_{700}	• P_{680}
• Main function	• $NADP^+$ reduction	• Photolysis of water

Process of light reaction

① Light absorption

By photosynthetic pigments
↓
Reaction centre of PS gets energised
↓
Electron pair is emitted
↓
Electrons pass through ETS (Electron Transport System)

② Photolysis of water

- Breakdown of water in the presence of light
- Associated with release of oxygen.

③ Photophosphorylation

• Non cyclic	• cyclic
• Involves PS II & PS I	• Involves only PS I
• Formation of $NADPH+H^+$ & ATP	• Formation of ATP only.

④ Chemiosmotic hypothesis

- Development of proton gradient for the formation of ATP
- Occurs in thylakoid membrane

LIGHT ABSORPTION

- Takes place inside thylakoids by chlorophyll, carotenoids etc.
- Pigments that capture energy are called Light Harvesting Complex / Photosystem.
  - ↳ consists of reaction centre + antenna molecules
  - Reaction centre → chl a
  - Antenna molecules → transfer energy to reaction centre.

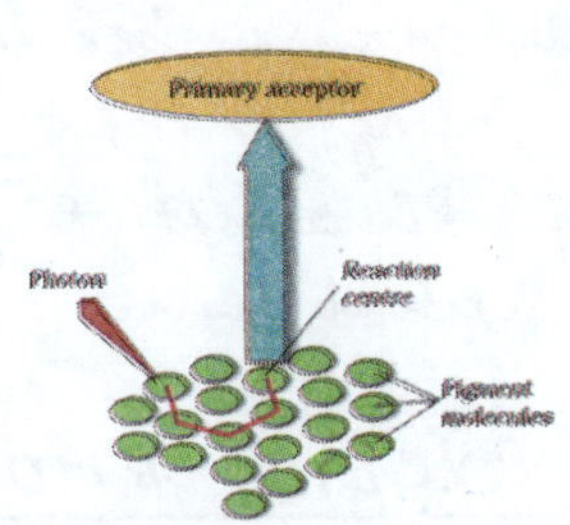

ELECTRON TRANSPORT SYSTEM

- Reaction centre becomes highly energised after absorbing light energy
- Photoexcited reaction centre releases a pair of electrons.
- These electrons are accepted by primary acceptor.
- Electrons then pass down through ETS.
- During passage of electrons,
  - reduction of NADP to NADPH + H^+ takes place.
  - Photophosphorylation (ADP → ATP) takes place.

PHOTOLYSIS OF WATER

- Photochemical oxidation of water $[2H_2O \longrightarrow 4H^+ + 4e^- + O_2]$
- Described by Van Niel.
- Electrons obtained from this reaction are passed to PS II

PHOTOPHOSPHORYLATION – Addition of P in the presence of light.

Non cyclic Photophosphorylation – Z scheme

- Primary acceptor passes e^- to plastoquinone (PQ)
- From PQ ⟶ cyt b_6f (e^- carrier)
  - ↓
  - PS I ⟵ Plastocyanin
- PS I also receives photons directly from sunlight.
- PS I gets excited & release e^-.
- These e^- are finally accepted by $NADP^+$ present in stroma.
- $NADP^+$ receives protons from splitting of water. $NADP^+ + 2e^- + 2H^+ \longrightarrow NADPH + H^+$

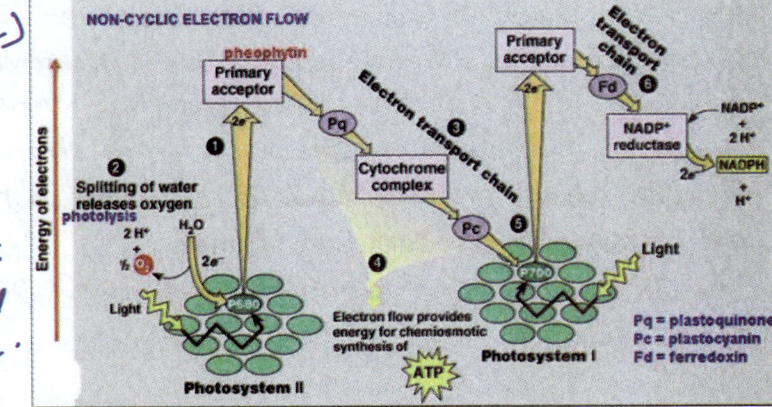

NEET SYNAPSE

- Non cyclic photophosphorylation is also called Z-scheme because the shape of path of e⁻ flow resembles the letter Z.
- This occurs because the components of ETS are arranged according to their redox potential.
- Eg. PC accepts e⁻ from cyt b6f - thus PC has more reduction potential can cyt b6f.

CYCLIC PHOTOPHOSPHORYLATION

> Formation of ATP only.

- Donor & acceptor of e⁻ is same - P700
- Occurs in stroma lamellae and unstacked thylakoids.
- Steps of process → e⁻ from P700 are accepted by primary e⁻ acceptor ⟶ Transferred to ferredoxin (Fd) ⟶ cyt b6f ⟶ PC ⟶ P700
- Formation of NADPH + H^+ does not occur.

Photosystem I

CHEMIOSMOTIC HYPOTHESIS

- ATP synthesis occurs due to proton gradient

NEET SYNAPSE - Proton gradient is created across thylakoid membrane. More protons inside lumen; lesser towards outside in stroma

- Development of proton gradient -
  - Splitting of water molecule - releases H^+ inside thylakoid lumen.
  - Through proton transporter - Plastoquinone (PQ) - During transportation down the chain cytochrome accepts only e⁻. ∴ protons are transported to the lumen by PQ (not accepted by cytochrome b6f)
  - Through NADP reductase - Reduction of $NADP^+$ to NADPH + H^+ requires H^+ which are taken up from stroma.

  All the above processes lead to reduction in H^+ conc. in stroma & an increase in H^+ conc in lumen.

  This proton gradient is broken by F_0-F_1 particles containing enzyme ATPase.

ATP synthase enzyme consists of two parts-

1) CF_0 - embedded in thylakoid membrane.
   - carries out facilitated diffusion of H^+ across the membrane.
2) CF_1 - protrudes on the outer surface of thylakoid membrane- towards the stroma.
   - it catalyses the formation of ATP from ADP.

NEET SYNAPSE

- The conc. of H^+ inside the lumen is high whereas it is low in stroma.
- ∴ H^+ should easily diffuse from lumen to stroma, given the gradient.
- But this diffusion does not happen as thylakoid membrane is impermeable to H^+. ∴ Facilitated diffusion of protons by CF_0 CF_1 particles takes place

Steps of ATP formation

- H^+ move from lumen to stroma

↓

- Configuration changes occur in CF_1 (ATPase unit)

↓

- ATP formation starts

↓

- 3 H^+ are required for the formation of 1 ATP molecule

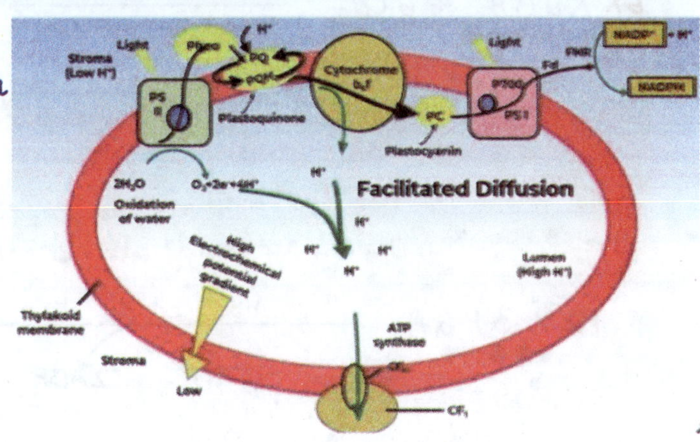

Products of light reaction

- ATP, NADPH+H^+, O_2
- Non cyclic photophosphorylation - ATP, NADPH+H^+, O_2
- Cyclic photophosphorylation - ATP only
- ATP & NADPH+H^+ are used up in dark reaction of Photosynthesis.
- Products of light reaction are also called assimilatory power, as they are used in carbon assimilation during dark reaction.

NEET SYNAPSE

O_2 evolved during photosynthesis comes from water molecules. Mn and Cl^- ions are crucial for photolysis of water.

DARK REACTION

- Involves biochemical reduction of CO_2 to form carbohydrates.
- Occurs in stroma of chloroplast.
- Discovered by Blackman, hence also called Blackman's reaction.
- Can occur through C_3 pathway, C_4 pathway or CAM.

C_3 PATHWAY | CALVIN CYCLE

- Discovered by Melvin Calvin - (Calvin cycle)
- First stable product is 3-carbon compound - (C_3 cycle)
- Stages of Calvin Cycle.

1. Carboxylation of RuBP (Ribulose 1,5- biPO4)

6X RuBP + 6 CO_2 —(RUBisCO / RuBP carboxylase)→ 12 X 3-PGA (Phosphoglyceric acid) (36C)

P 1 2 3 4 5 P

RuBisCO – Ribulose Biphosphate Carboxylase Oxygenase
- It can bind with CO_2 & O_2
- During carboxylation reactions - it binds with CO_2
- During oxygenation reactions - it binds with O_2

12 X 3PGA —(Phosphoglycerate kinase; 12ATP → 12ADP)→ 12 X 1,3 biPGA (36C)

2. Reduction of CO_2

12 X 1,3 BiPGA —(Phosphoglycerate dehydrogenase; 12 X NADPH → 12 X NADP+)→ 12 X PGAL (Glyceraldehyde 3-PO4) (36C)

2 X PGAL (6C) —(Aldolase)→ Fructose 1,6 biPO4 (6C)

Fructose 1,6 biPO4 (6C) ⟶ ⟶ Glucose (6C)

3. Regeneration of RuBP

10 X PGAL (30C) —(ATP → ADP)→ 6 X RuBP (30C)

P 1 2 3 4 5 P

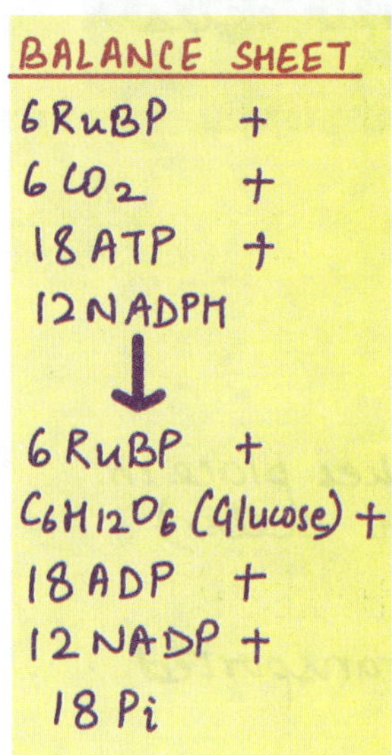

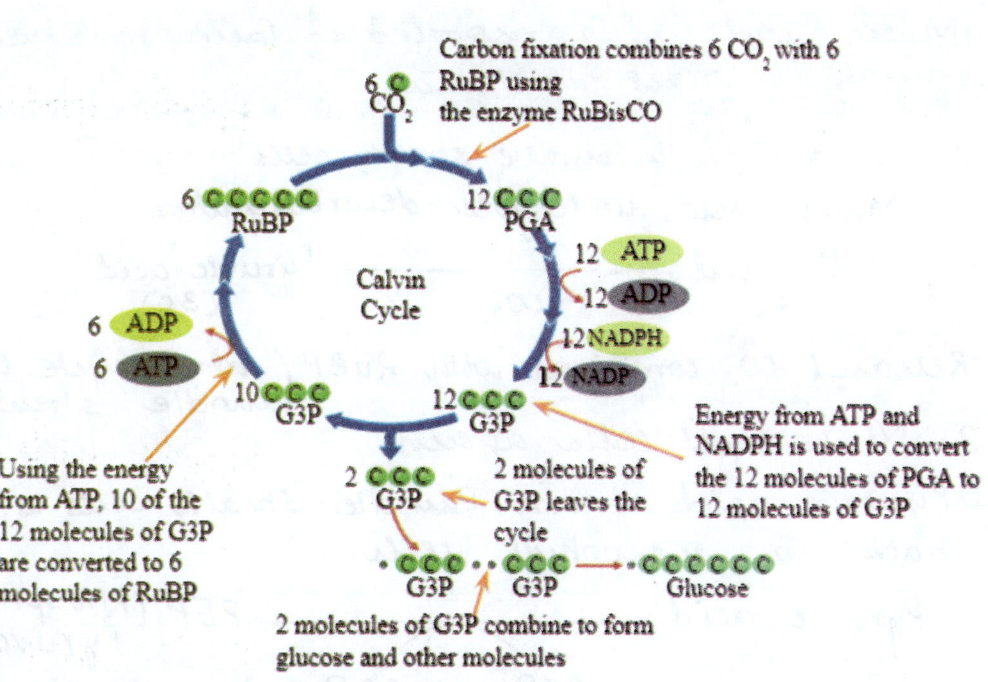

C_4 PATHWAY / HATCH AND SLACK CYCLE

- Discovered by Hatch & Slack
- First stable product is 4 carbon compound (C_4 cycle)
- Occurs in plants adapted for dry, tropical regions.
- Exhibited by plants having characteristic leaf anatomy - Kranz anatomy.
- Kranz anatomy-
  - Mesophyll region not divided into palisade & spongy parenchyma.
    ↳ Contains compactly arranged cells.
  - Vascular bundles surrounded by bundle sheath cells.
  - Chloroplasts of bundle sheath cells are larger & agranal.
  - chloroplasts of mesophyll cells are small & with grana.
- Steps of C_4 pathway

1. CO_2 fixation in mesophyll cells -

$$\underset{\text{Phospho enol pyruvate}}{\text{PEP (3C)}} + CO_2 \xrightarrow[\text{(PEPcase)}]{\text{PEP carboxylase}} \underset{\text{OxaloAcetic Acid}}{\text{OAA (4C)}}$$

$$\text{OAA (4C)} \longrightarrow \text{Malic acid (4C)}$$

NEET SYNAPSE - Mesophyll cells of C_4 plants lack RuBisCO. This reduces the chances of photorespiration ∴ increasing efficiency of photosynthesis.

Malic acid is transported to Bundle sheath cells through plasmodesmata.

2. CO_2 fixation in bundle sheath cells.

Malic acid undergoes decarboxylation.

$$\underset{(4C)}{\text{Malic acid}} \xrightarrow{\searrow CO_2} \underset{(3C)}{\text{Pyruvic acid}}$$

Released CO_2 combined with RuBP (Calvin cycle takes place in bundle sheath cells)

3. Mesophyll cells again

Pyruvic acid from Bundle sheath cells is transported back to mesophyll cells.

$$\text{Pyruvic acid} \xrightarrow[\text{ATP} \rightarrow \text{ADP}]{} \text{PEP (Phospho enol Pyruvate)}$$

NET REACTION

6 PEP + 6 RuBP + 6 CO_2 + 30 ATP + 12 NADPH

↓

6 PEP + 6 RuBP + 30 ADP + 30 H_3PO_4 + 12 $NADP^+$

BALANCE SHEET

For 1 Carbon fixed – 2 ATP used

For 1 Glucose (6C) – 12 ATP used

Total ATP used = 12 + 18 (C_3 cycle in bundle sheath cells) = 30 ATP

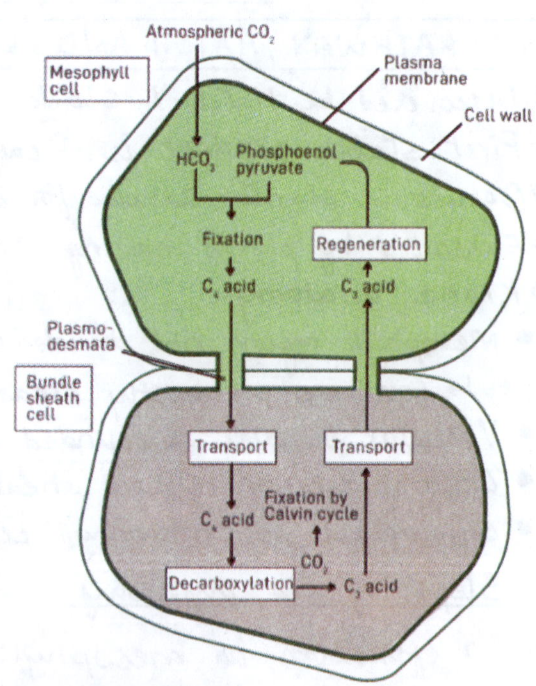

CAM PATHWAY – Crassulacean Acid Metabolism

- Present in succulent xerophytes
- Stomata remain closed during day & open during night.
- CO_2 is fixed at night; sugars are formed during day.
- This desert adaptation reduces water loss.

- Steps of CAM.

1. PEP + CO_2 ⟶ OAA
   OAA —(Malate dehydrogenase)⟶ Malic acid } at night

Malic acid is stored in vacuoles, thereby reducing the pH during day time
↳ releases CO_2 molecule ⟶ enters C_3 cycle ⟶ sugar formation

PHOTORESPIRATION

- Occurs when O_2 conc is high
- No synthesis of sugar or ATP
- It utilises ATP & releases CO_2
  ↳ considered wasteful process.
- It involves- chloroplasts, peroxisomes & mitochondria.
- Also called C_2 pathway-
  first stable product is 2C compound.

RuBP + O_2 —(RuBisCO / RuBP oxygenase)⟶ Phosphoglycolate (2C)

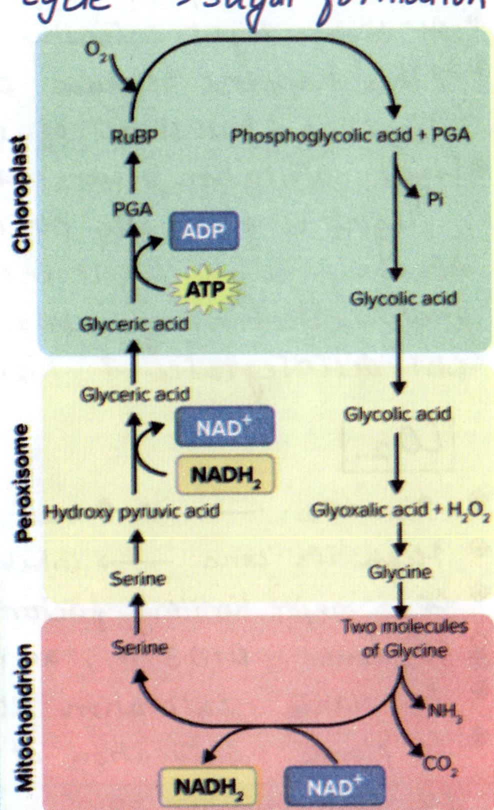

Peroxisomes are sites for synthesis of hydrogen peroxide in the cell.

NEET SYNAPSE

In C4 plants, mesophyll cells show very little photorespiration while bundle sheath cells do not show photorespiration because there is constant availability of CO_2 in bundle sheath cells due to decarboxylation, ∴ RuBisCO always binds with CO_2.

Bacterial Photosynthesis

- Pigments in photosynthetic bacteria- bacteriochlorophyll, bacterioviridin, bacteriophaeophytin and carotenoids.
- They utilise infra red radiation (870 nm – 1020 nm)
- Process does not evolve O_2.

Examples- Green sulphur bacteria
Purple sulphur bacteria

FACTORS AFFECTING PHOTOSYNTHESIS

LIGHT

- Effective wavelength - 400-700 nm
- Low light intensity - rate of photosynthesis is low.
- Linear relationship b/w incident light & rate of photosynthesis.
- At low intensity - as intensity ↑, PS ↑
- At higher light intensity - no further ↑ in PS
- ↳ This happens because other factors become limiting (fall short of requirement)
- Light saturation occurs at 10% of full sunlight
∴ Light is generally not a limiting factor.

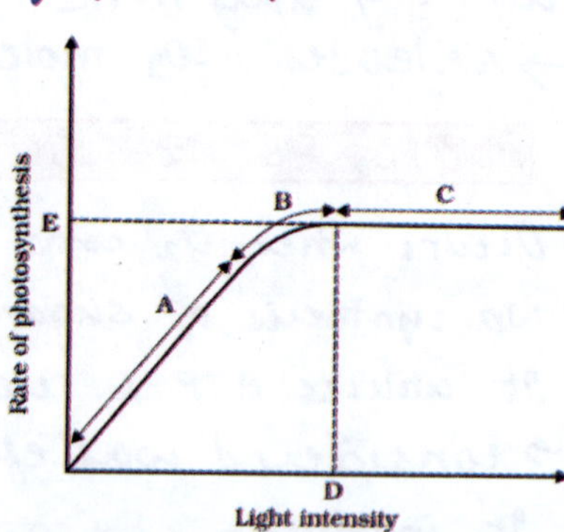

At very high light intensity - photooxidation of chlorophyll occurs - Chl disintegrates & hampers PS.

NEET SYNAPSE

C_4 plants are saturated with CO_2 at a lesser conc. than C_3 because C_4 plants fix CO_2 more efficiently than C_3 due to reduced photorespiration.

CO_2

- ↑ in CO_2 ⟶ ↑ rate of PS
- High CO_2 conc. ⟶ inhibits PS
- CO_2 - major limiting factor of PS
- CO_2 conc - 0.03%; an increase to 0.05% can ↑ PS
- C_4 plants - saturation at 360 ppm
- C_3 plants - saturation at 450 ppm.

CO_2 compensation point

A point at which CO_2 used during PS = CO_2 evolved through respiration.

TEMPERATURE

- Optimum range - 25-30°C
- Desert plants - can carry out photosynthesis even at 55°C
- Optimum temp. for tropical plants is higher than temperate plants

Blackman's Law of Limiting Factors.

When multiple factors control a process, the rate of process is limited by slowest factor.
∴ Rate of process is determined by the slowest factor.

WATER

- ↑ water content - ↑ rate of PS
- In wilted leaves (water stress) - reduction in PS occurs.

12. Respiration in Plants

- Cellular respiration - breakdown of C-C bonds of organic compounds to release ATP
- Respiratory substrates - organic compounds that are broken down during cellular respiration.
- ATP - Energy currency of cell

NEET SYNAPSE
Most common respiratory substrate - glucose.

DO PLANTS BREATHE?

- Plants carry out cellular respiration.
- They exchange gases through stomata (leaves) and lenticels (stem)
- They lack organs for respiration because -
  Every part of plant carries out its own gaseous exchange.
  Most gaseous exchange occurs through photosynthesis.
- Equation of cellular respiration

$$C_6H_{12}O_6 + 6O_2 \longrightarrow 6CO_2 + 6H_2O + ATP$$

Respiration can be

Aerobic	Anaerobic
complete oxidation	incomplete oxidation
occurs in presence of O_2	occurs in absence of O_2
end products - $CO_2 + H_2O$	end products - ethanol, lactic acid.

NEET SYNAPSE
Obligate anaerobes cannot survive in presence of O_2
Facultative anaerobes can survive in presence of O_2 if needed

- All living organisms can completely or partially digest glucose. First product of glucose digestion is pyruvic acid.

GLYCOLYSIS

- Breakdown of glucose (1) into pyruvic acid (2)
- Glyco - sugar ; lysis - break down.
- Also called Embden Meyerhof Parnas Pathway (EMP - Pathway)
- Occurs in cytosol or cytoplasm of all living organisms
- Common to both aerobic & anaerobic respiration.
- Fate of Pyruvic acid
  - presence of O_2 → aerobic respiration in mitochondria
  - absence of O_2 → lactic acid fermentation
    Alcoholic fermentation.

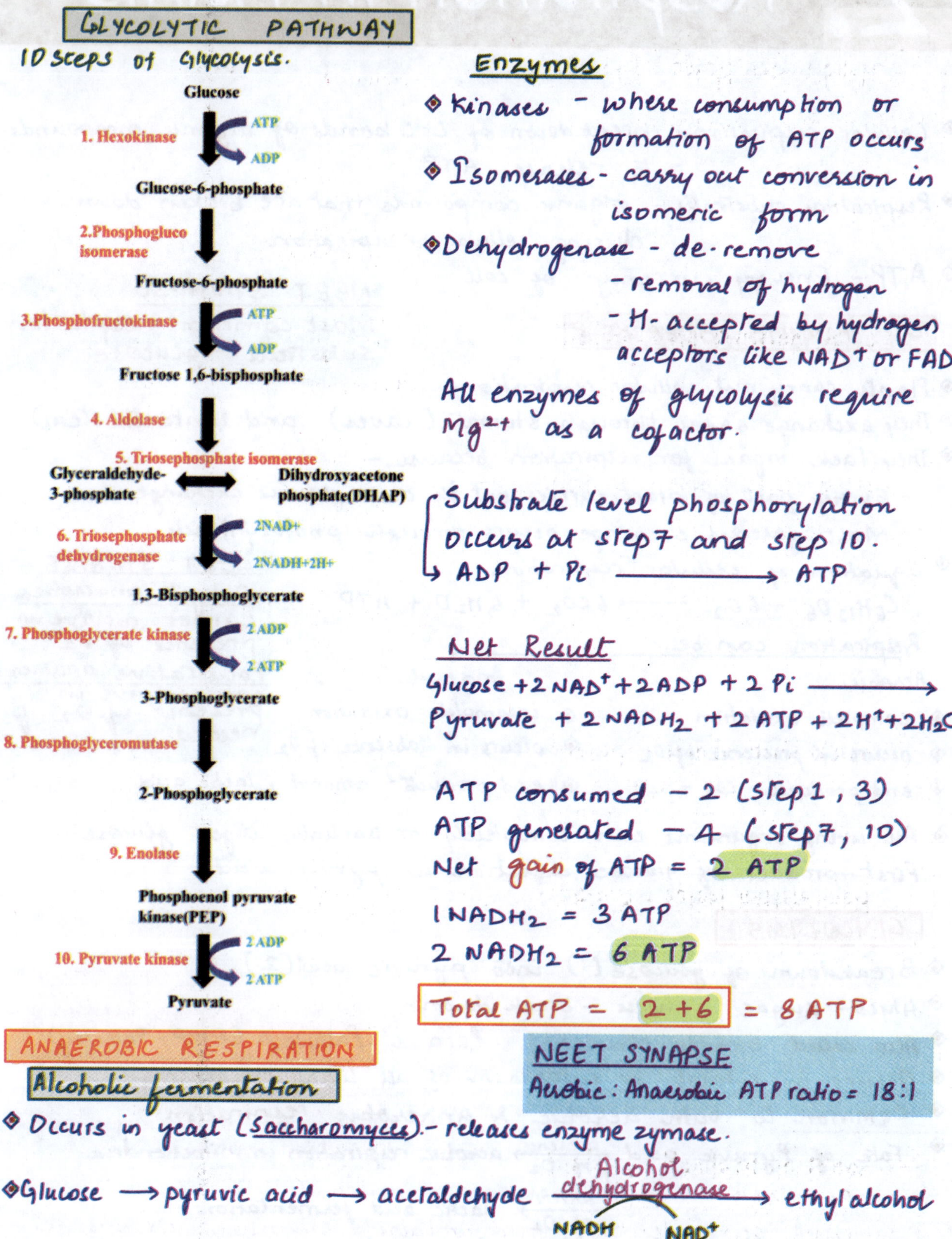

GLYCOLYTIC PATHWAY

10 steps of glycolysis.

Enzymes

- Kinases – where consumption or formation of ATP occurs
- Isomerases – carry out conversion in isomeric form
- Dehydrogenase – de-remove
  - removal of hydrogen
  - H- accepted by hydrogen acceptors like NAD^+ or FAD^+

All enzymes of glycolysis require Mg^{2+} as a cofactor.

Substrate level phosphorylation occurs at step 7 and step 10.
→ ADP + Pi ⟶ ATP

Net Result

Glucose + 2 NAD^+ + 2 ADP + 2 Pi ⟶
Pyruvate + 2 $NADH_2$ + 2 ATP + 2H^+ + 2H_2O

ATP consumed – 2 (step 1, 3)
ATP generated – 4 (step 7, 10)
Net gain of ATP = 2 ATP
1 $NADH_2$ = 3 ATP
2 $NADH_2$ = 6 ATP

Total ATP = 2 + 6 = 8 ATP

NEET SYNAPSE
Aerobic : Anaerobic ATP ratio = 18:1

ANAEROBIC RESPIRATION

Alcoholic fermentation

- Occurs in yeast (Saccharomyces) – releases enzyme zymase.
- Glucose ⟶ pyruvic acid ⟶ acetaldehyde $\xrightarrow{\text{Alcohol dehydrogenase}}$ ethyl alcohol (NADH → NAD^+)

Lactic acid fermentation

- It is seen in Lactic Acid Bacteria (LAB)
- Also present in muscles of our body.

Pyruvate + $NADH_2$ $\xrightarrow[\text{dehydrogenase}]{\text{Lactate}}$ Lactic acid + NAD^+

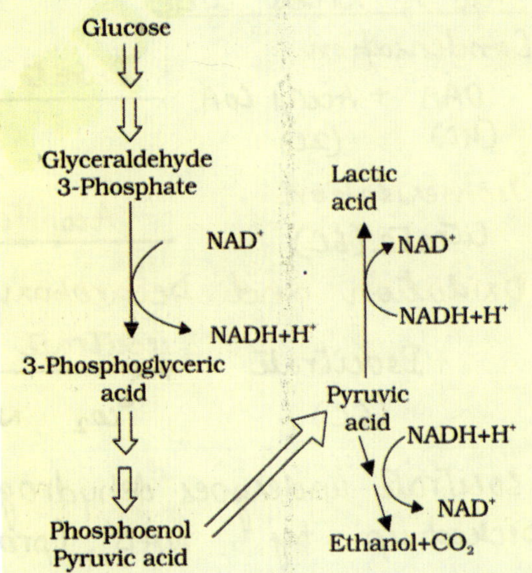

Applications of fermentation

- Production of antibiotics, dairy products, alcohol, vitamins etc
- In humans, lactic acid is formed in muscles during intense exercise due to anaerobic oxidation of glucose.

AEROBIC RESPIRATION

- Respiratory substrates completely broken down into CO_2 & H_2O, releasing energy (ATP)
- Steps of aerobic respiration
  - Oxidative Decarboxylation
  - Kreb's cycle.

NEET SYNAPSE

Oxidative decarboxylation is considered as link reaction between glycolysis and Kreb's cycle.

Oxidative Decarboxylation

- Pyruvic acid moves into mitochondrial matrix.
- decarboxylation - removal of CO_2
- oxidation - removal of H (dehydrogenation)

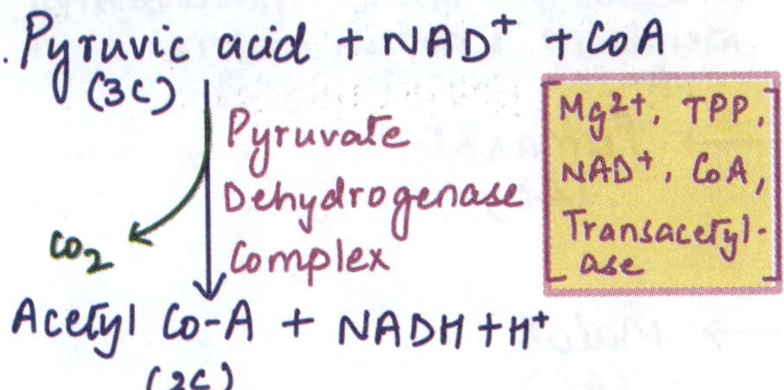

NEET SYNAPSE

Kreb's cycle is an amphibolic pathway - catabolic + anabolic.

Catabolic reaction - breaksdown Acetyl CoA into CO_2 & H_2O

Anabolic reaction - intermediate products act as building blocks for other molecules.

Krebs cycle

- Citric acid cycle - first stable product is citric acid.
- Tricarboxylic acid cycle - citric acid contains 3 carboxylic acid groups.
- Kreb's cycle - discovered by Hans Krebs.

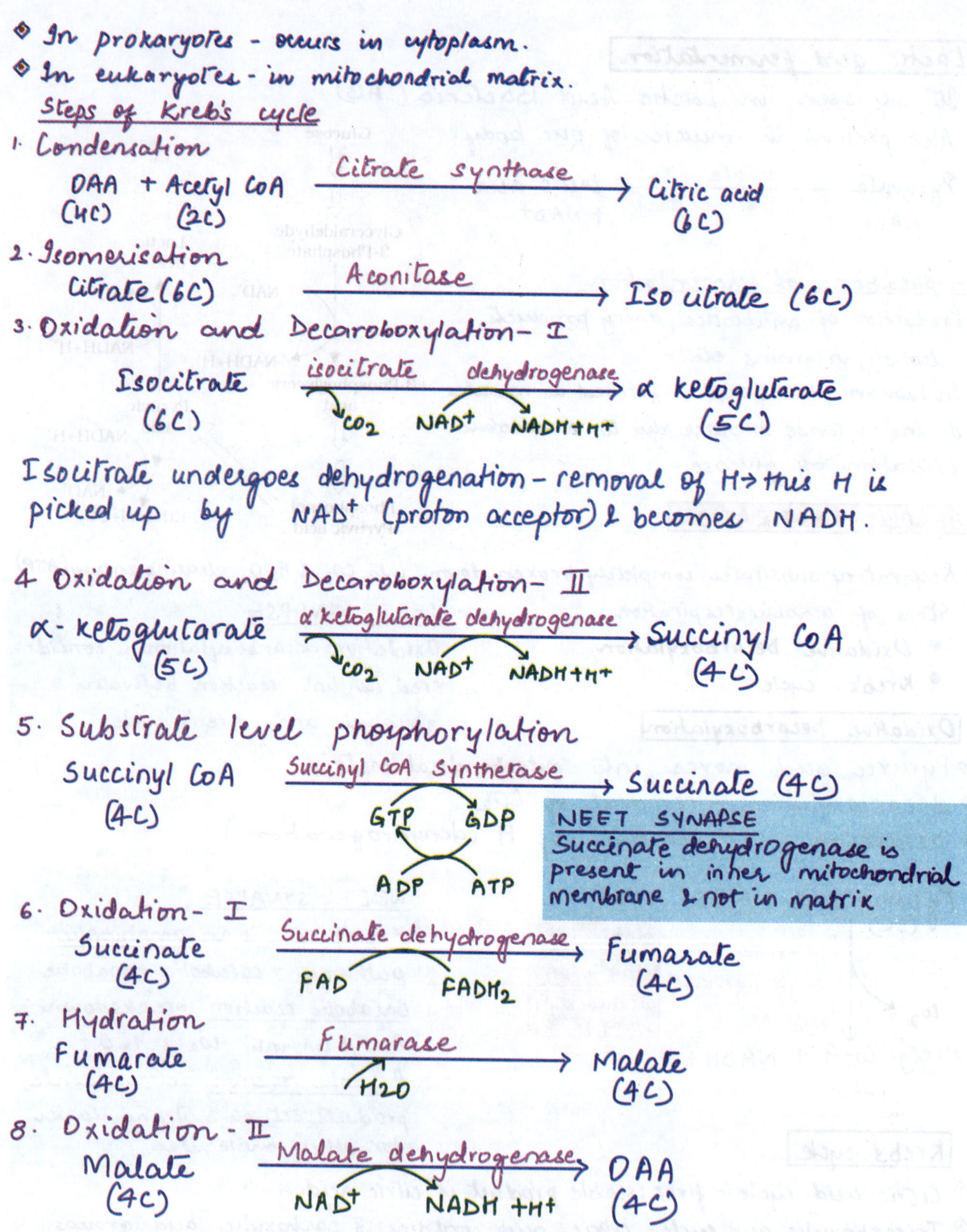

- In prokaryotes - occurs in cytoplasm.
- In eukaryotes - in mitochondrial matrix.

Steps of Kreb's cycle

1. Condensation

OAA (4C) + Acetyl CoA (2C) —Citrate synthase→ Citric acid (6C)

2. Isomerisation

Citrate (6C) —Aconitase→ Iso citrate (6C)

3. Oxidation and Decarboxylation- I

Isocitrate (6C) —isocitrate dehydrogenase→ α ketoglutarate (5C)

CO_2; NAD^+ → $NADH + H^+$

Isocitrate undergoes dehydrogenation - removal of H → this H is picked up by NAD^+ (proton acceptor) & becomes NADH.

4. Oxidation and Decarboxylation- II

α- ketoglutarate (5C) —α ketoglutarate dehydrogenase→ Succinyl CoA (4C)

CO_2; NAD^+ → $NADH + H^+$

5. Substrate level phosphorylation

Succinyl CoA (4C) —Succinyl CoA Synthetase→ Succinate (4C)

GTP → GDP; ADP → ATP

NEET SYNAPSE
Succinate dehydrogenase is present in inner mitochondrial membrane & not in matrix

6. Oxidation- I

Succinate (4C) —Succinate dehydrogenase→ Fumarate (4C)

FAD → $FADH_2$

7. Hydration

Fumarate (4C) —Fumarase→ Malate (4C)

H_2O

8. Oxidation - II

Malate (4C) —Malate dehydrogenase→ OAA (4C)

NAD^+ → $NADH + H^+$

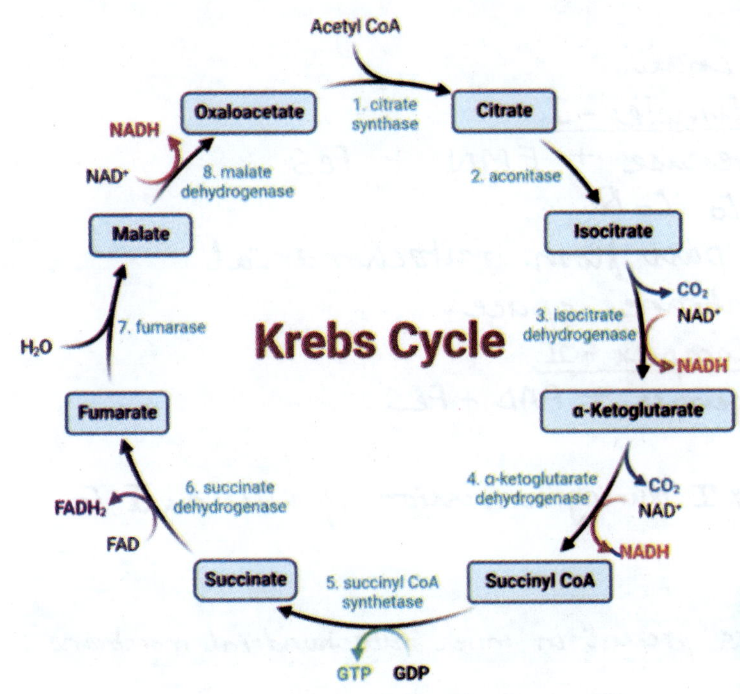

- **Summary**

  1 molecule of pyruvic acid undergoes - 3 decarboxylation, 5 oxidation

- **Net Result**

  Pyruvic acid + 4 NAD^+ + FAD^+ + 2H_2O + ADP + Pi ⟶ 3CO_2 + 4 NADH + H^+ + $FADH_2$ + ATP

- **Net gain of high energy compounds from 1 krebs cycle** - 3 NADH, 1 $FADH_2$, 1 GTP

NEET SYNAPSE

Glycolysis yields 2 molecules of pyruvic acid, thus for each molecule of glucose - 1 glycolysis, 2 link reactions and 2 kreb's cycles take place.

Photophosphorylation - ATP formation using light as energy source

Oxidative phosphorylation - ATP formation using NADH & $FADH_2$

ELECTRON TRANSPORT CHAIN

- Oxidation of NADH+H^+ & $FADH_2$ (high energy compounds) to release energy in the form of ATP.
- Involves 4 protein complexes - transfer H^+ & e^-
- Occurs in inner mitochondrial membrane.
- Electron carriers of ETS - NAD, FMN, FAD, Co Q, Cyt b, c_2, c, a & a_3
- H^+ & e^- are finally accepted by oxygen & water is formed.
- Formation of ATP takes place due to proton gradient.
- Functioning of complexes -
  - Complex I & II are alternate with each other.
  - At a given time either I, III, IV or II, III, IV work.
  - NADH + H^+ enters the chain through complex I
  - $FADH_2$ enters the chain through complex II

Complexes in respiratory chain

(i) NADH dehydrogenase / Complex - I

- Consists of NADH dehydrogenase + FMN + FeS
- Transfers e- from NADH to CoQ.
- During the transfer, 4 H^+ pass from mitochondrial matrix to the intermembrane space.

(ii) Succinate dehydrogenase / Complex - II

- Consists of succinate dehydrogenase + FAD + FeS
- Accepts e- from succinate.
- 2 e^- are accepted by Complex II during conversion of succinate to fumerate.

NEET SYNAPSE

CoQ & Cyt c are mobile carriers present in inner mitochondrial membrane

(iii) Cytochrome bc_1 complex / Complex III

- Consists of cyt b, cyt c_1, FeS and Haem prosthetic group.
- Also called cyt c reductase (reduces cyt c - adds e-)
- Transfers e- from $CoQH_2$ to cyt c.
- During transfer, it transports 4 H^+ into the intermembrane space.

(iv) Cytochrome c oxidase / Complex IV

- Consists of cyt a, a_3, haem and 2 Cu ions.
- Oxidises cyt c, takes its e^- and transfers them to O_2.
- Oxygen is the final e- acceptor. (aerobic oxidation)
- During transfer, it transports 2 H^+ into the intermembrane space.

(v) ATP synthase / F_0-F_1 complex / Complex V

- F_1 - ATPase - site for ATP synthesis.
- F_0 - forms a channel for passage of H^+ from intermembrane space to matrix.

Oxidative Phosphorylation

- 1 ATP molecule is synthesised when 4 protons cross the mitochondrial membrane.

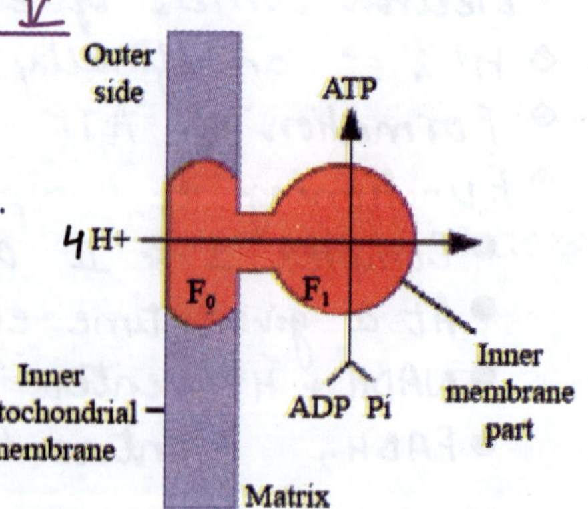

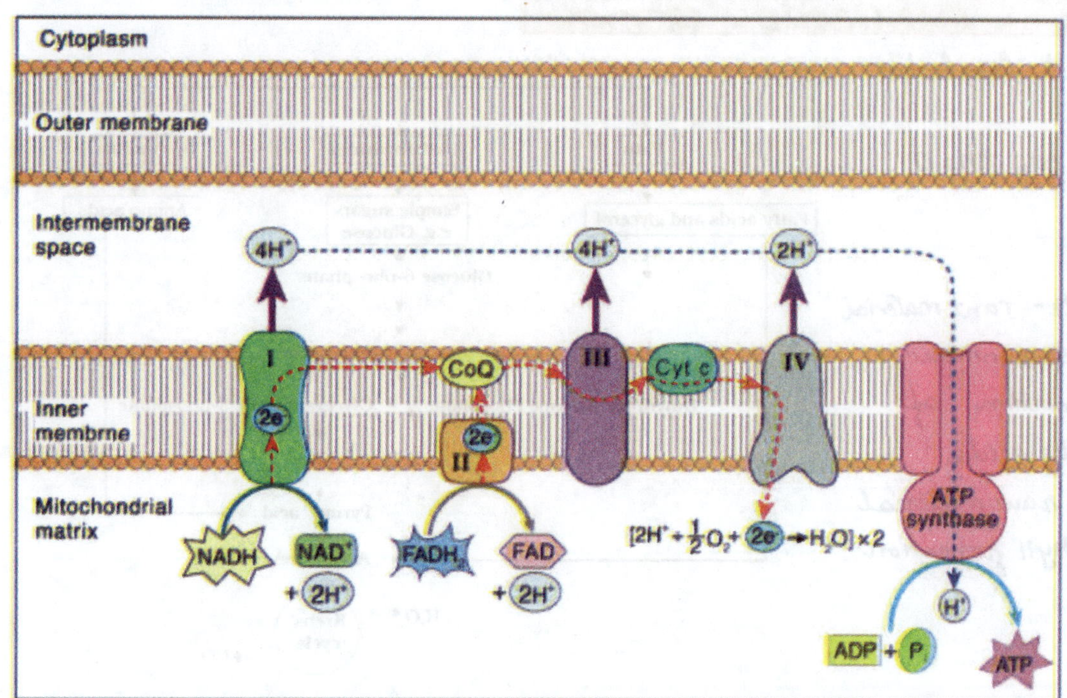

NEET SYNAPSE

$C_6H_{12}O_6$ ↓ Aerobic oxidation

CO_2 - released during Kreb's cycle
+
H_2O - formed in ETS
+
ATP - Glycolysis + Kreb's + ETS

Entry of NADH in ETS	Entry of $FADH_2$ in ETS
↓	↓
Protons transferred - 8	Protons transferred - 6
↓	↓
ATP synthesised = 2·5 ~ 3	ATP synthesised - 1·5 ~ 2

RESPIRATORY BALANCE SHEET - per 1 glucose molecule.

Glycolysis - 1 - Net gain - 2 ATP
$2NADH_2$ - 6 ATP

Link reaction - 2 - 2 NADH = 6 ATP

Kreb's cycle 2 - 6 NADH = 18 ATP
- 2 $FADH_2$ = 4 ATP
Substrate level = 2 ATP

38 ATP

RESPIRATION - AMPHIBOLIC PATHWAY

- Catabolic + Anabolic
- Catabolism -
  $C_6H_{12}O_6 \longrightarrow CO_2 + H_2O$
- Anabolism -
  α- ketoglutarate- raw material for amino acid synthesis.
  Acety CoA - formation of fatty acids.
  Succinyl CoA - raw material for chlorophyll formation.

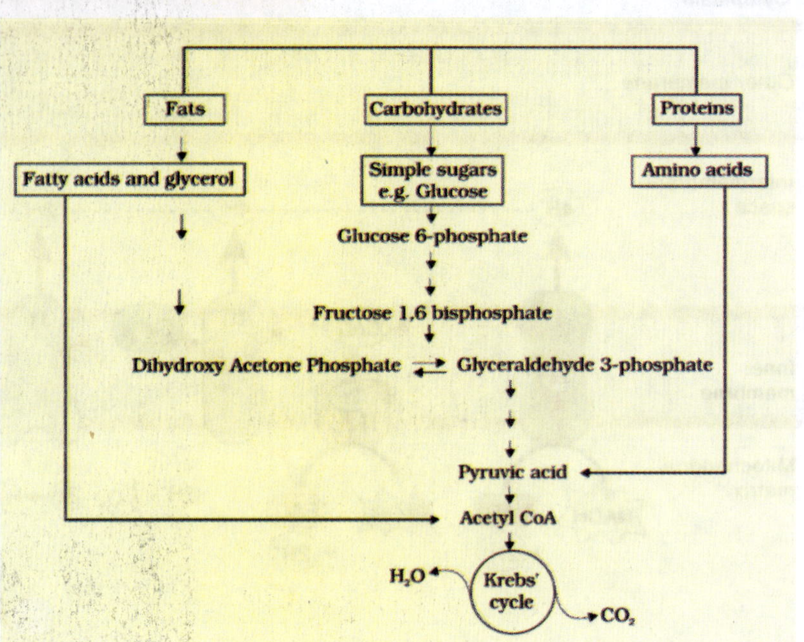

RESPIRATORY QUOTIENT

$$RQ = \frac{\text{Volume of } CO_2 \text{ evolved}}{\text{Volume of } O_2 \text{ absorbed}}$$

RQ for carbohydrates = 1 (O_2 absorbed = CO_2 evolved)

RQ for proteins = 0.9 (O_2 absorbed > CO_2 evolved)

RQ for fats = 0.7 (O_2 absorbed > CO_2 evolved)

RQ for organic acids = 1.33 (O_2 absorbed < CO_2 evolved)
(Malic acid, citric acid)

CAM plants (at night) = 0

Anaerobic oxidation = ∞

13. Plant Growth and Development

- Growth - increase in size, volume or weight
  - plant continues to increase in height & girth
  - leaves, flowers and fruits have limited growth.
  - fundamental and conspicuous characteristic
  - irreversible and permanent increase in size
  - involves anabolism & catabolism.
- Differentiation - acquiring specialised structure and function.
- Development = growth + differentiation.

PLANT GROWTH IS INDETERMINATE

- Plants grow throughout their life.
- ↳ due to presence of meristematic tissue.
  - ↳ open form of growth.

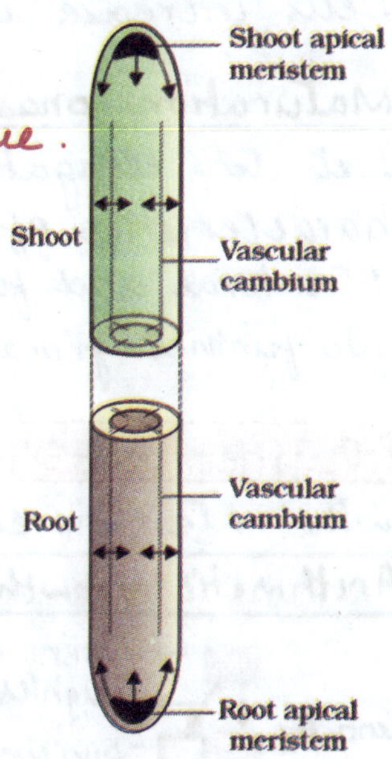

GROWTH IS MEASURABLE

- Attributes for measuring growth-
  - Increase in cellular dimensions
  - Increase in dry & fresh weight
  - Increase in volume of cells.
  - Increase in number of cells.

TYPES OF GROWTH

- Primary growth - formation of primary permanent tissues and organs.
  - Caused by apical & intercalary meristem.
  - contributes to increase in length of plant.
- Secondary growth - begins after primary growth
  - occurs by cambium
  - contributes to increase in girth of plant.
  - occurs mainly in dicots and gymnosperms.

PHASES OF GROWTH

1. Meristematic phase

- Growth occurs in meristematic regions – root & shoot apex.
- Characteristics of cells of meristematic phase –
  - small, dense protoplasm, large nucleus.
  - thin cellulosic, primary cell wall.
  - abundant plasmodesmata
  - rapid division with high respiratory rate.

2. Elongation phase

- Proximal to meristematic phase
- Characteristics of cells –
  - Highly vacuolated
  - Cell wall accumulates new material
  - Cells increase in length.

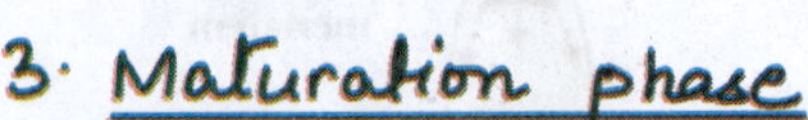

3. Maturation phase

- Next to elongation phase
- Characteristics of cells –
  - Structural and functional differentiation.
  - No further growth occurs after differentiation.

GROWTH RATES

Growth rate – increase in length or weight of plant per unit time.

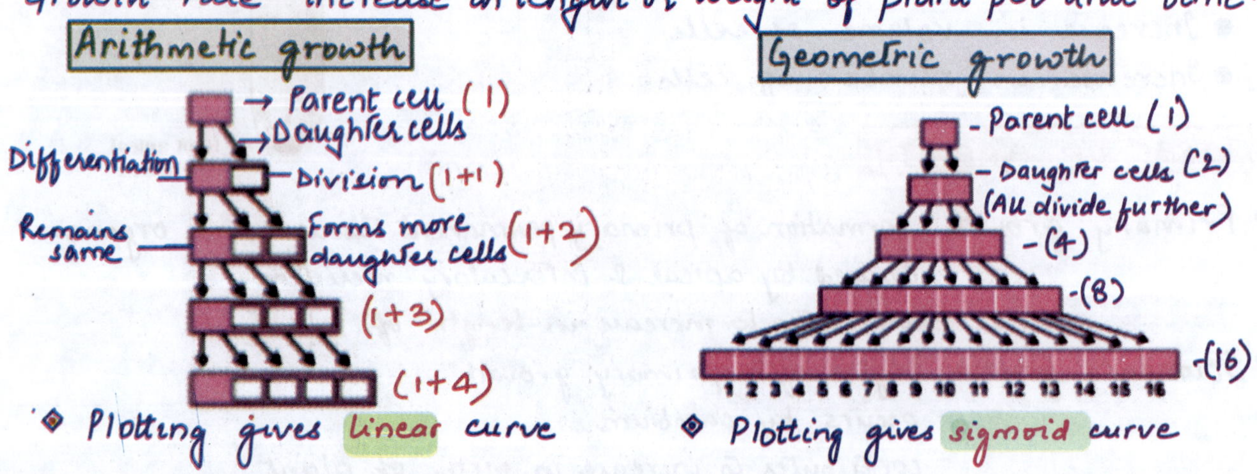

- Plotting gives linear curve
- Plotting gives sigmoid curve

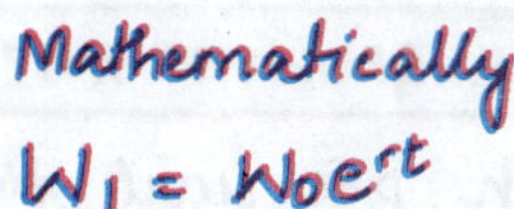

Mathematically

$L_t = L_0 + rt$

L_t - Length of plant after time 't'
L_0 - initial length (time = 0)
t - time taken for growth
r - Growth rate (growth per unit time)

Mathematically

$W_1 = W_0 e^{rt}$

W_1 - Final size
W_0 - Initial size
r - Growth rate
t - time
e - base of natural logarithm

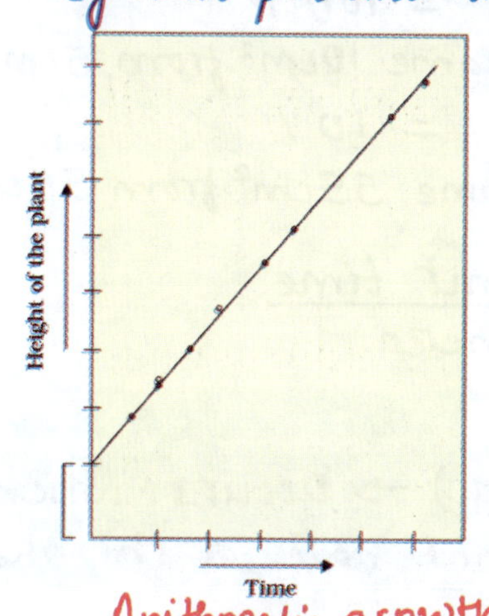

Arithmetic growth

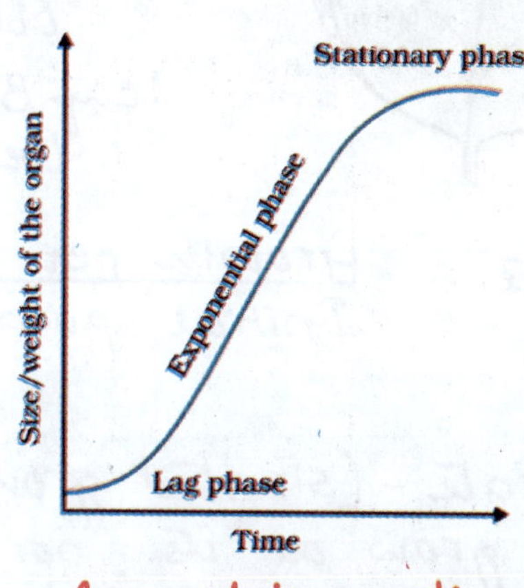

Geometric growth

Lag phase-
slow growth rate
represents beginning of growth
Log / Exponential phase
high growth rate
Stationary phase
Growth is slow & constant
Occurs due to shortage of food & space.

NEET SYNAPSE

Arithmetic growth
- Occurs during root & shoot elongation

Geometric growth
- typical for all cells, tissues & organs of a plant.

GROWTH RATE IN EMBRYO

Zygote divided
Geometric phase: all cells divide
= Cells capable of division
= Cells that lose capacity to divide
Arithmetic phase:
These cells divide
cells do not divide

Initially-
Geometric growth

Later
Arithmetic growth.

QUANTITATIVE COMPARISONS OF GROWTH RATE

ABSOLUTE GROWTH RATE

- Measurment of total growth per unit time.
- Graph for absolute growth rate is bell shaped.

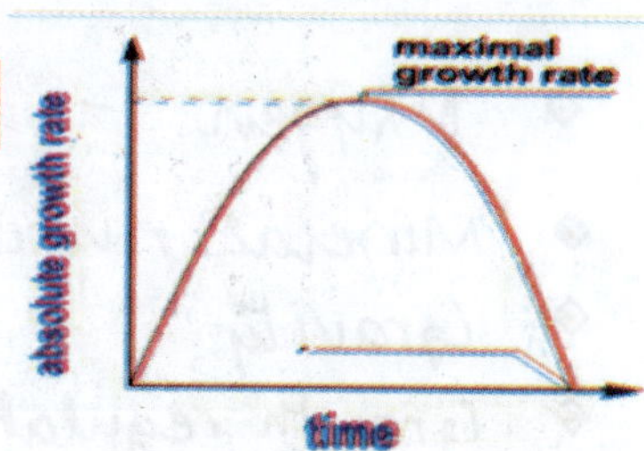

RELATIVE GROWTH RATE

- Growth per unit time per initial parameter.

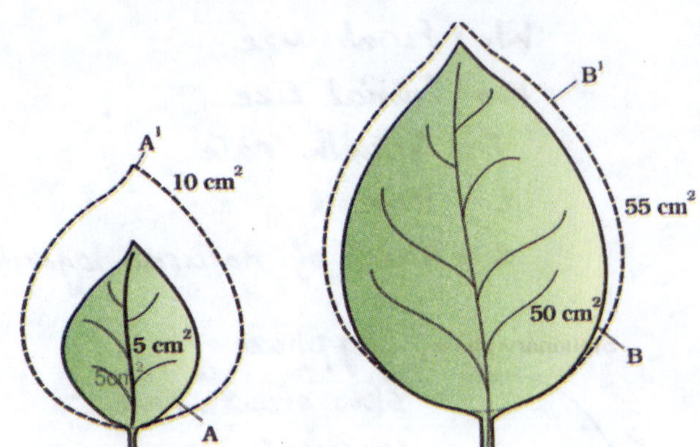

Absolute growth in both leaves is equal = 5 cm^2 in 7 days

Relative growth in both leaves
Leaf A = 100%
(became 10 cm^2 from 5 cm^2)
Leaf B = 10%
(became 55 cm^2 from 50 cm^2)

$$\text{Relative growth rate} = \frac{\text{Growth per unit time}}{\text{Initial parameter}}$$

NEET SYNAPSE

Negative growth rate - (stunted growth) → occurs when plant does not grow at its normal rate or shrinks.

CONDITIONS FOR GROWTH

- Light - required for tissue differentiation, photosynthesis, determination of direction of root & shoot growth
- Temperature - Optimum temperature - 20-35°C
  Higher temp. disrupt enzyme function, thus hampering growth.
- Water - Maintains turgidity; essential for growth - cell elongation.
- Oxygen - Required for aerobic respiration
- Mineral nutrients - Raw materials for cell protoplasm
- Gravity - Determines direction of growth.
- Growth regulators - Phytohormones - manufactured by cell.

DIFFERENTIATION, DEDIFFERENTIATION AND REDIFFERENTIATION

DIFFERENTIATION

- Act of obtaining maturity & specific function by a cell/tissue.
- Changes in structure & function take place.
- For example differentiation of tracheary elements involves
  - loss of protoplasm
  - Development of strong, elastic lignocellulosic secondary cell wall.
- Formation of guard cells involve differential wall thickenings
- Formation of root cap involves mucilage secretion.

DEDIFFERENTIATION

- Occurs when differentiated cells regain their dividing capacity.
- Ex- interfascicular cambium & cork cambium.
  They are formed from fully differentiated cells.

REDIFFERENTIATION

- Process where dedifferentiated cells again lose their dividing ability.
  Cells become specialised (permanent)
  Ex- secondary phloem & secondary xylem.
  They are formed from interfascicular cambium & cork cambium.

NEET SYNAPSE

Plant tissue culture involves redifferentiation of parenchyma cells under controlled laboratory conditions.

DEVELOPMENT

- Includes all events from formation to senescence.
- Starts from seed germination

1. Seed germination occurs due to imbibition of water which causes seed to swell & bursting of seed coat.
2. In epigeal germination - Hypocotyl elongates pushing the cotyledons above the ground.
   In hypogeal germination - Epicotyl elongates & seeds germinate under the ground.

NEET SYNAPSE
Seed viability – capacity of a seed to germinate
Seed vigour – ability of seed to establish in the soil.

PLASTICITY

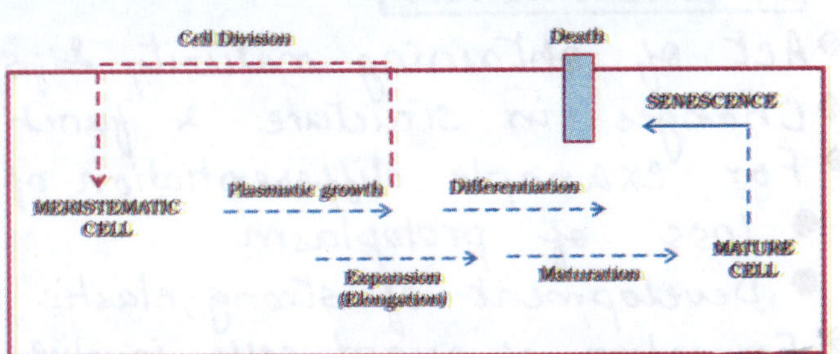

Figure 13.8 Sequence of the developmental process in a plant cell

Ability of a plant to modify its structures according to changes in the environment.

Ex. Heterophylly – presence of different types of leaves on the same plant.

Larkspur – juvenile leaves are broadly lobed; in adult plant leaves become pinnately divided in the region of flowers.

Buttercup – submerged leaves are dissected, emerged leaves are broad & lobed.

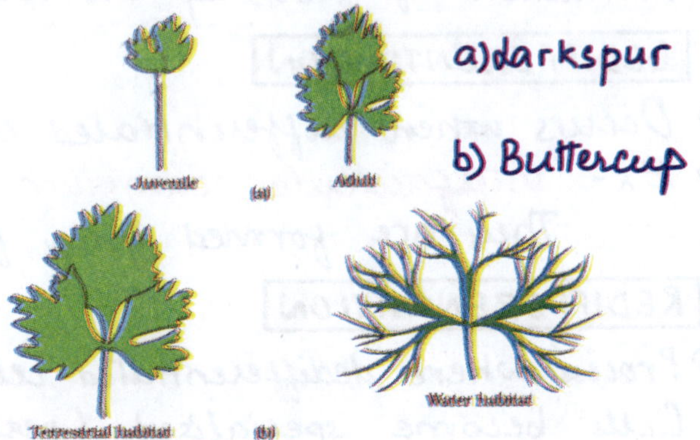

PLANT GROWTH REGULATORS – PGR's

- Responsible for physiological response of plant.
- Secreted in minute quantities
- Also called phytohormones / plant hormones.
- They can be –
  Growth promoters – Auxin, gibberellin, cytokinin
  Growth inhibitors – Abscisic acid, ethylene.

Ethylene also has growth promoting effects but to a lesser extent.

AUXIN

- Indole derivatives
- First PGR to be discovered.
- Produced by growing regions of plant – root & shoot apices.
- Derived from tryptophan.
- Exhibit polar transport.

Types of Auxin

Natural - Indole 3 Acetic Acid (IAA), Indole 3 Butyric Acid (IBA)
Synthetic - 2,4 Dichlorophenoxy acetic acid (2,4-D)
Naphthaline acetic acid (NAA)

Discovery of Auxin

- Charles Darwin & Francis Darwin observed that coleoptiles of canary grass were growing towards source of light (unilaterally)
- Darwin concluded the following-
  - Tip of coleoptile senses unilateral light stimulus.
  - Curvature occurs below the tip, ∵ rapid growth occurs here.
  - Tip of coleoptile was influencing the bending below it.
- F W Went isolated auxin from tip of coleoptiles of oat seedlings.

Functions

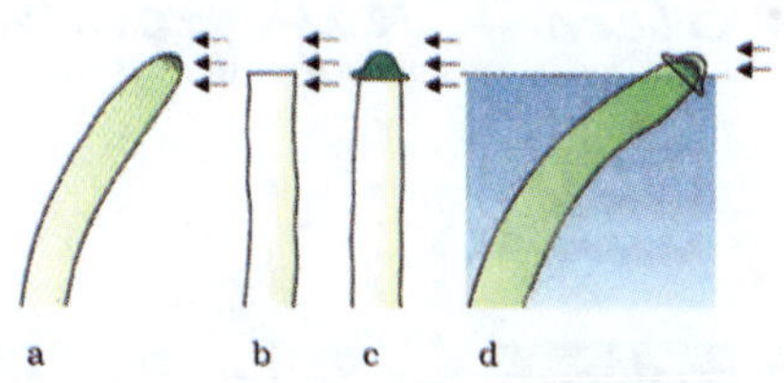

Experiment used to demonstrate that tip of the coleoptile is the source of auxin. Arrows indicate direction of light

- Cell elongation - loosens cell wall
  ↑ respiration
  solubilises carbohydrate reserve
- Cell division - in vascular cambium
- Apical dominance - presence of apical bud inhibits the growth of lateral buds.
- Xylem differentiation-
- Abscission - promotes falling of mature leaves & fruits.
  prevents falling of young leaves & fruits.
- Parthenocarpy - promotes development of seedless fruits.
  Eg- Tomato
- Flowering - induce flowering in pineapple
- Rooting - induces rooting in stem cuttings. (IBA, NAA)
- Herbicide - kills dicot weeds. (2,4-D)
- Nodule formation in legumes

NEET SYNAPSE

Decapitation - removal of shoot apex → results in growth of lateral buds.
- widely used in tea plantations & for hedge making.

GIBBERELLINS

- All gibberellins are terpenes
- They are weak acids called gibberellic acid.
- Synthesised in apices of young leaves, embryo, buds & roots.
- Transport in plant through xylem.

Discovery of Gibberellins

- Discovered in Japan from *Gibberella fujikuroi* (fungus)
- Fungus causes Bakanae disease (foolish seedling disease of rice)
- E Kurosawa - found active substance in fungal extract.
- GA_3 is the first discovered gibberellin.

Functions

- Stem & leaf growth - stimulate stem elongation in sugarcane, thereby increasing yield significantly.
  - stimulate axis elongation in grapes, thereby letting bunches become larger.
- Bolting - In rosette plants eg. cabbage - leaves are prominent while internodes are stunted.
  - Gibberelins cause internode elongation just before reproduction → increasing height.
- Delay senescence - delay ageing & ripening of fruits, extend shelf life & storage period.
- Seed germination - promote seed germination; break seed dormancy.
- Parthenocarpy - stimulate the formation of seedless fruits.
- Fruit growth - enlarges apples & bunches of grapes.
- Malting - enhances starch digestion ↑ malt production.
- Rapid maturity - cause quicker growth, used for commercially important plants.

NEET SYNAPSE
Gibberellins are used for increasing size, volume, surface area of fruits & vegetables

CYTOKININ

- Purine derivatives, basic in nature.
- Primary function - cell division
- Synthesised mainly in roots → travels upwards from roots.
- Also synthesised in seeds & developing fruits.
- Abundantly found in coconut milk and apple.

Discovery of cytokinins

- Skoog observed that callus proliferated only when something was added in addition to auxin
- Later cytokinins were discovered by Miller
- Miller added herring fish sperm DNA to tobacco pith culture
- Pith callus grew for longer duration.
- Miller isolated active substance & named it kinetin.
- Kinetin does not naturally occur in plants.
- First natural cytokinin was isolated in corn kernels & was called zeatin.

Functions of cytokinins

- Promotes cell division & organ formation - found in root apices, developing shoot buds & young fruits.
- Overcomes apical dominance - promote lateral bud development.
- Development of chloroplast - increase the rate of chlorophyll and grana formation.
- Flowering - They induce flowering in Wolffia.
- Promote breakage of seed dormancy.
- Delay senescence - delay ageing process of leaves & other organs.
- Morphogenesis - induce organ formation & cell division
  - used in tissue culture practices.
- Increase shelf life - keeps fruits and vegetables fresh for longer durations.
- Provide resistance to pathogens & extreme temperature.

NEET SYNAPSE

Auxin : Cytokinin ratio determines organ formation in tissue culture.
High Auxin/Cytokinin - favours root development
High Cytokinin/Auxin - favours shoot development.
Equal cytokinin/Auxin - forms undifferentiated mass of cells.

ETHYLENE

- Gaseous hormone
- Formed from methionine.
- Maximum synthesis occurs
  - during ripening of fruits
  - in tissues undergoing senescence.
- Commercial product of ethylene - Ethephon (liquid form)
  - → releases ethylene gas.
  - → helps in artificial ripening

Discovery of Ethylene

- HH Cousins observed ripening of unripe bananas when kept near ripe oranges, the gas was later identified as ethylene.

Functions of Ethylene

- **Root initiation** - promotes root growth in low concentration.
- Epinasty - drooping of leaves and flowers.
- **Horizontal growth** - promotes horizontal growth of seedlings.
  - inhibits vertical growth
  - induces growth of internodes & leaf bases.
- Flowering - usually inhibits flowering
  - but induces flowering in pineapple.
- **Fruit ripening** - stimulates ripening of tomatoes, oranges etc.
  - ↑ rate of respiration - respiratory climacteric.
  - causes dehiscence of dry fruits.
- **Abscission & senescence** - enhances abscission & senescence of leaves, fruits & flowers.
- Breaking dormancy - of different plant organs
  - but not of lateral buds.
- Storage organs - sprouting of storage organs like tubers, rhizomes etc. is enhanced by ethylene.

NEET SYNAPSE

Since ethylene has inhibitory as well as promotery effects, it is considered in both categories of PGR's. However, it has mainly inhibitory effects.

ABSCISIC ACID

- Also called stress hormone or dormin.
- Produced when plant is under stress.- lack of water, saline soil, frost.
  Derived from terpenes.
  In leaves, it is produced by chloroplast.

Discovery of Abscisic acid

- First growth inhibitor identified in dormant potato tuber - inhibitor B.
- Other researcher obtained from cotton fruits - abscission-II
- Another researcher isolated it from Betula leaves - dormin.
- Later established- all above were same - abscisic acid (ABA)

Functions of ABA

- Induces stomatal closure
- Induces bud dormancy
- Causes abscission of leaves, flowers & fruits.
- Induces geotropism in roots
- Causes carotenoid synthesis - applied to green oranges to turn them yellow.
- Regulates fruit drop
- Antagonist of all growth promoters -
  - Delays flowering
  - Delays cell division & elongation
  - Inhibits seed germination, development, maturation and dormancy.
  - Enhances senescence

14. Breathing and Exchange of Gases

- Cellular respiration - breakdown of respiratory substrates in the presence of O_2 to release energy along with CO_2.
- Breathing/Respiration - exchange of O_2 from atmosphere with CO_2 produced by cells

RESPIRATORY ORGANS

- Sponges (eg Sycon) - Plasma membrane
- Cnidarians (eg Hydra) - General body surface
- Platyhelminthes
  - Free living - General body surface
  - Parasitic - Anaerobic respiration
- Aschelminthes
  - Free living - General body surface
  - Parasitic - Anaerobic respiration
- Annelids (eg. Earthworm) - Skin (Cutaneous respiration)
- Arthropods
  - Crustaceans - Prawn/crayfish - Gills (Branchial respiration)
  - Insecta - Insects - Trachae
  - Arachnids - Scorpions, spiders - Book lungs
  - King crab - Book gills
- Molluscs (eg. snail) - Gills & pulmonary sac
- Echinoderms (eg. Starfish) - Tubefeet
- Hemichordates (eg. Balanoglossus) - Pharyngeal wall
- Chordates
  - Protochordates - Pharyngeal wall
  - Cyclostomes, fishes - Gills
  - Amphibians - Gills (in larva)
    - buccopharyngeal membrane
    - Lungs (Pulmonary respiration)
  - Reptiles, birds, mammals - lungs

HUMAN RESPIRATORY SYSTEM

CONDUCTING PART

External nostrils – Openings of nose

Nasal cavity
- Nasal passage – contains mucous lining & hair
  - prevents entry of dust particles
- Nasal chamber – present behind nasal passage

Pharynx
- Nasal chamber opens here
- common passage for food & air
- divided into nasopharynx, oropharynx & laryngopharynx.

Larynx
- commonly called voice box
- made up of 9 cartilages (3 paired, 3 unpaired)
- present at the level of 3rd – 6th cervical vertebrae.
- enlarges in boys during puberty – Adam's apple.
- first part of larynx – glottis
- Glottis covered by epiglottis (prevents entry of food during swallowing) ↳ made of elastic cartilage.

NEET SYNAPSE
Voice box of birds is called Syrinx

Trachea (windpipe)
- contains C-shaped rings (made of hyaline cartilage)
- length – about 10 cm
- divides at the level of 5th thoracic vertebrae
- branches are called bronchi (sing. bronchus)

Bronchi & bronchioles
- Trachea divides into right & left primary bronchi
- Each primary bronchus enters respective lung.
- Primary bronchi divides into secondary bronchi
- Secondary bronchi divide into tertiary bronchi
- Tertiary bronchi further divide into terminal & respiratory bronchioles.

1°
2°
3°
bronchioles
respiratory bronchioles

EXCHANGE

Alveoli
- Respiratory bronchioles divide to form alveolar ducts.
- Alveolar ducts open into alveolar sacs
- Alveolar sacs contain alveoli.

Alveoli – sites of gaseous exchange
- human lungs – approx. 300 million alveoli
- highly vascular, filled with air.
- Alveolar wall made of squamous epithelium.

Important points

Trachea, bronchi & initial bronchioles - supported by incomplete cartilaginous rings.

Epithelium of trachea - ciliated pseudostratified columnar

LUNGS

- Present in thoracic cavity.
- Paired - right lung shorter than the left (accomodates liver)
- Mediastinum - partition between lungs; lodges heart.
- Pleura - double layered covering of lungs.
  - Outer layer - Parietal pleura
  - Inner layer - Visceral pleura
  - Outer & inner layer separated by pleural cavity.
  - Pleural cavity - filled with pleural fluid.
  - Pleural fluid - provides lubrication
    - prevents friction during breathing.
- Right lung - has 3 lobes - superior lobe → separated by horizontal fissure
  - middle lobe } → separated by oblique fissure.
  - inferior lobe }
- Left lung - has 2 lobes - superior lobe → separated by oblique fissure.
  - inferior lobe
- Thoracic chamber is anatomically air tight chamber.
  - Boundaries -
  - Dorsal - vertebral column
  - Ventral - sternum (breast bone)
  - Lateral - ribs
  - Inferior - diaphragm.
- Diaphragm - dome shaped
  - muscular
  - separates thoracic cavity from abdominal cavity.

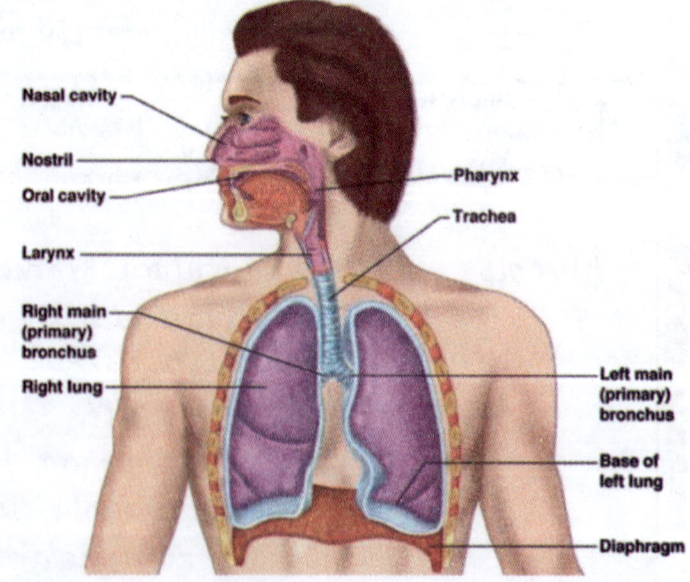

Steps involved in respiration

1. Pulmonary ventilation - drawing in O_2, expelling CO_2
2. Diffusion of gases - diffusion of O_2 & CO_2 across alveolar wall.
3. Transport of gases - occurs through blood.
4. Diffusion of gases between blood & tissues.
5. Utilisation of O_2 by cells (cellular respiration) and releasing CO_2.

MECHANISM OF BREATHING

INSPIRATION | INHALATION

- Active process (requires energy)
- Muscles involved - PEI
  Phrenic (diaphragm) External intercostals
- <u>Mechanism</u>
- Atmospheric pressure - 760 mm Hg
- { Diaphragm contracts → becomes flat
  { External intercostals contract → move upward & outwards
  ↳ Leads to increase in thoracic volume
  Thereby increasing pulmonary volume.

Volume $\propto \frac{1}{\text{Pressure}}$

- ∴ Intra pulmonary pressure decreases (756 mm Hg)
- When intra pulmonary pressure reduces to a lower value than atmospheric pressure ⟶ air moves from atmosphere (high pressure) into the lungs (low pressure)

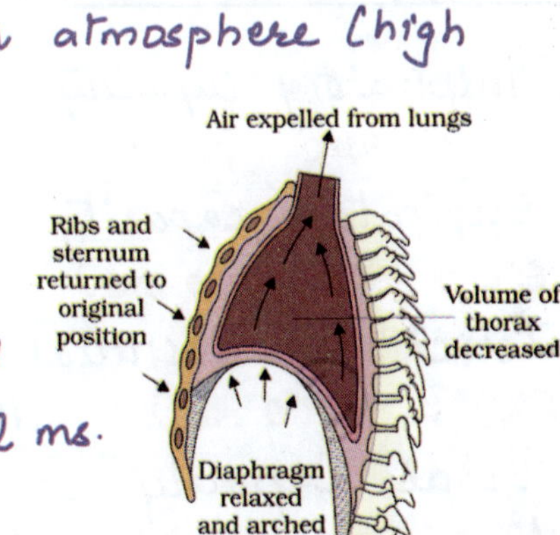

EXPIRATION / EXHALATION

- Passive process (does not require energy)
- Muscles involved [normal expiration - none actively
  [forceful expiration -
  diaphragm, internal intercostals, abdominal ms.
- <u>Mechanism</u>
- Diaphragm & <u>external intercostals</u> relax
  ↳ becomes dome shaped ↳ bring thoracic cavity downwards & inwards.
- Intra pulmonary volume reduces ; pressure increases.
- When intra pulmonary pressure > atmospheric pressure, air moves out of lungs (high ⟶ low pressure)

<u>NEET SYNAPSE</u> - contraction of abdominal ms. & internal intercostals leads to further reduction in pulmonary volume ; causing forceful expiration

LUNG VOLUMES AND CAPACITIES

LUNG VOLUMES

1. Tidal volume (500 ml) - amount of air inhaled or exhaled in normal respiration.

NEET SYNAPSE - 70% of tidal volume participates in gaseous exchange. 30% remains in conducting part

2. Inspiratory Reserve Volume (IRV) (2500 - 3000 ml) - extra volume of air inhaled during maximal inspiration.
3. Expiratory Reserve Volume (ERV) (1000 - 1100 ml) - maximum volume of air that can be exhaled during forceful expiration.
4. Residual Volume (1100 - 1200 ml) - volume of air remaining in lungs after forced expiration.

Anatomical dead space - portion that is inaccessible for gaseous exchange.

Physiological dead space - present in gas exchange zone, but no exchange takes place eg- alveolar duct, respiratory bronchiole

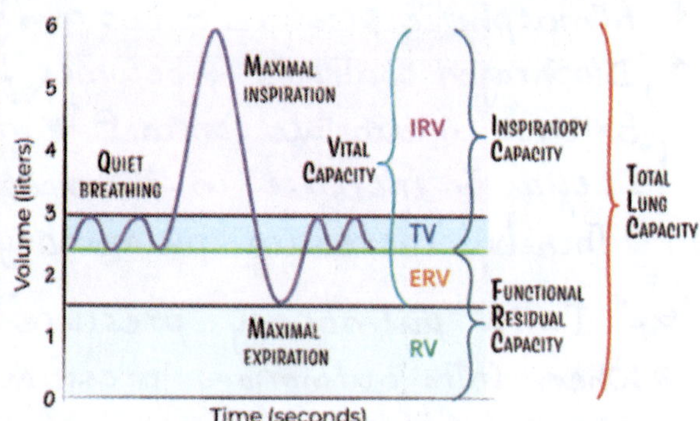

LUNG CAPACITIES

1. Inspiratory capacity (IC = 3000 - 3500 ml) - volume of air that can be inspired after normal expiration (TV + IRV)
2. Expiratory capacity (EC = 1500 - 1600 ml) - volume of air that can be exhaled after normal inspiration. (TV + ERV)
3. Functional Residual Capacity (FRC = 2500 ml) - volume of air that remains in lungs after normal expiration (ERV + RV)
4. Vital Capacity (VC = 3500 - 4000 ml) - maximum volume of air a person can breathe in after normal expiration (ERV + TV + IRV)
5. Total Lung Capacity (TLC = 5800 - 6000 ml) - total volume of air contained in lungs at the end of forceful inspiration (ERV + TV + IRV + RV) or (VC + RV)

NEET SYNAPSE

Lung volumes and capacities can be measured by spirometer. However, residual volume. RV, FRC & TLC cannot be measured.

EXCHANGE OF GASES

- Primary site- alveoli – O_2 taken in ; CO_2 given out
- Secondary site- tissues – O_2 taken from blood to tissues, CO_2 given from tissues to blood.
- Factors affecting diffusion of gases
  - Diameter of respiratory membrane – Thinner membrane, faster diffusion.
  - Partial pressure of gas - Movement of gas from high to low pressure.
  - Solubility of gases – Higher solubility, better diffusion
    CO_2 is 20-25 times more soluble than O_2.

Gaseous exchange at alveoli

- Alveolar diffusion membrane is less than 1 mm thick.
- It consists of
  - Alveolar epithelium (squamous epithelium)
  - Epithelial basement membrane
  - Thin interstitial space
  - Capillary basement membrane
  - Capillary endothelial membrane

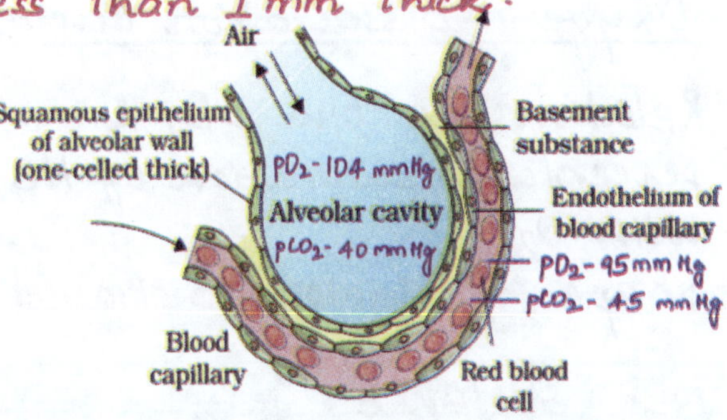

Figure 14.4 A Diagram of a section of an alveolus with a pulmonary capillary.

Exchange of O_2

- pO_2 in alveolar air - 104 mm Hg
- pO_2 in blood capillaries - 95 mm Hg
- Rapid diffusion of O_2 occurs from alveoli to capillaries.

Exchange of CO_2

- pCO_2 in blood capillaries - 45 mm Hg
- pCO_2 in alveolar air - 40 mm Hg
- Rapid diffusion of CO_2 occurs from capillaries to alveoli.

NEET SYNAPSE
Gaseous exchange occurs due to differential partial pressures.

Gaseous exchange at tissue level

Exchange of O_2

- pO_2 in respiring cell - 40 mm Hg
- pO_2 in blood capillaries - 95 mm Hg
- Rapid diffusion occurs from blood capillaries to respiring cell.

Exchange of CO_2

- pCO_2 in respiring cell - 45 mm Hg
- pCO_2 in blood capillaries - 40 mm Hg
- Rapid diffusion occurs from respiring cell to blood capillaries.

TRANSPORT OF GASES

TRANSPORT OF OXYGEN

1. **In dissolved form** – O_2 is sparingly soluble in plasma
   - about 3% is transported in this form.

2. **In combined form** – as oxyhaemoglobin (OxyHb)
   - Hb has 4 Fe^{2+} ions.
   - Each Fe^{2+} combines (reversibly) with 1 O_2 molecule.

   ∴ 1 Hb can bind with 4 O_2 molecules – forming oxy Hb.

Every 100 ml of blood can deliver 5 ml of O_2 to tissues under normal physiological conditions.

Oxygen Dissociation Curve

- Relationship b/w pO_2 & percentage saturation of Hb with O_2.
- Shape – sigmoid / S shaped.

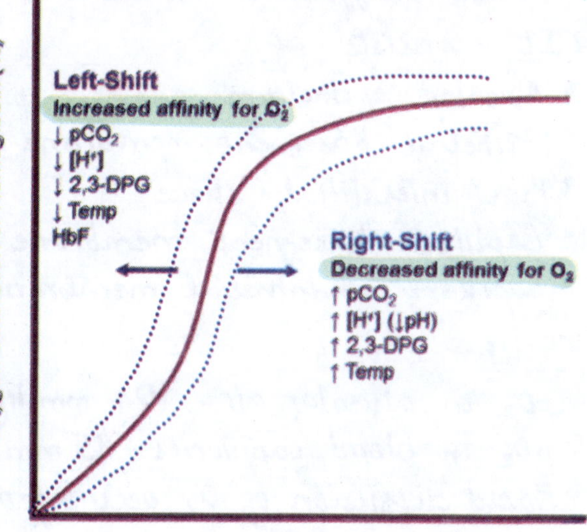

NEET SYNAPSE

- p50 – Oxygen tension at which Hb is 50% saturated with O_2.
- Higher p50 denotes decreased affinity of Hb for O_2.

TRANSPORT OF CARBON DIOXIDE

Dissolved state

- About 7% of CO_2 gets dissolved in plasma.

NEET SYNAPSE

Hb acts as buffer of blood as it binds H^+ ions & reduces acidity of blood

As Bicarbonates

- About 70%.
- In RBC –

$$CO_2 + H_2O \underset{}{\overset{CA}{\rightleftharpoons}} H_2CO_3 \rightleftharpoons H^+ + HCO_3^-$$

CA – Carbonic Anhydrase

H^+ (binds with Hb) ←

- CO_2 is released from HCO_3^- at alveoli.
- Alveoli – high pO_2, low pCO_2

As CarbaminoHb.

- 20 – 25% transported in association with Hb
- CO_2 combines with amino group of Hb.
- $Hb + CO_2 \underset{alveoli}{\overset{tissue}{\rightleftharpoons}} HbCO_2$
- Every 100 ml of deoxygenated blood delivers approx. 4 ml CO_2 to alveoli

Hamburger's effect / Chloride shift

HCO_3^- move out of RBC into plasma at alveoli (for releasing CO_2), this causes ionic imbalance. Thus to maintain balance Cl^- enter RBCs.

REGULATION OF BREATHING

NEURAL REGULATION

1. Respiratory Rhythm Centre - Located in medulla oblongata.
   - Regulates respiratory rhythm.
2. Pneumotaxic centre - Located in pons.
   - Regulates functioning of respiratory rhythm centre.
   - Reduces the duration of inspiration - alters respiratory rate.

CHEMICAL REGULATION

1. Chemosensitive area - situated near respiratory rhythm centre.
   - highly sensitive to change in pCO_2 & pH.
2. Chemoreceptors
   - present in medulla - mediate rapid breathing
   - present in carotid & aortic bodies - sensitive to CO_2 & H^+ concentration.

NEET SYNAPSE

Role of O_2 in regulating respiration is insignificant as no receptors for detecting pO_2 are present in carotid & aortic bodies.

RESPIRATORY DISORDERS

1. Asthma - allergic disorder; difficult expiration with wheezing, bronchial constriction due to smooth muscle spasm.
2. Emphysema - irreversible distension of alveolar walls.
   Occurs due to chronic smoking.
   alveoli always remain inflated, do not contract fully.
3. Occupational Lung Diseases - lead to inflammation & fibrosis.
   Silicosis - due to exposure to silicon dust
   Asbestosis - due to exposure to asbestos dust

15. Body Fluids and Circulation

BLOOD

- Main circulating fluid ; pH - 7.4 (slightly alkaline)
- Mesodermal in origin ; volume of blood in an adult - 5.5 L (approx.)

COMPOSITION OF BLOOD

Plasma — 55% ; 45% — Formed elements

55% ← Plasma
WBC + Platelets
45% ← RBC

PLASMA

- Straw / light yellow coloured fluid.
- Composition -
  - Water (92%)
  - Plasma proteins
    - Albumin - most abundant protein in body
      - maintains osmotic balance in body
    - Globulin - provides immunity (defence mechanism) forms immunoglobulins
    - Fibrinogen & Prothrombin - help in blood clotting
  - Inorganic contents - Na^+, Cl^-, K^+, Ca^{2+}, gases etc.

FORMED ELEMENTS

Erythrocytes (RBCs)

- 5 - 5.5 million / mm^3
- Red, contain Hb
- Circular & biconcave
- Mature RBC's - enucleated
- Formed in -
  - adult - bone marrow
  - foetus - liver
- Function - Transport O_2 & CO_2
- Hb - 12-16 gms/100ml
- Life span - 120 days
- Spleen - Graveyard of RBCs.

RBCs appear red due to Hb (Fe^{2+} containing protein)

Leucocytes (WBCs)

6000 - 8000 / mm^3

Granulocytes
- Eosinophils
  - Allergy, parasitic infection
- Basophils
  - secrete histamine, serotonin, heparin - inflammatory mediators
- Neutrophils
  - Phagocytosis

Agranulocytes
- Monocyte - Phagocytosis
- Lymphocytes - Phagocytosis, production of antibodies.

Thrombocytes

1.5 - 3 lakh / mm^3

- Platelets
- Colourless
- Non-nucleated
- Formed by fragmentation of megakaryocytes.
- Help in blood clotting.
- Life span - 7-10 days.
- Thrombus = clot

Blood

Plasma — Formed elements

Formed elements: RBCs, WBCs, Platelets

WBCs: Granulocytes, Agranulocytes

	Eosinophil	Basophil	Neutrophil	Monocyte	Lymphocyte (B, T)
	2-3%	0.5-1%	60-65%	2-10%	20-25%
Nucleus -	Bilobed	S-shaped	Multilobed	Bean shaped	

Important points

1. Neutrophils - also called PMNL (Poly Morpho Nuclear leucocytes)
   - they can have variously shaped nuclei.
2. Inflammatory mediators - Histamine - vasodilator
   - Serotonin - vasoconstrictor
   - Heparin - anticoagulant.
3. Monocyte - largest blood cell, nucleus eccentric.
4. TLC - Total leucocyte count

NEET SYNAPSE

All lymphocytes are leucocytes but all leucocytes are not lymphocytes.

BLOOD GROUPS

- Antigen - substances that have ability to generate immune response.
- Antibody - substances generated in body in response to antigen.

ABO Blood group

- Discovered by Karl Landsteiner
- Antigens are present on the surface of RBCs – Antigen A and antigen B
- Antibodies present in plasma - antibody A & antibody B.
- Types of blood groups present - A, B, AB & O -
- Blood groups are determined by gene I – alleles - I^A, I^B & I^O

Blood group	Antigen	Antibody	Can receive from	Can donate to
A (I^AI^A, I^AI^O)	A	anti-B	A, O	A, AB
B (I^BI^B, I^BI^O)	B	anti-A	B, O	B, AB
AB (I^AI^B)	A, B	—	A, B, AB, O	AB only
O (I^OI^O)	-	antiA, antiB	O only	A, B, AB, O

NEET SYNAPSE

If incorrect blood is transfused to a person, it causes agglutination (clumping) of RBCs which leads to haemolysis which can lead to death.

Eg. Antigen A + antibody A (present in person with blood group B ⟶ Clumping of RBCs

Rhesus Blood Group

- Discovered in Rhesus monkey.
- Antigen- Rh → person having antigen – Rh+ve
  person lacking antigen – Rh –ve

RH+ve is dominant over RH–ve

Rh incompatibility

- Rh-ve person exposed to Rh+ve blood → clumping of RBCs.
- During first pregnancy → mother Rh-ve Father Rh+ve
  ↓
  Foetus Rh+ve
- During pregnancy, maternal & foetal blood are separated by placenta.
- ∴ no exposure to Rh antigen takes place.
- While delivery, maternal blood comes in contact with baby's blood ⟶ mother's blood generates antiRh antibodies.
- During second pregnancy with Rh+ve foetus, mother's blood sends antiRh antibodies (formed during first delivery) through placenta to foetus.
- This causes agglutination reaction & haemolysis.
- Hence it is called Haemolytic disease of Newborn (HDN) or Erythroblastosis foetalis.
- To prevent HDN, a specific immunoglobulin – anti Rh antibodies, (RhoGAM) are injected in mother. They suppress immune response of Rh-ve individuals for Rh+ve RBC's.

BLOOD COAGULATION

Blood vessel injury
↓
Tissue exposed to blood
↓
Platelets adhere at injury site
↓
Form temporary plug
↓
Release of Ca^{2+}
↓

Cascade of reactions
↓ Thrombokinase
Prothrombin ⟶ Thrombin
↓
Fibrinogen ⟶ Fibrin
(Fibrin threads form a clot)

NEET SYNAPSE

- Vit K is essential for blood clotting.
- Serum is the clear fluid released from the blood clot.

Serum = [Blood – Formed elements + Clotting factors] or [Plasma – clotting factors]

LYMPH - Tissue fluid / Interstitial fluid

- Colourless or yellowish fluid ; flows in lymphatic vessels.
- Blood flows through capillaries (squamous epithelium).
↓
- Capillaries have minute fenestrations.
↓
- Water + water soluble substances from blood leak out of capillaries.
↓
- These reside in cells of tissues ; larger proteins & blood cells are unable to leak.
↓
- Hence tissue fluid / interstitial fluid has similar composition as that of plasma. but with less proteins.

NEET SYNAPSE
Lymph is rich in fats & poor in proteins

Functions of lymph

- Provides immunity as it contains lymphocytes.
- Transports some nutrients, hormones etc.
- Carrier of CO_2 & various other metabolic wastes.
- Absorption of fats occurs in lacteals (lymph vessels) in small intestine.

Lymphatic system

- Comprises lymph, lymph nodes, lymphatic capillaries & lymphatic vessels.
- Lymph nodes are solid structures present along lymphatic vessels.
- Lymphatic vessels empty in the subclavian veins.

CIRCULATORY PATHWAYS

Open Circulatory System	Closed Circulatory System
Blood flows in open spaces (sinuses).	Blood flows in vessels.
Respiratory pigment (if present) is dissolved in plasma.	Respiratory pigment (Hb) is present in RBCs.
Present in arthropods & molluscs.	Present in annelids, echinoderms, and all vertebrates.
Body's visceral organs bathe in blood.	Vessels supply blood to the deepest cells of the body.

SINGLE CIRCULATION

- Blood passes only once through the heart
- Present in fishes - Heart is 2 chambered (1 atrium, 1 ventricle)
- Ventricle —deoxygenated blood→ gills —oxygenated blood→ body organs —deoxygenated blood→ atrium

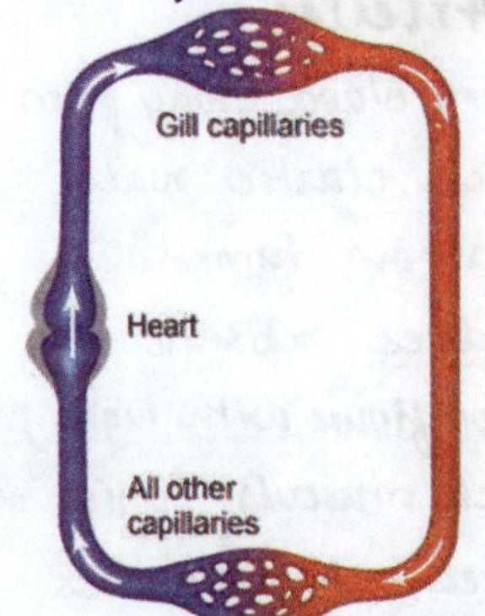

Single circulation

DOUBLE CIRCULATION

- Blood passes twice through heart.
- Blood flows in two loops – oxygenated & deoxygenated circuits
- Types

Incomplete / Mixed circulation	Complete double circulation
Found in amphibians & reptiles (except crocodile)	Found in crocodiles, birds & mammals.
They possess 3 chambered heart.	They possess 4-chambered heart.
2 auricles & 1 ventricle	2 atria & 2 ventricles.

Gills/lungs/skin —oxygenated blood→ left atrium
Body organs —deoxygenated blood→ right atrium
ventricle (mixed blood)

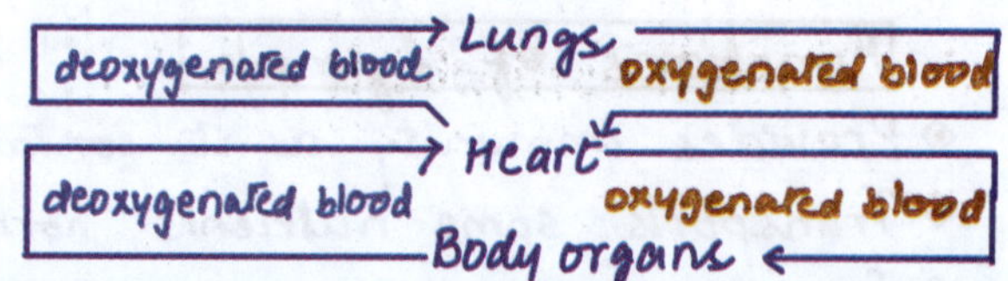

NEET SYNAPSE – Double circulation is necessary for maintaining homeostasis in warm blooded animals.

PORTAL CIRCULATION

- When blood flows from one organ to another bypassing the heart.
- Hepatic Portal circulation

  Nutrient rich blood flows from small intestine to liver via hepatic portal vein.
- Hypothalamo Hypophyseal portal system

  Blood containing hormones flows from hypothalamus to anterior pituitary gland.

CORONARY CIRCULATION

- Coronary arteries supply oxygenated blood to heart muscles.
- Coronary veins drain deoxygenated blood from heart muscles.

HUMAN CIRCULATORY SYSTEM

- Types of vesseles that are part of closed circulatory system–

Arteries	Veins	Capillaries
Carry blood away from heart	Carry blood towards heart	Very small
Thick elastic wall	Thin, scarcely elastic walls.	Lined by squamous epithelium
Narrow lumen	Wide lumen.	Transport blood from arteries to veins.
Valves absent	Valves present	Exchange of O_2 & CO_2
Blood flows with high pressure	Blood flows with low pressure	
Thick muscular tunica media	Thin, less muscular tunica media	
Gives out arterioles	Form from venules.	

Internal structure of arteries & veins

They are composed of –

- Tunica externa - outermost, fibrous (collagen), prevents overexpansion while stretching.
- Tunica media - middle, muscular (smooth muscles), rich in elastic fibres.
- Tunica interna/intima - innermost, contains squamous epithelium & thin elastic band.

HEART

- Mesodermal in origin, situated in mediastinum (between T5 - T8)
- Highly muscular - 4 chambered; apex tilted towards left.
- Size - approx. equal to clenched fist of individual.
- Coverings - double walled pericardium [outer - parietal pericardium; inner - visceral pericardium]
- Space b/w the two filled c̄ pericardial fluid.
- Chambers - 2 atria; 2 ventricles.

  Left side - Left atrium + left ventricle - oxygenated blood

  Right side - Right atrium + right ventricle - deoxygenated blood.

CHAMBERS OF HEART

ATRIA

- Right & left atrium separated by interatrial septum (thin & muscular)
- Septum prevents mixing of oxygenated & deoxygenated blood.
- Foramen ovale - small opening present between right & left atria before birth. It closes soon after birth (when baby breathes)

Atrium & ventricle of same side are separated by atrio-ventricular septum. (thick & fibrous).

VENTRICLES

- Bigger than atria; left ventricle slightly bigger than right ventricle.
- Right & left ventricles separated by interventricular septum (thick walled)

VALVES OF HEART

Valve	Location	Function
Tricuspid	B/w Right Atrium & Right Ventricle	Prevents backflow of blood from RV to RA during ventricular contraction
Bicuspid / Mitral	B/w Left Atrium & Left Ventricle	Prevents backflow of blood from LV to LA during ventricular contraction.
Pulmonary	B/w Right Ventricle & Pulmonary artery	Prevents backflow of blood from PA to RV during ventricular relaxation.
Aortic	B/w Left ventricle & Aorta	Prevents backflow of blood from Aorta to LV during ventricular relaxation.

INTERNAL STRUCTURE OF HEART

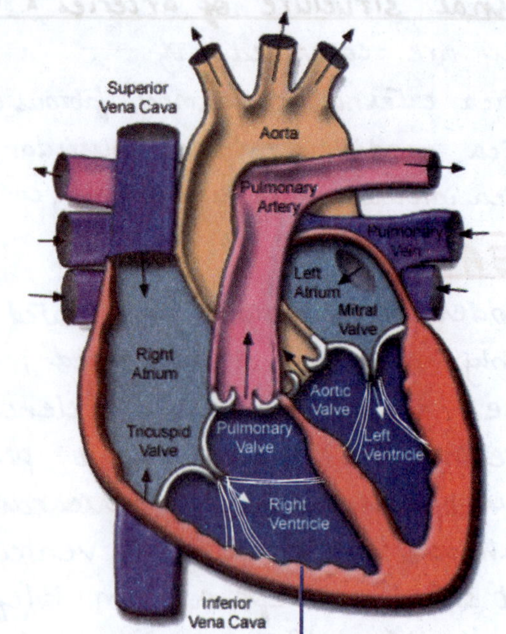

Superior vena cava - brings deoxygenated blood from head and neck to right atrium.
(Superior vena cava lacks valves)

Inferior vena cava - brings deoxygenated blood from lower part of body to right atrium.

Right atrium - receives deoxygenated blood from entire body.

Right ventricle - receives deoxygenated blood from right atrium

Pulmonary artery - carries deoxygenated blood from RV to lungs

Pulmonary vein - brings oxygenated blood from lungs to left atrium

Left atrium - receives oxygenated blood from lungs through pulmonary vein.

Left ventricle - receives oxygenated blood from left atrium.

Aorta - largest artery - carries oxygenated blood to entire body.

Papillary muscles - muscle tissue that projects inside from wall of ventricles.

Chordae tendinae - fibrous cords attached to flaps of bicuspid & tricuspid valves in the ventricles.

NEET SYNAPSE

Myocardium - thickest part of wall of heart, made of cardiac muscles

IMPULSE CONDUCTION IN HEART

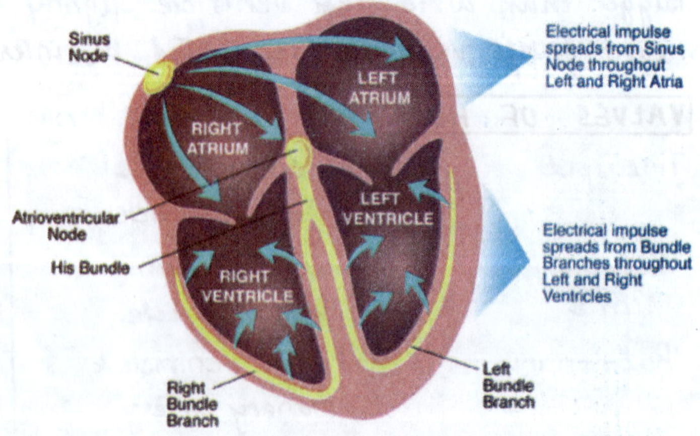

- Human heart is myogenic.
- Modified muscles of myocardium form nodal tissue which generates & propagates impulses.
- SA node generates impulses at the rate of 72/min.
- Flow of impulse

  SA node ⟶ AV node ⟶ Bundle of His ⟶ Purkinje fibres.

SA node - pacemaker; AV node - pacesetter

SA node - situated in right wall of right atrium.

AV node - situated in left wall of right atrium.

CARDIAC CYCLE

- Rhythmic contraction (systole) and relaxation (diastole) of heart chambers.
- Duration - 0.8 sec. It comprises-
  - Atrial systole - 0.1 sec
  - Ventricular systole - 0.3 sec
  - Ventricular diastole - 0.4 sec.

Duration of atrial diastole = 0.7 sec

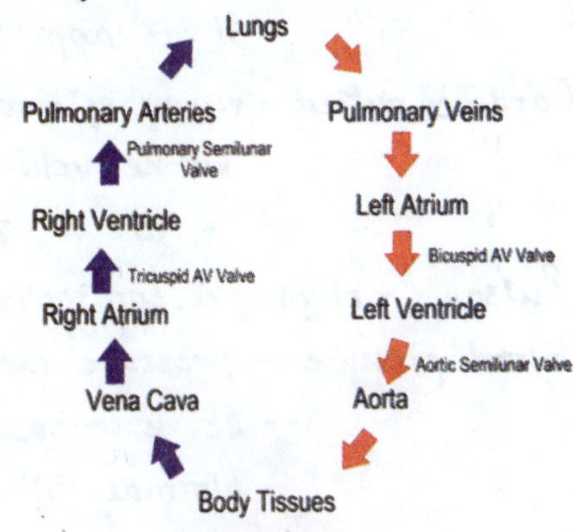

Phases

① Joint diastole-

- All 4 chambers are in relaxed state.
- Blood flows freely from venacava & pulmonary veins into RA & LA respectively.
- Pressure in atria increases.
- It causes bicuspid & tricuspid valves to open.
- Thus, free flow of blood also occurs from atria to ventricles (RA → RV ; LA → LV)

70% of ventricular filling occurs during JD.

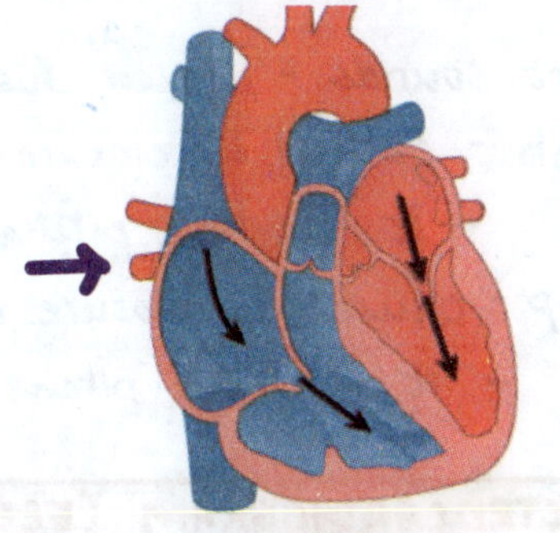

② Atrial systole

- SA node generates action potential.
- Both atria contract simultaneously.
- Increased pressure increases ventricular filling by 30%.

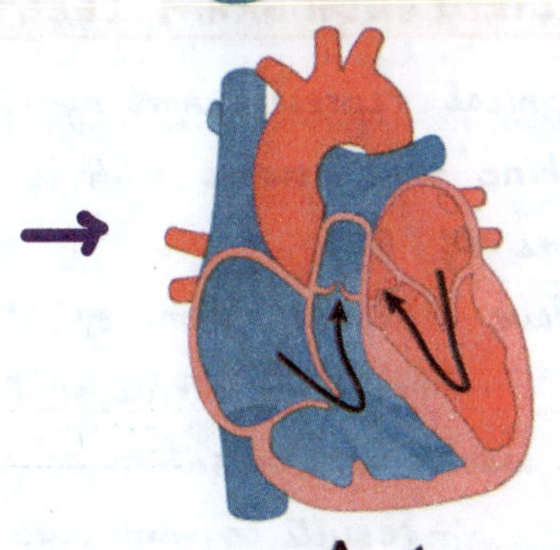

③ Ventricular systole

- Action potential travels further to AV node, Bundle of His & Purkinje fibres.
- This causes ventricular contraction
- Increased pressure leads to opening of AV valves.
- Blood flows from RV into pulmonary artery & from LV into aorta.
- Ventricular systole coincides with atrial diastole.

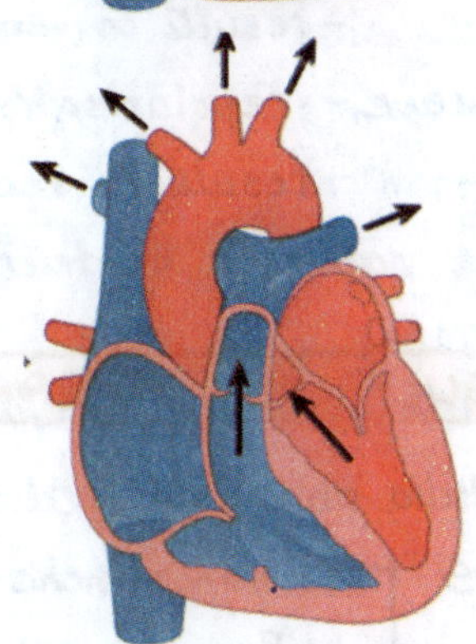

NEET SYNAPSE

Heart rate = 72/min = 72 times in 60 sec

∴ 1 Cardiac cycle = 60/72 = 0.8 sec.

STROKE VOLUME AND CARDIAC OUTPUT

- Stroke volume - Volume of blood ejected in each ventricular contraction.
  - It is approximately 70 ml
- Cardiac output - volume of blood pumped by each ventricle per minute.
  - stroke volume × heart rate
  - 70 × 72 = 5040 ml ≈ 5 L
- Pulse - rhythmic contraction & relaxation in aorta & main arteries.
- Blood pressure - pressure exerted by column of blood on the walls of arteries.
  - It is measured by sphygmomanometer.
  - Normal BP → systolic = 120 mm Hg
    diastolic = 80 mm Hg
- Heart sounds - caused due to closure of valves.
  - Lubb - caused by closure of bicuspid & tricuspid valves (Atrio ventricular valves)
    - it is low pitched
  - Dupp - caused by closure of pulmonary & aortic valves (Semi-lunar valves)
    - it is high pitched

ELECTROCARDIOGRAM (ECG)

- Graphical representation of electrical activity of heart.
- Machine that records ECG is electrocardiograph
- Waves of ECG
  - P-wave - depolarisation of atria
    - results in atrial contraction.
  - QRS wave - depolarisation of ventricles
    - results in ventricular contraction.
  - T wave - repolarisation of ventricles
    - results in ventricular relaxation; systole ends at the end of T wave

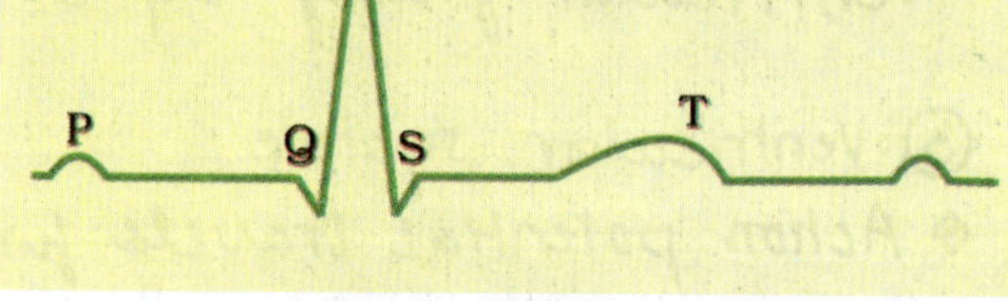

Diagrammatic presentation of a standard ECG

- Heart rate can be determined by counting the number of QRS waves in ECG.

REGULATION OF CARDIAC ACTIVITY

- Medulla oblongata mediates cardiac activity through Autonomic Nervous System (ANS)
- ANS
  - → Sympathetic supply - accelerates heart beat & strength of ventricular contraction.
  - → Parasympathetic supply - reduces heart beat & strength of ventricular contraction.
- Epinephrine & Nor epinephrine - increase cardiac output.
  (adrenaline & nor adrenaline)

DISORDERS OF CIRCULATORY SYSTEM

Hypertension (high blood pressure)

- Persistent increase in blood pressure above 140 mm Hg (systolic) & 90 mm Hg (diastolic)
- It can adversely affect heart, brain & kidneys.

Coronary Artery Disease (CAD)

- Irregular thickening of walls of coronary artery → causes narrowing of lumen.
- It occurs due to deposition of fats, cholesterol, calcium & fibrous tissues.
- It is called atherosclerosis.

Angina Pectoris

- 'Pain in the chest. It results from reduced blood supply to the heart.
- It precedes heart attack.

Heart Failure

- It occurs when heart is unable to pump blood sufficient for body's organs.
- Can be due to CAD, hypertension, diabetes/obesity, stress etc.
- It is also called Congestive Heart Failure (CHF) – congestion in lungs is a main symptom of disease.

Cardiac Arrest

- Heart suddenly stops beating; mainly due to loss of electrical activity.

Heart Attack

- Sudden damage to heart muscles caused due to inadequate blood supply.

Myocardial Infarction

- Inadequate blood supply to heart muscles.

16. Excretory Products and their Elimination

- Excretion - removal of nitrogenous wastes from the body.
- Osmoregulation - maintaining osmotic & ionic balance of body fluids.
- Excretion and osmoregulation maintain homeostasis in the body.

EXCRETORY PRODUCTS

AMMONIA	UREA	URIC ACID
Most toxic	less toxic	least toxic
Requires maximum water for excretion.	Requires less water for excretion	Almost insoluble in water.
Formed in liver by deamination	Formed in liver by ornithine /urea cycle	Excreted in semi-solid form.
Process - ammonotelism	Process - ureotelism	Process - uricotelism
Animals - ammonotelic	Animals - ureotelic	Animals - uricotelic
Eg. most bony fishes, aquatic amphibians, aquatic insects etc. (aquatic animals)	Eg - Elasmobranch fishes, adult amphibians, mammals. (Terrestrial + aquatic)	Eg - land reptiles, most insects, birds (Terrestrial)
		Conserves water.

Guanotelic animals - excrete guanine ; Eg. spiders.

NEET SYNAPSE

- Dual excretion - some animals excrete ammonia as well as urea depending upon water availability.
- Uric acid when increases, it crystallises within the body

Excretory Organs in Different Animals

Excretory Organ	Example
Contractile vacuole	Protozoans
General body surface	Sponges, Cnidarians
Renette cells	Aschelminthes
Protonephridia (flame cells)	Platyhelminthes, Cephalochordates, rotifers

Excretory Organ	Example
Nephridia	Annelids
Malpighian tubules	Insects
Coxal glands	Arachnids
Green glands	Crustaceans
Kidneys	Vertebrates

EXCRETORY SYSTEM OF HUMANS

- It comprises • 2 kidneys • 1 urinary bladder
  • 2 ureters • 1 urethra

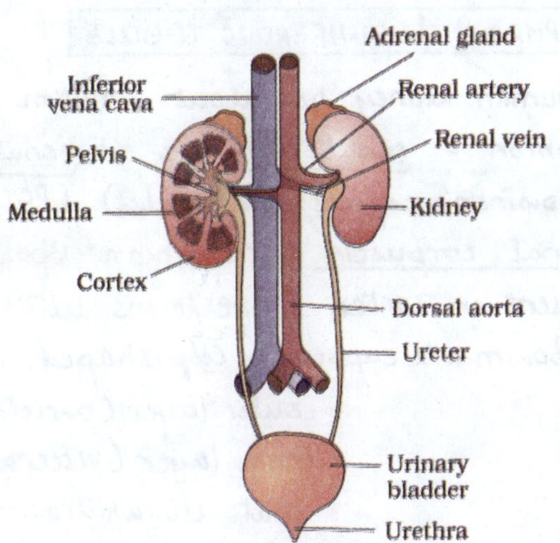

Human Urinary system

KIDNEYS

- Mesodermal in origin.
- Reddish brown, bean shaped, paired.
- Location - retroperitoneal; b/w - T12 & L3.
- Size - Length → 10-12 cm, width → 5-7 cm,
  Thickness → 2-3 cm
- Floating ribs (11th & 12th pair) protect kidneys.
- Left kidney is slightly above right kidney

Functions of Kidneys

- Excretion of metabolic wastes & foreign chemicals.
- Regulates body fluid osmolarity & electrolyte concentration.
- Regulates acid base balance of the body
- Secretes hormones - erythropoietin & renin.

Structure of Kidney

- Coverings - renal fascia (outermost),
  adipose capsule (middle),
  renal capsule (innermost).
- Hilum - concavity present on inner surface
  - passage for blood vessels & nerves.
  - Ureters exit kidneys from hilum.

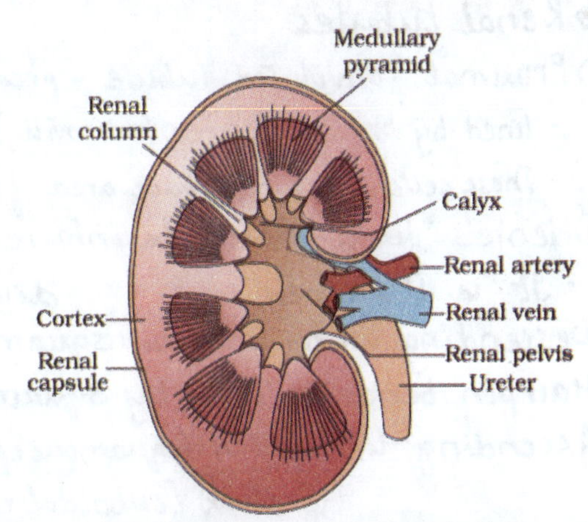

Longitudinal section (Diagrammatic) of Kidney

Internal Structure

- Divided into outer cortex and inner medulla.
- Medulla divided into 8-12 medullary pyramids
- Pyramids have broad base (towards cortex) and narrow apex (renal papilla) towards pelvis.
- Renal colums of Bertini - Extensions of cortex into medullary pyramids
- Each medullary pyramid contains nephrons (structural & functional units of kidneys)

Renal papilla opens into minor calyces (receive urine from renal pyramid)
Minor calyces open into 2-3 major calyces.
Major calyces drain urine into pelvis (funnel shaped space)
Pelvis transfers urine to ureters.

NEPHRON / URINIFEROUS TUBULE

- A human kidney has about 1 million nephrons (thin, tubular, highly convoluted)
- Nephron = renal corpuscle (Bowman's capsule + Glomerulus) + renal tubules (PCT, DCT, Loop of Henle)
- Renal corpuscle / Malpighian Body

Present in cortex ; performs ultrafiltration of blood during urine formation.

- Bowman's capsule - cup shaped, double walled structure.
  - outer layer (parietal) is lined with simple squamous epithelium.
  - inner layer (visceral) is lined with podocytes (create slits so that ultrafiltration can take place).
- Glomerulus - Tuft of capillaries present inside Bowman's capsule.
  - Capillaries are formed from afferent arteriole (wide diameter)
  All capillaries unite to form efferent arteriole (narrow diameter)

NEET SYNAPSE - Difference in diameter builds pressure in capillaries that helps in ultrafiltration.

- Renal tubules

① Proximal Convoluted Tubule - present in cortex region
- lined by brush bordered (microvilli) cuboidal epithelium
- These cells increase surface area for reabsorption.

② Henle's loop - descends into renal medulla.
- It is U shaped, divided into-

Descending limb - lined by squamous epithelium.
Hairpin bend - lined by squamous epithelium.
Ascending limb - thin (squamous epithelium)
- thick (cuboidal epithelium)

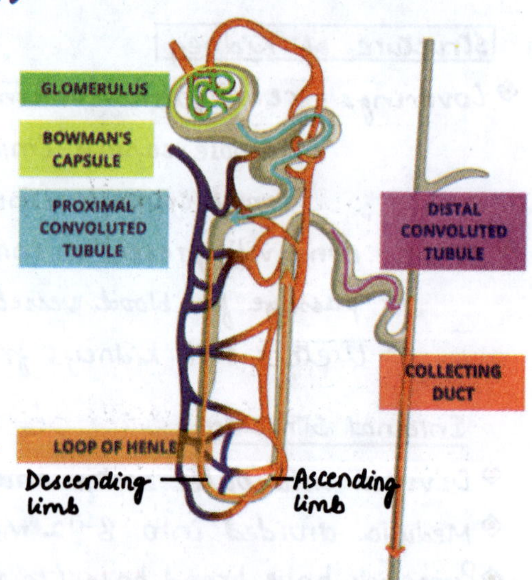

③ Distal Convoluted Tubule - present in cortex region
- lined by cuboidal epithelium.

- Collecting duct - extends from cortex to medulla
  - lined by cuboidal epithelium.

↓ It is continuous with nephron but not a part of it.

- Ducts of Bellini - collect urine from collecting ducts and transfer to minor calyces.
- Vasa recta - network of peritubular capillaries present around Loop of Henle, they form a U-shaped network.
  - responsible for counter current mechanism along with Loop of Henle.

TYPES OF NEPHRON

Cortical Nephron

- 2/3 part present in cortex
- 1/3 part present in medulla
- Have short loops of Henle
- Vasa recta highly reduced or absent
- Make up 80-85% of total nephrons.

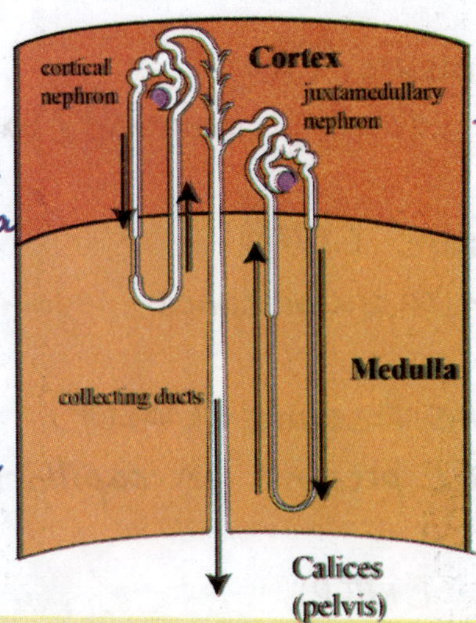

Juxtamedullary Nephron

- 2/3 part present in medulla
- 1/3 part present in cortex
- Have long loops of Henle
- Vasa recta are well developed
- Make up 15-20% of total nephrons.

Blood flow in kidney

Aorta → Renal artery → Afferent arteriole → Glomerulus → Efferent arteriole → Vasa recta → Renal venules → Renal vein → Inferior venacava → Heart → Aorta

URETERS

- Paired, muscular tubes – transfer urine from kidneys to urinary bladder.
- Length – 25-30 cm

URINARY BLADDER

- Pear shaped, reservoir of urine
- It is a muscular bag (smooth muscles)
- It is lined by transitional epithelium (has ability to stretch)

Ureter
Opening of ureter
Trigone
Internal urethral orifice
Urethra

URETHRA

- Extends from lower part of bladder & opens to outside.
- Males – length of urethra – 20 cm
- Females – length of urethra – 4 cm

MECHANISM OF URINE FORMATION

1. Glomerular filtration / Ultrafiltration

- 1100-1200 ml of blood (1/5 of cardiac output) is filtered by kidneys per minute
- Blood passes through glomerules to Bowman's capsule.
- Filtration through glomerulus occurs due to Net Filtration Pressure.

① Glomerular Hydrostatic pressure (GHP)
Pressure inside capillaries - positive pressure (favours filtration)
Value - 55 mm Hg

② Capsular Hydrostatic Pressure (CHP)
Pressure exerted by fluid in capsular space - negative pressure (opposes filtration)
Value - 15 mm Hg

③ Blood Colloidal Osmotic Pressure (BCOP)
Generated by large proteins present in capillaries (negative pressure)
Value - 30 mm Hg

Net Filtration Pressure (NFP)
= GHP - (CHP + BCOP) = 55 - (15 + 30)
NFP = 10 mm Hg

Glomerular filtrate contains all constituents of blood except blood cells, proteins, certain drugs etc.

Glomerular Filtration Rate - amount of filtrate formed by kidneys per minute. It is 125 ml/min

TUBULAR REABSORPTION

- Volume of filtrate formed per day = 180 L
- Volume of urine excreted per day = 1.5 L
- ∴ 99% of filtrate is reabsorbed by renal tubules.
- Reabsorption - absorption of useful substances from renal tubules into peritubular capillaries.
- Reabsorption can be → active (with expenditure of energy)
  → passive (without expenditure of energy)

Reabsorption in PCT

- Maximum reabsorption
- About 70-80% of electrolytes and water are reabsorbed here.
- Active reabsorption - Glucose, amino acids, NaCl
- Passive reabsorption - HCO_3^-, urea, water (Osmosis)
- PCT helps to maintain ionic balance & pH of body.

NEET SYNAPSE

Maximum reabsorption of water takes place in PCT among all renal tubules.

Reabsorption in Loop of Henle

- Minimum reabsorption
- LOH maintains high osmolarity in interstitial/medullary fluid.

Descending limb
- Permeable to water
- Impermeable to salts
- Water is reabsorbed passively (osmosis)
- Makes the filtrate concentrated ⟶ hypertonic to plasma

Hairpin bend
- Highly permeable to water
  ↓
- Concentrates the filtrate to its maximum (1200 mosmol/L)

Ascending limb
- Impermeable to water
- Permeable to salts
- Transport of electrolytes occurs actively & passively
- Diffusion of Na^+ & Cl^- occurs.
- Active secretion of NaCl occurs in medullary fluid.
- Filtrate becomes hypotonic to plasma.

Reabsorption in DCT

- Conditional reabsorption of Na^+ (condition- secretion of aldosterone)
- Reabsorption of HCO_3^- & Cl^- - Passive reabsorption.
- Reabsorption of water occurs when ADH/vasopressin is secreted
  ↳ makes filtrate isotonic.

Reabsorption in Collecting Ducts.

- Water is reabsorbed from here in the presence of ADH.
- Filtrate becomes hypertonic in this region.
- Diffusion of urea occurs – makes medulla hyperosmotic.

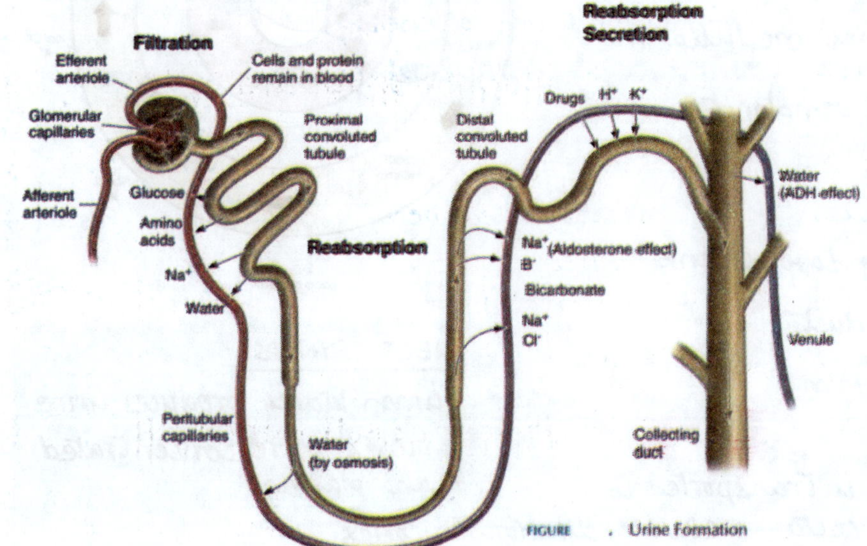

FIGURE . Urine Formation

NEET SYNAPSE
- ADH / Vasopressin acts on distal part of nephron- DCT & CD.
- It creates water channels or aquaporins which increase the rate of water reabsorption.

TUBULAR SECRETION

- Secretion of metabolic wastes by tubular cells into filtrate.
- Secretion in PCT
  - Selective secretion of H^+, NH_3, K^+, creatinine etc.
- Secretion in DCT
  - Selective secretion of H^+, K^+, NH_3 & certain drugs.
  - Regulates blood pH & $Na^+ - K^+$ levels.
- Secretion in Collecting Ducts
  - Selective secretion of H^+, K^+
  - Regulates ionic balance & blood pH.

COUNTER CURRENT MECHANISM

- Counter - opposite ; current - flow
- Flow of filtrate in limbs of Henle's loop - in opposite direction
  Flow of blood in capillaries of vasa recta - in opposite direction
  ∴ Henle's loop + vasa recta - exhibit counter current mechanism.

Osmolarity in cortex - 300 mOsm/L
Osmolarity in outer medulla - 600-900 mOsm/L
Osmolarity in inner medulla - 1200 mOsm/L
Osmolarity gradient occurs due to NaCl & Urea.

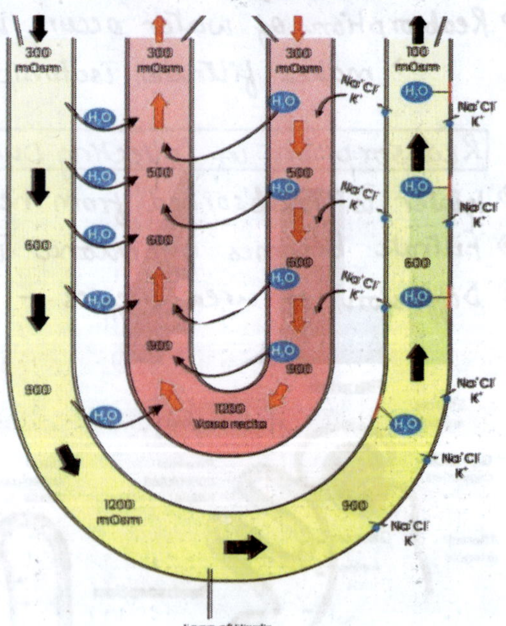

NaCl

NaCl transported by ascending loop of Henle is exchanged with descending limb of vasa recta.
↓
NaCl is returned to inner medulla
↓
Contributes to increased osmolarity in inner medulla.

Urea

Urea enters thin ascending Loop of Henle
↓
Transported to collecting duct
↓
Takes it back to interstitium

Water

Water reabsorbed by PCT is transported to ascending limb of vasa recta ⟶ causes dilution in cortex.

> **NEET SYNAPSE**
> Human kidney produces urine 4 times more concentrated than plasma.

REGULATION OF KIDNEY FUNCTION

CONTROL BY JGA

- Juxta Glomerular Apparatus – formed by cells of DCT + cells of afferent arteriole.
- It works through RAAS- Renin Angiotensin Aldosterone System.
- Mechanism

Angiotensin II – powerful vasoconstrictor – increases blood pressure.

Low Blood Pressure / GFR
↓
JGA releases Renin
Angiotensinogen ⟶ Angiotensin I —ACE→ Angiotensin II —Stimulates→ Adrenal cortex
↓ releases
Aldosterone

Aldosterone causes Na^+ & H_2O reabsorption from DCT. This increases blood volume, thereby increasing BP

NEET SYNAPSE
Angiotensinogen is a blood plasma protein & is produced by liver.

CONTROL BY ADH

- Secreted by posterior pituitary (neurohypophysis)
- Mechanism
- Reduction in blood volume / body fluid volume
  ↓
  Release of ADH / Vasopressin
  ↓
  Increases water reabsorption in DCT & CD.

CONTROL BY ANF

- Atrial Natriuretic Factor – secreted by walls of atria.
- Causes vasodilation (in case of high BP & blood volume)
- Causes increased excretion of Na^+ in urine → reduces blood volume & BP.
- Checks the activity of RAAS

All the above hormones together maintain osmolarity & homeostasis.

MICTURITION

- Act of passing urine; urine is carried by peristaltic waves from ureter to UB
- Results from contraction & relaxation of blader wall & urethral sphicter.
- Mechanism
- Urinary bladder fills with urine; activates stretch receptors
  ↓
  send sensory signals to CNS
  ↓
  CNS passes motor messages

contraction of smooth muscles of bladder | Relaxation of urethral sphincter.

This mechanism is called micturition reflex.

Human urine

Colour - pale yellow, straw coloured (pigment urochrome)
pH - 6, slightly acidic
Odour - pungent ammonia odour on standing.

- On an average, about 25-30 gms of urea is excreted per day.
- Glycosuria (glucose in urine) & Ketonuria (ketone bodies in urine) indicate diabetes mellitus.

ACCESSORY EXCRETORY ORGANS

1. Skin
   - Sudoriferous (sweat glands) - excrete NaCl, water, urea, lactic acid.
   - Sebaceous (oil glands) - secrete sebum - contains waxes, sterols, fatty acids etc
2. Lungs - excrete CO_2 & water (metabolic wastes)
   - Approx - 200 ml/min CO_2 is excreted.
3. Liver - excrete bile pigments like biliverdin & bilirubin (pass through faeces via alimentary canal)

DISORDERS OF EXCRETORY SYSTEM

1. Renal stones - also called renal calculi
   - insoluble crystallised salts like oxalates.
2. Nephritis (Bright's disease) - inflammation of glomeruli
   - can cause proteinuria or hematuria.
   - can be congenital or due to bacterial infection
3. Renal failure / kidney failure - total inability of kidney for excretion.
   - cause uremia (urea in blood)

Artificial kidney / Haemodialysis

- Blood is pumped from artery (after mixing it with anticoagulant & cooling it)
- Waste materials diffuse out into dialysing solution from blood
- Composition of dialysing fluid same as that of plasma except nitrogenous wastes
- Plasma proteins do not cross - too large for pores of cellophane tube.
- Clean blood is returned to veins.

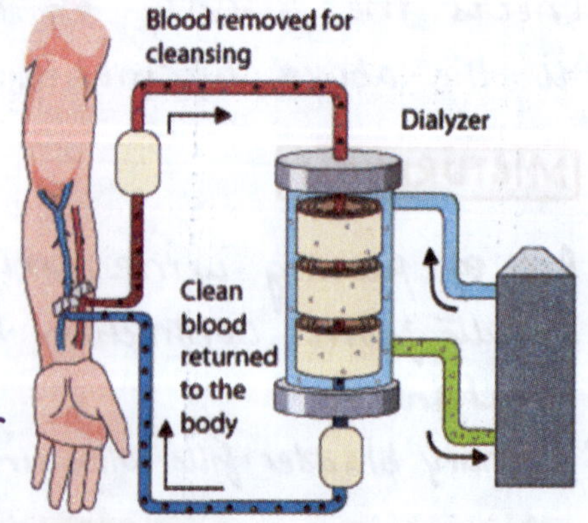

4. Kidney Transplant - replacement of non functional kidney by a functional healthy kidney. A person having a transplanted organ must take immunosuppresants throughout life.

17. Locomotion and Movement

- Movement - change in posture or position of any body part of a living organism
- Locomotion - change in place or location. It occurs as a result of movement.

Locomotion is a type of movement but all movements are not locomotary.
Hydra utilises its tentacles for capturing prey as well as for locomotion.

TYPES OF MOVEMENTS

1. Amoeboid or Pseudopodial Movement
- Pseudopodia (false feet) formed by protoplasmic streaming.
- Found in leucocytes (mainly macrophages) for changing shape and for squeezing out through capillaries (diapedesis)
- Change in shape occurs due to rearrangement of cytoskeletal elements.

2. Ciliary Movement
- Performed by cilia (short, numerous, hair like projections present on cell surface)
- Occurs in protozoans (eg. Paramoecium) & in internal tubular organs of higher animals (eg. trachea, fallopian tubes in humans)
- In Paramoecium, cilia help in moving food particles in gullet & also locomotion.
- In trachea of humans, they help in movement of mucus & dust particles and in fallopian tube, they assist in movement of ova.

3. Flagellar Movement
- Occurs due to flagella (few long hair like projections present on cell surface)
- Occurs in protozoans (eg. Euglena), sponges & coelenterates.
- In sponges, they line water canal system & help in water movement.
- In humans, sperm is the only flagellated cell → it swims through the female reproductive tract with the help of flagella.

Muscular Movement
- Used by majority of vertebrates including humans.
- Takes place through muscle tissue.
- Muscle fibres undergo contraction & relaxation to bring about movement & locomotion.

MUSCULAR SYSTEM

- Muscle - specialised tissue of mesodermal origin (majority of muscles)
- Muscles of - Iris, ciliary body & sweat glands → ectodermal in origin.
- Myocytes - cells of muscles. Characteristics of muscle tissue - contractility, excitability, extensibility, elasticity

TYPES OF MUSCLES

Skeletal muscles	Smooth muscles	Cardiac muscles
Fibre - cylindrical	Spindle shaped	Cylindrical
Multinucleate (syncitium)	Uninucleate	Uninucleate
Striated, unbranched	Unstriated, unbranched	Striated, branched
Attached to bones;	Present in visceral organs; Involuntary	Present in heart
Voluntary		Involuntary
Intercalated discs absent	Intercalated discs absent	Intercalated discs present
Fast contractions	Slow contractions	Moderate contractions.
Function - locomotion	Transportation of food, blood, gametes etc.	Pumping action of heart.

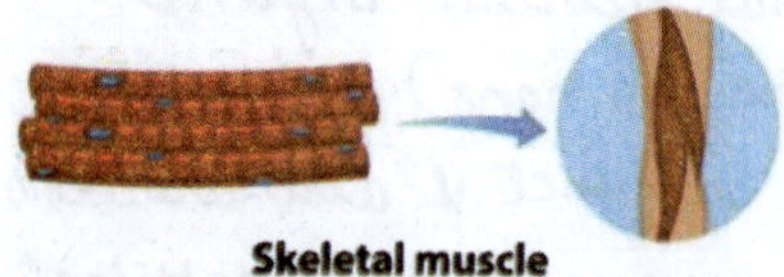
Skeletal muscle

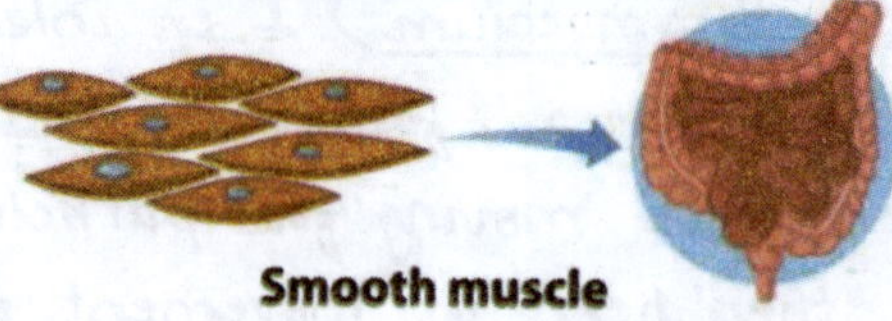
Smooth muscle

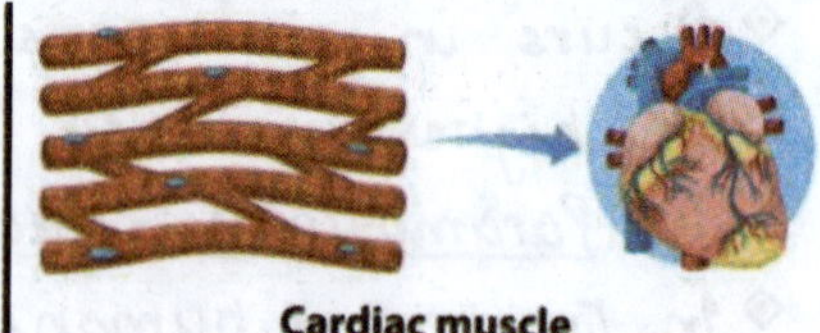
Cardiac muscle

SKELETAL MUSCLES

Muscle (covered by epimysium)
↑
Fascicles bound by fascia (collagenous connective tissue)
↑
Muscle fascicle (covered by perimysium)
↑
Muscle fibre (covered by endomysium)
↑
Myofibrils
↑
Actin + Myosin filaments

NEET SYNAPSE -
Sarcolemma - plasma membrane of muscle fibre
Endomysium - connective tissue layer around muscle fibre

Ultrastructure of skeletal muscle fibre

- Sarcolemma - plasma membrane of muscle fibre
- Sarcoplasm - cytoplasm of muscle fibre.
- Sarcoplasmic reticulum - ER of muscle fibre
  - contains Ca^{2+} reserves.
- Myofibrils - parallely arranged within sarcoplasm
  - contain alternate dark & light bands.

NEET SYNAPSE
Neurons that supply skeletal muscles are motor neurons

Dark bands

- Also called Aniosotropic (A-band)
- Does not let light pass through it
- Made up of myosin protein
- H-zone - Henson's zone
  Present at centre of A band (dark)
  comparatively light - due to the presence of myosin only. At other places on dark band, actin overlaps myosin.
- M-line - present at the centre of H-zone
- O-zone - Overlapping zone. Part of dark band outer of H-zone.

H zone
Z line
M line
Z line
Lighter I band
Darker A band
Lighter I band

Light bands

- Also called Isotropic (I-band)
- It allows light to pass through it.
- Made of actin protein.
- Z-line - zig zag line
  made of elastic fibre.
  - passes through centre of I-band

Sarcomere
- Portion b/w 2 successive Z-lines
- Comprises one full A-band and half of each adjacent I-bands.
- It is the functional unit of contraction of skeletal muscle.

Molecular Structure of Skeletal Muscle Fibres

- Myofibrils consist of myofilaments
  Myofilaments are made up of
  Contractile Proteins - actin & myosin
  - responsible for shortening of muscle fibre.

  Regulatory Proteins - tropomyosin & troponin
  - regulate the process of contraction.

Thick myofilaments - 150 A° diameter
Thin myofilaments - 70 A° diameter

NEET SYNAPSE - Dystrophin is a muscle protein that connects cytoskeleton of muscle fibre to extracellular matrix. It is present in all types of muscles.

Thick Myofilaments

- Consist of polymerised myosin protein
- Contributes to 55% of muscle protein by weight.
- Present in A band (dark band) only.
- Each myosin is composed of monomer meromyosin.
- Each meromyosin comprises
  - Heavy Meromyosin (HMM) – Head + short arm
  - Light Meromyosin (LMM) – tail part
- HMM extends outwards at regular distance and angle from each other from the surface of polymerised myosin forming cross arm.
- Head is globular & acts as ATPase – contains binding sites for ATP
- Cross arm forms bridges with actin during muscle contraction.

Thin Myofilaments

- Present in I band and extend to A band.
- It is composed of 3 different proteins

1. Actin

- globulin protein with low molecular weight.
- occurs in 2 forms
  - F-actin (Fibrous) – polymeric
  - G-actin (Globular) – monomeric
- G actin polymerises into two filamentous F-actins
- Polymerisation requires Mg^{2+}
- Two F-actins are helically wound over each other.

NEET SYNAPSE

G-actin contains myosin binding sites – allow cross bridge formation

2. Tropomyosin

Double stranded, helical, fibrous protein
Runs closely along the length of F-actin
Covers the myosin binding site on actin at resting muscle state.
Thus prevents formation of cross bridges at rest.

3. Troponin

Trimeric protein – contain 3 units
- TpI – inhibitory site
- TpT – tropomyosin site
- TpC – Ca^{2+} binding site.

Found at regular intervals on tropomyosin
Keeps tropomyosin in place during resting state of muscle

MECHANISM OF MUSCLE CONTRACTION

Explained by Sliding Filament Theory

Neural signal reaches Neuro Muscular Junction (junction of nerve & ms fibre)

↓

Impulses reach terminal ends of axons

↓

Vesicles containing neurotransmitter acetylcholine fuse with pre synaptic membrane (axonal membrane)

↓

Release of acetyl choline (Ach) in synaptic cleft

↓

Ach binds with Ach receptors present on sarcolemma

↓

Action potential generates in sarcolemma & travels through T-tubules to sarcoplasmic reticulum ⟶ Releases Ca^{2+} into sarcoplasm

↓

Ca^{2+} binds with TPC causing change in shape

↓

Troponin - tropomyosin complex displaced.

↓

Myosin binding sites exposed

NEET SYNAPSE

NMJ - junction of nerve & sarcolemma

Motor unit - junction of nerve & all ms. fibres that it supplies

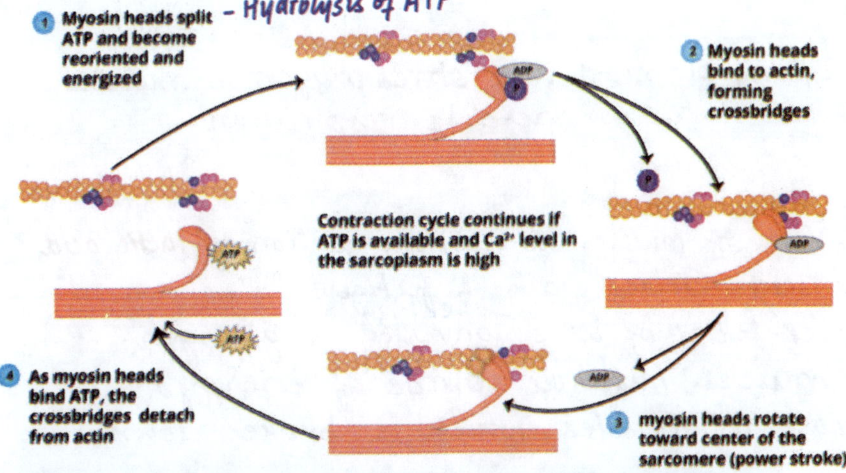

During sliding -

Myosin cross bridges undergo rotation

↓

Actin is pulled towards centre of A band

↓

Z-line pulling results in shortening of sarcomere

↓

Leads to contraction

↓

Myosin released ADP + Pi, this causes relaxation

↓

Binding of new ATP causes breaking of cross bridges

↓

New ATP hydrolyses & causes formation of cross bridges again

NEET SYNAPSE

Length of A band does not change during contraction

Length of I band reduces during contraction

Length of actin & myosin filaments does not change

↳ They only slide during contraction.

Mechanism of Muscle Relaxation

Ca^{2+} return to sarcoplasmic reticulum by active transport

↓

Ca^{2+} bind with calsequestrin (Ca^{2+} binding protein) present in sarcoplasmic reticulum.

↓

TpC becomes free, masks myosin binding sites on actin.

↓

Cross bridges do not form, causing muscle relaxation.

TYPES OF MUSCLE FIBRES

Red Muscle Fibres

- Dark red in colour due to presence of myoglobin.
- Thin fibres
- Do not fatigue easily
- Contain more mitochondria, thus carry out more aerobic respiration, hence called aerobic muscles
- Found in muscles that undergo prolonged contraction.
- Eg. extensor ms. of back.

White Muscle Fibres

- White or pale yellow in colour due to less or no myoglobin.
- Thick fibres
- They fatigue faster
- They contain lesser mitochondria hence carry out anaerobic respiration.
- Found in muscles that undergo faster contraction.
- Eg. muscles of eyeball

NEET SYNAPSE

Myoglobin is an Fe^{2+} containg pigment that stores oxygen in muscles. The stored oxygen is used later for aerobic respiration.

Muscle fatigue

- Repeated anaerobic contraction of muscles causes accumulation of lactic acid
- Deposition of lactic acid causes pain & fatigue.
- Lactic acid passes to liver & 80% of it is converted to glycogen.
- Glycogen is stored in muscles (used as source of energy)
- It is converted to glucose in muscles, which is broken down to release energy.

NEET SYNAPSE

Tetanus - Lack of relaxation b/w successive stimuli causing continuous ms. contractions.

Spasm - sudden involuntary contraction of a muscle or group of ms.

SKELETAL SYSTEM IN HUMANS

- Skeletal system = bones + cartilage (both are specialised connective tissues)
- Bones - hard matrix (contains Ca^{2+} salts)
- Cartilage - pliable matrix (contains chondroitin salts)

SKELETON

AXIAL - (80 bones)

Cranium -	8
Face	14
Hyoid	1
Ear ossicles	6
Vertebral column	26
Sternum	1
Ribs	24
	80

Cranial bones

Frontal	1
Parietal	2
Temporal	2
Occipetal	1
Sphenoid	1
Ethmoid	1
	8

Facial bones

Nasal	2
Maxillae	2
Mandible	1
Zygomatic	2
Lacrimal	2
Palatine	2
Inferior Nasal	2
Vomer	1
	14

APPENDICULAR (126 bones)

Pectoral girdle	
Clavicle	2
Scapula	2
	(4)
Forelimbs	
Humerus	2
Ulna	2
Radius	2
Carpals	16
Metacarpals	10
Phalanges	28
	(60)

Pelvic girdle	
Coxal bones	(2)
Hindlimbs	
Femur	2
Tibia	2
Fibula	2
Patella	2
Tarsals	14
Metatarsals	10
Phalanges	28
	(60)
Total	126

Bones of vertebral column will be discussed later in the chapter.

AXIAL SKELETON

- Present along middle longitudinal axis of body.

SKULL

- Skeleton of head ; has a large opening at base – foramen ovale.
- Consists of 29 bones – Cranium (8) + Ear Ossicles (6) + Hyoid (1) + Facial bones (14)

Cranium

- Composed of 8 bones
- held together by sutures.

> **NEET SYNAPSE**
> In infants, sutures are often movable and act as major growth centres in skull

Cranial Bones

Frontal bone (Unpaired)
Parietal bones (Paired)
Sphenoid bones (Unpaired)
Ethmoid bones (Unpaired)
Temporal bones (Paired)
Occipital bone (Unpaired)

Ear ossicles

- Malleus, Incus, Stapes (smallest bone of body)
- They are present in middle ear.

> **NEET SYNAPSE**
> Middle ear is an air cavity. Ear ossicles resonate & amplify sound

Hyoid bone

- U-shaped, present at base of buccal cavity
- It does not articulate with any other bone.
- It is the point of attachment of tongue & serves as floor of mouth.

Facial bones

- Constitute facial region. Facial muscles attach here.
- Mandible (lower jaw) is the only freely movable bone of skull.

VERTEBRAL COLUMN – Backbone

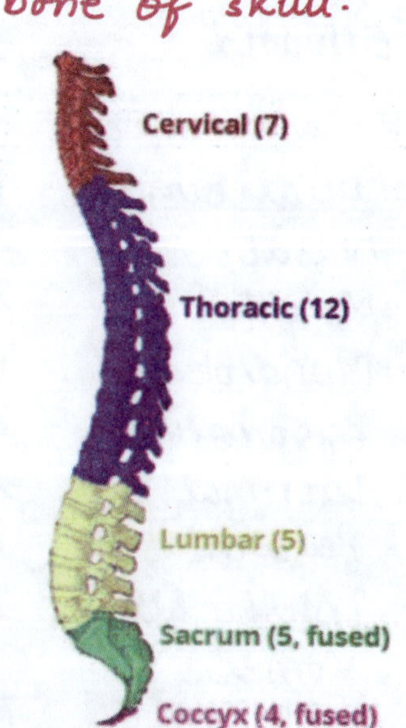

- Made up of 26 serially arranged bones. (vertebrae)
- Each vertebra has hollow central part for the passage of spinal cord.

Cervical (7) Atlas – first vertebra
Axis – second vertebra
Thoracic (12) located in chest region.
Lumbar (5) Lumbar vertebra – largest & strongest
Sacral (5) Female sacrum is wider than male sacrum
Coccyx (5) Also called tail bone

STERNUM - Breast bone

- Flat dagger shaped bone located in front of chest
- Helps during respiration.

RIBS

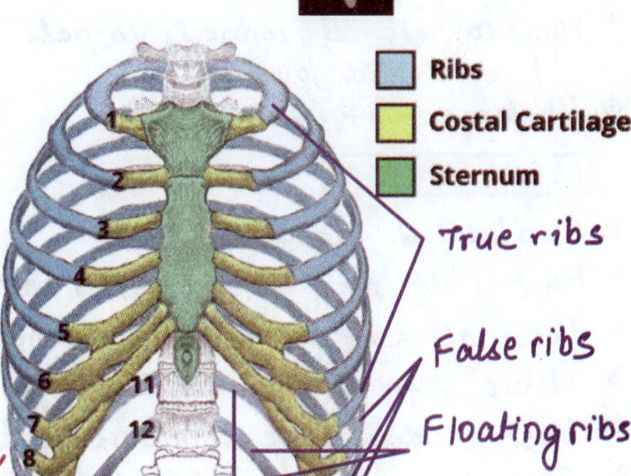

- Thin flat bones; 12 pairs
- Connected to dorsally- vertebral column
  ventrally- sternum
- Ribs are bicephalic - possess two articulation surfaces on dorsal end

Vertebrosternal Ribs (True Ribs)

- First 7 pairs - attach directly to sternum by costal cartilages
- Costal cartilages are hyaline cartilages

Vertebrochondral Ribs (False Ribs)

- 8th, 9th & 10th pairs
- They articulate with costal cartilage of 7th rib attached indirectly with sternum

Floating or Vertebral Ribs

- 11th & 12th pairs
- Their anterior ends are free floating
- They protect the kidneys.

NEET SYNAPSE
Hyaline cartilage is the most abundant cartilage in body. It is an articular cartilage- present at joints.

APPENDICULAR SKELETON

Includes pectoral girdle, pelvic girdle, forelimbs & hindlimbs.

PECTORAL GIRDLE

- Also called shoulder girdle
- It contains separate right & left halves
- Each half contains - 1 scapula & 1 clavicle
- Scapula possesses acromion & coracoid processes.
- Glenoid cavity - cup shaped cavity where head of humerus articulates.
- Clavicle is present anteriorly & articulates with acromion process of scapula.

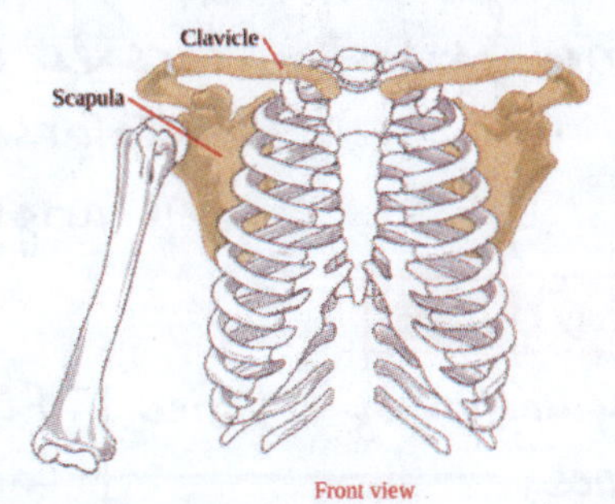

Human shoulder girdle or pectoral girdle

FORELIMB

- Has 30 bones
- Humerus – longest & largest bone of upper limb.
- Radius & ulna – bones of forearm
- Carpals – 8 small wrist bones
- Metacarpals – 5, connects carpals with phalanges.
  ↑↓ condyloid joint
- Phalanges – 14 (2, 3, 3, 3, 3)

Clavicle
Scapula
Humerus
Radius
Ulna
Carpals
Metacarpals
Phalanges

PELVIC GIRDLE

- Also called hip girdle
- Each half of pelvic girdle is called coxal / innominate bone.
- Two halves of pelvic girdle connect ventrally at pubic symphysis
- Pubic symphysis contains fibrous cartilage.
- Each coxal bone contains 3 bones – ilium, ischium & pubis.
- They form acetabulum (cavity where femur articulates)
- Pelvis in females is wider than in males to accomodate foetal development during pregnancy.

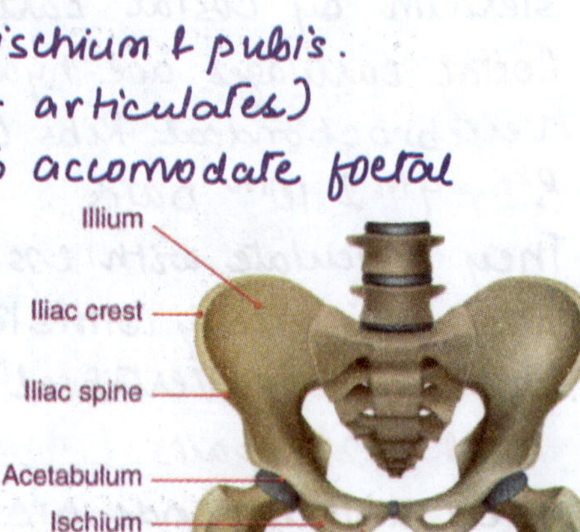

HINDLIMB

- It has 30 bones
- Femur – longest & largest bone of leg and body.
- Articulates with acetabulum on one end &
- with tibia (not fibula) on the other end.
- Patella – knee cap ; sesamoid bone
- **NEET SYNAPSE** – Sesamoid bones are formed by ossification of tendons.
- Tibia & fibula – present in shank region.
- Bones of foot – Tarsals (7) form ankle
  Metatarsals (5) form sole
  Phalanges (14) form toes

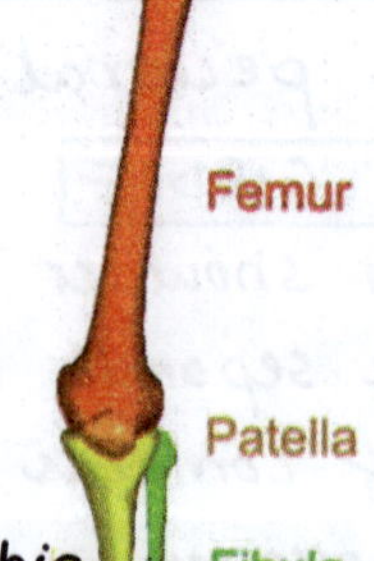

Tibia
Fibula
Tarsals (7)
Metatarsals (5)
Phalanges (14)

JOINTS

- Articulation of 2 bones
- Types
  - Fibrous – immovable
  - Cartilagenous – slightly movable
  - Synovial – freely movable

FIBROUS / IMMOVABLE JOINTS

- Articulating bones are joined by bundles of collagen fibres.
- Eg: Skull bones (sutures), teeth in mandible & maxillae.

CARTILAGINOUS / SLIGHTLY MOVABLE JOINTS

- Articulating bones have a pad of fibro cartilage between them.
- Allow very slight movement (amphiarthrosis)
- Slight movement occurs due to compression of cartilage discs.
- Eg: joints between pubic bones of pelvic girdle.
  joints between vertebrae (intervertebral discs)

SYNOVIAL / FREELY MOVABLE JOINTS

- Allow movement in one or more directions.
- Articulating bones are enclosed within synovial capsule.
- Synovial capsule is lined by synovial membrane.
- The synovial membrane encloses synovial cavity.
- This synovial cavity is filled with synovial fluid.
- Fluid reduces friction & allows free movement.

Types

> **NEET SYNAPSE**
> Joint b/w skull & first vertebra is condyloid joint.

Ball and Socket Joint

- Multiaxial joint (movement in more than one direction)
- Present in shoulder joint (Glenoid cavity & humerus)
  hip joint (Acetabulum & femur)

Hinge Joint

- Monoaxial joint (movement in one plane only)
- Present in ankle, knee, elbow, and b/w phalanges & digits

Pivot Joint

- Monoxial joint; primary movement is rotation
- Present in b/w humerus & radius, b/w radius & ulna,
  b/w atlas & axis (1st & 2nd vertebra)

Saddle Joint

- Biaxial joint; it possess saddle shape
- Present in b/w metacarpal of thumb and carpals.

Gliding Joint

- Monoaxial joint, articulating bones slide over each other.
- Present b/w radio-ulna and carpals, b/w sternum and clavicle.

DISORDERS OF BONES, MUSCLES AND JOINTS

1. Arthritis (Arthro- joint ; itis -inflammation)
   Pain & stiffness in joints.
   Main types
   - Osteoarthritis
   - Rheumatoid arthritis (autoimmune disorder)

2. Gout
   Inherited disorder of purine metabolism
   Deposition of uric acid crystals (sodium urate) in synovial joints.
   Restricting protein rich diet improves symptoms.

3. Osteoporosis
   Reduction in bone tissue mass ; excessive resorption of bones.
   Mostly occurs in post menopausal women & aged men.
   Major cause- hormonal imbalance - calcitonin & parathormone.
   - estrogen.

4. Myasthenia Gravis
   Weakening and paralysis of skeletal muscles.
   Autoimmune disorder - antibodies destroy Ach receptors.

5. Tetany
   Muscle cramps, rapid spasms, inability to relax between contractions.
   Caused due to hypocalcemia (low Ca^{2+} levels)
   Can be treated with calcium supplements

NEET SYNAPSE

Tetanus- Bacterial infection (Clostridium tetani)-causes full body nerve stimulation. It requires emergency treatment.

6. Muscular Dystrophy
   Genetic disorder - lack of protein dystrophin
   Progressive degeneration & weakness of skeletal muscles.

18. Neural Control and Coordination

NEURAL OR NERVOUS SYSTEM

- Specialised excitable tissue ; can perceive and respond to stimuli.
- Basic unit - neuron (nerve cell)
- Lower invertebrates possess simplest nervous system.
- True neuron first appeared in coelenterates eg. Hydra (nerve net)
- Insects have well developed neural system
- Human brain has about 10^{11} neurons.

HUMAN NERVOUS SYSTEM

Nervous System
- CNS
- PNS
  - Somatic Nervous System
  - Autonomic Nervous System
    - Sympathetic Nervous System
    - Parasympathetic Nervous System

Central Nervous System

- Present in central axis of body
- Comprises brain & spinal cord

Peripheral Nervous System

- Consists of nerves & ganglion originating from brain & spinal cord.
- Connects CNS with the body
- Consists of cranial nerves (12 pairs) & spinal nerves (31 pairs)
- Nerve fibres can be
  - Afferent (sensory) - Bring impulses from organs to CNS
  - Efferent (motor) - Take impulses from CNS to organs.

Somatic Nervous System

- Relays impulses from CNS to skeletal muscles & voluntary organs.

Autonomic Nervous System

- Relays impulses from CNS to involuntary organs & smooth muscles.

Sympathetic Nervous System

- Responds to emergency or stressful situations - fight / flight.

Parasympathetic Nervous System

- Balances the actions of sympathetic Nervous System.

Eg. Symp - ↑ Heart rate ; Parasympathetic - ↓ Heart rate.
It promotes rest & digest functions.

Visceral Nervous system

Part of PNS– comprises nerves, ganglia & plexuses.
They supply the viscera (internal organs of body)

Nervous tissue contains – Neuron & Neuroglial cells.

NEURON

- Structural and functional unit of nervous system.
- It consists of–
  Cell body / Cyton / Perikaryon / Soma
- contains nucleus & cytoplasm
- Nucleus has distinct nucleolus
- Neuroplasm contains Nissl's granules

NEET SYNAPSE
Nissl's granules are modified RER and carry out protein synthesis

- Other organelles like mitochondria,
- Golgi bodies etc. are also present.

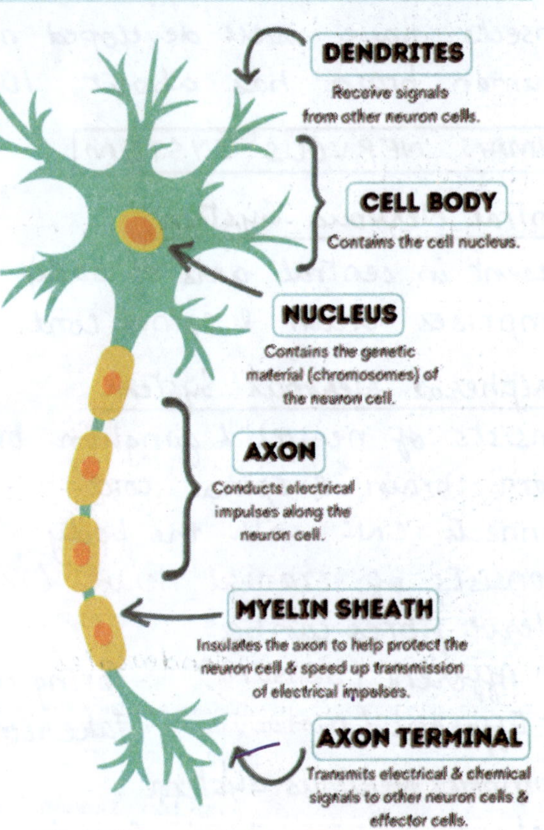

Dendrites – afferent processes

- Outgrowths from cyton.
- Conduct impulses towards cyton
  Contains Nissl's granules

Axon – efferent process

- Single, long cylindrical projection
- Axon hillock – part of cyton where axon arises.
- Telodendria – branched ends of axon
- Axoplasm – cytoplasm of axon
- Axolemma – cell membrane of axon
- Myelin sheath – insulating layer around axon (medullated neurons)
  – neurons without myelin sheath (non-medullated neurons)
- Schwann cells – form myelin sheath in CNS by wrapping around axon.
- Nodes of Ranvier – spaces where myelin sheath is absent.
  – electrical conduction takes place here.

Neurilemma – present around myelin sheath of axons.

Non medullated neurons also possess schwann cells but they do not wrap around to form myelin sheath.

TYPES OF NEURONS

Apolar	Unipolar	Pseudounipolar	Bipolar	Multipolar
◆ lack dendrite or axon. ◆ Nerve impulses radiate in all directions ◆ Present in Hydra, they form nerve net	◆ Single nerve process extends from cell body ◆ Present in invertebrates (insects) & embryonic life of humans	◆ Cell body gives out one extension, which splits into two, one behaves as axon, one as dendrite. ◆ Present in dorsal root ganglion of spinal cord.	◆ One axon, one dendrite distinctly arise from cell body. ◆ Present in retina of eye, olfactory epithelium	◆ One axon, multiple dendrites arise from cell body. ◆ Most common. Present in human brain. Cerebral cortex

Sensory / Afferent Neurons	Motor / Efferent Neurons	Interneurons
◆ Connect receptor cells to CNS ◆ Exteroreceptors - present on skin (cutaneous sense organs) ◆ Interoreceptors - present in muscles, ligaments, tendons, bone joints etc.	◆ Connect CNS to the effectors (muscles & glands). ◆ They conduct motor impulses.	◆ Occur only in CNS ◆ Connect two or more neurone for distant transmission of impulses. ◆ Can adjust with afferent as well as efferent systems.

NEUROGLIAL CELLS

Astrocytes	Oligodendrocytes	Microglia	Schwann cells	Ependymal cells
◆ Most abundant ◆ Form BBB - blood brain barrier ◆ Provide repair mechanism.	◆ Have fewer processes. ◆ Oligo - few ◆ Form myelin sheath in CNS.	◆ Mesodermal origin. ◆ Specialised macrophages Scavengers	◆ Form myelin sheath in PNS. ◆ Provide insulation.	◆ Secrete cerebro spinal fluid in CNS. ◆ Line the ventricles of brain.

PHYSIOLOGY OF NERVE IMPULSE CONDUCTION

- **Stimulus** - any disturbance in the surroundings to which a response is generated in the body
- **Impulse** - sum of mechanical, chemical & electrical disturbances generated in the body in response to a stimulus.
- **Nerve fibres** - axons of neurons make up nerve fibres.

NEET SYNAPSE

Impulse conduction through nerve fibres is an electrochemical process. Electrical gradients are created due to ionic changes (chemical part).

MEMBRANE POTENTIALS

- Resting potential - potential at which axon is at rest
  - it is −70 mV
- Action potential - potential when conduction of impulse takes place.
- ECF - large amount of Na^+ - positively charged
- ICF - K^+ & negatively charged proteins → negatively charged.

ACTION POTENTIAL

- **At rest** - Resting potential | Polarised Stage

  Membrane is impermeable to
  - Na^+ (ECF)
  - negatively charged proteins (ICF)

  It is freely permeable of K^+ → diffuse out (efflux of K^+)

  This leads to development of ionic gradient across axolemma.

  $Na^+ - K^+$ pump - maintains electrical gradient across membrane

  It transports 3 Na^+ outwards (from ICF to ECF)
  2 K^+ inwards (from ECF to ICF)

  Resting Membrane Potential
  - Postive outside (ECF);
  - negative inside (ICF / axoplasm)

NEET SYNAPSE

Diffusion of ions across membrane occurs through 'leaky channels'

Memory trick

NOKIA
Na^+ Outside K^+ Inside

RMP = −70 mV

- **Depolarisation stage**

Stimulus arrives at the axolemma,

↓

Causes reduction in potential difference across the membrane

↓

Voltage gated Na^+ channels open

↓

Sudden influx of Na^+
(ICF becomes positively charged (+ve)) } - reversal of polarity
(ECF becomes negatively charged (−ve)) }

↓

Action potential is generated

↓

Depolarisation spreads along the length of axon initiating more action potentials.

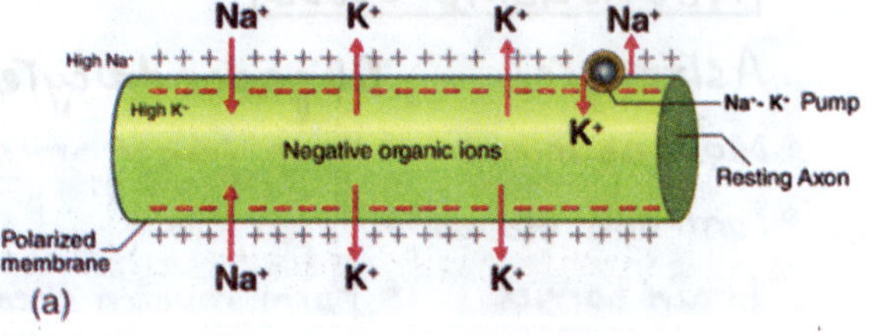

(a)

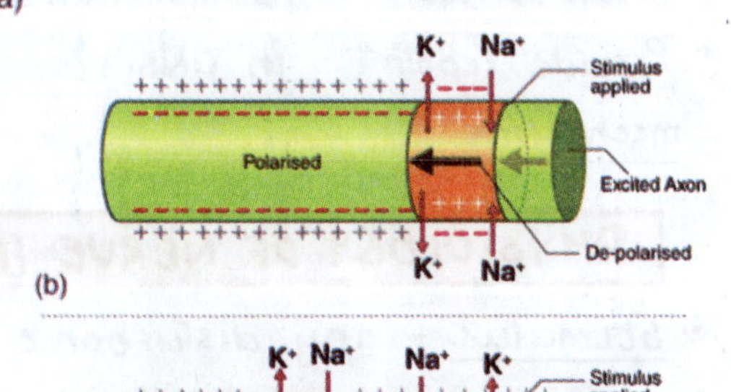

(b)

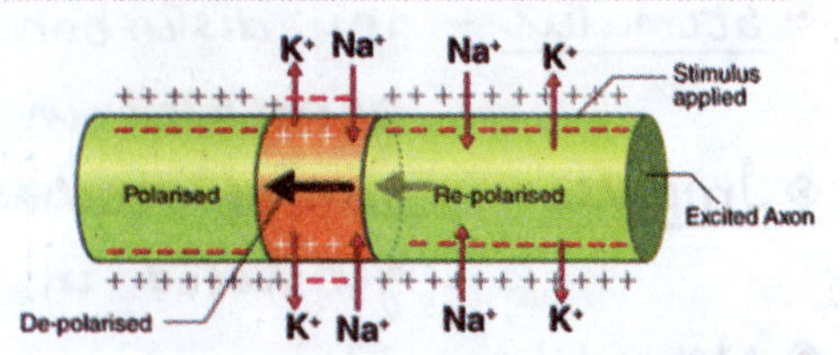

- **Repolarisation Stage**
  Rapid efflux of K^+ ions due to opening of voltage gated K^+ channels
  It establishes polarised state.

NEET SYNAPSE
Saltatory Conduction - When conduction occurs from one Node of Ranvier to another. Also called Jumping conduction.

SYNAPSE

- Junction of two neurons; transmission of impulse takes place here.

TYPES OF SYNAPSES

Electrical	Chemical
Transmission occurs through gap junctions.	Transmission occurs through synaptic cleft
Faster conduction	Slow conduction
Rare in humans	Common in humans
Neurotransmitters are not involved	Neurotransmitters are involved in transmission. Eg. Acetylcholine (Ach)
Two way transmission possible	Two way transmission does not occur.
Pre & Post synaptic membranes are in very close proximity	

- **Chemical Synapse**

Action potential arrives at axon terminal
↓
Depolarisation causes voltage gated Ca^{2+} channels to open
↓
Ca^{2+} triggers fusion of Ach vesicles to pre synaptic membrane
↓
Ach released in synaptic cleft
↓
Ach binds to its receptors on post synaptic membrane.
↓
Depolarisation of post synaptic neuron occurs
↓
Action potential is generated in post synaptic neuron.

SYNAPTIC DELAY – Release of Ach and binding delays the process of transmission responsible for slow conduction

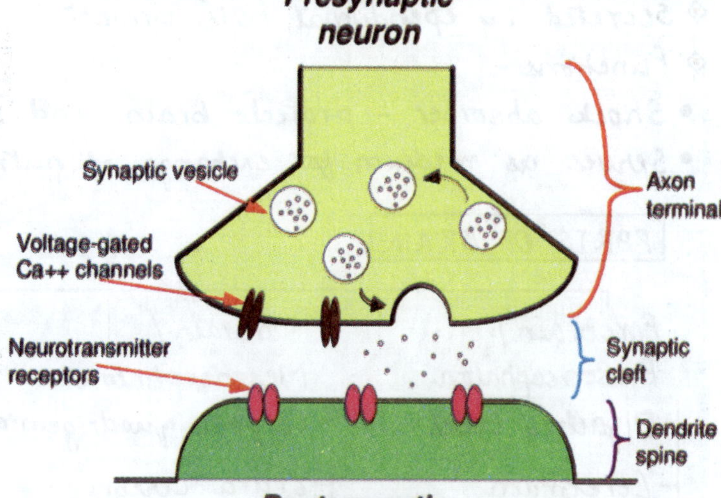

Ach is broken down and components are taken back by pre synaptic neuron. Ach is recycled.

CENTRAL NERVOUS SYSTEM

- Site of processing information & controlling activities.
- It includes brain & spinal cord.

BRAIN

- Command and control centre of the body.
- Protected by bony skull.
- B/w the skull & brain, membranous coverings called meninges are present.

MENINGES

- Made up of connective tissue ; 3 in number.

- Space between skull and dura mater is called epidural space.

1. Dura mater - outermost
   - thick, tough, made of collagen fibres

- Space between dura & arachnoid is called subdural space

2. Arachnoid mater - soft, non vascularised, contains CSF (cerebro spinal fluid)
   - appear as 'spider web'.

- Space between arachnoid & piamater is called sub arachnoid space.

3. Pia mater - very soft, highly vascularised
   - directly in contact with surface of brain.

CEREBROSPINAL FLUID

- Colourless, slightly alkaline fluid
- Secreted by ependymal cells present in choroid plexus in ventricles of brain.
- Functions -
  - Shock absorber - protects brain and spinal cord
  - Serves as medium for exchange of nutrients and waste products.

PARTS OF BRAIN

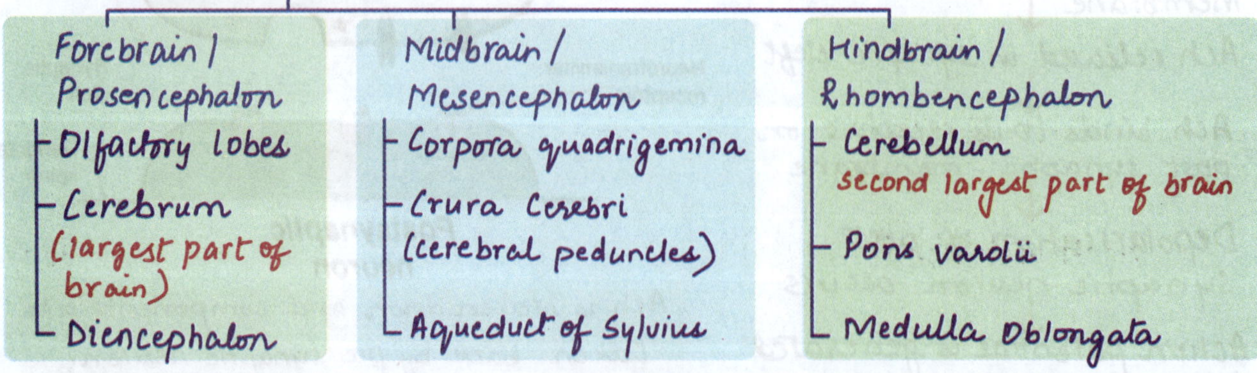

FOREBRAIN

1. Olfactory lobe – functionally related to smell.

- Paired ; differentiated into [olfactory bulb, olfactory tract] } send impulses to olfactory area present in temporal lobe.

2. Cerebrum

- Divided into right and left cerebral hemispheres.
- Corpus callosum – horizontal tract of nerve fibres connecting the cerebral hemispheres.
  – characteristic feature of mammals
- Sulci & gyri – folds of surface of cerebral hemispheres
  sulci – clefts or depressions
  gyri – ridges or elevations
- Each cerebral hemisphere is divided into 4 lobes

Frontal lobe – contains prefrontal area, premotor area & motor area.

- centre of knowledge, wisdom, logic, intelligence, reasoning, creativity.
- Motor area controls voluntary motor activities. Also contains –
- Broca's area – motor speech area
  ↳ translates thoughts into speech
- Pre motor area – planning & organising actions.
- Prefrontal / association area – establishes coordination b/w sensation & movements. Also responsible for memory & communication.

lobes of cerebral hemisphere

Parietal lobe – centre for perception of pain, pressure, taste, touch and temperature – general sensory perception.

Temporal lobe – present close to ear. It contains –

- Olfactory association area – smell interpretation
- Auditory association area – hearing interpretation
- Wernicke's area – sensory speech area (understanding spoken words)

Occipetal lobe – contains visual association area – for visual interpretation

NEET SYNAPSE – Association areas are neither sensory nor motor. They are responsible for intersensory associations, memory & communication.

General Structure of Cerebrum

- Cortex and Medulla
  - Cortex- outer portion of cerebrum, forms about 80% of brain mass
  - Medulla- inner portion of cerebrum.
- Grey matter and white matter
  - Cortex of cerebrum appears grey in colour due to concentration of cell bodies, dendrites & axon terminals of non myelinated neurone
  - Medulla of cerebrum appears white in colour due to concentration of cell bodies, dendrites & axon terminals of myelinated neurons.
- Basal nuclei / basal ganglia
  - Scattered masses of grey matter bulging into white matter.
  - They control and regulate motor activities.
- Limbic system (emotional brain)
  - It surrounds corpus callosum and thalamus.

  Its main components are

  Hippocampus - resembles sea horse.
  - converts short term memory into long term memory.
  - its normal functioning requires acetylcholine.

  Amygdala - almond shaped
  - associated with emotions, jealousy, rage

  Septal nuclei - associated with sexual arousal

  Cingulate gyrus- associated with emotional pain.
  Its activity increases in jealousy.

NEET SYNAPSE
Deficiency of Acetylcholine is associated with Alzheimer's disease

3. Diencephalon

It consists of

NEET SYNAPSE
Hypothalamus is also a part of limbic system

- **Thalamus** - mass of grey matter, lies under each cerebral hemisphere.
  - called as relay centre - centre for sensory & motor signalling.
  - All sensory inputs from hindbrain pass through it.
- **Hypothalamus**- contains neurosecretory cells- secrete hormones
  - contains hunger, satiety & thirst centres
  - maintains homeostasis & osmoregulation
  - Thermostat - maintains body temperature.
- **Epithalamus** - Associated with pineal gland.
  - Forms anterior choroid plexus - exchanges chemicals b/w CSF & blood

MIDBRAIN

Located between hypothalamus (forebrain) & pons (hindbrain)

- **Corpora quadrigemina**
  4 round bodies
  - superior colliculi (2) - sight
  - inferior colliculi (2) - hearing
- **Crura cerebri**
  Thick nerve bands that criss cross and connect forebrain & hindbrain
- **Cerebral aqueduct / Duct of Sylvius**

Lateral ventricles (Forebrain)
↓ Foramen of Monro
Third ventricle (Mid brain)
↓ cerebral aqueduct
Fourth ventricle (Hindbrain)

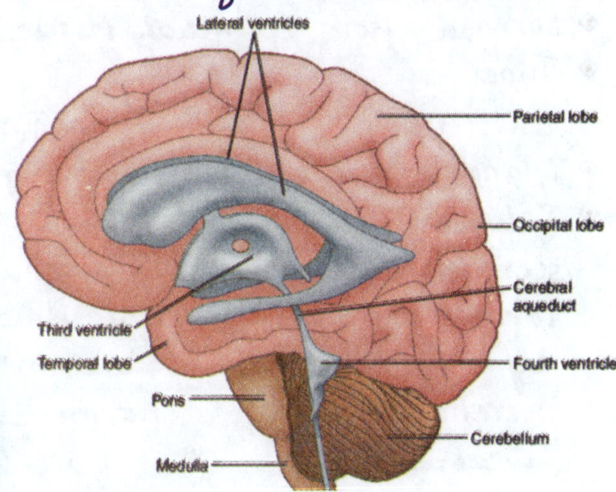

> **NEET SYNAPSE**
> Parkinson's disease – deficiency of dopamine due to loss of secretory activity of substantia nigra (source of dopamine)

HINDBRAIN

- **Cerebellum**
  - Highly convoluted surface to accomodate more neurons
  - Also called small brain or little cerebrum.
  - Internal structure looks like highly branched tree (Arbor vitae)
  - Cerebellum is divided into 2 cerebellar hemispheres
  - They are attached by vermis (worm like)
  - Cerebellar cortex - white matter
  - Cerebellar medulla - grey matter
  - It's main function is to maintain posture & balance
  - It also controls fine motor activities of the body.
- **Pons varolii**
  - Serves as link between cerebral cortex & cerebellum.
  - It controls breathing through Pneumotaxic centre
- **Medulla Oblongata**
  - Last part of hind brain - connected to spinal cord.
  - Controls involuntary mechanisms like respiration, cardiovascular reflexes, gastric secretions etc.

19. Chemical Coordination and Integration

- Endocrine System- network of glands that produces & releases hormones.

GLANDS

- Formed from epithelial tissue.
- Types

Exocrine	Endocrine	Heterocrine
• Glands with ducts • Release their secretion to the target organ by a duct. • Secretion can be sweat, sebum, saliva, milk etc.	• Ductless glands • Release their secretions in surrounding interstitial fluid • Secretions are called hormones. • They are transported by blood.	• Contain both tissues- exocrine + endocrine • Secrete hormone as well as exocrine secretion. • Eg. Pancreas, gonads

HORMONES

- Non nutrient chemicals - do not provide nutrition
- Act as intercellular messengers - communication method b/w cells.
- Secreted in minute quantities - usually nanograms.
- Released from one part of body and act on another (Target organ)
- Can also be produced by organs other than endocrine glands; eg GIT, kidneys etc.

- **TYPES OF HORMONES**

1. Peptide /Protein hormones - all pituitary hormones, PTH, all pancreatic hormones, hCG & relaxin
2. Iodothyronine - Thyroxine secreted from thyroid gland.
3. Steroids - derived from cholesterol. eg - sex hormones, hormones of adrenal cortex
4. Amines - amino acid derivative - tyrosine, adrenaline, serotonin etc

HUMAN ENDOCRINE SYSTEM

HYPOTHALAMUS

- Link between nervous & endocrine system.
- It is a part of brain with neurosecretory cells.
- It releases hormones that are associated with pituitary gland.
- It is connected to anterior pituitary by hypothalamo-hypophyseal portal circulation.
- It is connected to posterior pituitary by nerve endings.
- It releases two types of hormones
  - Tropic hormones (Releasing)
  - Inhibitory hormones

Eg. Somatotropin - Growth hormone - Releasing Hormones (RH) (GHRH)

Somatostatin - inhibits the release of growth hormone from pituitary. (GHIH) (IH)

HYPOTHALAMIC HORMONES AND THEIR TARGET ORGANS

Hypothalamus	Anterior Pituitary	Target Organ
• Thyrotropin RH (TRH)	• Thyroid Stimulating Hormone (TSH)	• Thyroid gland (Thyroxine T_3, T_4)
• Adrenocorticotropin RH (ACTH-RH)	• Adrenocorticotropic Hormone (ACTH)	• Adrenal cortex (Cortisol)
• Gonadotropin RH (GnRH)	• Luteinizing hormone (LH) • Follicle Stimulating Hormone (FSH)	• Testes, ovaries → Testosterone, Progesterone, Estrogen
• Growth Hormone RH (Somatotropin)	• Growth Hormone (GH)	• Most body organs.
• Growth Hormon IH (Somatostatin)	• Inhibits secretion of GH.	• Most body organs.
• Prolactin RH (PRH)	• Prolactin	• Mammary glands (causes milk formation)
• Prolactin IH (PIH)	• Inhibits Prolactin secretion	
• Melanocyte Stimulating H. (MSH-RH)	• Melanocyte Stimulating Hormone (MSH)	• Melanocytes (skin pigment cells)

HYPOTHALAMO – HYPOPHYSEAL AXIS

Neurosecretory cells of hypothalamus synthesise hormones

Transport through portal circulation → **Anterior Pituitary** → Responds to the hypothalamic hormones by secreting other hormones.

Transport through axons of neurons → **Posterior Pituitary** → Releases the hypothalamic hormones as it is when need arises.

PITUITARY GLAND

- Lodged in cavity called sella turcica present in sphenoid bone.
- Parts
  - Pars distalis / Anterior lobe } Adenohypophysis
  - Pars intermedia / Middle lobe } Adenohypophysis
  - Pars nervosa / Posterior lobe } Neurohypophysis.

Adenohypophysis

Hormones of Pars Distalis

i) Growth Hormone (GH)

- Anabolic hormone
- Stimulates protein synthesis
- Disorders caused by abnormal secretion of GH

Hyposecretion

Dwarfism

- People have short stature. Occurs before puberty

NEET SYNAPSE

Hypersecretion of GH after epiphyseal plate closure does not cause further increase in height.

Hypersecretion

Gigantism

- before puberty
- excessive growth of long bones

Acromegaly

- after puberty
- Enlarged hands, feet, jaws, nose, ears etc

ii) Gonadotropic Hormones

FSH –

In females

- growth of ovarian follicles

In males

- development of seminiferous tubules
- spermatogenesis

LH

In females

- Responsible for ovulation

In males

- Stimulates leydig cells to release testosterone

iii) Prolactin
- Stimulates mammary glands for milk production. Also called lactogenic hormone

(iv) Adrenocorticotropic Hormone
- Stimulates synthesis & secretion of glucocorticoids & sex corticoids from adrenal cortex.

v) Thyroid Stimulating Hormone
- Stimulates synthesis & secretion of thyroxine from thyroid gland.
- Promotes growth.

Hormones of Pars Intermedia

Melanocyte Stimulating Hormone (MSH)
- Stimulates synthesis and dispersal of melanin in skin.

Melanogenesis
formation of melanin - caused by MSH

Neurohypophysis

- Posterior lobe of Pituitary gland - Pars Nervosa

i) Oxytocin
- Acts on smooth muscles of uterus & mammary glands
- Uterus - initiates vigorous contractions to induce childbirth
  Also called birth hormone.
- Mammary glands - causes ejection of milk by contraction of smooth muscles of mammary glands.

ii) Vasopressin /ADH (AntiDiuretic Hormone)
- Causes contraction of blood vessels
  ↳ Increases blood pressure
- Aids in reabsorption of water in nephrons.
  ↳ Results in concentrated urine

Disorder caused by abnormal ADH secretion -
- Diabetes Insipidus - deficiency of ADH ⟶ less reabsorption of water from nephrons ⟶ excretion of excess water (dilute urine ↓ hypotonic) ⟶ causes excessive thirst

NEET SYNAPSE
Diabetes Insipidus
Polyuria - excessive urination
Polydipsia - excessive thirst

PINEAL GLAND

- Unpaired, attached to epithalamus.
- Secretes melatonin
  - maintains sleep-wake cycle (circadian rhythm)
  - has antagonistic action to MSH
  - influences metabolism, skin pigmentation, menstrual cycle and defense capability.

THYMUS

- Located between lungs ; behind sternum & ventral to aorta.
- Secretes peptide hormone thymosin
- Thymosin - promotes proliferation & maturation of T-lymphocytes, thus helps in cell mediated immunity
  - promotes antibody production, thus helps in humoral immunity.
- Thymus starts degenerating after puberty ; ∴ old people have weaker immune systems.

THYROID GLAND

- Situated in neck ; between trachea & larynx.
- Bilobed - 2 lobes connected by narrow isthmus.
- Contains
  - Follicles - functional units. Thyroglobulin is present in each follicle ; it forms thyroxine
  - Stroma - ground substance.
- Main hormones
  - T_3 - Triiodothyronine
  - T_4 - Tetraiodothyronine - Thyroxine (T_4)
- Specialised cells secrete TCT (Thyrocalcitonin)

FUNCTIONS OF THYROID HORMONE

- Control metabolism of carbs, fats, proteins.
- Regulate BMR (Basal Metabolic Rate)
- Help in maintaining water & electrolytes.
- Support erythropoiesis (formation of RBC's)

NEET SYNAPSE
- T_3 is the active form
- T_4 is abundant.
- T_4 is converted to T_3 by deiodination
- T_4 acts like a reservoir of T_3.

DISORDERS OF THYROID HORMONES

Hypersecretion

Exophthalmic goitre (Grave's disease)
- protrusion of eyeballs, ↑ BMR, weight loss.
- Thyroid gland enlarges. Swelling in the neck region.

NEET SYNAPSE
Hashimoto's disease - autoimmune disorder of thyroid gland.

Hyposecretion

Cretinism - present in children
- Stunted growth, mental retardation, low IQ, deaf-mutism etc.

Myxoedema - occurs in adults

Simple goitre - occurs due to deficiency of iodine in diet.
- Endemic goitre - when people of a particular area show goitre.

PARATHYROID GLAND

- Four in number. Located posterolaterally on thyroid gland.
- Secretes parathormone (PTH)
- Action - hypercalcemic & hypophosphatemic

Regulation of Blood Calcium levels

2 Antagonistic Hormones regulate blood Ca^{2+} levels.
PTH & TCT

Blood Ca ↑

- TCT is released from thyroid
- Reduces Blood Ca level by depositing Ca^{2+} on bone.
- Calcitonin makes bones strong.
- Calcitonin - Hypocalcemic

Blood Ca ↓

PTH - acts on

- Gut
  - ↑ Ca^{2+} absorption from diet
- Kidneys
  - ↑ Ca^{2+} reabsorption from renal tubules.
- Bones
  - ↑ resorption of bones to release Ca^{2+} in blood

ADRENAL GLAND

- Present on upper side of kidney. [adjacent to renal (kidney)]
- Internally, gland is differentiated into
  - Cortex
  - Medulla

Adrenal Cortex - All hormones are steroid hormones.

- Has 3 layers
  - Zona Glomerulosa (outermost) - secretes mineralocorticoids
  - Zona Fasciculata (middle) - secretes glucocorticoids
  - Zona Reticularis (innermost) - secretes sex corticoids
- Mineralocorticoids ⟶ maintain body fluid volume, osmotic pressure & blood pressure.
  - Aldosterone is most common.
    - ↳ Regulates electrolyte balance in the body.
    - ↳ When Na^+ falls ⟶ more aldosterone is secreted ⟶ causes reabsorption of Na^+
    - ↳ Promotes excretion of K^+ & Phosphate ions.
  - Deficiency of aldosterone causes Addison's disease
    - ↳ Disruption of carbohydrate metabolism.
    - ↳ Causes weakness & fatigue.

NEET SYNAPSE

Secretion of aldosterone is influenced by blood Na^+ levels. RAAS mechanism stimulates it. It is not controlled by ACTH.

◆ Glucocorticoids

- They include cortisol, cortisone & corticosterone.
- Cortisol is the main glucocorticoid (95%)
- Their secretion is controlled by ACTH (Ant. Pituitary)
- Functions
  - Gluconeogenesis - synthesis of glucose from non carbohydrate sources.
  - Glycolysis - breakdown of glycogen to release glucose.
  - Proteolysis - breakdown of proteins
  - Lipolysis - breakdown of lipids
  - Inhibits cellular uptake & utilisation of amino acids
    ↳ converts them into carbohydrates by deamination
  - Anti-inflammatory response - suppresses immune system.
  - Stimulates RBC production
  - Maintains cardiovascular system and kidney functions.

◆ Sex corticoids

- Androgenic steroids secreted by zona reticulosa
- They play a role in growth of axial, pubic and facial hair during puberty.
- Excessive secretion of sex corticoids causes virilism.

ADRENAL MEDULLA

◆ Contains special cells called chromaffin cells.

◆ Chromaffin cells are modified postganglionic cells of sympathetic nervous system.

Hormones of Adrenal Medulla

◆ Adrenaline / Epinephrine

Emergency hormone / hormone of fear, fight and flight

Functions- increases blood pressure, heart rate & energy level.

◆ Nor adrenaline / Nor epinephrine

Together adrenaline & nor adrenaline are called catecholamines.

They are rapidly secreted in blood in response to stress in the body and restores the body to balanced condition.

NEET SYNAPSE

During stressful conditions, adrenaline increases heart rate and cortisol narrows the arteries. Together they force blood to pump harder and faster.

PANCREAS

- Present in abdominal cavity in the curve of duodenum
- Heterocrine gland
  - Exocrine part - produces pancreatic juice.
  - Endocrine part - secretes hormones.

Endocrine part of Pancreas

- Called Islets of Langerhans
- Secrete 3 hormones

Insulin and Glucagon are antagonistic hormones

Insulin	Glucagon	Somatostatin
• Secreted by β-cells • Acts mainly on hepatocytes & adipocytes. • Glycogenesis - formation of glycogen from glucose • Hypoglycemic action ↳ Lowers blood glucose level • Anabolic effects- • Promotes protein & lipid synthesis	• Secreted by α-cells • Acts mainly on hepatocytes. • Glycogenolysis- break-down of glycogen to release glucose. • Hyperglycemic action Raises blood glucose level • Gluconeogenesis - • Breaksdown protein & lipid • to release glucose	• Secreted by δ-cells • Inhibits the secretion of insulin & glucagon. • Contributes to regulation of blood glucose levels. • Reduces gastric secretion. • Inhibits release of other digestive enzymes.

NEET SYNAPSE

- Deficiency of insulin causes diabetes mellitus.
- Insulin reduces ⟶ blood glucose raised ⟶ excess glucose excreted in urine - glycosuria
- Insulin reduces ⟶ cellular uptake of glucose (for respiration) reduces ⟶ cells use fats for producing energy ⟶ causes production ketone bodies ⟶ excess ketone bodies excreted in urine ⟶ Ketonuria

GONADS

- Heterocrine glands
  - Exocrine part - gametes
  - Endocrine part - hormones
- Gonads in males- Testes
- Gonads in females- Ovaries

TESTES

- Paired, present in scrotal sac
- Contain seminiferous tubules & interstitial tissue

OVARIES

- Paired structures, located in abdomen.
- Contain ovarian follicles & stromal tissue
- Mature follicle releases ovum & is converted into corpus luteum

Hormones of Testes

- Leydig cells (present in interstitial tissue) produce androgens.
- Testosterone is the main androgen.
  - ↳ Secretion starts at puberty
  - ↳ Initiates development of secondary sexual characters in males - beard, moustache, body & facial hair, broadening of chest, muscle growth, hoarse voice etc
  - ↳ Stimulate spermatogenesis.
  - ↳ Influences male sexual behaviour.
  - ↳ Promotes protein synthesis & increases muscle mass.

NEET SYNAPSE

Estrogen increases bone turnover i.e. it increases osteoblastic activity.
∴ Post menopausal women in whom estrogen level reduces are at a higher risk of osteoporosis.

Hormones of ovaries

- Follicles present in ovary secrete hormones

(i) Estrogen - Main female sex hormone.
- ↳ secreted by growing follicles
- ↳ influenced by FSH.
- ↳ Initiates development of secondary sexual characters in females -
- ↳ development of mammary glands
- ↳ development of female body pattern - wider hips high pitch voice & regulation of female sexual behaviour.

(ii) Progesterone
- ↳ Secreted by corpus luteum
- ↳ influenced by LH
- ↳ causes temporary changes in endometrium (uterine lining)
- ↳ Supports pregnancy
- ↳ Stimulates formation of alveoli in mammary glands - alveoli store milk in mammary glands.

Estrogen & Parathormone play a significant role in osteoporosis

HORMONES OF HEART, KIDNEY & GIT

HEART

- Secretes ANF Atrial Natriuretic Factor - checks RAAS
- Released during hypertension.
- It decreases blood pressure by causing vasodilation.
- Maintains blood volume

KIDNEY

- Secretes erythropoietin
- Stimulates RBC production.
- Secretes renin
  - Part of RAAS
  - Maintains osmotic balance of body
- Secretes calcitriol
  Promotes Ca^{2+} absorption

GIT

- Gastrin - stimulates release of gastric juice
- Secretin - promotes exocrine pancreas to release HCO_3^- & water
- CCK - stimulates pancreas and gall bladder to release enzymes & bile
- GIP - suppresses gastric secretion & motility.

Secretin was the first hormone to be discovered.

MECHANISM OF HORMONE ACTION

- Hormones bring about their action by binding to receptors.
- Types of receptors -

Membrane bound receptors / Extracellular receptors
- present on cell membrane

Nuclear receptors / Intracellular receptors
- present inside target cells.

Receptors are specific to only one hormone.

Hormone + receptor = hormone receptor complex.

Mechanism of action of Peptide Hormones

- Peptide hormones are lipid insoluble, hence cannot enter the cell directly through cell membrane.

∴ They bind to extracellular receptors

Hormone (first / primary messenger) binds with its receptor
↓
Form hormone - receptor complex
↓
Complex activates adenylate cyclase
↓
Converts ATP ⟶ cAMP (cyclic AMP) - second messenger
↓
Second messenger conveys information to inside of cell.
↓
Activation of enzyme system
↓
Enzymes carry out desired reaction in cell.
(Physiological response)

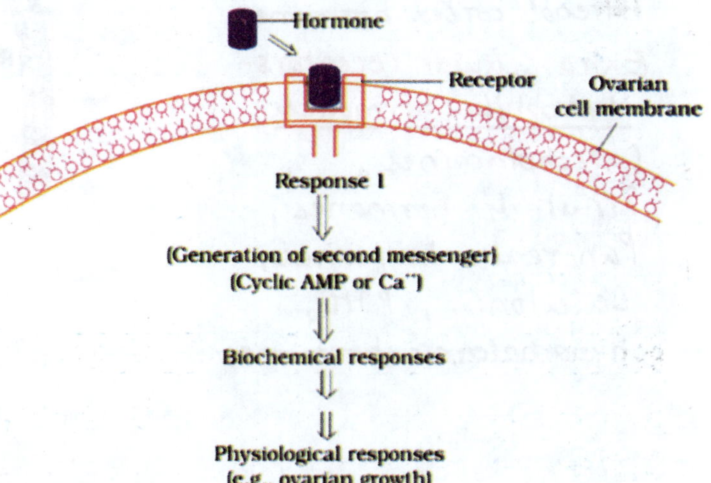

NEET SYNAPSE

cAMP, Ca^{2+} & IP_3 act as second messengers.

IP_3 - Inositol tri PO_4

Mechanism of action of Steroid Hormones

- Steroid hormones are lipid soluble
- ∴ they directly cross cell membrane
- They bind with intracellular receptors /nuclear receptors.

↓

Steroid hormone passes through cell membrane

↓

Binds with receptor present in cytoplasm or on nucleus.

↓

Hormone receptor complex enters nucleus

↓

Binds with DNA, causes gene transcription

↓

Transcription is followed by translation

↓

Protein synthesis is induced

↓

Physiological response takes place.

NEET SYNAPSE

Intracellular receptors - Lipophilic hormones

Thyroid hormone,
Steroid hormone
Adrenal cortex hormones

Extra cellular receptors - Hydrophilic hormones

Catecholamines,
Pituitary hormones,
Pancreatic hormones,
Calcitonin, PTH,
Hypothalamic hormones

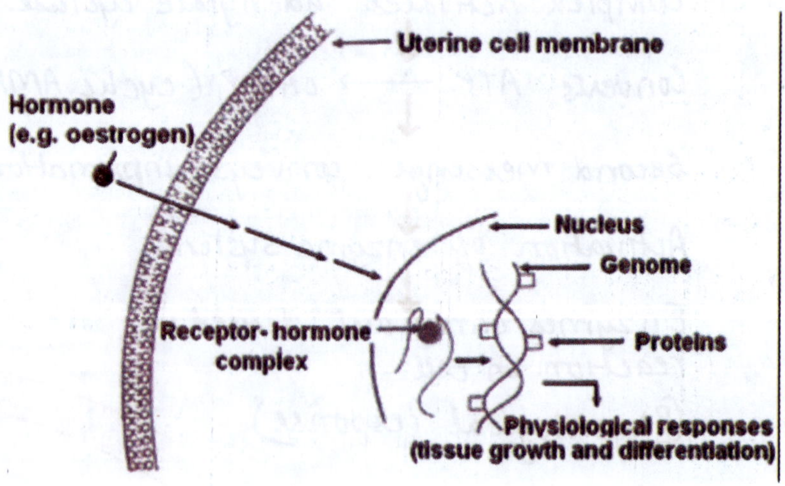

20. Sexual Reproduction in Flowering Plants

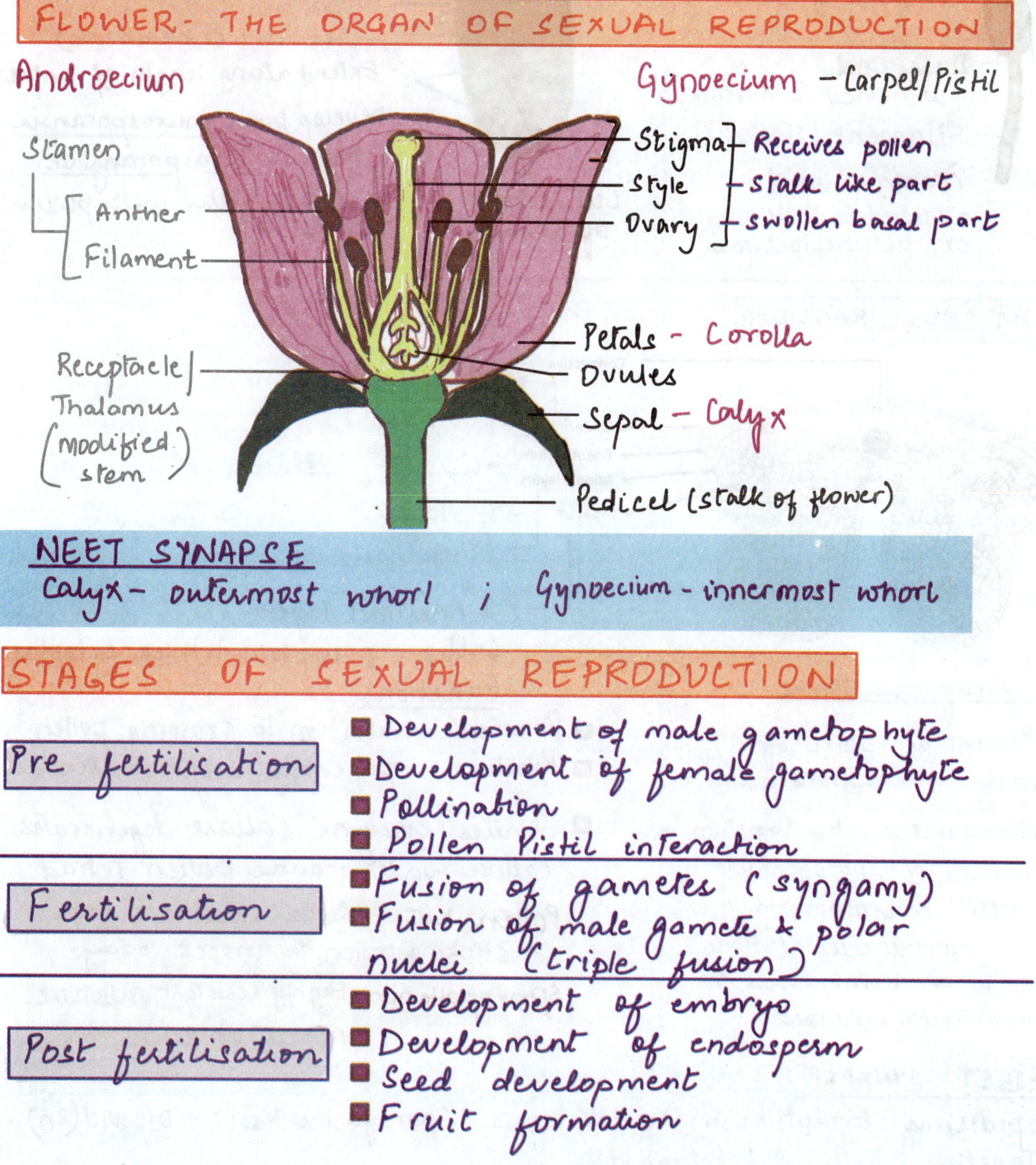

FLOWER- THE ORGAN OF SEXUAL REPRODUCTION

NEET SYNAPSE

Calyx - outermost whorl ; Gynoecium - innermost whorl

STAGES OF SEXUAL REPRODUCTION

Pre fertilisation
- Development of male gametophyte
- Development of female gametophyte
- Pollination
- Pollen Pistil interaction

Fertilisation
- Fusion of gametes (syngamy)
- Fusion of male gamete & polar nuclei (triple fusion)

Post fertilisation
- Development of embryo
- Development of endosperm
- Seed development
- Fruit formation

STAMEN, MICROSPORANGIUM AND POLLEN GRAIN

STAMEN

- Anther (fertile)
- Distal end (attached to anther)
- Filament (stalk like)
- Proximal end (attached to thalamus or petal-epipetalous)

Pollen sacs:
- Extend along length of anther
- Develop from microsporangia
- Anther is tetrasporangiate
- Sacs are filled with pollen grains

MICROSPORANGIUM

- Connective → Sterile tissue
- Epidermis → Outermost; single celled layer
- Endothecium → Inner to epidermis; hygroscopic; helps in dehiscence.
- Middle layers → 2-3 layers; parenchymatous → degenerate when anthers mature
- Tapetum → Innermost layer
  Cells - polyploid + thick cytoplasm
  Functions
  - Provides nutrition to growing pollen
  - Produces pollenkitt & sporopollenin
  - Secretes enzyme-callase degenerates callose wall around pollen tetrad

Pollen kitt - sticky substance helps in sticking pollen to insect body.
Sporopollenin - Highly resistant substance - makes up exine

Sporogenous tissue
- Present in centre of each microsporangium
- Surrounded by tapetum
- Consists of sporogenous cells - microspore/pollen mother cells (PMC)
- Cells are homogenous & compactly arranged

NEET SYNAPSE

Epidermis; Endothecium; middle layers; Sporogenous tissue - Diploid (2n)
Tapetum cells - Polyploid

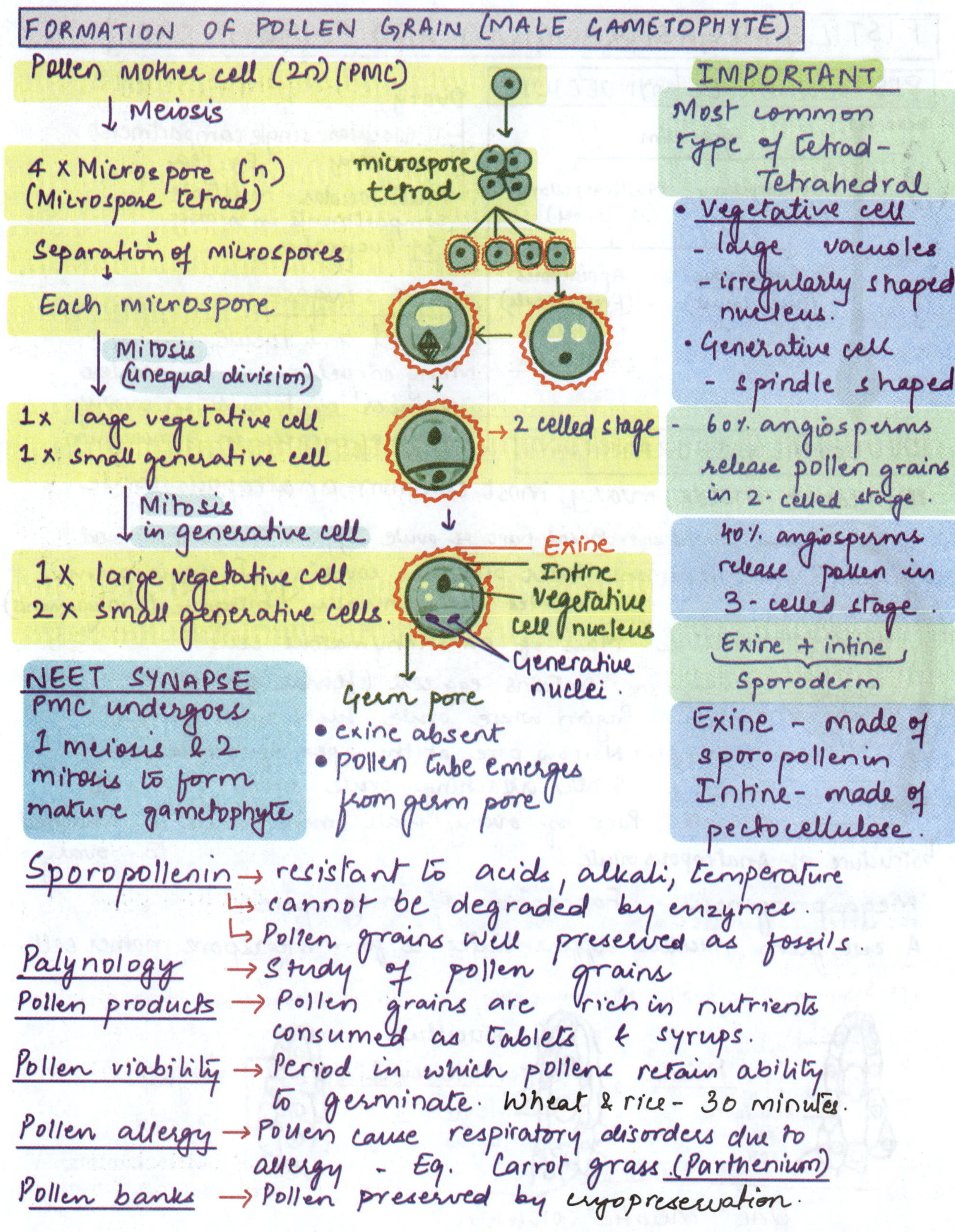
FORMATION OF POLLEN GRAIN (MALE GAMETOPHYTE)
Pollen mother cell (2n) (PMC)
Meiosis
4 x Microspore (n)
(Microspore tetrad)
microspore tetrad
Separation of microspores
Each microspore
Mitosis
(unequal division)
1x large vegetative cell
1 x small generative cell
2 celled stage
Mitosis
in generative cell
1 X large vegetative cell
2 X small generative cells.
Exine
Intine
Vegetative cell nucleus
Generative nuclei.
Germ pore
• exine absent
• pollen tube emerges from germ pore
NEET SYNAPSE
PMC undergoes 1 meiosis & 2 mitosis to form mature gametophyte
IMPORTANT
Most common type of tetrad - Tetrahedral
• Vegetative cell
- large vacuoles
- irregularly shaped nucleus.
• Generative cell
- spindle shaped
60% angiosperms release pollen grains in 2-celled stage.
40% angiosperms release pollen in 3-celled stage.
Exine + intine
Sporoderm
Exine - made of sporopollenin
Intine - made of pectocellulose.
Sporopollenin → resistant to acids, alkali, temperature
↳ cannot be degraded by enzymes.
↳ Pollen grains well preserved as fossils.
Palynology → Study of pollen grains
Pollen products → Pollen grains are rich in nutrients consumed as tablets & syrups.
Pollen viability → Period in which pollens retain ability to germinate. Wheat & rice - 30 minutes.
Pollen allergy → Pollen cause respiratory disorders due to allergy - Eg. Carrot grass (Parthenium)
Pollen banks → Pollen preserved by cryopreservation.

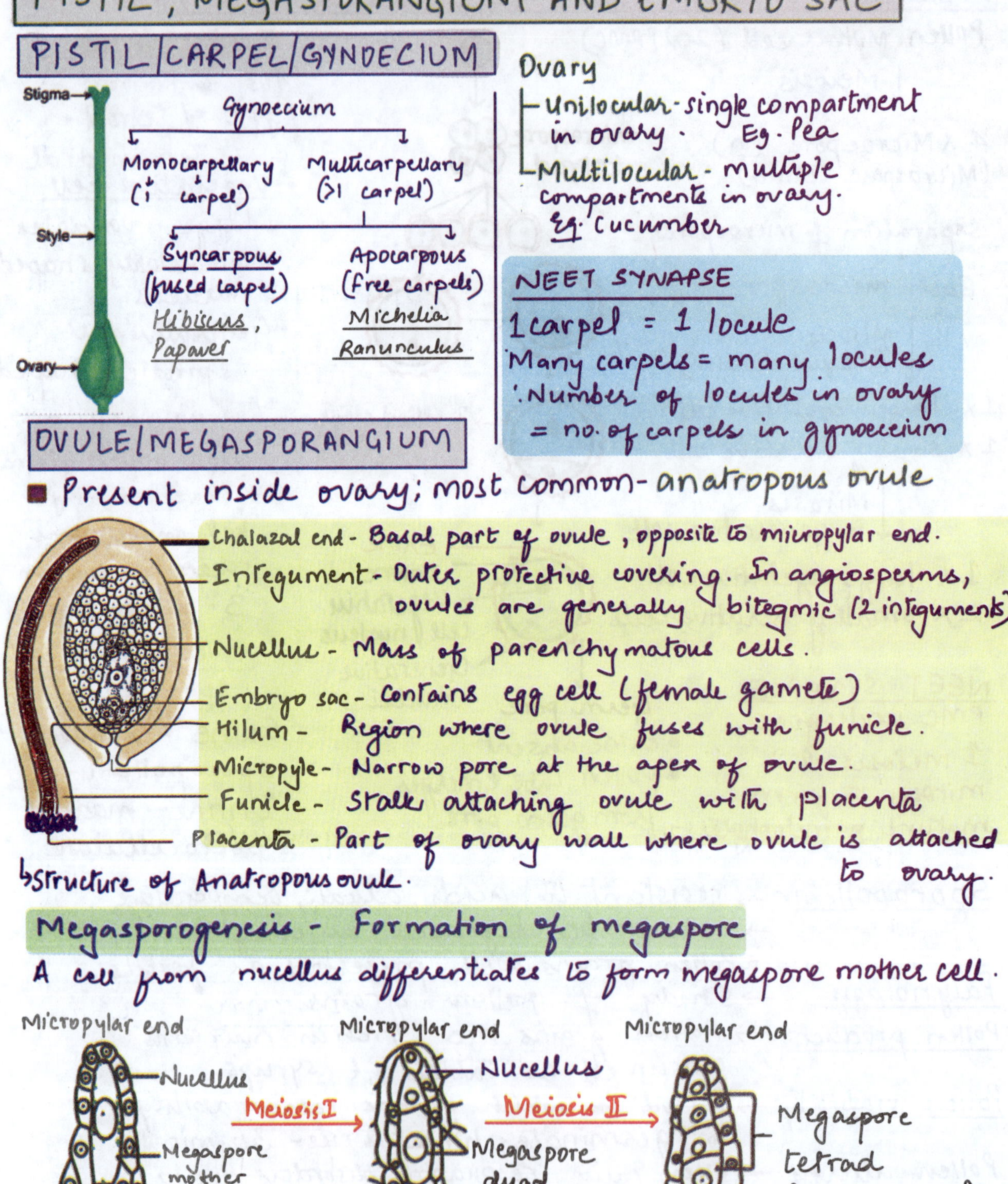

PISTIL, MEGASPORANGIUM AND EMBRYO SAC

PISTIL/CARPEL/GYNOECIUM

Gynoecium
- Monocarpellary (1 carpel)
- Multicarpellary (>1 carpel)
  - Syncarpous (fused carpel) Hibiscus, Papaver
  - Apocarpous (free carpels) Michelia, Ranunculus

Ovary
- Unilocular - single compartment in ovary. Eg. Pea
- Multilocular - multiple compartments in ovary. Eg. Cucumber

NEET SYNAPSE

1 carpel = 1 locule

Many carpels = many locules

∴ Number of locules in ovary = no. of carpels in gynoecium

OVULE/MEGASPORANGIUM

- Present inside ovary; most common - anatropous ovule

Chalazal end - Basal part of ovule, opposite to micropylar end.

Integument - Outer protective covering. In angiosperms, ovules are generally bitegmic (2 integuments)

Nucellus - Mass of parenchymatous cells.

Embryo sac - Contains egg cell (female gamete)

Hilum - Region where ovule fuses with funicle.

Micropyle - Narrow pore at the apex of ovule.

Funicle - Stalk attaching ovule with placenta

Placenta - Part of ovary wall where ovule is attached to ovary.

↳ Structure of Anatropous ovule.

Megasporogenesis - Formation of megaspore

A cell from nucellus differentiates to form megaspore mother cell.

EMBRYO SAC/FEMALE GAMETOPHYTE

Out of 4 megaspores 3 degenerate

Monosporic development

→ Only 1 remains usually at chalazal end – Functional megaspore

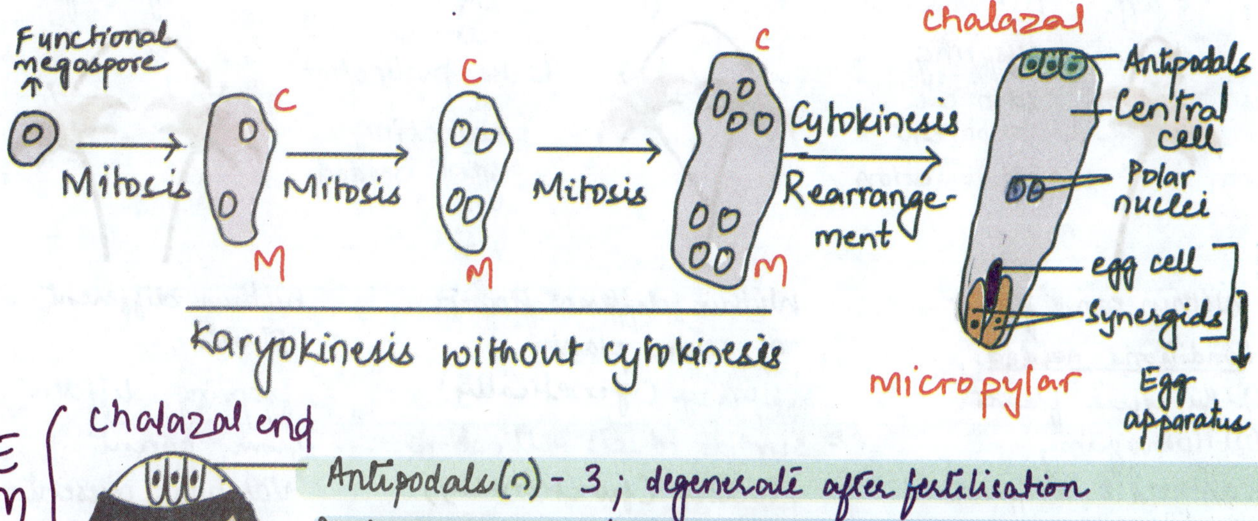

EMBRYO SAC

Chalazal end

- Antipodals (n) – 3 ; degenerate after fertilisation
- Central cell – 1 ; large ; contains 2 polar nuclei (Only diploid cell of embryo sac)
- Polar nuclei (n) – haploid – fuse during fertilisation – n+n = 2n
- Egg cell (n) – female gamete
- Synergids (n) – form filiform apparatus

Egg cell + Synergids = Egg apparatus

- Filiform apparatus – guides pollen tube towards egg cell.

micropylar end

NEET SYNAPSE

Megaspore mother cell

↓ 1 meiosis + 3 mitosis

Female gametophyte / Embryo sac

Polygonum type embryo sac

Embryo sac

7 celled 8 nucleate

	7 celled	8 nucleate
Antipodals	3	3
Synergids	2	2
Egg cell	1	1
Central cell	1	2 (polar nuclei)
Total	7	8

POLLINATION

- Transfer of pollen grains from anther to stigma.
- Male & female gametes in angiosperms are non-motile.

Types of Pollination

Autogamy (self pollination)

- offspring identical to parent
- No variation

Within same flower

Conditions needed

1. Bisexual flower
2. Homogamy - anthers & stigma mature simultaneously

- **Cleistogamous**
  - Closed flower
  - Assured seed set even in the absence of pollinators.
- **Chasmogamous**
  - open flower
  - self pollination as well as cross pollination can take place

Commelina ; Oxalis, Viola — possess cleistogamous as well as chasmogamous flowers.

Geitonogamy

Within different flowers of same plant

offspring (genetically)
- similar to self pollination

process (functionally)
- similar to cross pollination

Ex. Maize

Xenogamy

Within different plants.

- offspring different from parent
- Varitions present

Ex. Papaya

Geitonogamy, Xenogamy → Cross pollination → pollinating agent needed

Allogamy

Includes both geitonogamy & xenogamy

NEET SYNAPSE

Monoecious plant
- Bisexual flowers
- Autogamy can take place.
- Unisexual flowers geitonogamy can take place.

Dioecious plant
- has unisexual flowers
- only xenogamy can occur

AGENCIES OF POLLINATION

ABIOTIC

→ Wind (Anemophily)

Adaptations

- Large number of pollen grains
- Pollen - dry, light weight, very small, non sticky
- Stamens - well exposed
- Stigma - large, feathery, bushy, long
- Flowers - small, inconspicuous colourless, no scent, no nectar. have single ovule in ovary. Numerous flowers arranged in an inflorescence

well exposed stamens

Example - tassels of cob in maize are stamens.

BIOTIC

Pollination by Bats - Chiropterophily
Birds - Ornithophily Insects - Entomophily

Adaptations

- Flowers are showy, colourful, scented & conspicuous
- Small flowers group together to form inflorescence.
  Floral rewards
  → Pollen grains & nectar
- Sticky pollen grains due to presence of pollen kit
- Foul odour - pollination by flies or beetles.
- Some flowers provide safe place to insects to lay eggs

Eg. Amorphophallus
Yucca plant

→ Water - hydrophily

Adaptations of Hydrophily

- Flowers
  - Inconspicuous, small
  - colour, odour, netar absent
  - whorls coated with wax
  - Stigma unwettable; sticky
- Pollen grains -
  - light weight, small, non sticky
  - Possess mucilagenous coating to avoid sinking during transfer.

Eg. Vallisneria (epihydrophily)

- Dioecious
- Female flowers develop under water but at the time of pollination, they reach surface by elongation of stalk.
- Male flowers flow with water current to reach female flowers

- Zostera (hypohydrophily) Pollination takes place under water

- Pollen grains of Zostera are long, ribbon like. They reach stigma passively through water current.

Pollen/Nectar robbers – Insects that feed on nectar/pollen without carrying out pollination.

NEET SYNAPSE
Water hyacinth & water lily are pollinated by wind or insects though they live in aquatic habitat.

Ornithophilous flowers – abundant nectar; edible parts
Chiropterophilous flowers – open at night, conspicuous, colourless, foul smell.

OUTBREEDING DEVICES

- Natural mechanisms of flowers to promote cross pollination.

① Dicliny / Unisexuality	unisexual flowers prevent autogamy but not geitonogamy. Diecy – plant is either male or female. – prevents self pollination.
② Dichogamy	In bisexual flower, male & female parts do not mature at same time. Protoandry – male part develops first. Protogyny – female part develops first
③ Heterostyly	Anther & stigma positioned at different height; so pollen does not land on stigma.
④ Self incompatibility	Genetic barrier – prevents the germination of pollen grains on stigma even when both belong to same plant.
⑤ Herkogamy	Physical barrier present between anther & stigma.

POLLEN PISTIL INTERACTION

Pollen lands on stigma

Compatible pollen

- Pistil allows germination
- Pollen from same flower or same plant or plant of same species

Incompatible pollen

- Pistil does not allow germination
- Pollen tube not formed.

① Germination of pollen on stigma

Pollen grains absorb sugary solution from stigma

↓

Intine expands

↓

Pollen tube emerges from germ pore.

↓

Vegetative cell moves ahead followed by generative nucleus.

- In 2 celled pollen → generative cell first undergoes mitosis during the growth of pollen tube

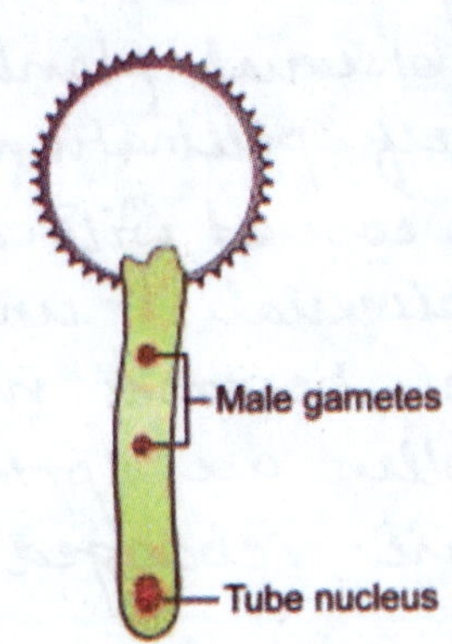

② Entry of pollen tube into ovule

- Porogamy - entry through micropyle
- Chalazogamy - entry through chalaza
- Mesogamy - entry through integuments

③ Entry of pollen tube into embryo sac.

- Guided by filiform apparatus
- Upon entry, one or both synergids start disintegrating

↓

Pollen tube bursts

↓

Releases gametes in embryo sac

DOUBLE FERTILISATION

Concept given by Nawaschin
Fertilisation takes place twice

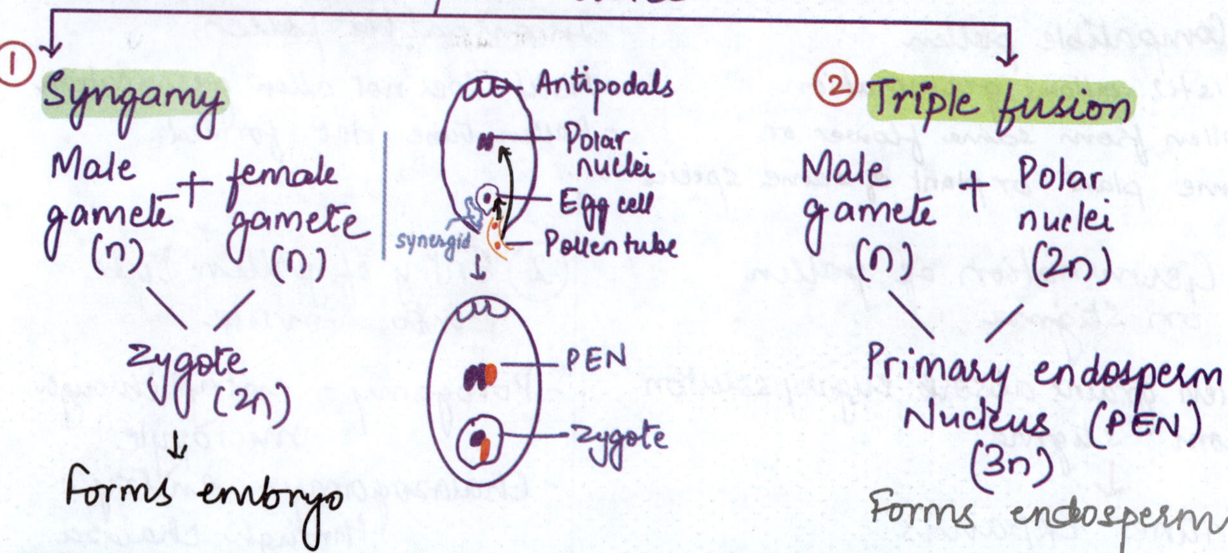

NEET SYNAPSE

Zygote forms first ; endosperm forms later
Endosperm develops first , zygote develops later (to nourish the growing embryo)

ARTIFICIAL HYBRIDISATION

Desired pollen used for pollination.

① Emasculation
- Removal of anthers in immature state.
- Done in bisexual plants
- Prevents self pollination

② Bagging
- Stigma is covered with butter paper
- Done in bisexual & unisexual flowers
- When carpel becomes mature & receptive, desired pollen are sprinkled on stigma
- Flowers are rebagged until fruit is formed.

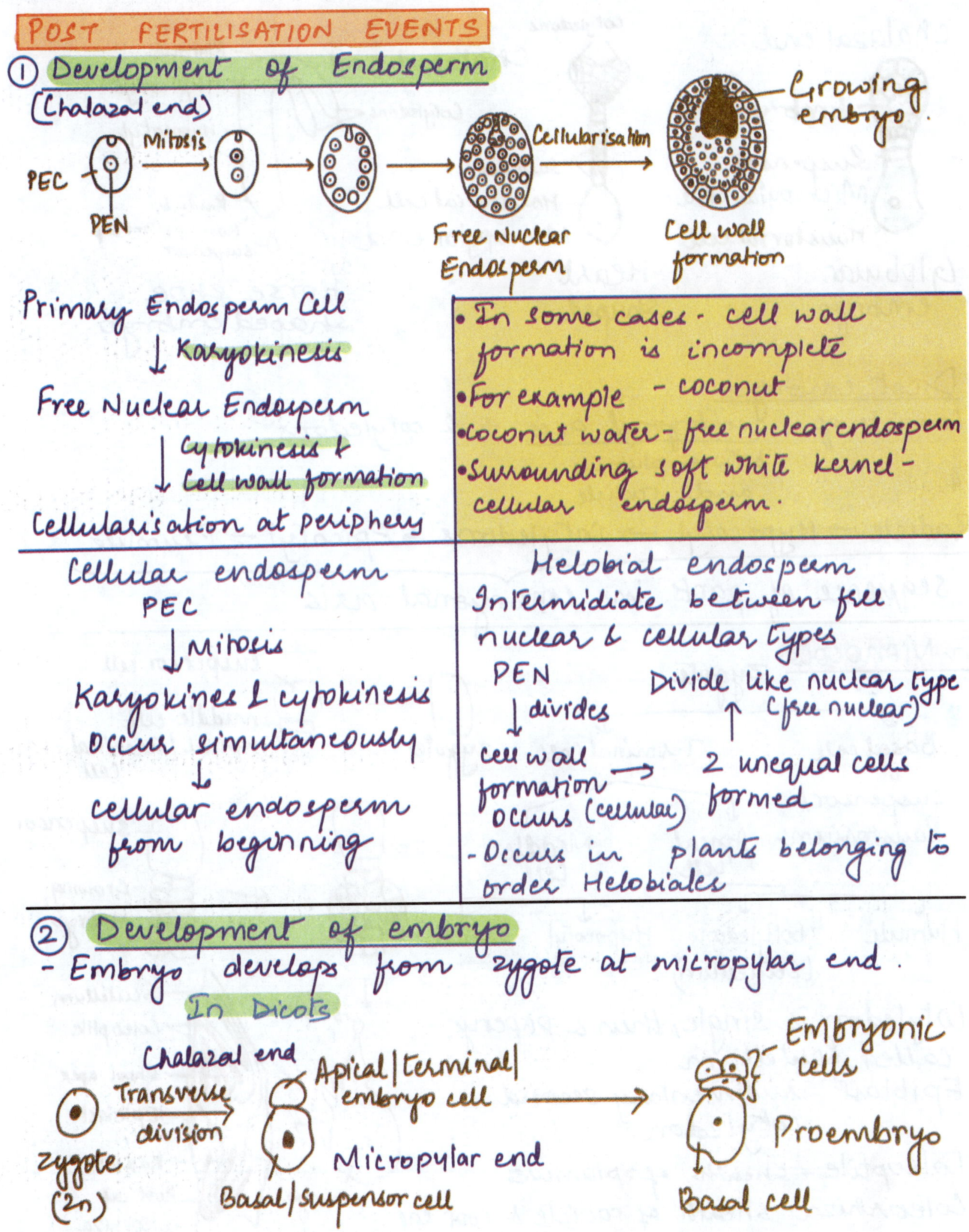

POST FERTILISATION EVENTS

① Development of Endosperm

(Chalazal end)

PEC —Mitosis→ → → Free Nuclear Endosperm —Cellularisation→ Cell wall formation

PEN

Growing embryo.

Primary Endosperm Cell

↓ Karyokinesis

Free Nuclear Endosperm

↓ Cytokinesis & Cell wall formation

Cellularisation at periphery

- In some cases - cell wall formation is incomplete
- For example - coconut
- Coconut water - free nuclear endosperm
- Surrounding soft white kernel - cellular endosperm.

Cellular endosperm

PEC

↓ Mitosis

Karyokines & cytokinesis occur simultaneously

↓

cellular endosperm from beginning

Helobial endosperm

Intermidiate between free nuclear & cellular types

PEN

↓ divides

cell wall formation occurs (cellular) → 2 unequal cells formed ↑ Divide like nuclear type (free nuclear)

- Occurs in plants belonging to order Helobiales

② Development of embryo

- Embryo develops from zygote at micropylar end.

In Dicots

zygote (2n) —Transverse division→ Chalazal end; Apical/terminal/embryo cell; Micropylar end; Basal/suspensor cell → Embryonic cells; Proembryo; Basal cell

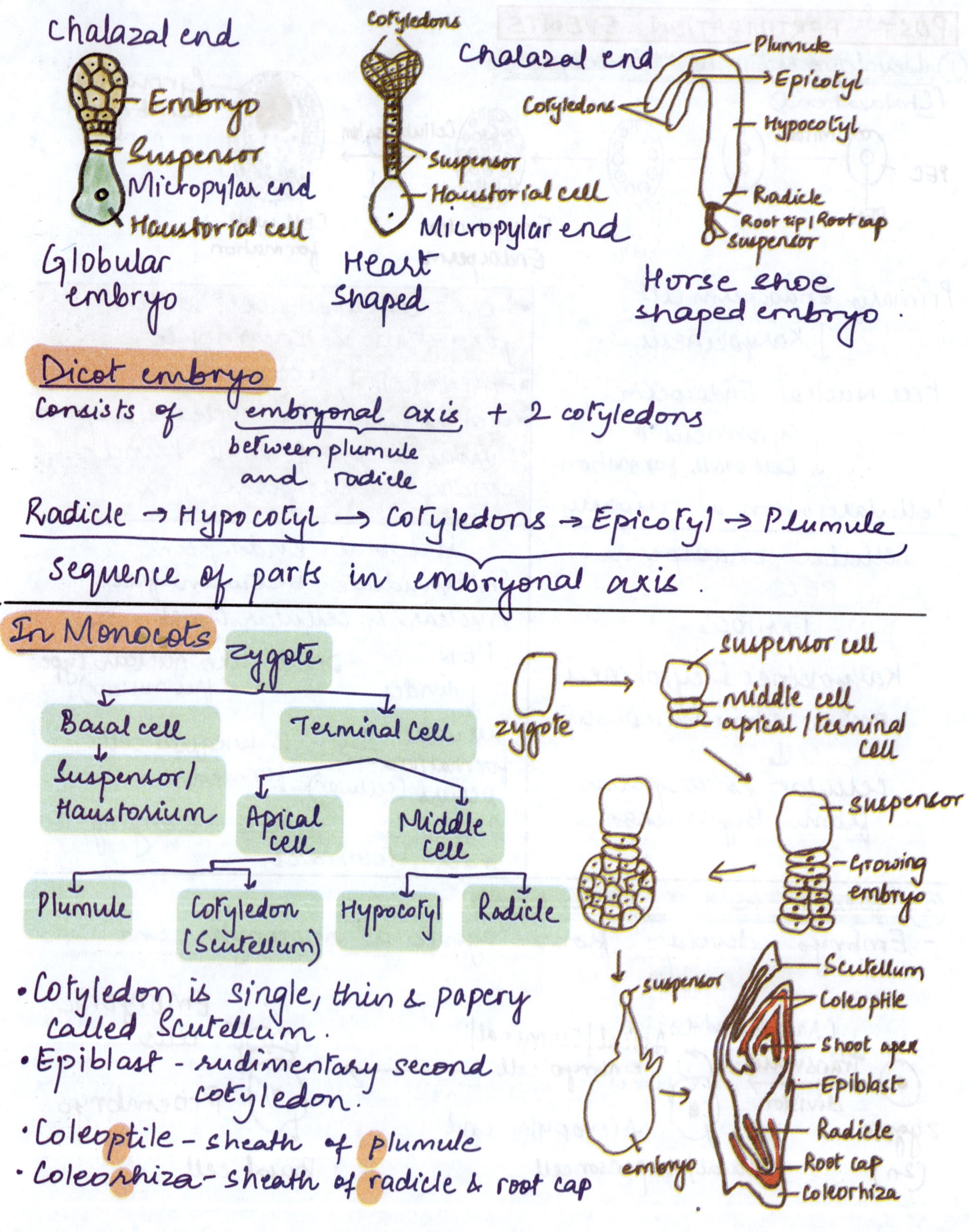

Dicot embryo

Consists of embryonal axis + 2 cotyledons
(embryonal axis: between plumule and radicle)

Radicle → Hypocotyl → Cotyledons → Epicotyl → Plumule

(sequence of parts in embryonal axis.)

In Monocots

- Cotyledon is single, thin & papery called Scutellum.
- Epiblast - rudimentary second cotyledon.
- Coleoptile - sheath of plumule
- Coleorhiza - sheath of radicle & root cap

DEVELOPMENT OF SEED

- Ovule —Fertilisation→ seed
  - Embryo – links two generations
  - Cotyledons – contain food reserves
  - Seed coat – formed from integuments
    - outer – Testa
    - inner – Tegmen
- Micropyle – remains in seed
  - entry of water & oxygen takes place during germination
- Water content – 10–15 %
- Dormancy – inactive state; seed viable
  - breaks when favourable conditions are present – suitable temperature, oxygen & moisture.

NEET SYNAPSE

Exceptions

In Dicots
Castor – albuminous

In monocots
Orchids – non albuminous

Mature seed

Non albuminous/ Ex albuminous	Albuminous
• Endosperm absent	• Endosperm present
• Consumed during embryo development	• Not consumed completely.
• Usually found in dicot plants	• Usually found in monocot plants.
Eg. Pea, beans, groundnut	Eg. wheat, maize, barley.

Perisperm – remnants of nucellus are persistent.
Eg. Black pepper; sugar beet

FORMATION OF FRUIT

Ovary —Fertilisation→ Fruit [True fruit]

Ovary + Other floral parts → Fruit [False fruit]
Eg. Apple (Thalamus), strawberry, cashews

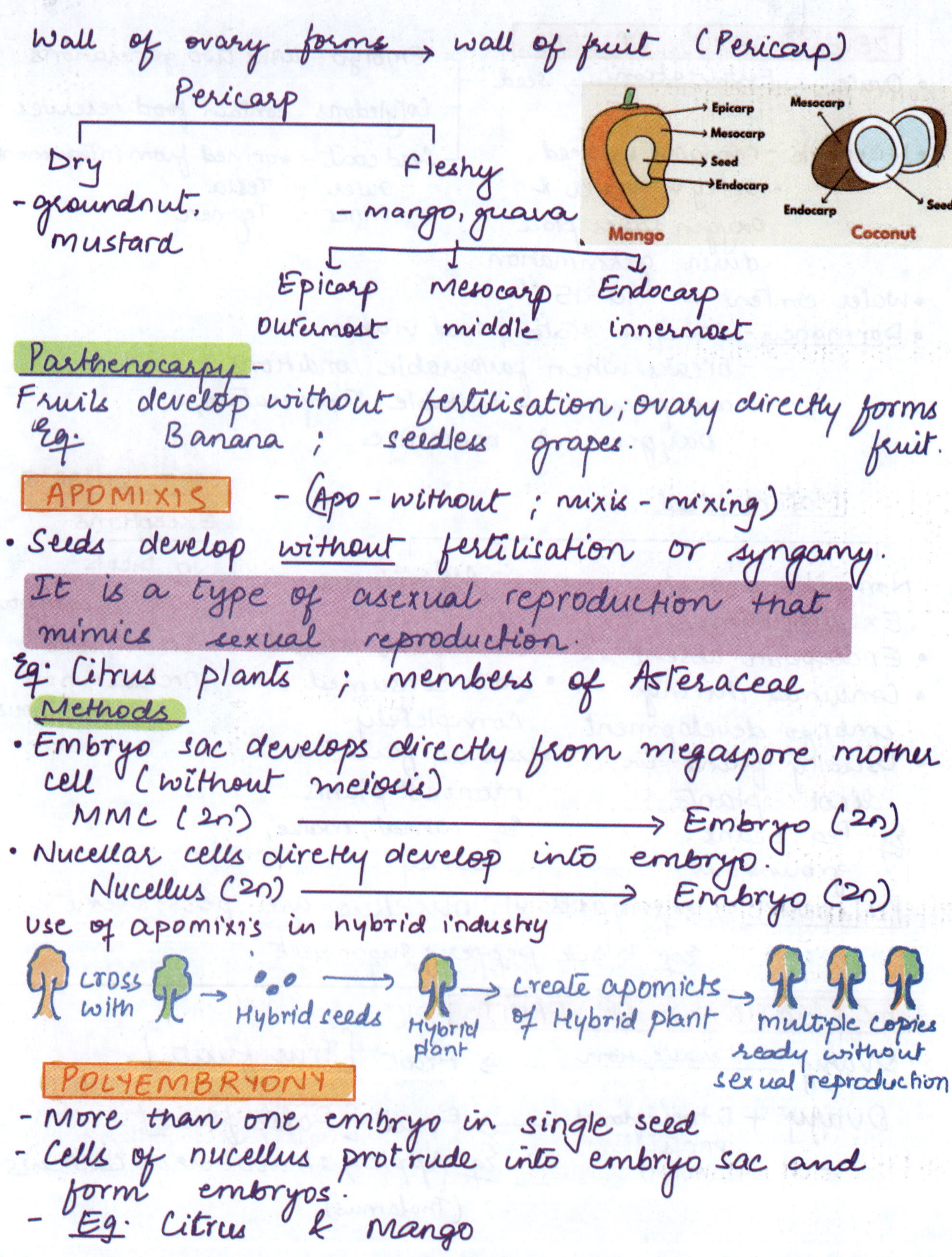

Wall of ovary forms → wall of fruit (Pericarp)

Pericarp
- Dry – groundnut, mustard
- Fleshy – mango, guava
  - Epicarp – outermost
  - Mesocarp – middle
  - Endocarp – innermost

Parthenocarpy –
Fruits develop without fertilisation; ovary directly forms fruit.
Eg. Banana ; seedless grapes.

APOMIXIS – (Apo - without ; mixis - mixing)
- Seeds develop without fertilisation or syngamy.

It is a type of asexual reproduction that mimics sexual reproduction.

Eg: Citrus plants ; members of Asteraceae

Methods
- Embryo sac develops directly from megaspore mother cell (without meiosis)
  MMC (2n) → Embryo (2n)
- Nucellar cells directly develop into embryo.
  Nucellus (2n) → Embryo (2n)

Use of apomixis in hybrid industry

POLYEMBRYONY
- More than one embryo in single seed
- Cells of nucellus protrude into embryo sac and form embryos.
- Eg. Citrus & Mango

21. Human Reproduction

Humans - sexual reproduction
- viviparous.

Puberty →

Gametogenesis
Formation of gametes
♂ Spermatogenesis ♀ Oogenesis

Insemination
Transfer of sperms into female reproductive tract

Fertilisation
Fusion of male & female gamete (sperm) ♂ ♀ (ovum)
zygote

Implantation
Attachment of embryo to uterine wall

Gestation
Embryonic development in womb / uterus.

Parturition
Delivery of baby

REPRODUCTIVE EVENTS

REPRODUCTIVE SYSTEMS

	Male	Female
Primary sex organs	**Testes** - Formation of sperms - Secrete testosterone	**Ovaries** - Formation of ova - Secrete estrogen & progesterone
Secondary sex organs	- Male accessory ducts - Male accessory glands - External genitalia	- Female accessory ducts - Female accessory glands - External genitalia - Mammary glands

MALE REPRODUCTIVE SYSTEM

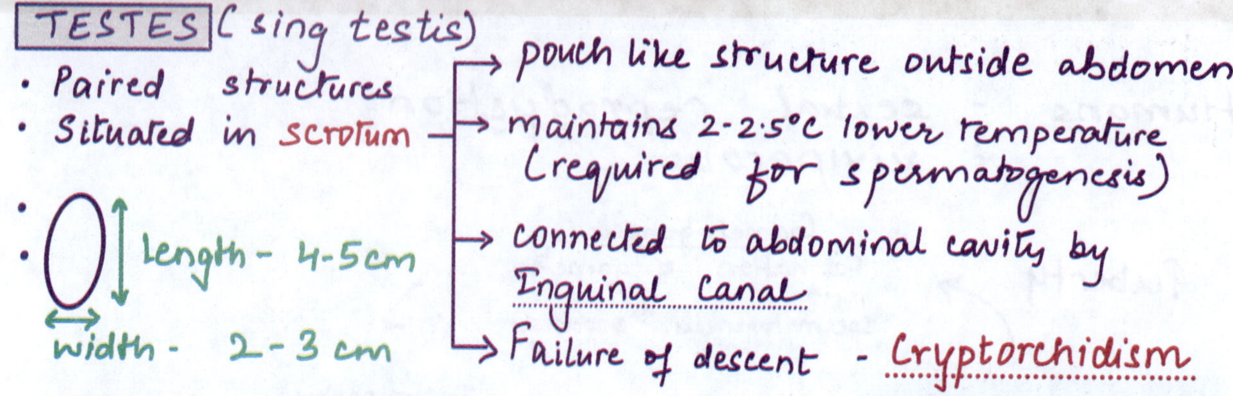

TESTES (sing testis)

- Paired structures
- Situated in scrotum
  - → pouch like structure outside abdomen
  - → maintains 2-2.5°C lower temperature (required for spermatogenesis)
  - → connected to abdominal cavity by Inguinal canal
  - → Failure of descent - Cryptorchidism
- length - 4-5cm
- width - 2-3 cm

Internal Structure of Testis.

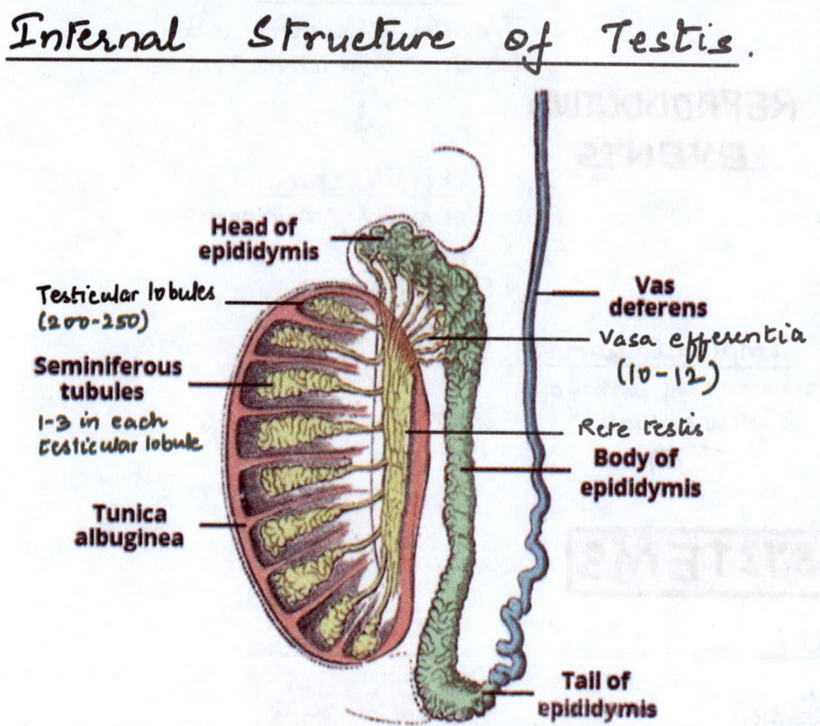

NEET SYNAPSE

Flow of sperms

Seminiferous tubules
↓
Tubuli recti
↓
Rete Testis
↓
Vasa efferentia
↓
Epididymis
↓
Vas deferens
↓
Ejaculatory duct
↓
Urethra

Internal structure of Seminiferous Tubule

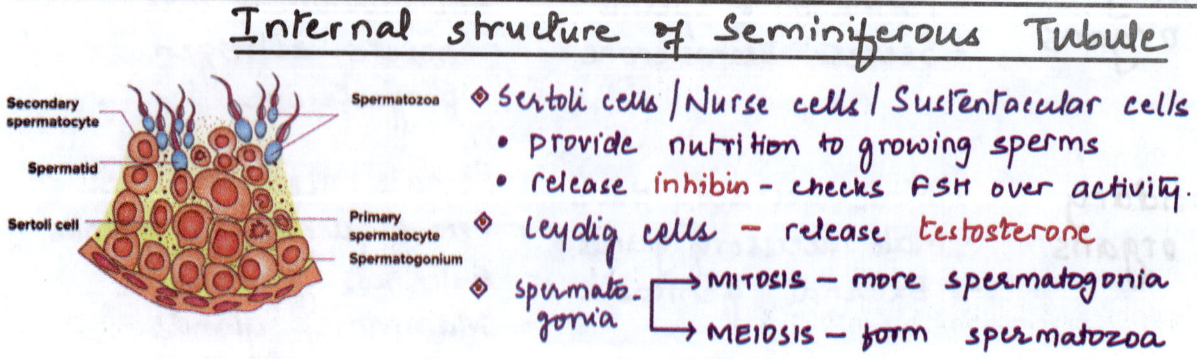

- ◈ Sertoli cells / Nurse cells / Sustentacular cells
  - provide nutrition to growing sperms
  - release inhibin - checks FSH over activity.
- ◈ Leydig cells – release testosterone
- ◈ spermatogonia
  - → MITOSIS – more spermatogonia
  - → MEIOSIS – form spermatozoa

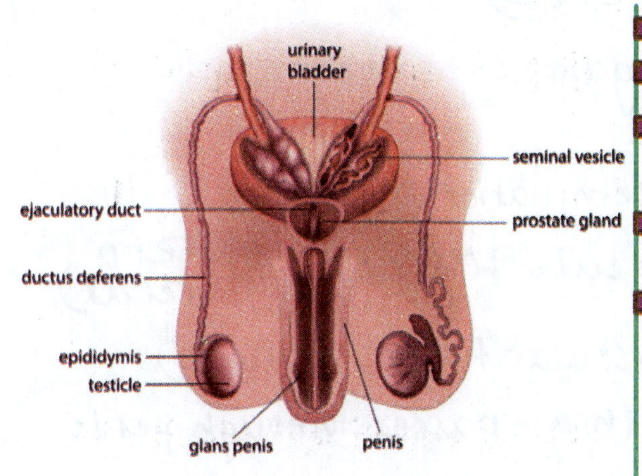

- Testes - production of sperms
- Epididymis - storage of sperms
- Vas deferens - takes sperms to abdomen
- Vas deferens + Seminal vesicle duct
- Ejaculatory duct ↓ Passes through prostate gland & enters urethra. ↓ Releases sperms.

Male Accessory Ducts

- **Intra testicular duct system**
  - Seminiferous tubules
  - tubuli recti
  - rete testis
- **Extra Testicular duct system**
  - Vasa efferentia
  - Epididymis
  - Vas deferens
  - Ejaculatory duct.

Male Accessory Glands

Seminal vesicle
- Paired
- Secrete viscous fluid
- Secretion contains fructose, inositol, prostaglandins
- Contribute 60-70% of seminal plasma

Prostate gland
- Single
- Secrete alkaline fluid; provide odour
- Secretion contains Ca^{2+}, PO_4, fibrinolysin.
- Contribute 20-25% of seminal plasma

Bulbourethral/ cowper's glands
- Paired
- Secrete viscous fluid
- Acts as lubricant
- Secretion contains mucus
- Contributes 5-10% of seminal plasma

EXTERNAL GENITALIA (PENIS)

- Copulatory organ
- Erectile tissue
- Facilitates insemination

corpus cavernosa (muscular tissue - 2 - postero lateral)

corpus spongiosum (muscular tissue - single)

urethra - penile urethra - passes through penis

prepuce (foreskin) - fold of skin ; covers glans penis

glans penis] Corpus spongiosum
urethral opening]

SEMEN

- Sperms + seminal plasma
  (Testes) (Accessory glands)
- Volume - 2.5 - 5 ml / ejaculate
- Sperm count - 200 - 300 million
- For normal fertility -
  60% sperms must have normal shape & size
  40% out of above must have vigorous motility.
- Infertility - < 20 million/ml

NEET SYNAPSE

- pH of semen - alkaline (7.2-7.7)
- Alkaline pH neutralises
  - acidity of urethra (urine)
  - acidity of vagina (female reproductive tract)

FEMALE REPRODUCTIVE SYSTEM

Ovaries	Accessory ducts	Accessory glands	External genitalia (vulva)	Mammary glands (Breasts)
Primary sex organs	Fallopian tubes	Bartholin's glands	Mons pubis	Secrete milk
Produce ova	Uterus (Womb)	Skene's glands	Labia majora	Glandular + Adipose tissue
Secrete female sex hormones	Vagina		labia minora	
			Vestibule	
			Clitoris	
			Hymen	

OVARIES

Paired structures ; Almond shaped ; 2-4 cm in length

Internal structure

- Germinal epithelium (cuboidal cells)
- Tunica albuginea (connective tissue)
- Cortex (ovarian follicles)
- Medulla (blood vessels + nerves + smooth ms.)

} STROMA

- Ovarian follicle
- Ovum
- Granulosa cells (follicular granulosa)

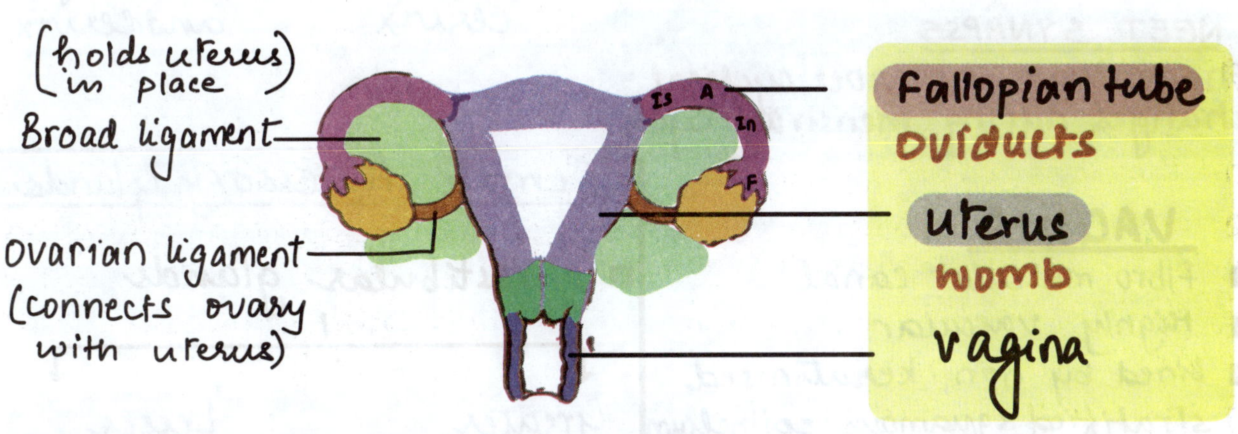

Female Accessory ducts

FALLOPIAN TUBES (OVIDUCTS)

↓

- Paired, muscular,
- ciliated epithelium
- length → 10–12 cm
- Join ovary to uterus

(proximal)

Isthmus - closest to uterus

Ampulla - fertilisation

Infundibulum - funnel shaped (distal) - closest to ovary

Ovary

Fimbriae - finger like projections

Pick up ovum through ostium

UTERUS (womb)

- Single & hollow
- Inverted pear shaped
- Suspended by mesometrium
- Wall of uterus

CAVITY

Perimetrium (outermost; fibrous)

Myometrium
- muscular (smooth ms.)
- Thickest

Endometrium
- highly vascular
- glandular

NEET SYNAPSE

Endometrium undergoes cyclical changes during menstrual cycle.

Parts of uterus

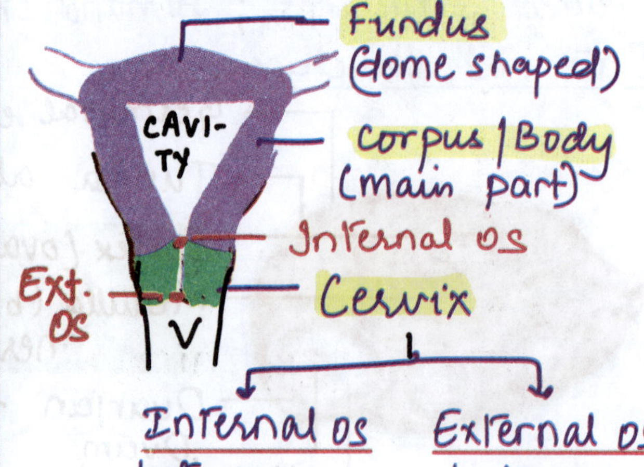

Cervix

Internal os	External os
- between body of uterus & cervix	- between vaginal opening and cervix

VAGINA

- Fibro muscular canal
- Highly vascular
- Lined by non keratinised stratified squamous epithelium
- Mucus membrane has folds called rugae
- Vaginal orifice partially covered by hymen.
- Vagina

Copulation canal	Birth canal
Receives semen during copulation	Vagina + cervix & passage for delivering baby

Female Accessory Glands

- Vestibular glands

Greater vestibular glands	Lesser vestibular glands
Bartholin's glands	Skene's glands
- present on each side of vaginal orifice.	- present between urethral & vaginal orifices.

FEMALE EXTERNAL GENITALIA (vulva)

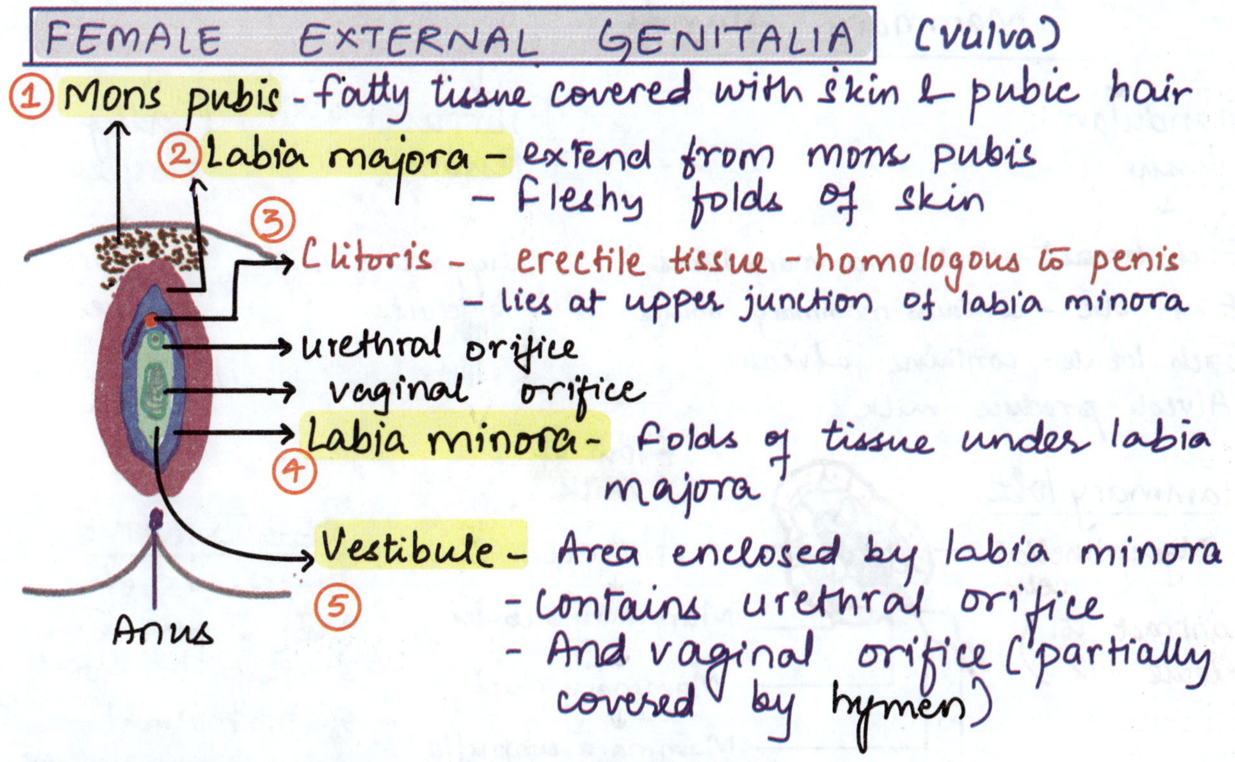

1. Mons pubis - fatty tissue covered with skin & pubic hair
2. Labia majora - extend from mons pubis
   - Fleshy folds of skin
3. Clitoris - erectile tissue - homologous to penis
   - lies at upper junction of labia minora

urethral orifice

vaginal orifice

4. Labia minora - Folds of tissue under labia majora
5. Vestibule - Area enclosed by labia minora
   - Contains urethral orifice
   - And vaginal orifice (partially covered by hymen)

Anus

MAMMARY GLANDS / BREASTS

- Develop at puberty
- Modified sweat glands
- Present on Pectoralis major muscle
- Nipple is surrounded by areola.
- Areola possesses many sebaceous glands called areolar glands.
- Main function - Lactation secretion & release of milk

Milk composition

Fat
Casein (milk protein)
Lactose (milk sugar)
Minerals & vitamins

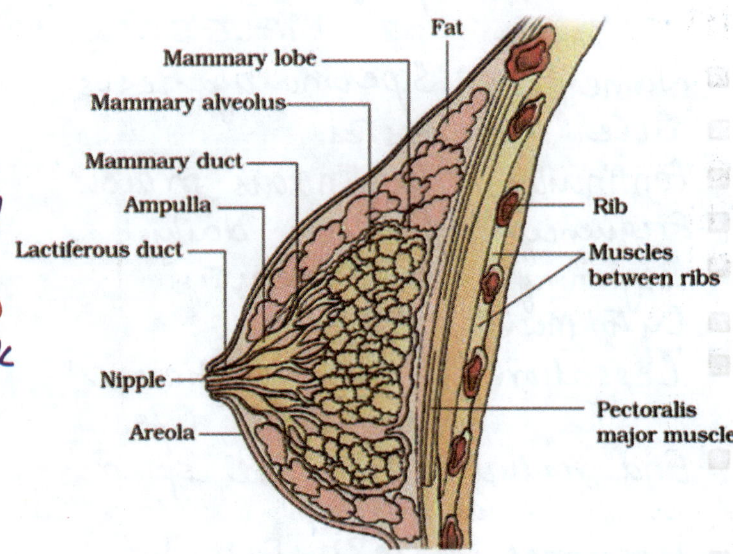

Mammary glands

- **Glandular tissue**
  - Each breast → 15-20 mammary lobes
  - Each lobe - contains mammary lobules
  - Each lobule - contains alveoli
  - Alveoli produce milk
- **Fibrous tissue** → supports alveoli & ducts.
- **Fatty tissue** → Adipose tissue → present between lobes

Mammary lobe

Myoepithelial cells (contract to release milk)

Flow of milk

Alveoli
↓
Mammary tubules
↓
Mammary duct
↓
Mammary ampulla
↓
Lactiferous duct

> **NEET SYNAPSE**
> Expression of milk is due to synergistic effect of hormones - oestrogen, progesterone, prolactin & oxytocin.

GAMETOGENESIS

- Process of formation of gametes

	MALES	FEMALES
Name	Spermatogenesis	Oogenesis
Site	Testes	Ovaries
Continuity	Continuous process	Discontinuous process
Frequency	Occurs daily	Once in 28 days
Beginning	At puberty	In embryonic stage
Cytokinesis	Equal	Unequal
Cessation	Never, continues throughout life	Stops at menopause (45-50 yrs of age)
End product	4 equal sperms	1 large ovum & 2 polar bodies
Hormones involved	GnRH, FSH, LH, Testosterone	GnRH, FSH, LH, Estrogen, Progesterone

SPERMATOGENESIS

Spermatogonia (germinal epithelium) → mitosis → more spermatogonia
Spermatogonia (germinal epithelium) → meiosis → spermatozoa (sperms)

Spermatogonium — 44+XY (46) 2n
↓ Growth — Spermatocytogenesis
Primary spermatocyte — 44+XY (46) 2n
↓ Meiosis - I (Reduction in chromosome number)
Secondary spermatocytes — 44+X (23) n; (23) n 44+Y
↓ Meiosis - II (Same chr number)
Spermatids — 44+X (23) n, 44+X (23) n, (23) n 44+Y, (23) n 44+Y
↓ Differentiation — Spermiogenesis
Spermatozoa — n, n, n, n

NEET SYNAPSE

Spermatogenesis → Spermatogonia → Spermatozoa
Spermiogenesis → Spermatid → Spermatozoa
Spermiation → Release of sperms from seminiferous tubules

Spermiogenesis

- Process of differentiation
- Nucleus becomes compact
- Golgi bodies → acrosome
- Centrioles rearrange - proximal & distal centrioles
- Mitochondria - spiral arrangement
- Cytoplasm reduced
- Flagellation - in tail part
- Overall weight reduction of cell.

Hormonal control

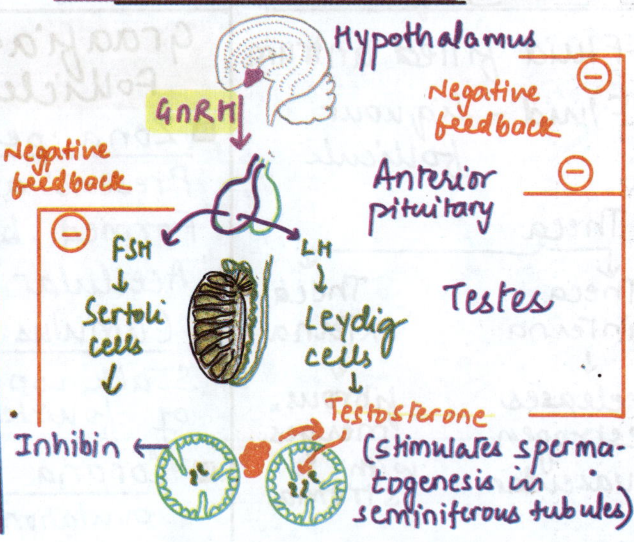

OOGENESIS

- In each ovary A million primary follicles present at birth

↓ Follicular atresia

60000 - 80000 primary follicles are left at onset of puberty

↓

At puberty.

2° → 3°

↓

Graafian follicle

↓

ruptures to release 2° oocyte

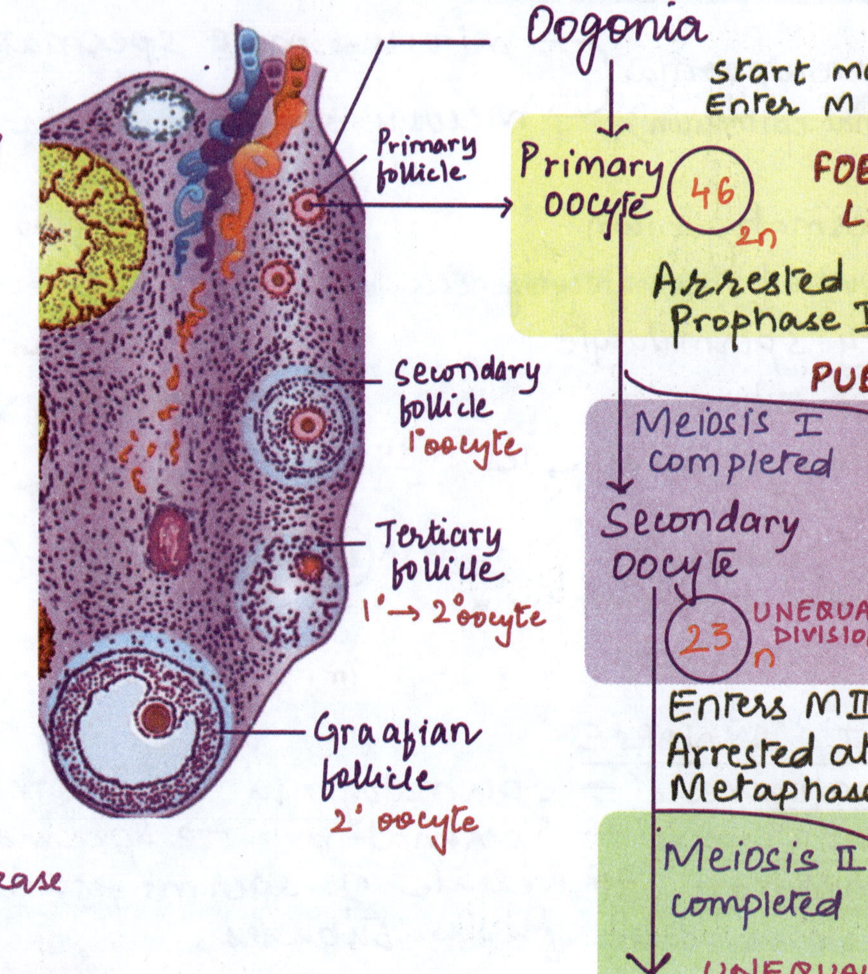

Oogonia

↓ Start meiosis Enter M I

FOETAL LIFE

Primary oocyte (46, 2n)

Arrested at Prophase I

PUBERTY

Meiosis I completed

Secondary oocyte (23, n) — UNEQUAL DIVISION — 1st Polar body (n)

Enters M II

Arrested at Metaphase II

Meiosis II completed

UNEQUAL DIVISION

(23, n) ovum — 2nd PB (n)

FERTILISATION

Tertiary follicle

- Fluid filled antrum
- Fluid - Liquour folliculi
- Theca
  - Theca interna ↓
    - releases estrogen
    - vascular
  - Theca externa ↓ fibrous, merges with stroma

Graafian follicle

- **Zona pellucida**
  Present around secondary oocyte
  Formed by secondary oocyte
  Acellular; made of glycoproteins
- **Cumulus oophorus**
  Stalk connecting oocyte with wall of follicle.
- **Corona radiata** - formed after ovulation - from granulosa cells.

Structure of sperm

Head

- Little cytoplasm
- Haploid nucleus
- Acrosome
  modified golgi bodies
  contains sperm lysins
  ↓
  help in penetrating ovum

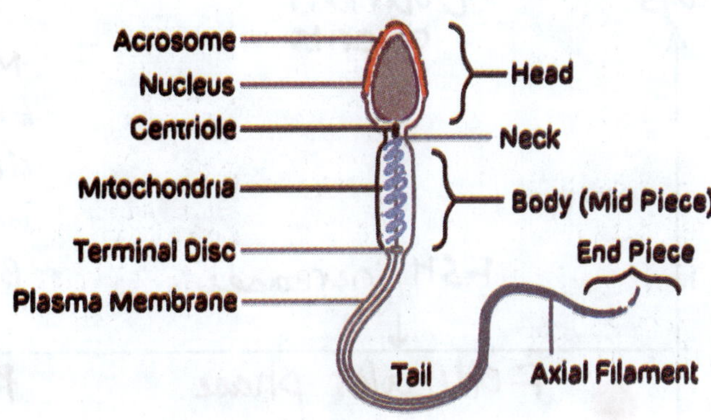

Neck

- Proximal centriole → helps in cleavage
- Distal centriole → gives rise to axial filament

Middle piece

- Spirally arranged mitochondria (Nebenkern) – produce energy for sperm movement.

Tail

- Contains central axial filament surrounded by cytoplasm.
- Helps in sperm motility

Structure of ovum

- Non cleidoic (no shell); Alecithal (no yolk)
- Contains haploid nucleus
- Surrounded by 3 layers –
- Corona radiata – outermost
  – cellular
- Zona pellucida – Acellular
  – Glycoproteinaceous
  – Disintegrates at implantation
- Vitelline membrane – innermost, thin, transparent
  – provides protection

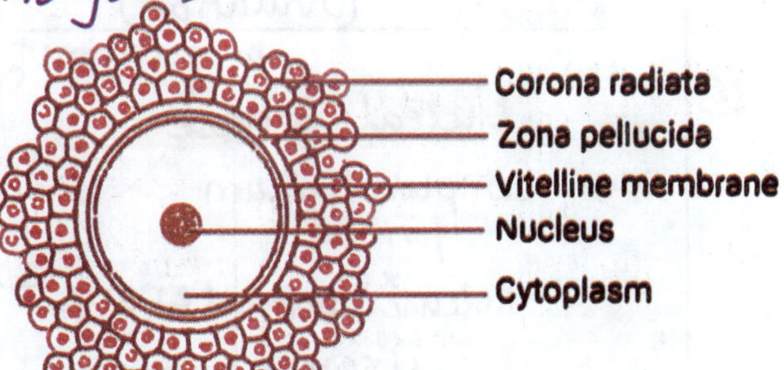

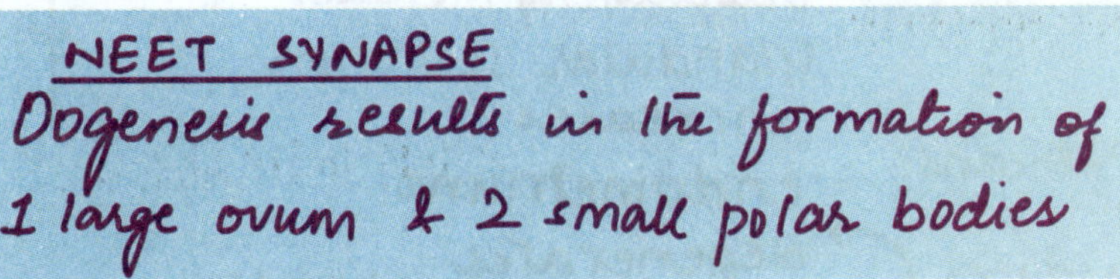
NEET SYNAPSE

Oogenesis results in the formation of 1 large ovum & 2 small polar bodies

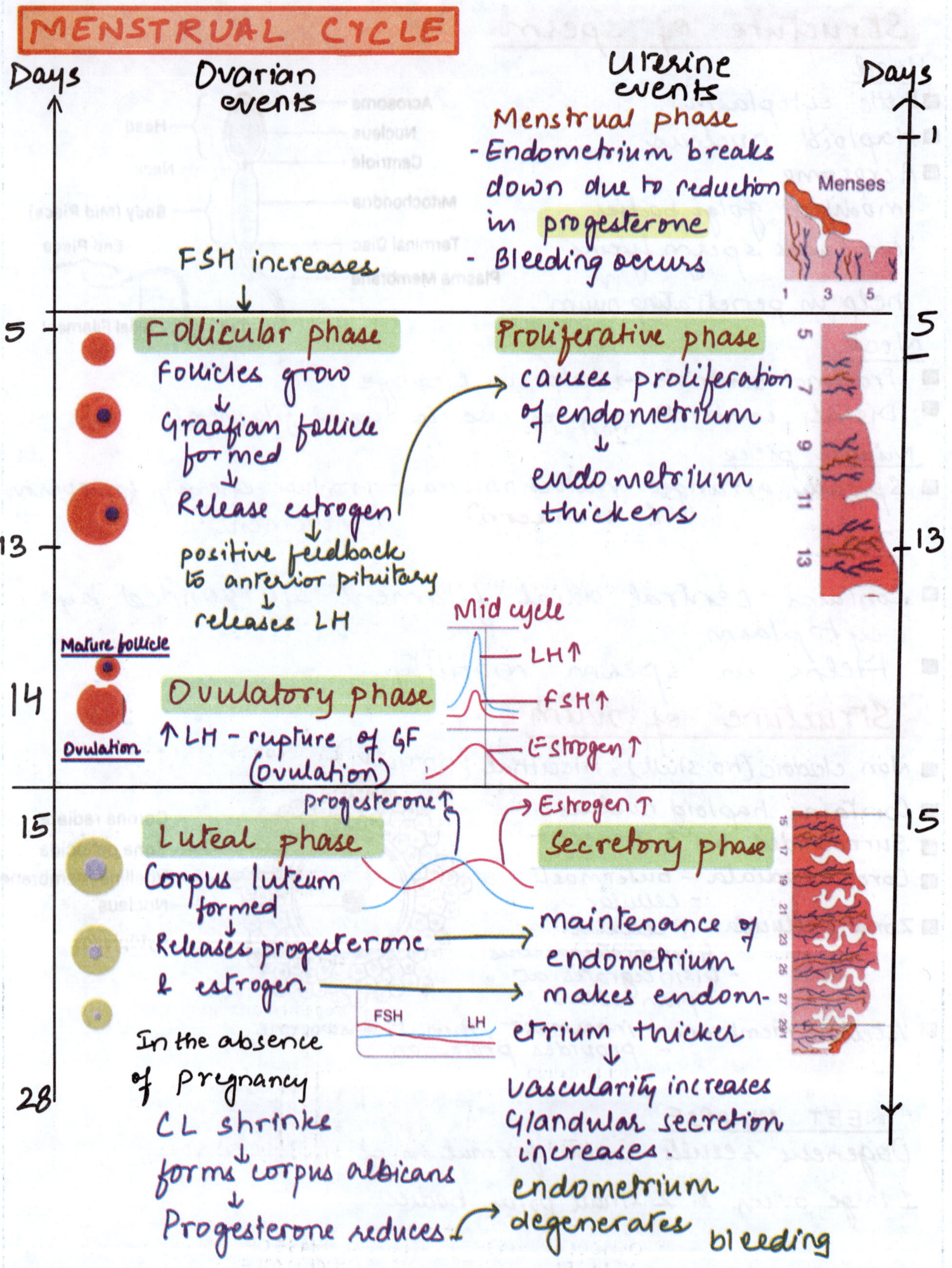
MENSTRUAL CYCLE
Days
Ovarian events
Uterine events
Days
Menstrual phase
- Endometrium breaks down due to reduction in progesterone
- Bleeding occurs
Menses
1
3
5
FSH increases
5
Follicular phase
Follicles grow
Graafian follicle formed
Release estrogen
positive feedback to anterior pituitary
releases LH
Proliferative phase
causes proliferation of endometrium
endometrium thickens
5
7
9
11
13
13
13
Mid cycle
LH↑
FSH↑
Estrogen↑
Mature follicle
14
Ovulatory phase
↑LH - rupture of GF (ovulation)
Ovulation
progesterone↑
Estrogen↑
15
Luteal phase
Corpus luteum formed
Releases progesterone & estrogen
Secretory phase
maintenance of endometrium
makes endometrium thicker
vascularity increases
Glandular secretion increases
endometrium degenerates
bleeding
15
17
19
21
23
25
27
28
FSH
LH
In the absence of pregnancy
CL shrinks
forms corpus albicans
Progesterone reduces
28

Important points

- Reproductive cycle of primates.
- Menarche – beginning of cycle – at puberty
- Menopause – cessation of cycle – 45-50 years of age.
- Duration – 28 days
- One ovum is released in each cycle from alternate ovary
- LH surge – causes ovulation
- Day of ovulation ⇒ number of days in cycle – 14
- Luteal phase duration remains fixed.

Hormonal control of Menstrual cycle

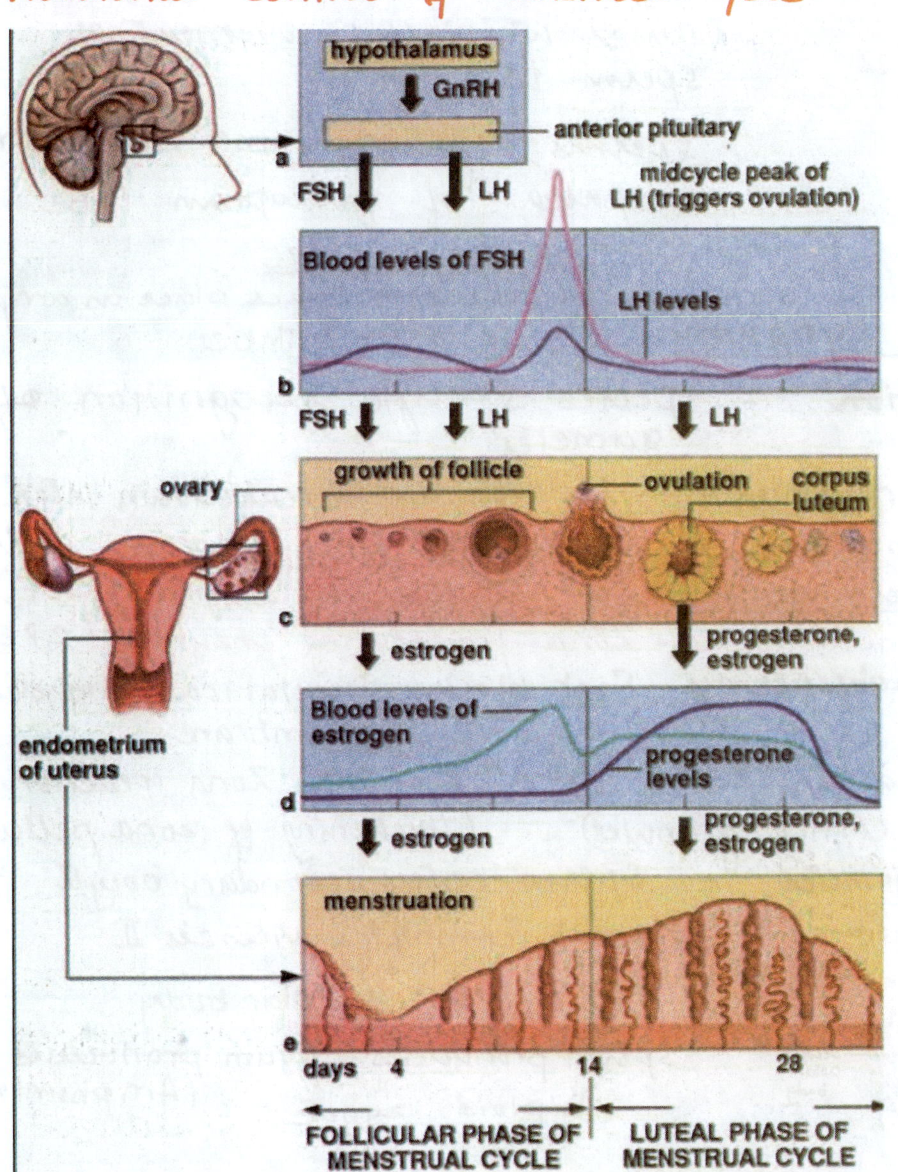

FERTILISATION AND IMPLANTATION

Insemination - release of semen into female reproductive tract.
- Sperms live for 48-72 hrs.

EVENTS OF FERTILISATION

① Capacitation - Acrosome exposed
- Entry of Ca^{2+} into sperms
↓
Causes whiplash movement of sperm tail
↓
Sperms vigorously move towards ampulla of fallopian tube.

2° oocyte simultaneously reaches ampulla by ciliary action

② Syngamy

NEET SYNAPSE
Fertilisation takes place in ampulla of fallopian tube

Steps of syngamy

a) **Agglutination** - species specific recognition of gametes.

b) **Acrosomal reaction** -
Acrosome bursts
↓
Releases sperm lysins →
- Hyaluronidase - breaksdown inter cellular substance of corona radiata
- Corona digesting enzyme (CDE)
- Zona penetrating enzyme (ZPE)

c) **Block of polyspermy**
Fast block - Depolarisation of ovum membrane
Slow block → Zona reaction (thickening of zona pellucida)
Slow block → Cortical reaction (extrusion of cortical granules)

d) **Fusion of gametes** - Sperm enters secondary oocyte
↓
2° oocyte completes Meiosis II
↓
Ootid (ovum) + Polar body
↓
Sperm pronucleus + ovum pronucleus (Amphimixis)
↓
Diploid zygote

Sperms
Ovum
Second polar body

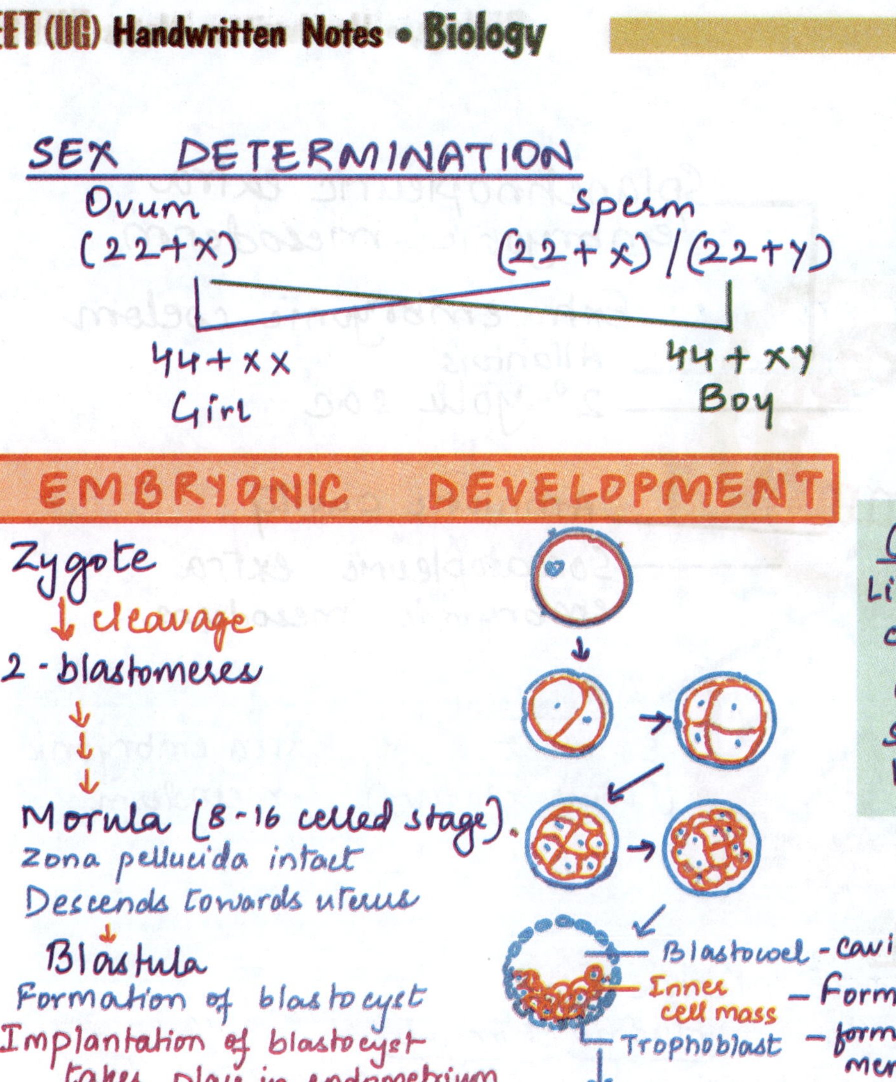

NEET Synapse
Father is responsible for determining sex of the baby

Cleavage
Like mitosis but cytoplasmic content remains same ∴ size of daughter cells keep on reducing

Gastrula
Formation of 3 germ layers

Hypoblast (cuboidal cells)
Epiblast (columnar cells)
cytotrophoblast
syncytiotrophoblast
embeds in endometrium
IMPLANTATION

Extra embryonic mesoderm
Primary yolk sac

All germ layers arise from EPIBLAST
Sequence of formation
① Endoderm
② Mesoderm
③ Ectoderm

Hypoblast
Epiblast
Invaginating mesoderm cells
Primitive streak

GASTRULATION
- Epiblast forms primitive streak
  ↓
  cells invaginate
  ↓
  integrate into hypoblast
  ↓
  Form endoderm
- Migrating cells form mesoderm
- Remaining cells form ectoderm

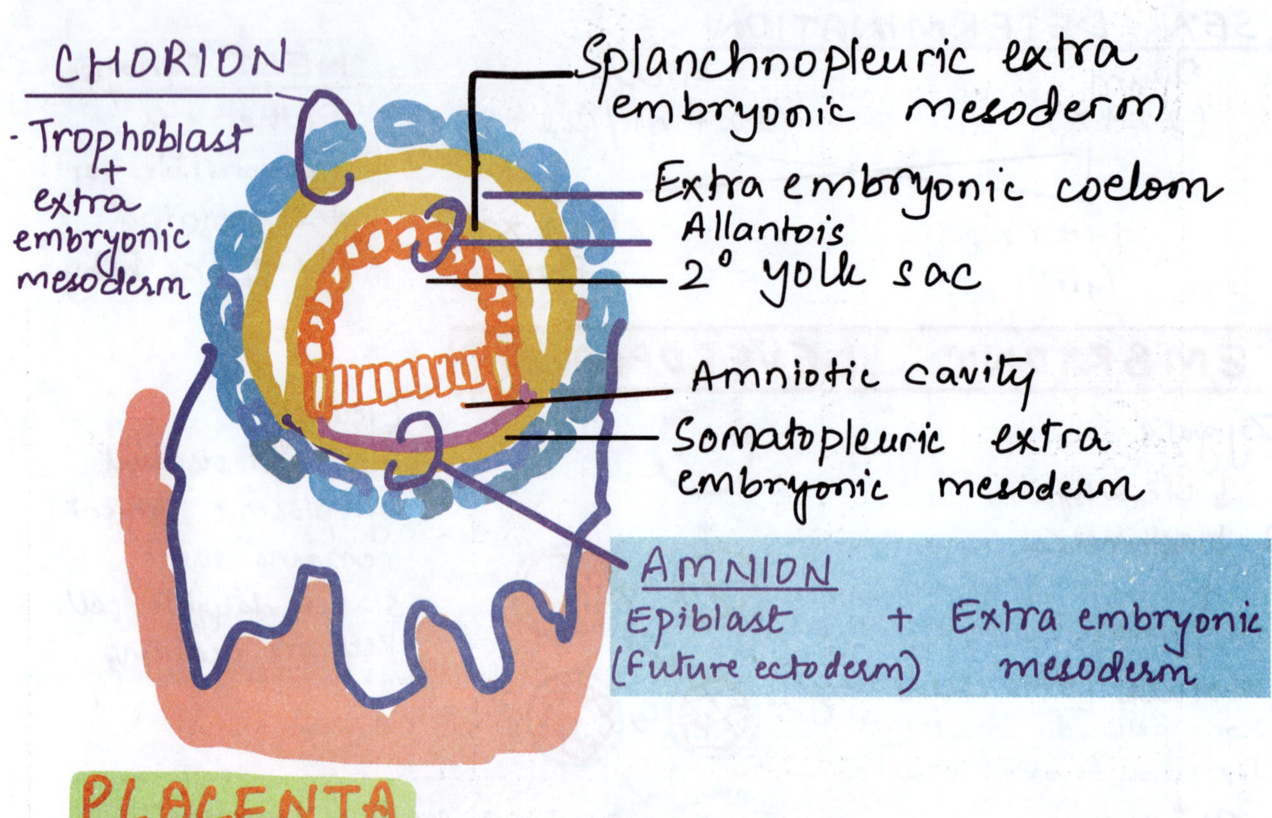

PLACENTA

- Connects foetus to uterine wall
- Human placenta – Haemo (Mother's blood) chorial (Foetal chorion)
- Functions of placenta

Mother: O_2, Nutrients ↓ Foetus; Foetus ↑ CO_2, N_2 wastes to Mother

- Acts as diffusion membrane
- Acts as temporary endocrine gland
- Hormones of placenta
- hCG – Human Chorionic Gonadotropin [Detected in pregnancy test]
- hPL – Human Placental Lactogen/ Chorionic somato mammotropin] Growth of mammary glands
- Chorionic thyrotropin
- CRH – Corticotropin Releasing Hormone/chorionic corticotropin
- Relaxin – secreted during later stages of pregnancy
  ↳ secreted by ovary to relax pubic symphysis
- Estrogen & Progesterone

hCG, hPL & relaxin – produced only during pregnancy

GESTATION

- Period of pregnancy → from conception to birth.
- Human gestation period- 9 months / 38 weeks / 266 days
- Divided into 3 trimesters

Milestones of embryonic development

1 month end	Heart is formed
2 month end	Limbs & digits are formed.
3 month end (First trimester end)	Major organ systems are formed (Limbs & external genital organs well developed)
5th month	Baby's first movements Appearance of hair on head
6 month end (second trimester end)	Body covered with fine hair (Lanugo) Eye lids separate Eye lashes are formed
9 month end (Third trimester end)	- Baby is fully formed.

PARTURITION

Birth of baby

Stages of birth

1. Dilation of cervix
2. Birth of baby
3. Delivery of placenta

NEET SYNAPSE

Human chorionic gonadotropin
↓ chorion, gonads, stimulate

- hCG stimulates the ovaries to maintain Corpus Luteum
- hCG behaves as LH
- Corpus luteum secretes large amounts of progesterone to maintain pregnancy

NEET SYNAPSE

First formed milk is colostrum- thick & yellow. It is rich in calories & antibodies IgA

- Oxytocin is the birth hormone.

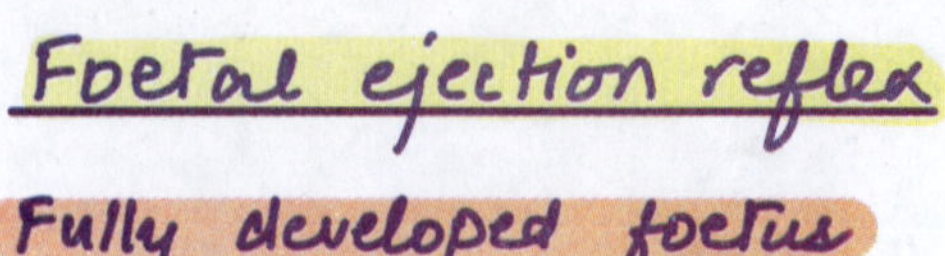

Foetal ejection reflex

Fully developed foetus + Placenta

Fetal stress → ↑ CRH in fetal blood ← Maternal timelines

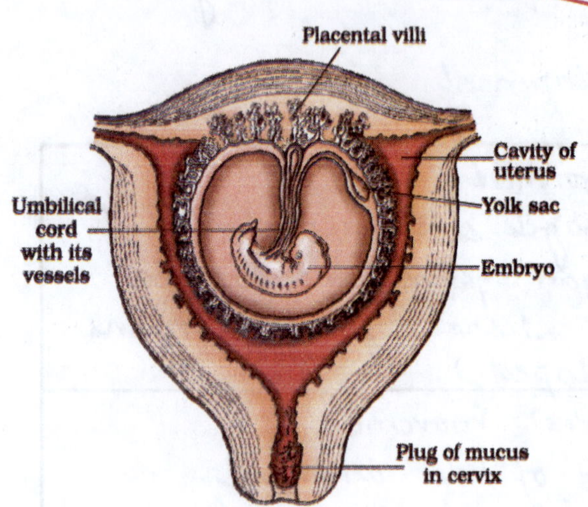

↑ CRH in fetal blood

↓

↑ Fetal ACTH secretion

↓

↑ Fetal cortisol

↓

Travels through placenta

↓

Estrogen ↑ ; Progesterone ↓ in maternal blood

↓

↑ Estrogen

- ↑ Oxytocin production by placenta
- ↑ Oxytocin receptors in myometrium
- ↑ Uterine production of prostaglandins

↓

Uterine contractions (+ve feedback → ↑ Uterine production of prostaglandins)

↓

Postive feedback to maternal pituitary

↓

More oxytocin

↓

Vigorous contractions

↓

Birth

NEET SYNAPSE

- Placental villi are formed by Chorion.
- Umbilical cord connects placenta with foetus

LACTATION

- secretion & release of milk
- Anterior pituitary
  ↓
  releases Prolactin
  ↓
  causes formation of milk
- Placenta
  ↓
  hCS / hPL
  ↓
  enhances milk formation
- Posterior pituitary
  ↓
  Oxytocin
  ↓
  ejection of milk / let down of milk

NEET SYNAPSE

Lactation is an example of synergistic effect of hormones

1. Prolactin – formation of milk
2. Estrogen – Progesterone increase in number & size of milk ducts
3. Oxytocin – ejection of milk

TWINS

Identical (monozygotic)

ovum + sperm → zygote → embryo → splitting of embryo → ♀ ♀

Same gender
Same features

Fraternal (dizygotic)

ovum + sperm → zygote → embryo → ♀
ovum + sperm → zygote → embryo → ♀

- Features are different.
- Can be same or different genders
- Formed when 2 ova are simultaneously released by both ovaries & fertilised.

22. Reproductive Health

Reproductive and Child Healthcare Programme (RCH)

- Also called Family Planning Program
- Started in 1951

Objectives of RCH

- Awareness about STI's
- Knowledge about birth control & pregnancy
- Prevention of female foeticide
- Prevention of sex abuse & related crimes
- Child immunisation
- Sex education
- Research on reproduction related areas
- Development of new techniques in reproductive care

POPULATION EXPLOSION

- Sudden & rapid increase in population in short span of time
- In 2011 - population growth rate - < 2%. (20/1000/year)

CAUSES

Decrease in	Increase in
Death rate (mortality)	Medical facilities
MMR (Maternal mortality rate)	Average life span
IMR (Infant mortality rate)	Number of individuals in reproductive age group
	Care of new mothers & new born children

BIRTH CONTROL METHODS

Ideal contraceptive

Should be	Should NOT
User friendly / easy to use	Interfere with libido
Easily available	Interfere with sexual act
Highly effective	Have side effects
Reversible	

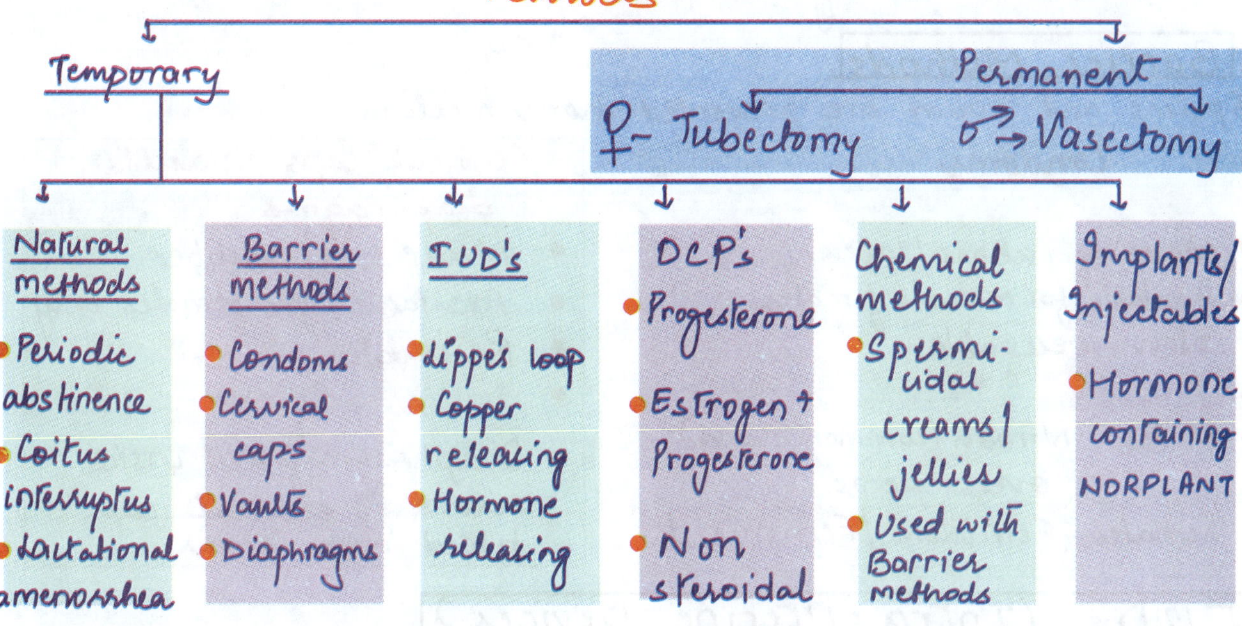

Natural methods

High failure rate ; No side effects

Rhythm method / Periodic Abstinence / Calender method

Avoid coitus during fertile period → 10-17 days of menstrual cycle

Coitus interruptus withdrawal method

Withdraw penis from vagina before ejaculation (Pre ejaculation may happen)

Lactational amenorrhea

- Absence of menses during intense lactation – upto 6 months after birth

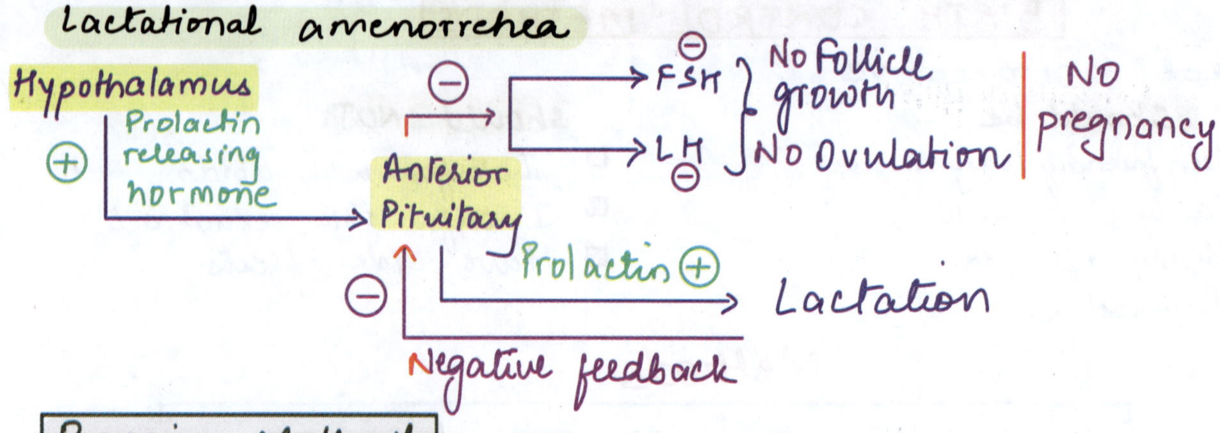

Barrier Methods.

Sperms and ovum are prevented from meeting.

Condoms

- Made of rubber/latex
- Available for males & females
- Non reusable
- Prevent STIs
- Males - Nirodh (common brand)
  - covers penis
- Females - Femidom / Femshield

Cervical caps, vaults, diaphragms

- Made of rubber
- Available for females only
- Reusable
- Do not prevent STIs.
- Diaphragm fitted inside cervix ; cervical cap fitted over cervix.

IUDs (Intra-Uterine Devices)

- Very commonly used ; best for spacing children
- Not user friendly ; inserted by medical professionals.

Lippe's loop

- Inert
- Non medicated
- Increases phagocytosis of sperms

Copper releasing

- Release Cu ions
- Suppress sperm motility
- Suppress fertilisation capacity of sperms
- eg. CuT, Cu7 Multiload 375

Hormone releasing

- Make uterus unsuitable for implantation
- Make cervical mucus thick - hostile to sperms
- Cause anovulation (absent ovulation)

Progestasert, LNG-20

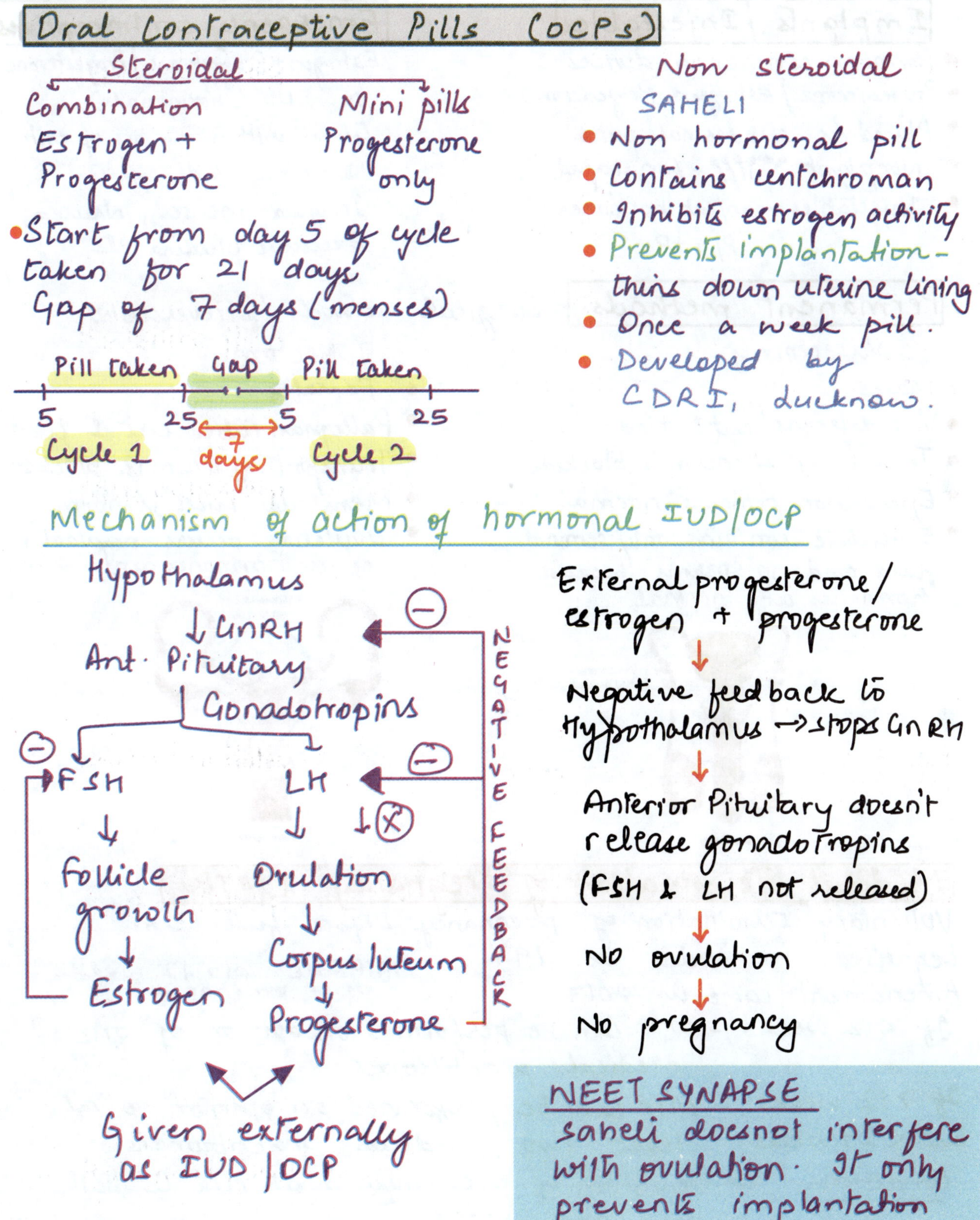
Oral Contraceptive Pills (OCPs)
Steroidal
Combination
Estrogen + Progesterone
Mini pills
Progesterone only
• Start from day 5 of cycle taken for 21 days
Gap of 7 days (menses)
Pill taken
Gap
Pill taken
5
25
5
25
7 days
Cycle 1
Cycle 2
Non steroidal
SAHELI
• Non hormonal pill
• Contains centchroman
• Inhibits estrogen activity
• Prevents implantation - thins down uterine lining
• Once a week pill.
• Developed by CDRI, Lucknow.
Mechanism of action of hormonal IUD/OCP
Hypothalamus
GnRH
Ant. Pituitary
Gonadotropins
FSH
LH
Follicle growth
Estrogen
Ovulation
Corpus luteum
Progesterone
NEGATIVE FEEDBACK
Given externally as IUD/OCP
External progesterone/ estrogen + progesterone
Negative feedback to Hypothalamus → stops GnRH
Anterior Pituitary doesn't release gonadotropins (FSH & LH not released)
No ovulation
No pregnancy
NEET SYNAPSE
Saheli doesnot interfere with ovulation. It only prevents implantation

Implants / Injectables

- Hormone containing devices
- Progesterone / Estrogen+ Progesterone
- Placed as subdermal patch
- Norplant – fan shaped.
- Injectables – inject hormones P/E+P

Emergency contraceptives

Estrogen+ Progesterone / Progesterone or IUD (hormonal)
Given within 72 hrs of coitus
Numerous side effects – Irregular menses, Nausea, Excessive bleeding etc.

Permanent methods – Surgical methods / Irreversible

Vasectomy

- Males
- Vas deferens cut & tied
- Transport of sperm is blocked
- Ejaculation remains normal
- Ejaculate contains only seminal fluid and no sperms because hormones are normal

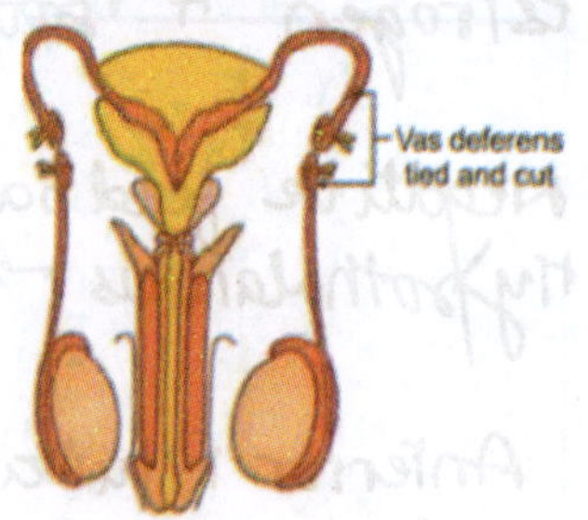

Vasectomy

Tubectomy

- Females
- Fallopian tubes cut & tied
- Transport of ovum is blocked
- Menstrual cycle is normal
- Ovulation occurs regularly. because hormones are normal

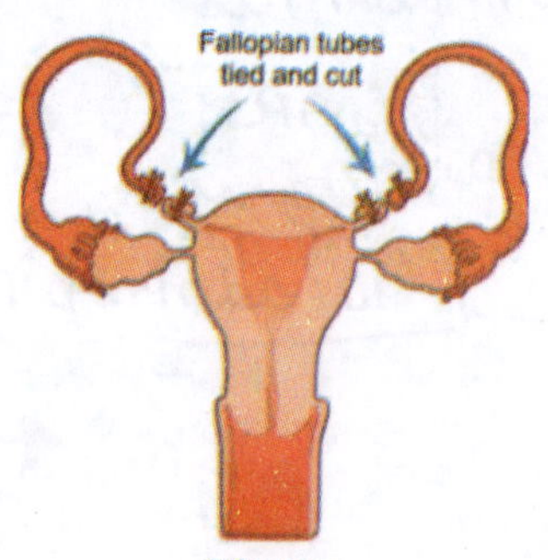

Tubectomy

Medical Termination of Pregnancy (MTP)

Voluntary termination of pregnancy before full term.
Legalised in India in 1971.
Amendment came in 2017

MTP safe upto 12 weeks of pregnancy

If <12 weeks – MTP can be performed on opinion of one medical practitioner

If >12 weeks but <24 weeks – MTP can be performed on opinion of at least two medical practitioners.

Conditions – continuation of pregnancy is at risk to both mother and child.
– Chances of mental or physical handicap.

Amniocentesis

Prenatal diagnosis of genetic abnormalities.

Process - Amniotic fluid withdrawn from amniotic sac
↓
Foetal DNA examined for genetic abnormalities.

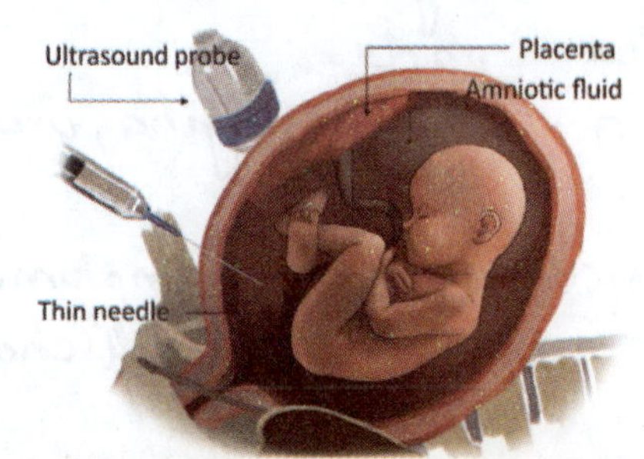

MISUSE OF AMNIOCENTESIS

Female foeticide - As gender of foetus can be determined by this procedure, some people abort the pregnancy when foetus is female

In India, there is a statutory ban on amniocentesis to prevent female foeticide

SEXUALLY TRANSMITTED INFECTIONS

- Also called Venereal diseases / Reproductive Tract Infections
- Spread through sexual intercourse.
- Occur mainly in age group → 15-24 yrs
- If left untreated, can lead to abortions, still birth, ectopic pregnancy, PID (Pelvic Inflammatory disease), infertility & even cancer of reproductive tract.

Bacterial STIs

Syphilis - Treponema pallidum
Gonorrhea - Neisseria gonorrheae
Chlamydiasis - Chlamydia trachomatis

Viral STIs

AIDS - HIV
Genital herpes - Herpes Simplex Virus
Genital warts - Human Papilloma Virus
Hepatitis B - Hepatitis B virus

Protozoan STIs

Trichomoniasis - Trichomonas vaginalis

NEET SYNAPSE

AIDS, Hepatitis B & Genital herpes are incurable STI's

Symptoms

- Itching & burning sensation in genital region.
- Infected parts
  Women - vulva, vagina, urethra
  Men - urethra
- Women - Generally asymptomatic
  - may have fluid discharge
- Men - Fluid discharge
  mild pain.

Prevention

- Avoid coitus with multiple partners
- Use a condom
- Use sterlised needles & syringes
- Knowledge about STI's should be imparted at school level.
- Any symptoms should be addressed immediately

INFERTILITY

- Couple unable to conceive despite unprotected sexual cohabitation for 1-2 yrs.

Assisted Reproductive Technologies (ART)

1. **In Vitro Fertilisation (IVF) / Test Tube Baby**

- Fertilisation outside the body.
- Egg and sperm are collected from partners / donors
- Fertilisation takes place in a petridish in laboratory
- Zygote is formed → incubated in culture plate
  ↓
  embryo is formed.

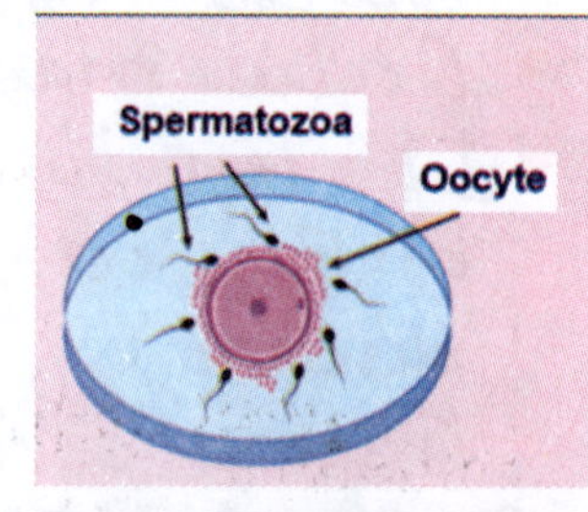

IVF is followed by ET (Embryo Transfer)

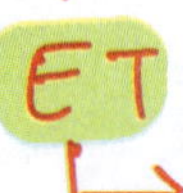

→ ZIFT (Zygote Intra fallopian Transfer)
Either zygote or embryo <8 blastomeres is transferred to fallopian Tube

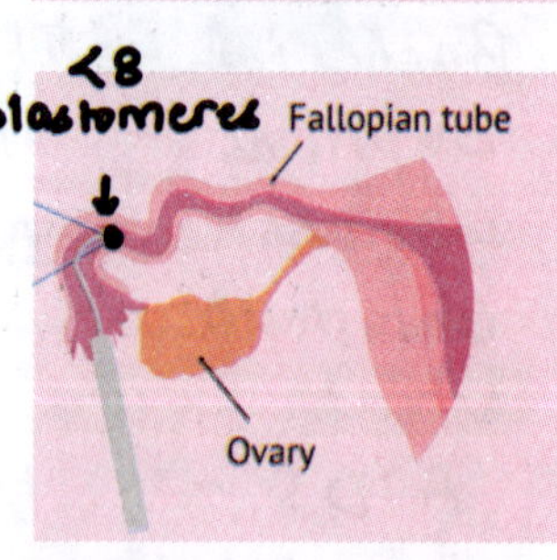

→ IUT (Intra Uterine Transfer)
Embryo >8 blastomeres is transferred to uterus of mother.

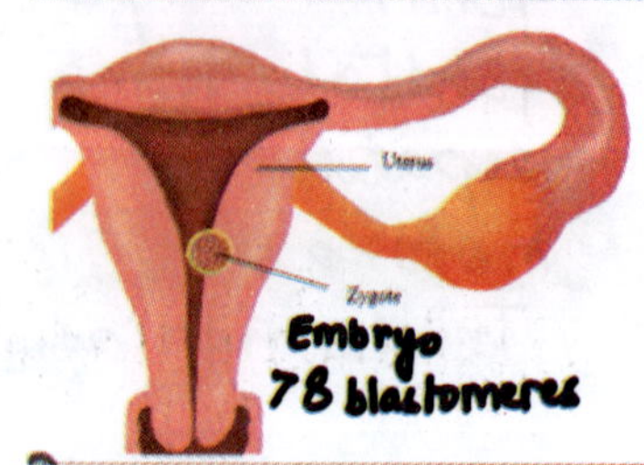

2. Gamete Intra Fallopian Transfer (GIFT)

Indication – women who can't produce eggs but have healthy uterus for carrying foetus.

Process – Egg taken from donor
↓
Placed in fallopian tube
↓
Fertilisation takes place normally

In vivo fertilisation

3 Intra Cytoplasmic Sperm Injection (ICSI)

Sperm is directly injected in the cytoplasm of ovum

Fertilisation is in vitro

It is a precise technique of fertilisation.

4. Artificial Insemination

Intra Uterine Insemination

Indication – Low sperm count

Semen is concentrated and injected in the female reproductive tract.

In vivo fertilisation

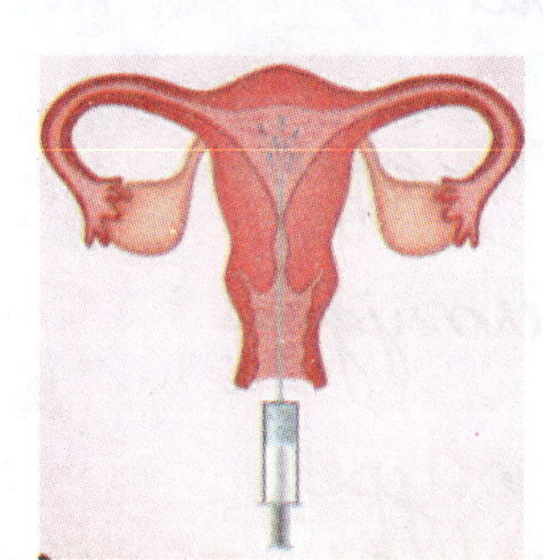

ART Summary

Infertile couple

- Reason identified
  - Female infertility
    - Not able to produce gamete – GIFT
    - Able to produce gamete but uterus not healthy – Surrogacy
  - Male infertility
    - Low sperm count – IUI
    - Low sperm count & motility – ICSI / IVF
- Reason unidentified
  - IVF followed by Embryo Transfer
    - ZIFT: <8 blastomeres
    - IUT: >8 blastomeres

23. Principle of Inheritance and Variations

Important Terms

Genetics	Study of inheritance & variation
Inheritance	Process by which characters pass from parents to progeny
Variations	Differences observed within a population.
Gene	Unit of inheritance. Segment of DNA carries information of protein.
Alleles	Alternate forms of a gene
Character	Characteristic of individual eg- colour, height, shape etc.
Trait	Attributes of a character - Eg. Tall & dwarf for height.
Homozygous	Both alleles of a trait in an individual are same Eg: TT
Heterozygous	Two alleles of a trait in an individual are different; Eg Tt
Genotype	Genetic constitution
Phenotype -	Physical appearance.

MENDELIAN INHERITANCE

Gregor Johann Mendel- Father of Genetics
He did experiments on Pisum sativum (pea plant) for 7 years.
Why Mendel chose pea plant for experiments?

① Flowers are bisexual & self pollinating
② 7 pairs of contrasting characters are present.
③ Life span is short, so more generations can be studied in less time.
④ Plants are short & easier to maintain

7 contrasting characters of pea plant as given below are located on 4 different chromosomes

Character	Traits	
	Dominant	Recessive
Flower color	Purple	White
Flower position	Axial	Terminal
Seed color	Yellow	Green
Seed shape	Round	Wrinkled
Pod shape	Inflated	Constricted
Pod color	Green	Yellow
Stem length 	Tall	Dwarf

Mendel selected 14 true breeding pea plants - Each plant exhibiting a contrasting trait for 7 characters.

Eg: For height he took 2 plants
Pure breeding Tall – TT
Pure breeding Dwarf – tt

Continuous self pollination was done to obtain true breeding plants.

He then cross pollinated the true breeding tall & dwarf
TT x tt

Cross pollination in self pollinated plants

This was done by emasculation & bagging

- Emasculation ↓ Removal of anthers to prevent self pollination.
- Bagging ↓ Covering the stigma to avoid undesired pollination

This flower becomes female parent.

Male plant with desired trait is true bred & pollen are selected.

↓

These pollen are dusted on stigma of female parent.

MONOHYBRID CROSS

Mono- single
Hybrid- mixing

Crossing of 2 plants is done to study the inheritance of 1 character.

↓

The 2 plants possess different traits of the same character.

Eg: one is dwarf, one is tall

Punnett Square (PS)

Grid devised by RC Punnett

Mendel's laws of Inheritance

① Law of Dominance

- Characters are controlled by factors
- Factors occur in pairs
- In a dissimilar pair of factors - heterozygotic condition; one allele dominates over the other i.e. one allele expresses itself & suppresses the expression of another allele. The one that expresses is dominant & the one that gets suppressed is recessive.

Concept of Dominance

Dominant allele = Unmodified → Produces functional enzyme

Represents original phenotype

Recessive allele - Modified

- less efficient enzyme
- Non functional enzyme
- No enzyme

(Non functional enzyme / No enzyme) Trait solely depends on functioning of dominant allele.

Mendel's Monohybrid Cross

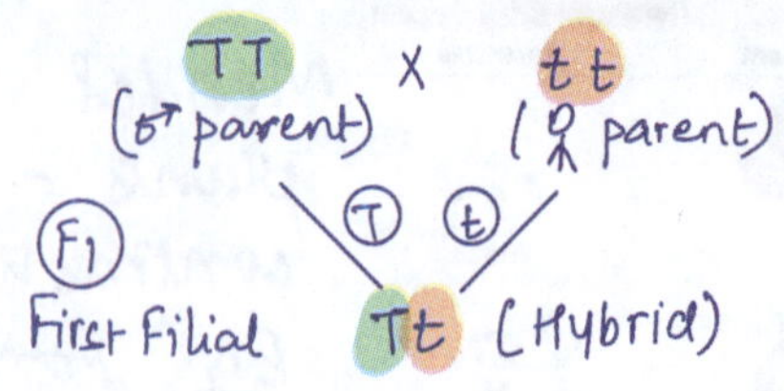

F2 Second Filial - Formed by selfing of Offsprings of F1

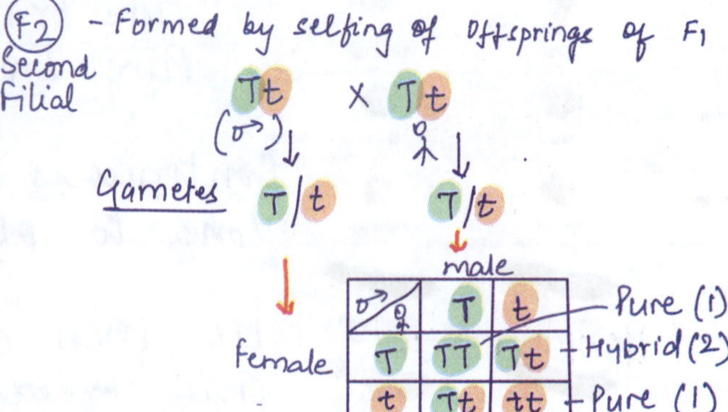

3 possible genotypes

TT : Tt : tt
1 : 2 : 1
Genotypic ratio

2 phenotypes

Tall : Dwarf
3 : 1
Phenotypic ratio

TEST CROSS

- To identify genotype of a phenotypically dominant plant.
- Example - Tall - TT/Tt (genotype)
- Seeds of plants to be tested are crossed with recessive parent

TT × tt - progeny - All tall

Tt × tt - progeny - 50% tall 50% dwarf

Tall

♂/♀	t	t
T	Tt	Tt
t	tt	tt

→ Tt : tt - Test cross ratio
1 : 1

Deviation from law of Dominance

① Incomplete Dominance

F₁ shows mixture of traits of parents - blending of traits.

Eg. 4 O'clock plant (*Mirabilis jalapa*)
Snapdragon (*Antirrhinum majus*)

Parents - RR (Red flower) rr (White flower)

Gametes R r

F1 Rr (pink flower)

F2 - Rr X Rr (selfing F1)

♂ / ♀	R	r
R	RR	Rr
r	Rr	rr

Genotypic ratio
1 : 2 : 1
RR Rr rr

Phenotypic ratio
1 : 2 : 1
Red : Pink : white

Traits do not blend, rather Each allele expresses itself partially - R - red ; r - white
Therefore - incomplete dominance

③ Multiple alleles

- Multiple forms of a gene occupy same locus in a pair of homologous chromosomes.
- An individual has only 2 alleles out of the multiple options
- Multiple alleles are observed at population level.
- Eg. ABO blood group.

② Co-dominance

Both alleles in heterozygous state express themselves completely.

Eg. ABO blood group in humans.
Gene controlling blood group = I
Alleles of I gene
I^A ; I^B ; i
I^A, I^B → Produce antigens; i → does not produce antigen

I^A & I^B are dominant over i

I^A & I^B are codominant - when present together - both express themselves completely.

Heterozygotes	Blood groups
$I^A i$	A
$I^B i$	B
$I^A I^B$	AB

NEET SYNAPSE

ABO blood group system exhibits
1. Dominance → I^A & I^B over i
2. Co dominance → I^A & I^B
3. Multiple allelism - more than 2 alleles regulate gene expression

Predicting blood group of a child $i = I^O$

Parent	I^AI^A	I^BI^B	I^AI^B	ii	I^Ai	I^Bi
I^AI^A	AA	AB	AA AB	AO	AA AO	AB AO
I^BI^B	AB	BB	AB BB	BO	AB BO	BB BO
I^AI^B	AA, AB	AB BB	AA BB AB	AO, BO	AA AB AO, BO	AB BB AO, BO
ii	AO	BO	AO BO	OO	AO OO	BO, OO
I^Ai	AA AO	AB BO	AA AB	AO, OO	AA OO	AB AO BO OO
I^Bi	AB	BB	AB BO	BO, OO	AB OO	BB OO

ABO blood group system

Genotypes - 6 - I^AI^A, I^AI^o (A) I^BI^B I^BI^o (B) I^AI^B (AB) I^oI^o/ii (O)

Phenotypes - 4

Law of segregation

- Law of purity of gametes
- During gamete formation the 2 alleles of a character separate from each other. Each allele passes to one gamete.
  ∴ gamete is haploid - pure for a particular trait.

T t → T ; t

- This takes place during meiosis/reduction
- Law of segregation is universal i.e. it has no exceptions.
- Segregation (separation) of alleles is a random process ∴ there is a 50% chance of a gamete containing either allele.

POLYGENIC INHERITANCE

Quantitative inheritance

Polygenic - Many genes responsible for inheritance of 1 character.

- Each allele has cumulative effect on the phenotype.

Eg. Human skin colour - 3 genes

AABBCC - very dark

AaBbCc - intermediate

aabbcc - very fair

Parents AABBCC very dark (ABC) aabbcc very fair (abc)

F_1 AaBbCc

F_2 AaBbCc X AaBbCc

↳ 7 phenotypes are seen

1:6:15:20:15:6:1

PLEIOTROPY

1 gene - many effects.

This gene affects metabolic pathways.

Eg ① Phenylketonuria

Gene for enzyme phenylalanine hydroxylase is faulty.

Phenylalanine —phenylalanine hydroxylase (×)→ Tyrosine

Tyrosine → Thyroxine (×) → Hypothyroidism

Tyrosine → Melanin (×) → Vitiligo

Eg ② Starch synthesis in pea seed.

B gene controls

Shape of seed	Starch grain size
BB - round	BB - large
Bb - round	Bb - intermediate
bb - wrinkled	bb - small
Law of Dominance	Incomplete Dominance

INHERITANCE OF TWO GENES (DIHYBRID CROSS)

- Cross is carried out between two pea plants that differ in traits of two characters. The other traits are same.
- Seed shape and seed colour were studied.

Round (R) (dominant) Wrinkled (r) (recessive) Yellow (Y) (dominant) Green (y) (recessive)

Parents RRYY (Round & yellow) → RY rryy (wrinkled & green) → ry

F1 (all heterozygous) RrYy

F2 - selfing of F1 RrYy X RrYy

Genotypic ratio

	YY	Yy	yy
RR	RRYY 1	RRYy 2	RRyy 1
Rr	RrYY 2	RrYy 4	Rryy 2
rr	rrYY 1	rrYy 2	rryy 1

Total genotypes - 9
Total phenotypes - 1

Phenotypic ratio
9 : 3 : 3 : 1
(9 - Parental; 3 : 3 - Hybrids; 1 - Parental)

Hybrids - 6/16 ~ 37.5%
Parental - 10/16 ~ 62.5%

F2 generation

Round Yellow (RrYy) × Round Yellow (RrYy)

	RY	Ry	rY	ry
RY	RRYY	RRYy	RrYY	RrYy
Ry	RRYy	RRyy	RrYy	Rryy
rY	RrYY	RrYy	rrYY	rrYy
ry	RrYy	Rryy	rrYy	rryy

Phenotypic Ratio
- Round/Yellow: 9
- Wrinkled/Yellow: 3
- Round/Green: 3
- Wrinkled/Green: 1

Phenotypic ratio → 9 : 3 : 3 : 1

Law of Independent assortment

- When 2 pairs of traits are combined in a hybrid, segregation of one pair of trait is independent of other pair of trait

- 2 pairs of traits - (R, Y) (r, y) ; combined in a hybrid (Rr, Yy)

segregation

R & r segregate independent of segregation of Y & y →

R ⟵ Segregation of one pair ⟶ r
independent of
Y ⟵ Segregation of another pair ⟶ y

R - 50% chance of combination with Y & 50% chance of combination with y

R —50%— Y - RY
R —50%— y - Ry

r - 50% chance of combination with Y & 50% chance of combination with y

r —50%— Y - rY
r —50%— y - ry

∴ The inheritance of one gene is not dependent on the other i.e. they assort independently.

Had independent assortment not been there in the above case; R would always combine with Y, and there would be no chance of variation.

NEET SYNAPSE

Types of gametes = 2^n
Numbers of different phenotype - 2^n
Numbers of different genotype - 3^n

] n = number of heterozygous pairs.

CHROMOSOMAL THEORY OF INHERITANCE

- Given by Sutton & Boveri
- It states that there is a close similarity between the behaviour of chromosomes and that of genes.

During gamete formation – Meiosis takes place

MI - Anaphase I - separation of homologous chromosomes takes place

MII - Anaphase II separation of chromatids of a chromosome takes place.

1 diploid parent cell

Homologous chromosomes

G₁ G₂ Meiosis I anaphase Meiosis II anaphase Germ cells

Bivalent

2n=4 2n=4

n n n n } Four Haploid daughter cells.

During metaphase I of Meiosis I, two chromosome pairs align independently.

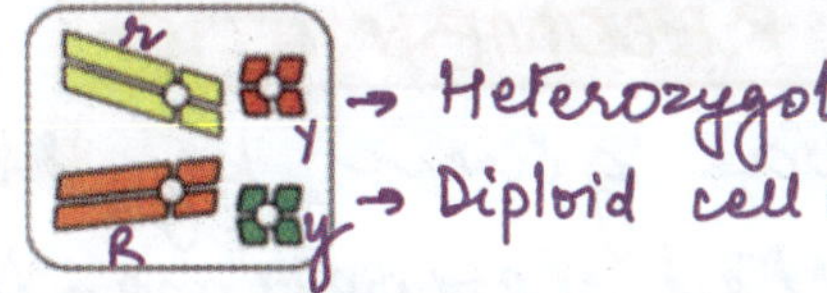

→ Heterozygotes R & Y

→ Diploid cell with replicated chromosomes

Possibility 1 Possibility 2

Chromosomes with R & y at one pole & r & Y at another

chromosome with R & y segregating independently of r & Y

-2 types of germ cells – Ry & rY

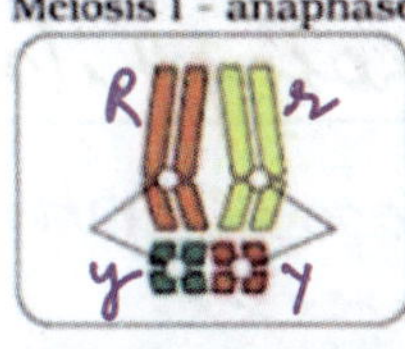

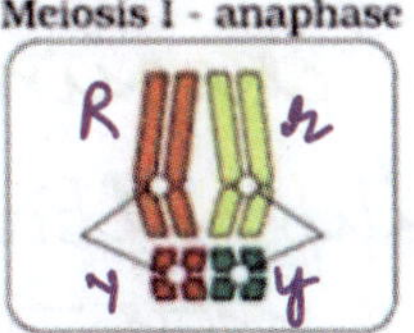

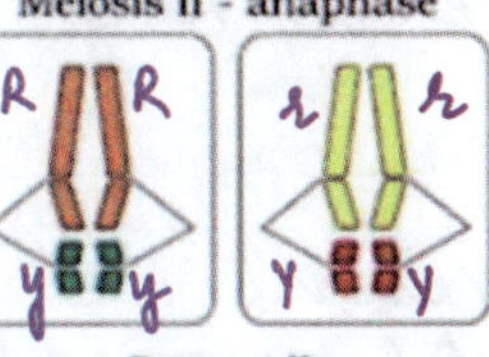

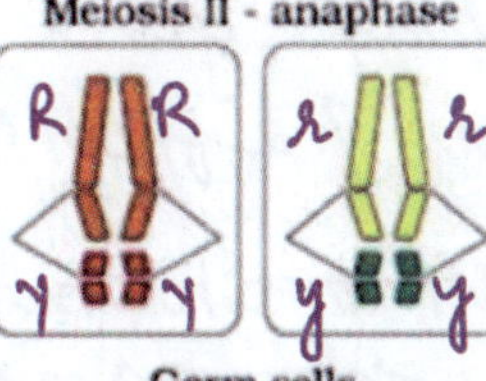

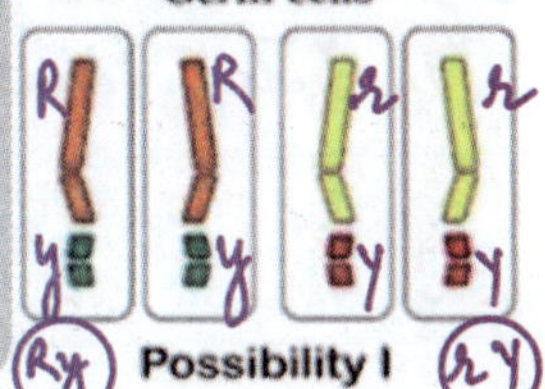

Germ cells

(Ry) Possibility I (rY) (RY) Possibility II (ry)

Independent assortment of chromosomes

Chromosomes with R & Y at one pole & r & y at another.

chromosome with R & Y segregating independently of r & y

-2 types of germ cells – RY & ry

Difference between Gene & Chromosome

Chromosome	Gene
• Occur in pairs	• Occur in pairs
• Segregate at the time of gamete formation such that only one of each pair is transferred to the gamete.	• Segregate at gamete formation and only one of each pair is transferred to the gamete
• Independent pairs segregate independently of each other.	• One pair segregates independently of another pair.

LINKAGE & RECOMBINATION

- Linkage was given by Morgan.
- He conducted experiments on Drosophila melanogaster

• Reasons for choosing Drosophila

1. Can be easily cultivated on synthetic medium
2. Short life cycle – 2 weeks
3. Single mating gives rise to large number of progeny / offsprings.
4. Sexual dimorphism present
5. Exhibit wide range of variations that can be observed with low power microscope.

Dihybrid crosses were conducted by Morgan

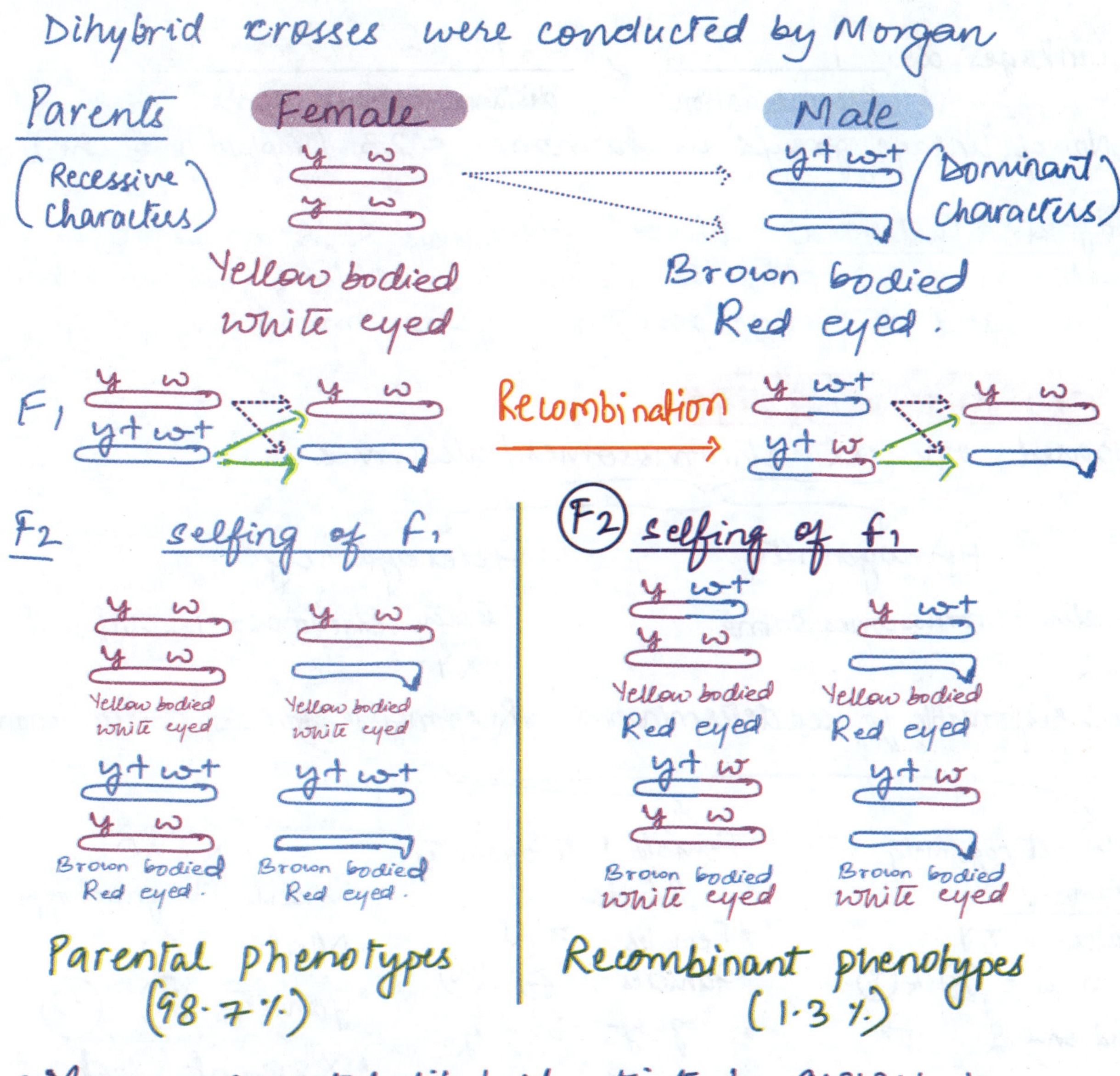

- Morgan expected dihybrid ratio to be 9:3:3:1 i.e 37.5% hybrids and 62.5% parental types, but he got 1.3% hybrids and 98.7% parental types.
- ∴ he concluded that some genes are linked, i.e, they are inherited together.
- They do not assort independently.
- Thus linkage is an exception of independent assortment.

$$\text{Linkage} \propto \frac{1}{\text{Recombination}} \propto \frac{1}{\text{distance between genes}}$$

No. of linkage groups in humans = 23 (haploid no. of chr.)

- Alfred Sturtevant – utilised frequency of recombination between gene pairs to determine distance between them.
- It is used to map position of genes on chromosomes.

SEX DETERMINATION

- Based on sex chromosomes / allosomes.

Homogamety
- Both chromosomes same
  XX
- Not responsible for sex determination

Heterogamety
- chromosomes different
  XY
- Responsible for sex determination

Male heterogamety
- Humans
- Males – XY
- Gametes – (X) & (Y)
- children – ♀ ♂
- females – XX
- Gametes – (X) (X)
- Children ♀/♂ ♀/♂

Male determines gender of the offspring.

Female heterogamety
- Birds
- Females – ZW
- Gametes – (Z) (W)
- Progeny – ♂ ♀
- Males – ZZ
- Gametes (Z) (Z)
- Progeny – ♀/♂ ♀/♂

Female determines gender of the offspring

XX – XO
Insects like grass hopper
- Males – XO
- Gametes (X) (O)
- X present X-absent
- females – XX. homogamety.

Male determines the gender of offspring

Drosophila
- Males – XY
- Females – XX

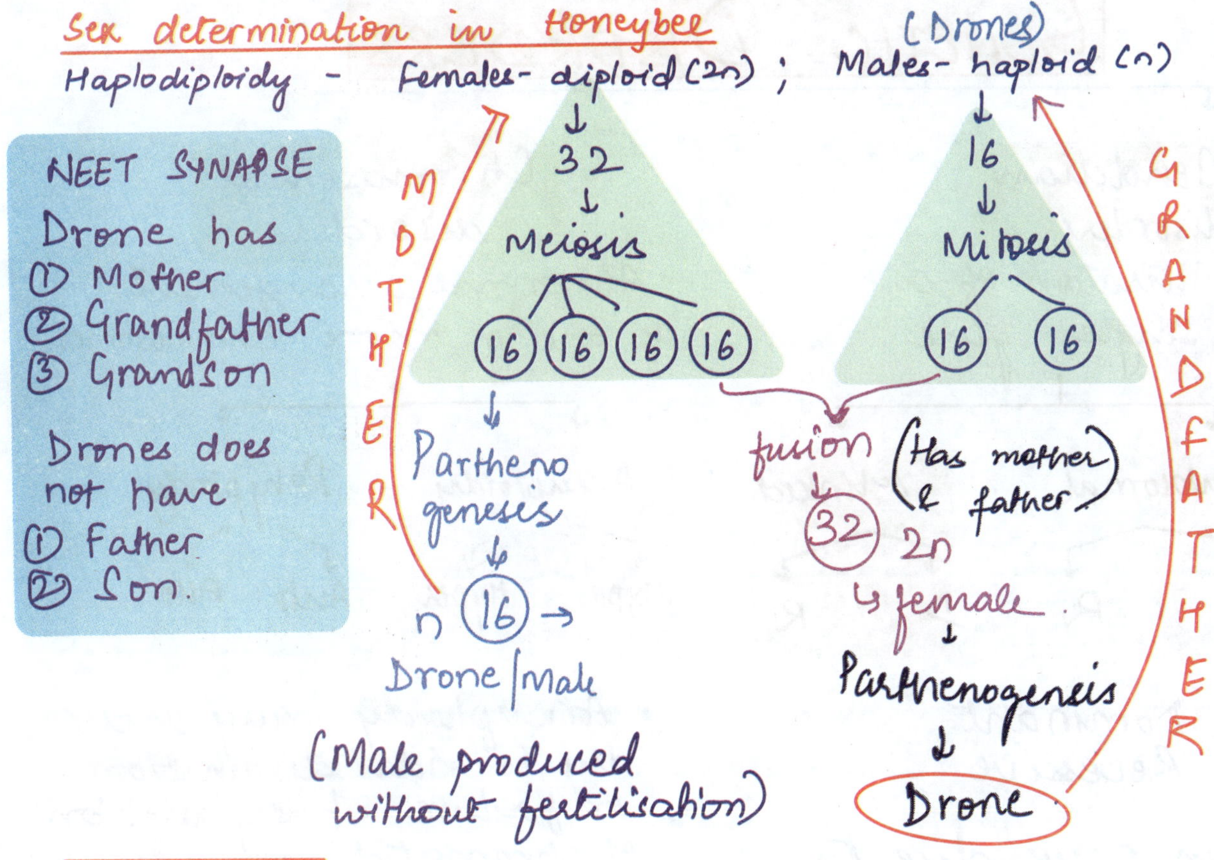

MUTATION

Sudden inheritable change in DNA or RNA

Frame shift mutation

- Addition or deletion of single base
- Change in reading frame

delete

AGG CTA GAC TTA

AGG CTA GAT TA

Reading frame changed ahead of mutation.

Point mutation

- Mutation due to change in single base pair.
- Can be - deletion, addition, substitution.

Eg: Sickle cell anaemia - Substitution mutation.

GENETIC DISORDERS

Mendelian disorders

- Alteration of a single gene

Autosomal
- D
- R

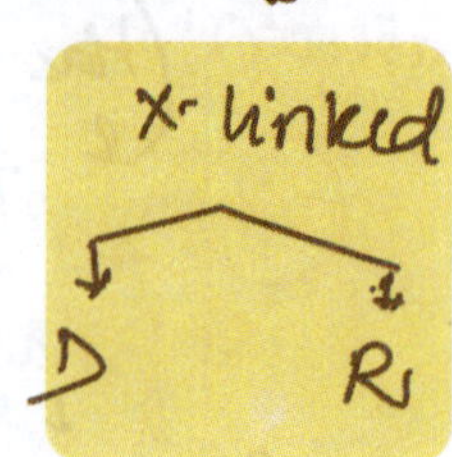

D = Dominant
R = Recessive

- Can occur due to mutation in genes
- Can be studied by pedigree analysis

Chromosomal disorders

- Abnormal arrangement of one or more chromosomes.

Aneuploidy
- Hypo
- Hyper

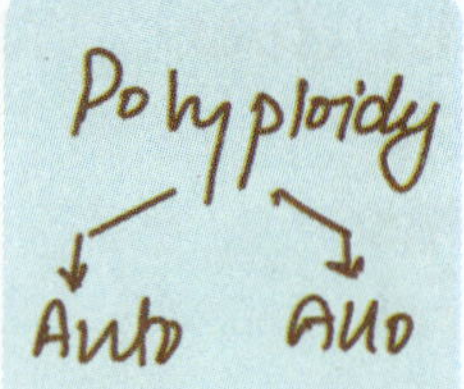

- Aneuploidy may occur due to non-disjunction or failure of separation of chromatids
- Polyploidy may occur due to failure of cytokinesis after telophase

PEDIGREE ANALYSIS

Study of inheritance of a trait in a family.

■	Male
●	female
◆	sex unspecified
■ ● ◆ (shaded)	affected individuals
■—●	mating
■═●	mating between relatives (consanguineous mating)
■—●, children below	parents above and children below (in order of birth-left to right)

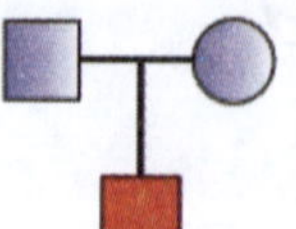

parents with male child affected with disease

five unaffected offspring

MENDELIAN DISORDERS

Autosomal	44 + XX	X-linked

Autosomal

- Mutated gene present on autosomes

A A — Homozygous dominant - diseased in autosomal dominant disorder

A a — Heterozygous dominant diseased in autosomal dominant disorder

a a — Homozygous recessive diseased in autosomal recessive disorder

X-linked

- Mutated gene present on X-chromosome.

X^c X^c - Diseased

X^c X - Carrier

X X - Normal

X Y - Diseased.

Identify the disorder.

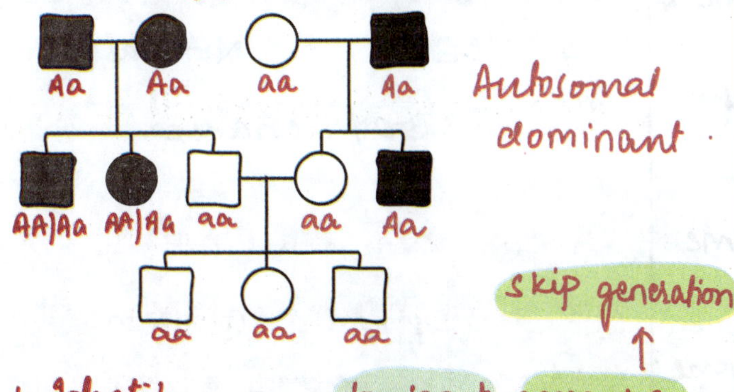

Autosomal dominant.

1. Identify - dominant or recessive → skip generation
   ↓ present in almost every generation

2. Identify - autosomal or X-linked
   - autosomal ↓ almost equally distributed among sons & daughters.
   - X-linked ↓ look for criss cross inheritance

Criss cross inheritance

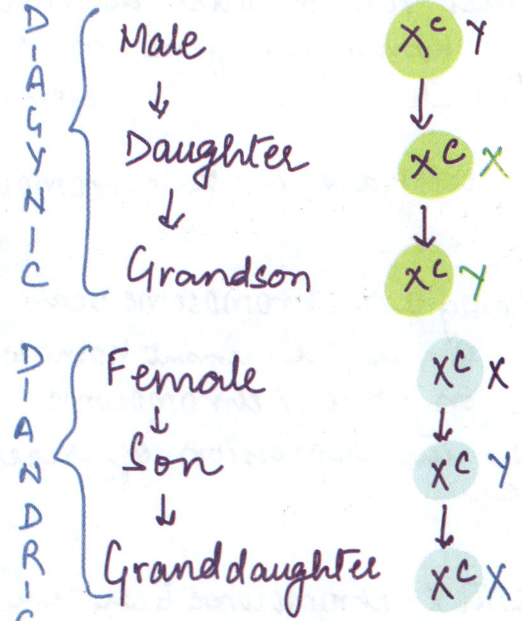

1. COLOUR BLINDNESS (CB)

- Sex linked recessive
- Inability to distinguish b/w green & red colour
- Occurs due to mutation in gene coding for one of the primary cone pigments.

Inheritance

- Occurs in 8 % males and 0.4 % females
- XY
  Males have 1 X chromosome & 1 Y chromosome
- X^cY
  Gene for CB lies on X chromosome & produces the disorder as there is no homologous gene on Y chr to check its expression
- XX
  Females have 2 - X chromosome
- X^cX
  If only 1 X chromosome bears gene for CB, its dominant homologous gene on other X chromosome checks the expression of recessive gene.
- X^cX^c
  If both X-chromosome bear gene for CB, female will be CB

"The son of a woman who carries the gene has a 50 % chance of being colour blind".

Woman in this case carries – X^cX

during gamete formation segregation will occur

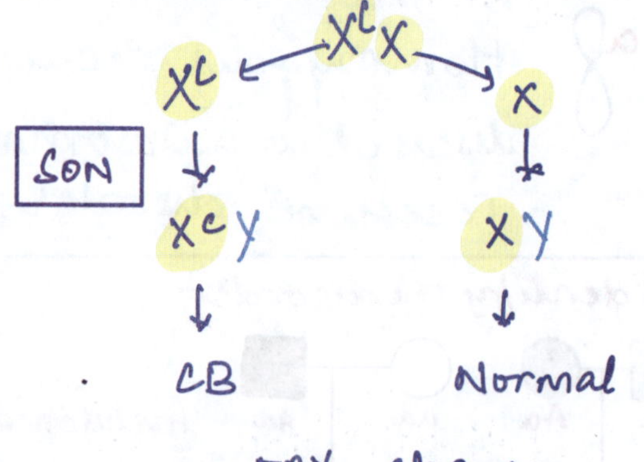

50% chance.

"A daughter will not be CB unless her mother carries the gene & her father is CB

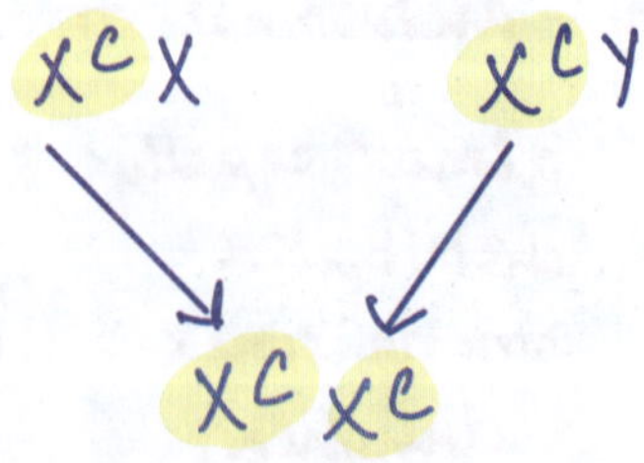

2. HAEMOPHILIA

- Sex linked recessive
- Blood defect which prevents its clotting.
- Gene controls synthesis of protein needed for blood clotting.

Factor VIII - Anti Haemophilic factor

Factor IX - Christmas factor.

- A simple cut may cause non stop bleeding
- Haemophilia also called
  Royal disease
  Christmas disease
  Bleeder's disease
- Inheritance

Females rarely affected as she must have haemophilic father (chances of survival to that stage are unlikely)

- Females are carriers - X^hX
- Haemophilic (X^hX^h) females do not survive.

NEET SYNAPSE

Genetic disorders related to blood

1. Haemophilia - X-linked recessive
2. Sickle cell anaemia - qualitative
   (Autosomal recessive | Abnormal Hb synthesis)
3. Thallesemia - quantitative

3. SICKLE CELL ANAEMIA (SCA)

- Autosomal recessive trait
- Characterised by sickle shaped RBC's under low O_2.
- Qualitative problem of synthesis of Hb

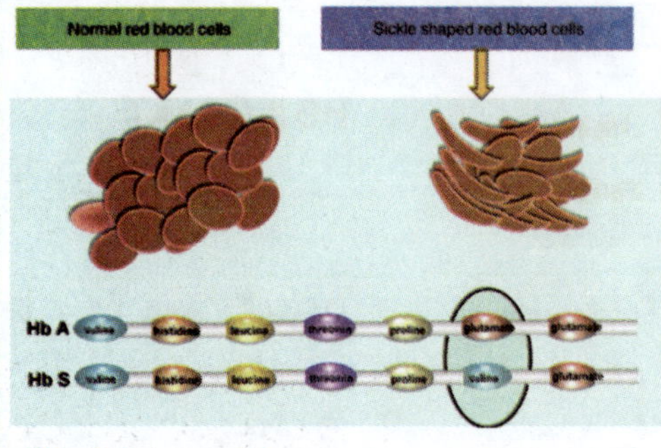

At 6th position of β-chain of Hb

Glutamic acid - GUG

↓ Point mutation/substitution

Valine - GAG

Pleiotropic gene effects

Change in shape of RBC (sickle shaped)

↓

RBC become inflexible

↓

Unable to pass through small capillaries

↓

Poor circulation

↓

Anaemia

THALASSEMIA

- Autosomal recessive trait
- Quantitative defect of Hb synthesis
- Reduced synthesis of α or β chains of Hb

Hb → α chain; β chain

α chain: HBA1, HBA2 (chromosome 16), HBA1, HBA2 (chromosome 16)

β chain: HBB (chromosome 11), HBB (chromosome 11)

Defect can be in 1 or all 4 genes.

Defect can be in 1 or both genes

CHROMOSOMAL DISORDERS

1. Down's syndrome

- Trisomy 21 — 21 21 21 } Total Chromosomes 47
  - → 3 copies instead of two
- Described by Langdon Down

Symptoms

- short stature ; small round head
- furrowed tongue ; continuous drooling
- partially open mouth
- broad palm with crease
- physical & mental retardation

2. Turner's syndrome

- 44 + XO (deficiency of 1 X chr)
- Total chr – 45
- Features – rudimentary ovaries, underdeveloped breasts, no menstruation

PHENYLKETONURIA

- Autosomal recessive trait
- Defect in gene producing enzyme phenylalanine hydroxylase

Phenylalanine —X→ Tyrosine

Phenylalanine ↓ converts into Phenylpyruvate

- Accumulation of phenylpyruvate in brain ; excretion
  - in brain ↓ mental retardation
  - excretion ↓ urine turns black on standing
- PKU also shows pleiotropy.

NEET SYNAPSE

Nullisomy → 2n – 2

Monosomy → 2n – 1

Trisomy → 2n + 1

3. Klinefelter's syndrome

- extra X chr. present
- 44 + XXY – Total chr – 47
- Phenotype – Male ; but show secondary sexual characters.
- Usually sterile

Features

- Gynaecomastia (male breast)
- Small testes
- Tall stature
- less body hair
- Feminine voice.

24. Molecular Basis of Inheritance

DNA

- Genetic material in most organisms.
- Present in [eukaryotes – in nucleus, mitochondria & chloroplast
  prokaryotes – in cytoplasm
- It is a polymer of deoxyribonucleotides
- It's length is defined as number of nucleotides or base pairs.
- Length of DNA is characteristic feature of an organism

Organism	Length of DNA	Arrangement of DNA
ϕ X174	5386 nucleotides	circular, ss DNA
Bacteriophage λ	48502 bp	linear, ds DNA
E. coli	4.6×10^6 bp	circular, ss DNA
Human (haploid content)	3.3×10^9 bp	linear, ds DNA

Hall of fame

Friedrich Meischer – discovered DNA, called it 'nuclein' (1938)

Watson and Crick – gave structure of DNA (1953)

This structure was based on –

i) X-ray diffraction pattern – Wilkins and Franklin

ii) Rule of complimentarity – Erwin Chargaff.

STRUCTURE OF DNA

- Double helical structure – right handed helix
- Two strands coiled around each other
- Each strand – polymer of deoxyribonucleotides
- Structure resembles a twisted ladder
  - ↳ Railing of ladder – alternating sugar & PO_4
    Steps of ladder – nitrogenous bases

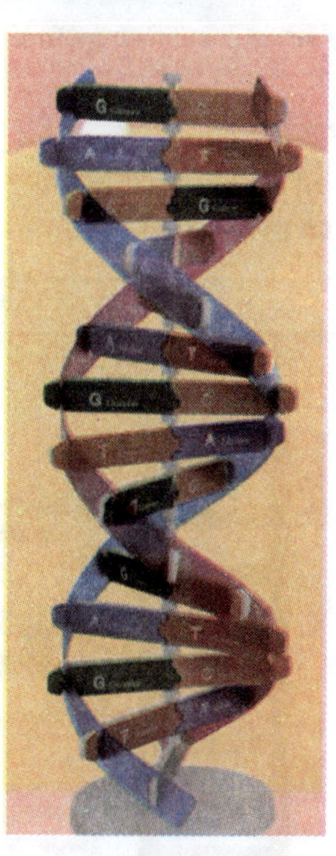

Double helical structure of B-DNA

NEET SYNAPSE

Types of DNA ⟶ A-DNA, B-DNA, C-DNA, D-DNA, Z-DNA

Only Z-DNA has a left handed helix.

NUCLEOTIDE

- Consists of
  - Pentose sugar
  - N_2 base
  - PO_4 group

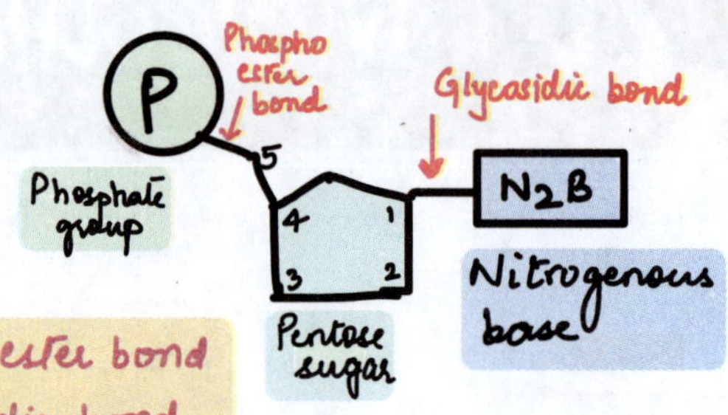

PO_4 attached at 5'OH of pentose sugar – phosphoester bond
N_2 base attached at 1'OH of pentose sugar – glycosidic bond

Pentose sugar

Ribose

- Reactive OH group present at 2'C
- Component of ribonucleotide (monomer of RNA)
- ∴ RNA is called polyribonucleotide

Deoxyribose

- Reactive OH group absent at 2'C
- Component of deoxyribonucleotide (monomer of DNA)
- ∴ DNA is called polydeoxyribonucleotide

Nitrogenous bases

Purines

Heterocyclic
Dicyclic
N-atom – 1,3,7,9C

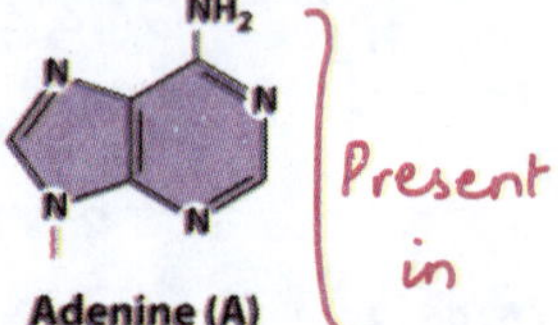

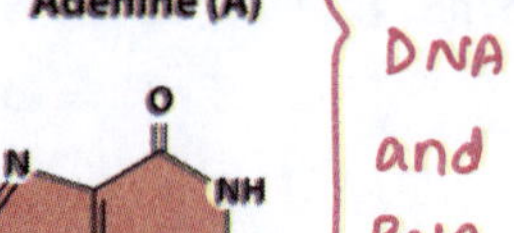

Present in DNA and RNA

Pyrimidines

Heterocyclic
Monocyclic
N-atom at 1,3C

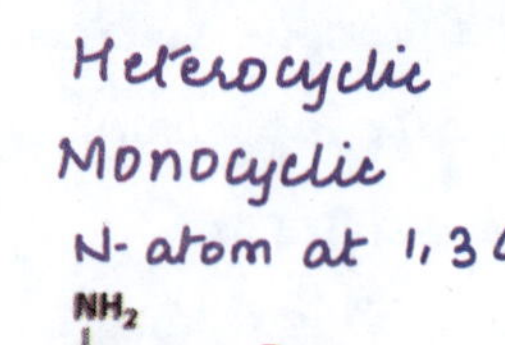

Present in DNA & RNA

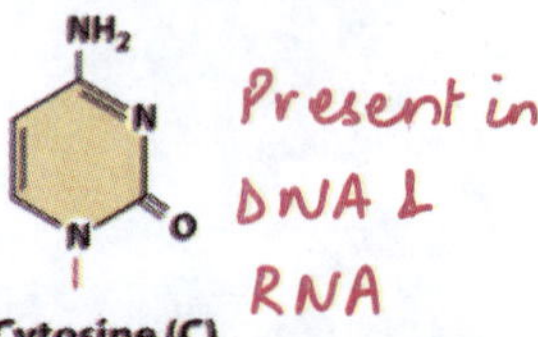

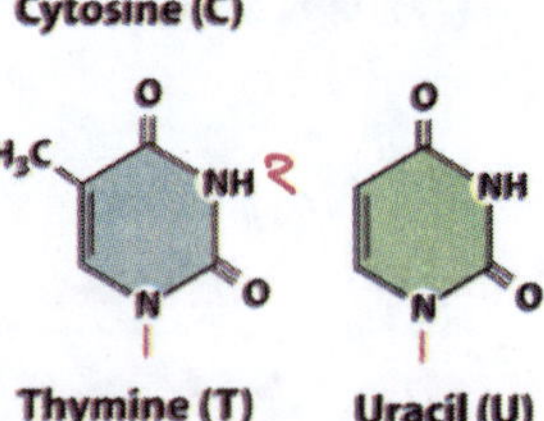

Thymine – DNA only
Uracil – RNA only

SALIENT FEATURES OF DNA DOUBLE HELICAL STRUCTURE

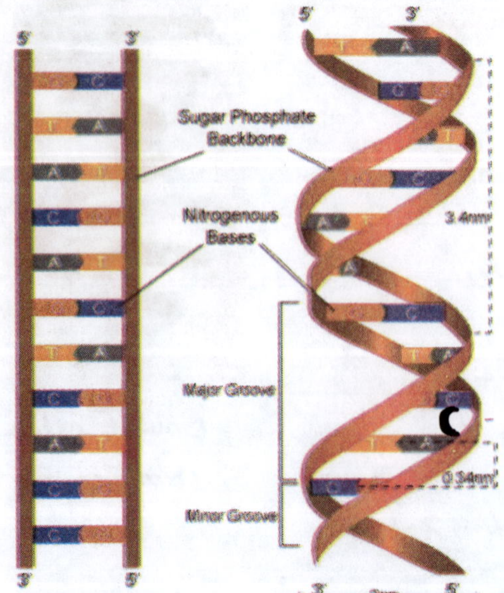

- Two strands run in antiparallel direction
- (5'→3'), (3'→5')
- Pitch of the helix (one complete turn) = 3·4 nm
- No. of base pairs in 1 pitch = 10
- Distance between 2 base pairs = 0·34 nm
- Rule of complimentarity G≡C ; A=T
- Angulation b/w two successive base pairs = 36°
- Width b/w 2 strands = 2 nm
- Twisting of strands creates major & minor grooves.

NEET SYNAPSE

Chargaff's rules – A=T ; G=C
A+G = C+T } purines = pyrimidines ; $\frac{A+G}{C+T} = 1$
Chargaff's rules are not applicable to RNA

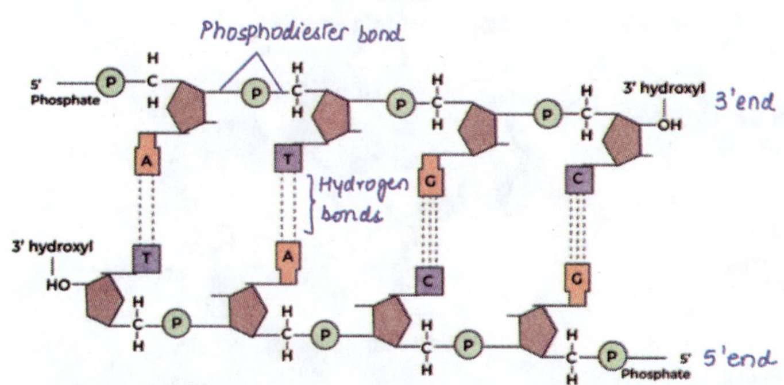

Phosphodiester bond
- Joins 2 nucleotides of the same strand
- Formed between 5'OH of one nucleotide & 3'OH of another nucleotide

Hydrogen bond
- Joins nucleotides of 2 strands.
- H-bond joins 2 strands of DNA

3'end - 3'OH not bonded with next nucleotide ; it is free
5'end - 5'OH not bonded with next nucleotide ; it is free.

NEET SYNAPSE
Sugar placement decides the polarity of the 2 antiparallel DNA strands

PACKAGING OF DNA HELIX

- Length of DNA in a human diploid cell = 2.2m $(6.6 \times 10^9 \text{ bp} \times 0.34 \times 10^{-9} \text{m})$
- Size of a typical nucleus - 10^{-6}m ∴ DNA has to be accomodated in small area.
- Packaging of DNA involves folding and compaction.

DNA PACKAGING IN PROKARYOTES

- DNA is present in prokaryotes in cytoplasm in supercoiled state.
- Coils are maintained by RNA & non histone proteins (histone proteins absent)
  The packaged structure is called nucleoid.

DNA PACKAGING IN EUKARYOTES

- DNA double helix is packed into nucleosomes.
- Nucleosome - 200 bp long DNA wrapped around octamer of histone proteins
- Histone proteins - positively charged, basic proteins
  ↳ rich in basic amino acids - lysine & arginine
- Positively charged histones attract the negatively charged DNA (due to PO_4^{3-} ions)
- Nucleosomes condense to form chromatin (thread like)
- Nucleosomes in chromatin resemble 'beads on a string' appearance.
- Further folding occurs due to Non Histone Chromosomal (NHC) proteins.
- Chromatin fibres condense further during metaphase to form chromosomes.

NEET SYNAPSE
- Histone proteins in nucleosome - H_2A, H_2B, H_3, H_4 (x2) & H_1 (for linker DNA)
- Association of H_1 with nucleosome indicates that DNA is condensed into chromatin fibre

Heterochromatin	Euchromatin
◆ Densly packed	◆ Loosely packed
◆ Inactive	◆ Transcriptionally Active
◆ Darkly stained	◆ Lightly stained

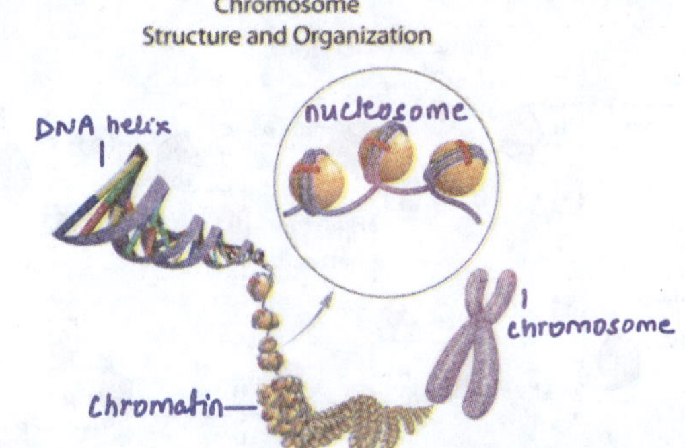

THE SEARCH FOR GENETIC MATERIAL

GRIFFITH's EXPERIMENT

◆ He used Streptococcus pneumoniae & mice
◆ 2 strains of bacteria were used

S-strain	R-strain
◆ Smooth colonies (mucopolysaccharide coat)	◆ Rough colonies (No coat)
◆ Virulent (caused pneumonia)	◆ Non virulent (no disease)

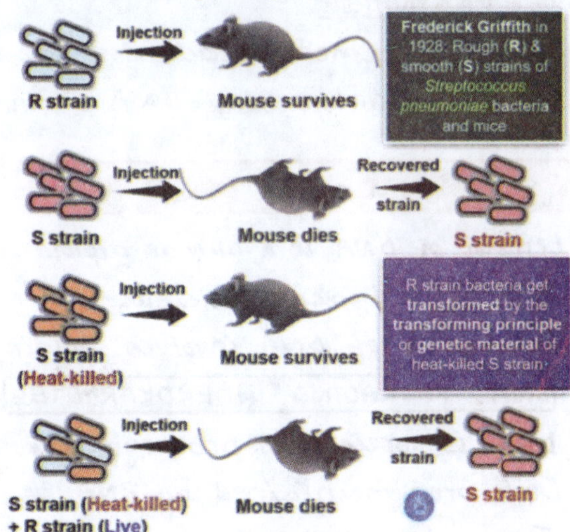

Key points

◆ Heat killed S-strain – non virulent as heat destroys disease causing proteins.
◆ Heat killed S + live R – virulent because heat does not destroy DNA which transforms the live R → hence S type colonies are recovered from R type.

BIOCHEMICAL CHARACTERISATION OF TRANSFORMING PRINCIPLE

◆ Avery, McLeod & McCarty conducted experiment to identify transforming molecule of Griffith's experiment.
◆ They took R & S strains and observed transformation in various set-ups using –
Proteases – digest proteins
RNases – digest RNA
DNases – digest DNA
◆ When DNA was digested, transformation did not occur which proved that DNA is the genetic material.

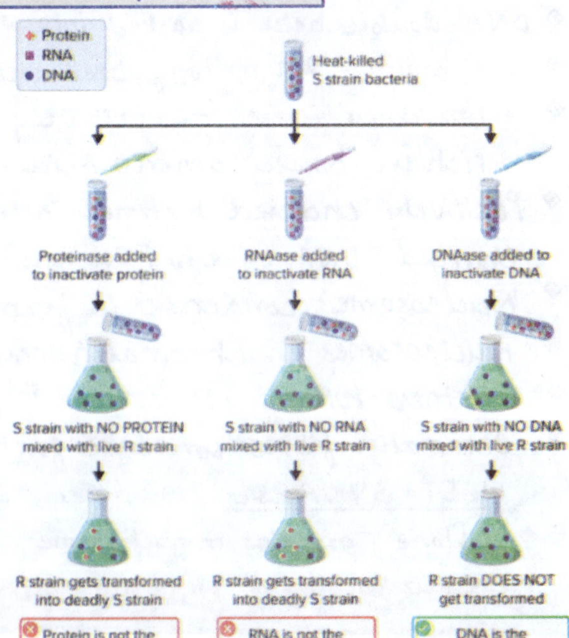

HERSHEY AND CHASE EXPERIMENT

- Bacteriophage & E. coli were used.
- Bacteriophage ┌ ^{32}P - radioactive DNA
  └ ^{35}S - radioactive protein coat
- DNA labelled with ^{32}P entered bacterial cell. whereas protein coat labelled with ^{35}S did not enter.
- Thus it was concluded that DNA was the infective part of bacteriophage.
- Hence it was proved that DNA is the genetic material.

RADIOACTIVE LABELLING: S^{35} labelled phage protein | P^{32} labelled phage DNA
INFECTION:
BLENDING:
CENTRIFUGATION:
OBSERVATION: S^{35} labelled phage protein found in the supernatant | P^{32} labelled phage protein found in the pellet

RNA WORLD

- RNA is the genetic material in some viruses
- It was the first genetic material to be discovered.
- DNA evolved from RNA
- RNA catlyses some essential biochemical reactions.

NEET SYNAPSE

Ribozyme catalyses-
1. Cleavage - Ribonuclease P
2. Splicing - snurps
3. Peptide bond formation - Peptidyl transferase

CHARACTERISTICS OF GENETIC MATERIAL

- DNA is less reactive - absence of 2'OH group
- DNA is more stable - presence of thymine instead of uracil
  - presence of double helix
- DNA undergoes slow mutation (more stable); RNA - faster mutation (single stranded)
- DNA is the genetic material but RNA is required for gene expression.
- DNA is biochemically less susceptible to changes (due to stability)

REPLICATION OF DNA

- Occurs during S-phase of interphase of cell cycle
- Essential for restoration of DNA content in daughter cells.
- DNA replication doubles DNA content but not chromosome number.

Semi conservative mode of DNA replication

- Idea was given by Watson & Crick.
- One strand of the newly synthesised ds DNA is synthesised de novo; while another strand is of parent DNA.

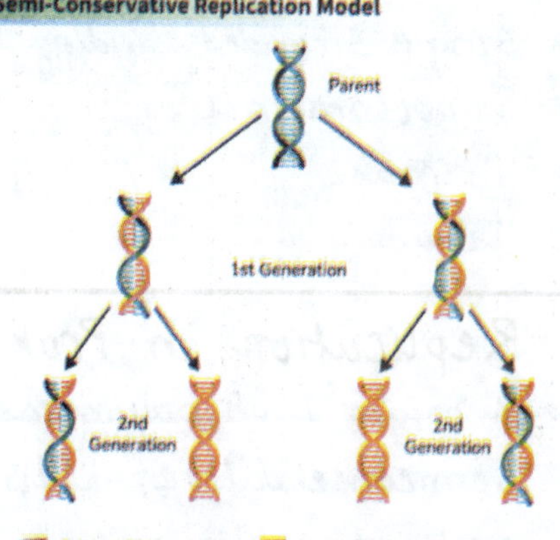

MESELSON AND STAHL EXPERIMENT

- Cultured E.coli in a medium containing $^{15}NH_4Cl$ for many generations
- This led to integration of ^{15}N in bacterial DNA
- Later medium was replaced by $^{14}NH_4Cl$
- After 20 min, sample was subjected to CsCl based centrifugation.
- Bacterial DNA showed intermediate density $^{15}N^{14}N$
- In next cycle, after 40 min, sample contained DNA with both intermediate ($^{15}N^{14}N$) and light ($^{14}N^{14}N$) densities

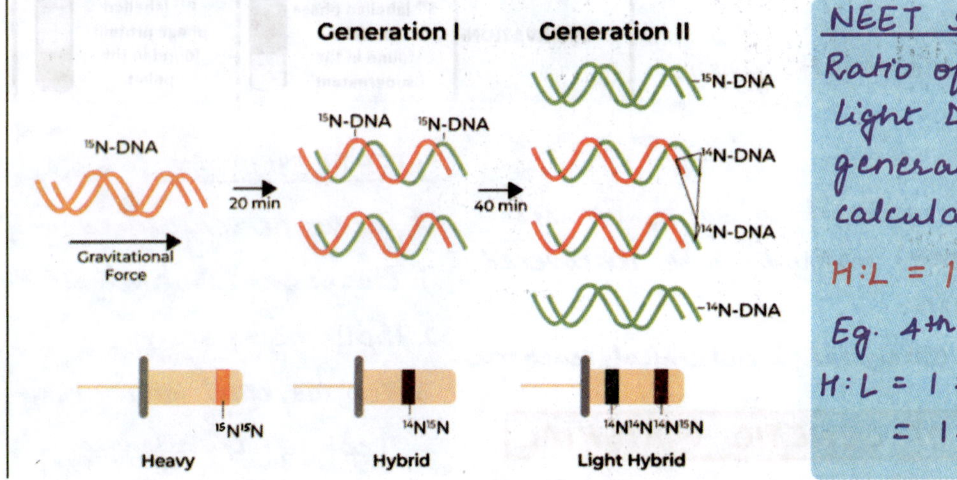

NEET SYNAPSE

Ratio of hybrid & light DNA after n generations can be calculated by -

$H:L = 1 : (2^{(n-1)} - 1)$

Eg. 4th generation

$H:L = 1 : (2^{(4-1)} - 1) = 1 : (2^3 - 1)$

$= 1 : 7$

In 1969, Taylor proved semiconservative mode of DNA replication in eukaryotes in Vicia faba (faba beans)

MACHINERY OF DNA REPLICATION

Enzymes used

Enzyme	Function
1. DNA dependent DNA Polymerase	polymerisation
2. Helicase	unwinding of DNA helix
3. Single Stranded Binding Protein (SSBP)	stabilises single stranded DNA
4. Topoisomerase	reduces supercoiling in DNA
5. Primase	synthesis of primers
6. Ligase	binding of DNA strands.

Replication in Prokaryotes	Replication in Eukaryotes
◆ 3 major DNA polymerases - I, II, III	◆ 5 types of DNA polymerases
◆ Semiconservative, bidirectional and discontinuous.	◆ Semiconservative, bidirectional and discontinuous.

MECHANISM OF DNA REPLICATION

Initiation

- Helicase cleaves DNA strand at ORI (origin of replication)
- Topoisomerase reduces supercoiling
- 2 single strands are created as replication fork opens.
- They are stabilised by SSBP

Elongation

- Primase enzyme synthesises primers
- DNA polymerase adds dNTPs (according to complimentary base pairing) at 3'OH end of primers
- Direction - 5' → 3'
- Leading strand - continuous (3' → 5')
- Lagging strand - discontinuous (5' → 3')
- On Lagging strand, DNA synthesis restarts many times as helix unwinds
- This results in formation of small fragments called Okazaki fragments
- These are joined by DNA ligase

REPLICATION FORK

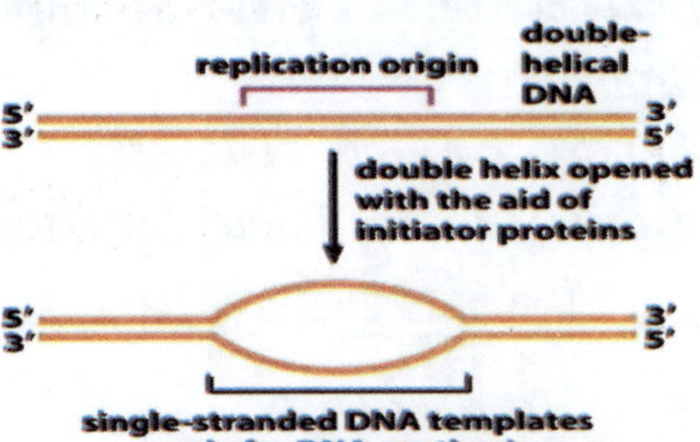

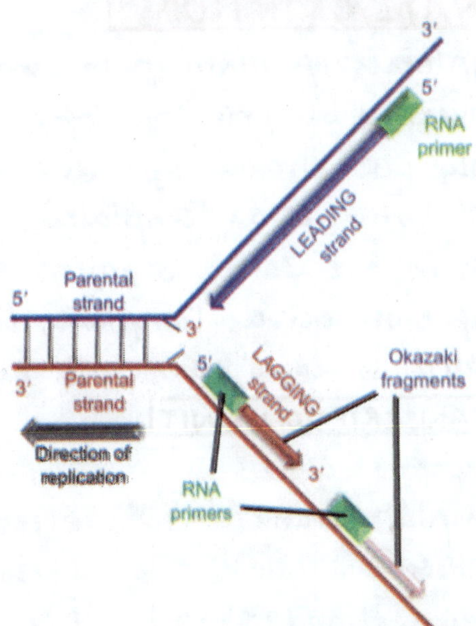

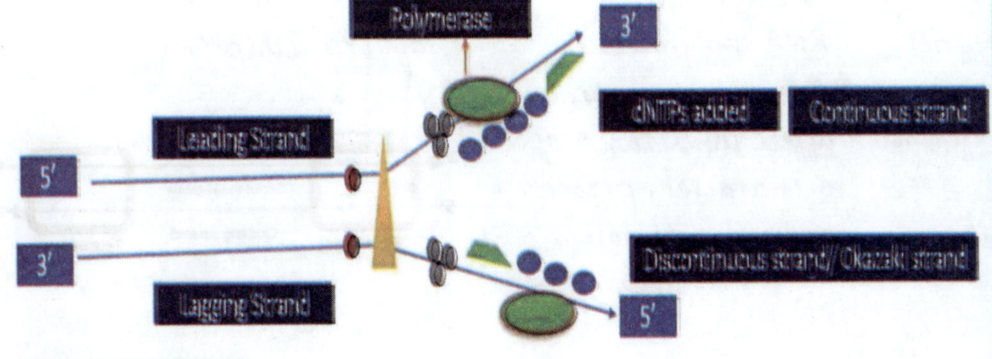

NEET SYNAPSE

- DNA polymerase polymerises at the rate of 2000 bp/sec.
- Primers are 7-12 nucleotide long RNA sequences.

Termination

- DNA replication ends when the two strands fuse.

DNA replication results in the formation of 2 daughter molecules - one old and another newly synthesised.

CENTRAL DOGMA OF MOLECULAR BIOLOGY

- Unidirectional flow of information from DNA to RNA to polypeptide.
- Teminism
  Central Dogma reverse
  Discovered by Temin & Baltimore

DNA ⇄ RNA ⟶ Protein (Transcription: DNA → RNA; Reverse Transcription: RNA → DNA)

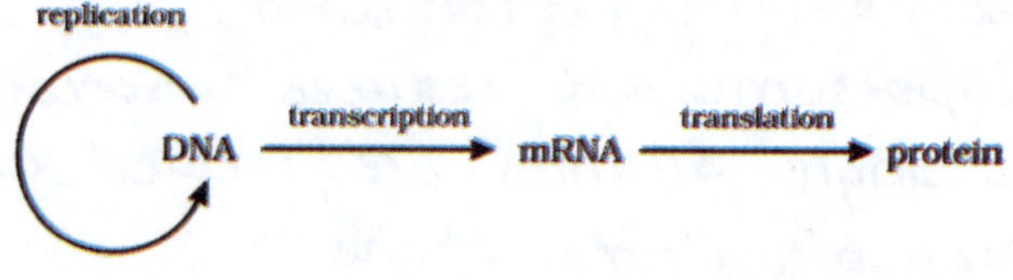

Representation of Central Dogma

TRANSCRIPTION

- Synthesis of mRNA from template strand of DNA.
- Governed by principle of complimentarity (exception A pairs with U)
- Only one strand of a ds DNA acts as template because–
  - If both act as templates, two different RNA transcripts will be formed from the same segment of DNA – this will complicate translation.
  - If both act as template, two RNA transcripts that will be complimentary to each other will be formed forming double stranded RNA.

TRANSCRIPTION UNIT

Structural Gene
- Template strand (3'→5') (Antisense strand)
- Coding strand (5'→3') (Sense strand)
- Coding strand does not code for anything
- It is used as a reference point for parts of transcription unit

Promoter
- Present 'Upstream' (before structural gene)
- At 5' of coding strand
- Binding site for RNA polymerase
- Regulatory sequences - affect inheritance of a character, present around promoter

Terminator
- Present 'Downstream' (after structural gene)
- At 3' of coding strand
- Defines the end of transcription.

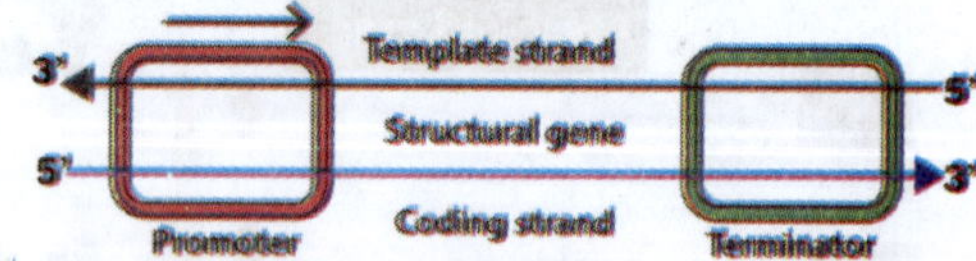

CISTRON

- Structure gene in a transcription unit that codes for a polypeptide.
- Monocistronic (eukaryotes) - These genes code for only one polypeptide - They contain only 1 initiation site
- Polycistronic (prokaryotes) - They code for more than one polypeptide - They contain several genes of a metabolic pathway

PROCESS OF TRANSCRIPTION

IN PROKARYOTES

- Occurs in cytoplasm
- Single RNA polymerase controls the synthesis of all types of RNAs.
- Steps of Transcription in Prokaryotes

Initiation

- Sigma (σ) factor directs RNA polymerase to bind with Promoter
- It polymerises NTPs in template dependent manner
- RNA polymerase opens helix and continues elongation.
- It drops σ factor after initiation.

Elongation

- Occurs in 5' ⟶ 3' direction
- RNA polymerase core enzyme carries out elongation all by itself, no cofactors are required.

Termination

- Rho (ρ) factor binds to RNA polymerase at terminator site.
- It facilitates termination.
- Nascent RNA & RNA polymerase fall off.

NEET SYNAPSE

RNA polymerase (core enzyme) + σ factor = RNA polymerase holoenzyme

Transcription & Translation can be coupled in prokaryotes as both occur in same compartment.

IN EUKARYOTES

- Occurs within the nucleus
- 3 separate RNA polymerases
  - RNA Polymerase I - rRNA (28S, 18S, 5.8S)
  - RNA Polymerase II - mRNA (hn RNA)
  - RNA Polymerase III - tRNA (5srRNA, snRNA)
- Process of transcription leads to formation of hnRNA (heterogenous nuclear RNA)
  ↳ precursor of mRNA

Post Transcriptional Changes

1. Capping - modification of GTP at 5'end to 7methyl guanosine
   - protects mRNA from degradation by nucleases
   - Translation initiates from this end.
2. Splicing - Removal of introns (non coding regions)
3. Tailing - Addition of poly A tail (200-300 bases) at 3'OH end.

EXON 1	INTRON 1	EXON 2	INTRON 2	EXON 3

primary transcript

5' cap	EXON 1	EXON 2	EXON 3	—AAAAAAA

mRNA transcript.

GENETIC CODE

- Nucleotide sequence of nitrogenous bases which specifies the amino acid sequence in a polypeptide.
- Only 20 amino acids are used in protein synthesis.
- Gamow gave the possibility of codons.
- $4 \times 4 \times 4 = 64$ (4 bases A, T, C, G - arranged in sequences of $3 = 4^3$)
- Nirenberg & Matthaei proved triplet codon existence.
  - ↳ They used cell free system - used Severo Ochoa enzyme (synthesise mRNA without template) and translated homopolymer of RNA (UUU)
- Har Gobind Khorana - defined combination of bases - co & homopolymers.

FEATURES OF GENETIC CODE

- Codon is triplet - sequence of 3 bases - no punctuation (commaless)
- Universal - codons code for same amino acids in living organisms.
- Non ambiguous - a codon always codes for same amino acid.
- Degenerate - more than one codon can code for same amino acid.
- Start codon - AUG, GUG
- Stop codon - UAA, UAG, UGA

Wobble hypothesis - 3' base can change, it lacks specificity.

MUTATION

- Spontaneous change in base sequence
- Point Mutation - mutation at a single nucleotide.
  - Substitution - a base replaced by another base.
    - Eg. Sickle cell anaemia (GAG ⟶ GUG)
  - Frame-shift - addition or deletion of a base can change reading frame.
    - Eg. AUG AUG GUA GUU CCG ⟶ AUG UGG UAG UUC CG (change in reading frame)
    - ↑ delete (A)

t-RNA - ADAPTER MOLECULE

- Adapter - can bind to mRNA as well as amino acid.
- Also called - soluble RNA (soluble in 1M NaCl)
  - smallest RNA
- Clover leaf structure (2D)
- Inverted L (3D)
- Anticodon site binds complementarily with codon
- Amino acid binding site 3' end - ACC sequence.

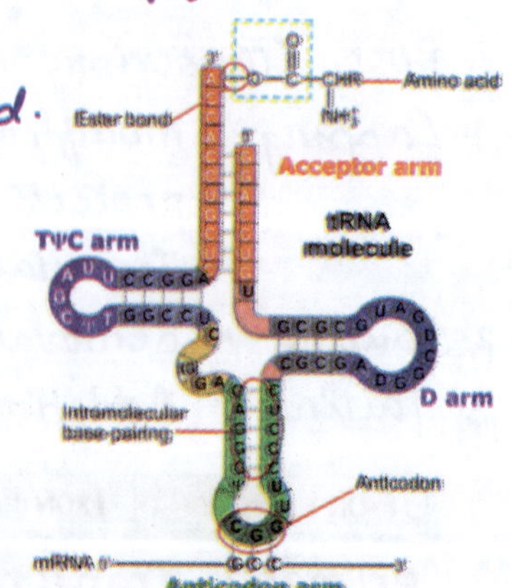

TRANSLATION

- Process of protein synthesis from mRNA
- Amino acids are arranged according to sequence of codons present on mRNA

MACHINERY OF TRANSLATION

1. mRNA - carries genetic information from nucleus to ribosomes (cytoplasm)
2. Amino acyl tRNA synthetase - catalyses amino acid attachment to 3' end of tRNA
3. Ribosome - protein factory - made of 2 subunits -
   - Small subunit - Translation begins when mRNA attaches to small subunit of ribosome.
   - Large subunit - possesses sites that allow binding of amino acids during polypeptide formation.
4. UTR's (untranslated regions) - additional sequences on mRNA that do not get translated.

STAGES OF TRANSLATION

1. Activation of amino acids / aminoacylation of tRNA / Charging of tRNA

$$\text{Amino acid} + \text{ATP} \xrightarrow[\text{tRNA synthetase}]{\text{Amino acyl}} \text{Amino acyl-AMP} + \text{Pi}$$

- $$\text{Aminoacyl AMP} + \text{tRNA} \xrightarrow[\text{tRNA synthetase}]{\text{Amino acyl}} \text{Aminoacyl tRNA} + \text{AMP}$$
- Enzyme is specific for its amino acid - there are 20 enzymes for 20 a.a.

NEET SYNAPSE

When 2 charged tRNAs come close enough, formation of peptide bond takes place due to high energy.

2. Initiation of Polypeptide Chain Synthesis

- Activated amino acyl tRNA attaches to AUG (initiation codon) on mRNA
- Small ribosome unit attaches to mRNA
- Larger subunit joins the assembly later to form translation
- initiation complex.

Polysome - When many ribosomes attach to mRNA

Large subunit has -

(i) P site (Peptidyl site) - elongation of polypeptide occurs here
(ii) A site (amino acyl site) - accepts the new incoming amino acid.
(iii) E site (Exit site) - the empty tRNA exits ribosome from this site.

- First amino acid tRNA complex occupies P-site of ribosome
- The other amino acids occupy A site as they enter ribosome.

3. Elongation of Polypeptide Chain

- Amino acids are added one by one to the first amino acid
- Codon recognition - codon on A site forms H-bond with tRNA anticodon.
- Peptide bond formation - ribosome catalyses the formation of peptide (Peptidyl transferase) bond b/w amino acids.
  - Polypeptide extending from P site moves to
  - A-site to accept new amino acid.

Translocation - tRNA with polypeptide at A site is translocated to P-site
- tRNA at P site moves to E-site & leaves the ribosome
- Ribosome moves down mRNA in 5' ⟶ 3' direction

4. Termination of Polypeptide chain.

- When A site reaches a stop codon.
- Stop codon does not code for any amino acid
- ∴ no new amino acid is added to the polypeptide chain.
- Stop codon is identified by release factors
- Release factors detach and release the chain from the ribosome.

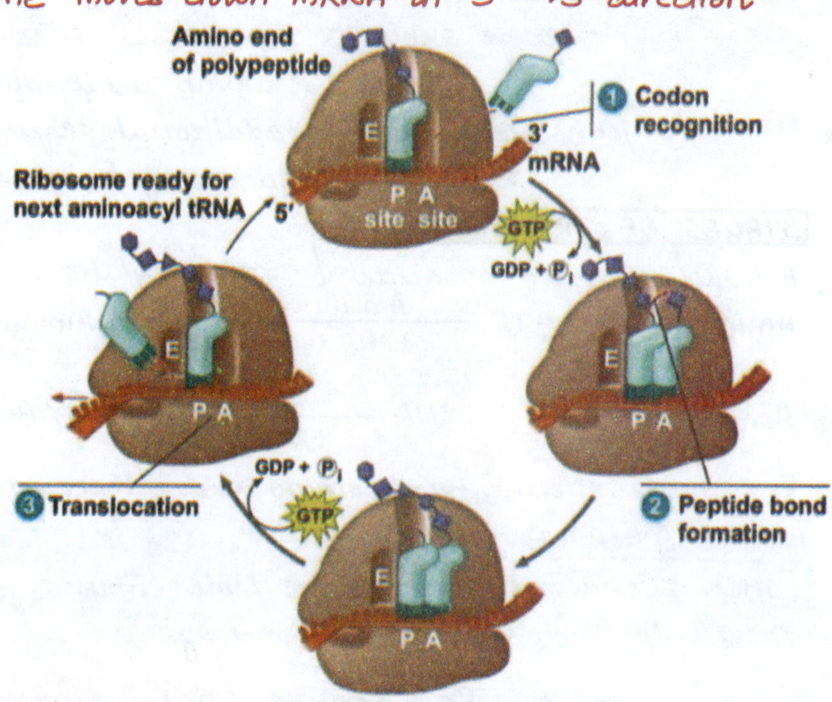

REGULATION OF GENE EXPRESSION

- Levels of gene expression - Transcription and Translation

GENE EXPRESSION IN PROKARYOTES

- Most expression occurs at transcription level.
- It is mediated by regulatory proteins (activators or repressors)
- Polycistronic - multiple genes, single transcript, single promoter.
- Operon - Gene cluster + promoter + operator - function together in regulation. Eg. lac operon, trp operon, his operon etc.

LAC OPERON

Elucidated by Jacob & Monod

1. Structural genes
   - lac z - codes for β galactosidase (hydrolysis lactose)
   - lac y - codes for permease (allows entry of lactose in cells)
   - lac a - codes for transacetylase (transfers acetyl group)
2. Operator gene
   - controls functioning of structural genes
   - repressor has affinity for operator
   - operator works like on & off switch of protein synthesis.
3. Promotor gene - RNA polymerase binds here to start transcription.
4. Regulatory gene - i-gene - inhibitory gene - codes for repressor protein.
   it is a constitutive gene (works all the time)
   Repressor is inactivated by inducer.

In lac operon - lactose or allolactose act as inducer

Lactose stops the activity of repressor so that operon can remain in switch off state.

→ Lac operon is an inducible operon

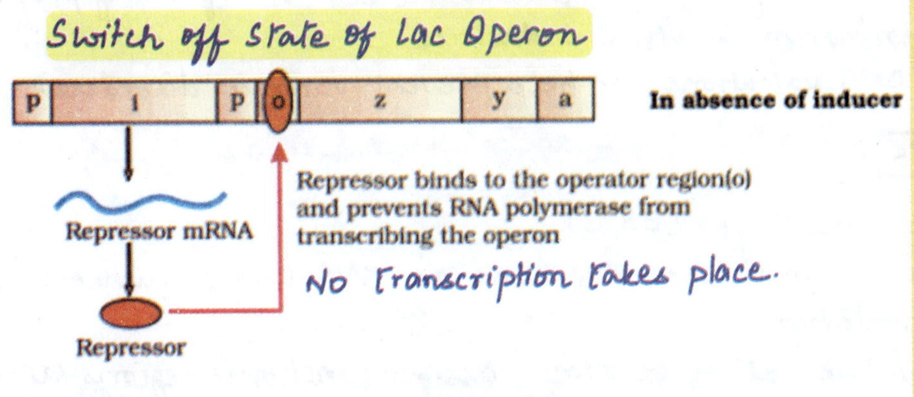

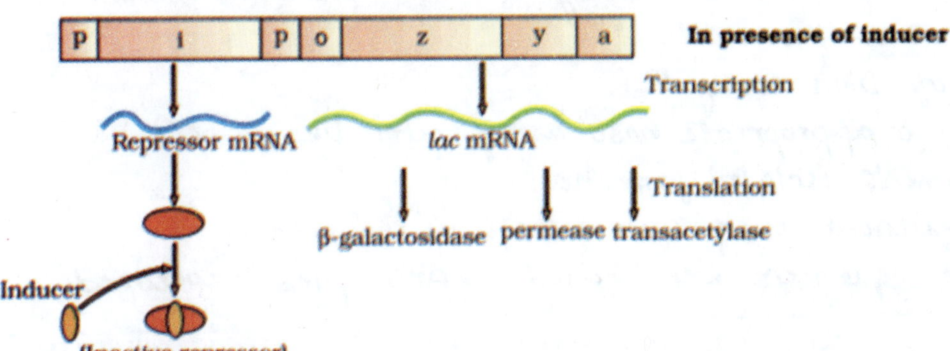

- Glucose is the preffered source of energy for bacteria.
- In absence of glucose, bacteria uses lactose for metabolism.
- Thus when lactose enters, it induces the formation of its own digestive enzymes.

HUMAN GENOME PROJECT

- A mega project to get complete knowledge of organisation, structure and function of human genome.
- Human genome – 3×10^9 base pairs.
- Bioinformatics – branch of biotechnology that involves high speed computation devices for storage, retrieval & analysis of large amount of data.
- HGP was launched in 1990 and completed in 2003
- Sequencing of chr. no. 1 completed in 2006.
- Coordinated by US Department of Energy and National Institute of Health
- Wellcome Trust (UK) was a major partner in beginning

GOALS OF HGP

- Mapping the human genome at the level of nucleotide sequences.
- Store the information in databases and develop tools of analysis.
- Solve any Ethical, Legal or Social Issue (ELSI) regarding project.
- Transfer the information to other industries.
- Understanding DNA variations can help prevent various disorders.

METHODOLOGIES

1. Expressed Sequence Tags (ESTs)
   Identify all genes that were expressed as RNA and sequence them.
2. Sequence Annotation
   Sequence the whole set of genome – assign functional regions later.
   Steps of Sequencing

i) Extraction of cell from human body
ii) Extraction of DNA from cell
iii) Amplification of DNA using PCR
iv) Transfer DNA to appropriate host using vectors like BAC & YAC
v) Resulting fragments isolated from host.
vi) They were sequenced using automated DNA sequencers
vii) automated DNA sequencers were based on principles developed by F. Sanger.
viii) Alignment of overlapping sequences was done using specialised computer based program.

Salient features of HGP

- Human genome contains 3164.7 million bp
- Human genome has about 30000 genes
- 99.9 % of DNA is exactly same in all humans.
- An average gene has about 3000 bases.
- Dystrophin gene - 2.4 million bases
- Function of 50% genes is unknown
- Less than 2% genes code for proteins
- Highest numbers of genes - Chromosome no. 1 - 2968
  Lowest number of genes - Chromosome Y - 231
- Repeated sequences make up very large portion of genome.
- Satellite DNA - part of genome possessing repetitive sequences.
- Minisatellite - 11-60 bp long; they are VNTR's used in DNA fingerprinting.
- Micro sattelite - 5-8 bp long sequences - called junk DNA.
- Single Nucleotide Polymorphisms (SNPs) - 1.4 million sites of single base variation.

APPLICATIONS AND FUTURE CHALLENGES

- HGP can lead to development of a new approach to biological research.
- Understanding of interconnecting networks of genes & proteins.

DNA FINGERPRINTING - DNA Profiling

- Given by Alec Jefferey
- Method used to identify individuals based on their unique DNA characteristics.
- Principle - 0.1% DNA differs in different individuals - makes them unique
  - This 0.1% is present in the form of repetitive sequences.
  - Repetitive sequences are variable in different individuals.
  - These sequences do not code for proteins.
  - They are present at many places in the genome.
  They are called VNTR's (Variable number Tandem Repeats)
  size ↓ 0.1 - 20 kb (Kilobases) - 1 kb = 1000 bases
  - They show very high degree of polymorphism (arises due to mutations)
  - These sequences form the basis for fingerprinting.

NEET SYNAPSE

RFLP - Restriction Fragment length Polymorphism - when DNA of 2 individuals is digested with same RE, the length of fragments differ due to repetitive sequences.

STEPS OF DNA FINGERPRINTING

1. DNA Extraction
   DNA can be taken from blood, semen, hair follicle etc.
   Cell lysis is followed by treatment with specific enzymes to obtain DNA.
2. Restriction Enzyme Digestion
   DNA is subjected to digestion by Restriction Endonucleases.
   This results in the formation of small DNA fragments.
3. Gel Electrophoresis
   DNA fragments are separated using Gel Electrophoresis
   DNA being negatively charged is attracted to positive terminal (anode)
   This separates DNA fragments based on size (larger DNA has more -ve charge)
4. Southern Blotting
   Transferring of separated DNA fragments on a nitrocellulose / nylon sheet.
   DNA is first denatured (made single stranded) then blotted on membrane
5. Hybridisation
   Radioactive labelled probes are injected on membrane.
   These probes bind to complimentary DNA sequences on the fragments.
   Thus specific sequence of VNTR's can be identified.
6. Autoradiography
   Nylon membrane with radioactive probes is exposed to X-ray film.
   Radioactive probes create specific bands, exhibiting the pattern of VNTRs
   This pattern varies significantly among individuals.
   This can help in identification of unique DNA pattern.

NEET SYNAPSE

Southern blot - detects specific DNA sequences
Northern blot - detects specific RNA sequences
Western blot - detects specific protein sequences

APPLICATIONS OF DNA FINGERPRINTING

Paternity Testing - 50% RFLP pattern of child matches with father and rest 50% with mother.

Criminal Identification - DNA matching can help with identifying suspect with the help of DNA sample.

25. Evolution

ORIGIN OF UNIVERSE

BIG BANG THEORY

- Explains the origin of universe.
- Universe formed 20 billion years ago as a result of one big explosion- Big Bang
- Universe was hot & dense ⟶ it expanded & later cooled down.
- Hydrogen & Helium were formed.
- Gravity led to formation of galaxies, stars & planets.

Our galaxy- Milky Way (has about 100 billion stars)

ORIGIN OF EARTH

- Earth formed 4·5 billion years ago
- Early state - molten, high temperature (5000-6000°C), no atmosphere.
- Cooling of Earth resulted in emission of gases like CO_2, CH_4, NH_3 & water vapours
- UV rays (from Sun) + water vapour ⟶ H_2 & O_2
- H_2 (light)- escaped ; O_2 combined with CH_4 & NH_3 to form CO_2, H_2O, N_2 etc.

As free oxygen was not present in primitive atmosphere, it was called reducing atmosphere

ORIGIN OF LIFE

- Life appeared on Earth 4 billion yrs ago, i.e. after 500 million years of its formation.

NEET SYNAPSE

Chronology of events

Universe - 20 bya

Earth - 4·5 bya

Life - 4 bya

THEORIES OF ORIGIN OF LIFE

- Theory of Special Creation
  Given by Father Suarez
  States that life was created by a supernatural power
- Panspermia Theory
  States that pansperms from space were brought to earth by asteroids or meteors.
  It is an extension of theory of Cosmozoic origin
- Theory of Cosmozoic Origin
  States that life came from other parts of universe in the form of spores, seeds etc.
- Theory of Spontaneous Generation
  States that life originated from decaying & rotten matter like straw mud etc
  Implies- life originates spontaneously.
  Also called 'theory of abiogenesis'

Theory of Biogenesis

- States that life originated from pre-existing life (omnis vivum e vivo)
- It was supported by Louis Pasteur.

Swan Neck Flask Experiment

- Louis Pasteur disproved the theory of spontaneous generation by performing this experiment.
- When the neck was S-shaped or swan shaped, bacteria could not enter the broth & it remained free of microbes
- When the neck was broken, air entered the flask, and growth of microbes was seen.

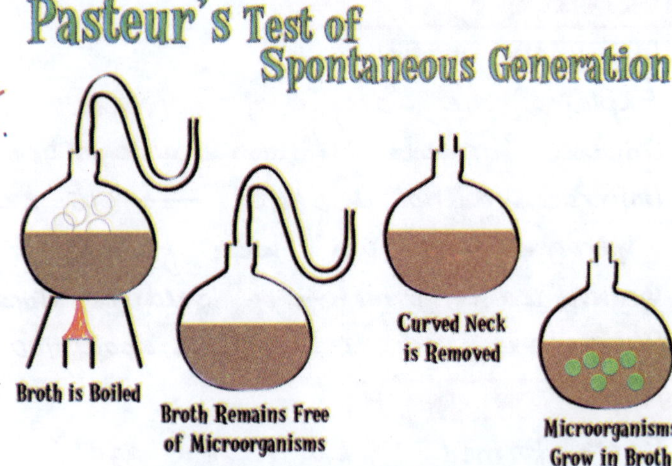

NEET SYNAPSE
- First non cellular life forms could have originated 3 billion years back.
- All life forms originated in water.

Modern Theory of Origin of Life

- Given by Oparin & Haldane
- Chemogeny

Inorganic molecules led to the formation of organic molecules.

CH_4, NH_3, H_2O —(high temperature, volcanic storms, reducing atmosphere)→ Nucleotides, amino acids, simple carbohydrates

polymerisation ↓

Nucleic acids, proteins, complex carbohydrates

- First replicating organic molecule - RNA (forerunner of life)
- Later protein - lipid microspheres enclosing RNA must have formed
- First cell like structures were called protocells.

Urey & Miller's Experiment

- Miller built a glass apparatus
- He created atmospheric conditions similar to primitive atmosphere - CH_4, NH_3, H_2 in ratio of 2:1:2
- Energy source - tungsten electrodes -
- 800°C temperature was maintained
- Vapours were made to condense
- Mixture of amino acids was obtained (glycine, alanine, aspartic acid etc)

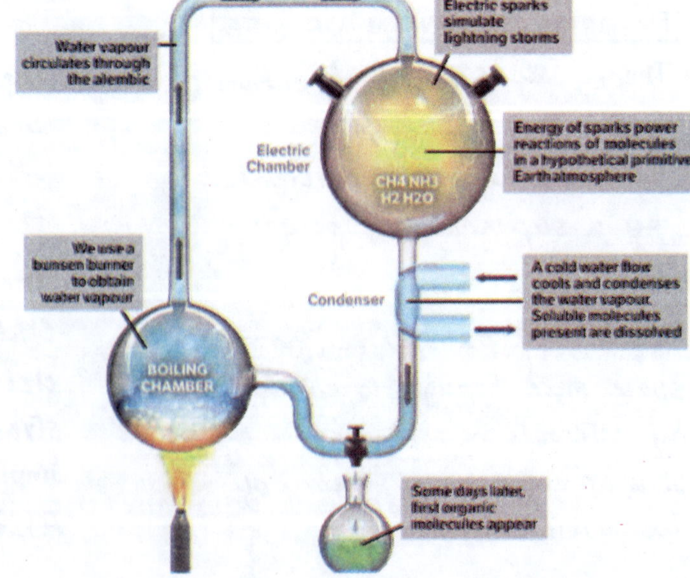

EVIDENCES OF EVOLUTION

COMPARATIVE ANATOMY AND MORPHOLOGY

1. Homologous & Analogous organs

Homologous organs & homology -

- Homologous organs - same origin, different function
- Homology - Relationship b/w structures of different groups of organisms.
- Occurs as a result of divergent evolution
- Divergent evolution - when species diverge from a common ancestor.
  - occurs due to different adaptations.

Homology in Animals

- Forelimbs of Vertebrates -
  Flippers of whale, wings of bat, forelimbs of cat & horse and arms of humans - all share similar bone structure.
  They are functionally dissimilar - whale swims, bat flies etc.

HOMOLOGOUS STRUCTURES

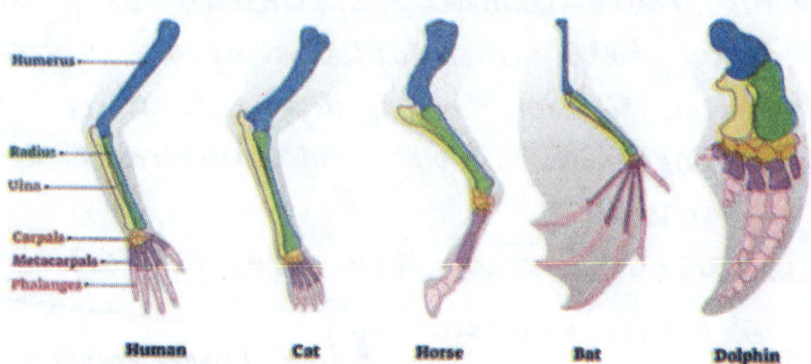

- Brain in Vertebrates -
  Brain comprises similar parts - from fishes to mammals.
- Hearts of vertebrates -
  From fishes to mammals - heart comprises similar basic plan.
  - it only differs according to habitat & energy requirements.

Homology in Plants

- Modified leaves in Bougainvillea (thorns) and Cucurbita (tendrils)
  same origin - different functions → protection → climbing
- Modified leaves in cactus & Venus fly trap.

Analogous organs & Analogy

- Analogous organs - different origin, same function
- Analogy - Relationship b/w structures of different groups of organisms.
- Occurs as a result of convergent evolution.
- It does not indicate common ancestry.

Analogy in Animals

- Wings of insects, bats and birds - all are adapted for flight (same function)
  Origin of insect wings - exoskeleton of chitin
  Origin of bat and bird wings - forelimbs
- Flippers of dolphins, penguin & shark - adapted for swimming.
- Eyes of Octopus and mammals - adapted for vision.

Analogy in Plants

- Sweet potato (modified root) & potato (modified stem) - adapted for food storage.

ADAPTIVE RADIATION

ADAPTIVE RADIATION - DIVERGENT EVOLUTION

- Development of different functional structures from a common ancestor.
- An organ becomes specialised to perform different functions.
- This helps in adaptation of an organism in new habitat.
- Process of evolution of different species in a given geographical area starting from a point and radiating to other habitats (geographical areas)

Examples

(i) Darwin's finches - these birds had a common ancestor - seed eating

New species as a result of adaptation to different foods present in the new habitat. → Insect eaters, Cactus eaters, Bud eaters.

1 2 3 4

(ii) Marsupials of Australia
- number of species evolved from same ancestral stock, each within the Australian subcontinent

NEET SYNAPSE

Adaptive radiation and adaptive convergence both exhibit independent evolution of similar traits due to environmental pressures.

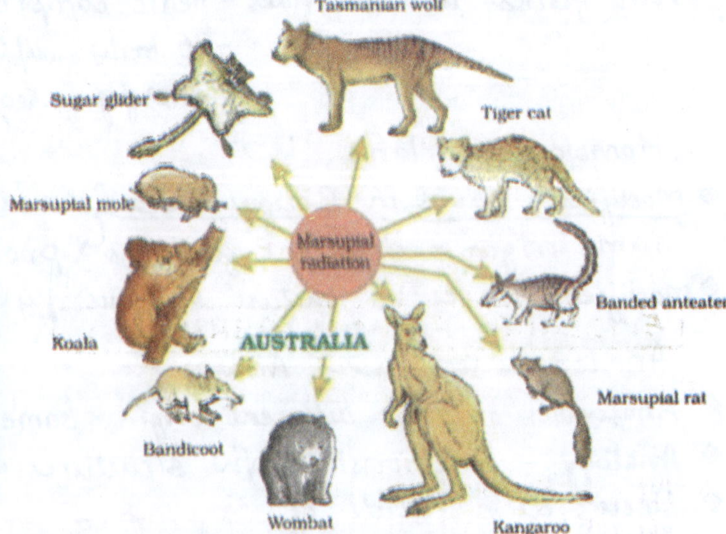

Adaptive radiation of marsupials in Australia

ADAPTIVE RADIATION - CONVERGENT EVOLUTION

- Adaptive Convergence- unrelated organisms develop similar characteristics in response to similar environmental conditions.
- Organisms from different habitats radiate (more than one adaptive radiation) and reach a certain geographical area. Due to common selective pressure, they tend to develop similar features.
- Adaptive convergence leads to convergent evolution.

Example

Australian marsupials & placental mammals.

- Different species of marsupials in Australia have evolved traits that are similar to placental mammals on other continents (eg. North America)
- This has occured because they occupy similar ecological niches & face similar environment pressures
- This has led to similarities in their appearance and behaviour.

EVIDENCES FROM BIOCHEMICAL PROCESSES

- DNA & protein similarities
- Organisms with similar DNA sequences are more closely related to each others.
- Biochemical pathways
- Pathways like Kreb's cycle are universally present.
- Formation of proteins universally occurs by polymerisation of amino acids.

EVIDENCES FROM EMBRYOLOGY

- Ernst Haeckel - gave 'Recapitulation theory'/ Biogenetic law
  It states 'Ontogeny repeats Phylogeny'
  - Development of embryo exhibits repetition of ancestral sequence.

  Karl Ernst Von Baer disproved this theory.

NEET SYNAPSE
Similarities in embryonic stages- Presence of notochord, gill slits in vertebrate embryos

PALAEONTOLOGICAL EVIDENCES

- Palaeontology - study of fossils.
- Rocks of varying ages contain fossils of different life forms, that died during the deposition of a particular sediment.
- Older fossils are found in deeper layers

Geological time scale - Chronological order in which different organisms existed. Consists of eons, eras, periods & epochs.

Determination of Age of fossils

1. Radiocarbon Dating
   Measures decay of $C^{14} \longrightarrow C^{12}$
   C^{14} is taken up by living organisms during their life. Its decay starts after death.
   Half life of C^{14} - 5730 yrs.

2. Uranium-Lead Method
   Measures decay of $U^{238} \rightarrow Pb^{206}$
   Half life of U^{238} - 4.5 by

3. Potassium - Argon Method
   Measures decay of $K^{40} \longrightarrow Ar^{40}$
   Half life of K^{40} - 1.25 by

4. Electron Spin Resonance (ESR) - Most accurate
   Measures trapped e^- in fossils exposed to natural radiation over time.

Geological Time Scale

ERA	PERIOD	EPOCH / AGE	Million Years Ago	EVENTS
CENOZOIC *Age of Mammals* 65.5 mya – present day	*Quaternary*	*Holocene*	Today – 0.01	Ice Age ends Humans are dominant
		Pleistocene	1.6	Earliest Humans appear Ice Age begins
	Tertiary	*Pliocene*	5.3	Hominids (human ancestors) appear
		Miocene	23.7	Grass becomes widespread
		Oligocene	36.6	Mammals are dominant
		Eocene	57.8	Eocene – Oligocene extinction event
		Paleocene	65.5	First large mammals appear
MESOZOIC *Age of Reptiles* 245 mya – 65.5 mya	*Cretaceous*	*Extinction of Dinosaurs*	144	K-T extinction event Earth looks closer to present-day Flowering plants appear
	Jurassic		208	First Birds appear Pangaea splits into Laurasia, Gondwanna Dinosaurs are dominant
	Triassic	*First Dinosaurs*	245	Pangaea cracks First mammals appear Reptiles are dominant
PALEOZOIC 570 mya – 245 mya	*Permian*	*Age of Amphibians*	286	Permian – Triassic extinction event Pangaea forms
	Carboniferous		360	First reptiles appear First large cartilaginous fishes appear
	Devonian	*Age of Fishes*	408	Late Devonian extinction event First land animals appear First amphibians appear
	Silurian		438	First land plants appear First jawed fishes appear First insects appear
	Ordovician	*Age of Invertebrates*	505	Ordovician – Silurian extinction event First vertebrates appear
	Cambrian		570	End Botomian extinction event First fungi appear Trilobites are dominant
PRECAMBRIAN 4600 mya – 570 mya	*Proterozoic Eon*		2500	First soft-bodied animals appear First multicellular life appear
	Archean Eon		3800	Photosynthesizing cyanobacteria appear First unicellular life appear
	Hadean Eon	*Priscoan Period*	4600	Atmosphere and oceans form Oldest rocks form as Earth cools
Formation of Earth				

NEET SYNAPSE

There have been 5 mass extinctions in past. The 6th mass extinction is in progress. It is the fastest extinction & is happening due to anthropogenic activities.

EVIDENCES FROM ANTHROPOGENIC EVOLUTION

- Evolutionary changes due to human activities.
- Human activities may include habitat destruction, environmental alterations, pollution etc
- Anthropogenic evolution through artificial selection
  - Selective breeding of certain plants & animals.
  - Domestication of numerous wild species & development of unique breeds within the same species.
  - Eg. - various breeds of dogs
    - various forms of mustard family - kale, kohl rabi, cauliflower etc.
- Anthropogenic evolution through natural selection

Industrial Melanism

- Industrial revolution took place in Great Britain during 19th century.

Aspect	Before Industrialisation	After Industrialisation
Environment	Unpolluted, tree trunks covered with lichens	Polluted, tree trunks covered with soot
Common moth	Biston betularia - light grey or white	Biston carbonaria, dark coloured, melanic moths.
Camouflage	Light coloured moths blend with lichen covered trees.	Dark coloured moths blend with soot covered trees
Predation	Light coloured moths have better camouflage ∴ less predation. - Dark moths predated	Dark coloured moths have better camouflage, hence less predation. Light moths predated
Natural selection	favours light coloured moths, hence their population increased	favours dark coloured moths, hence their population increased.

Anthropogenic activity - pollution influenced natural selection of moths.

Anti Microbial Resistance

- Over & rampant use of antibiotics has led to development of resistance in microbes. They no longer respond to antimicrobial drugs.
- Superbugs - micro organisms that develop antimicrobial resistance.

NEET SYNAPSE

Evolution is not a directed process in the sense of determination.
It is a stochastic process - relying on chance events in nature.

THEORIES OF EVOLUTION

LAMARCKISM

- Theory of Inheritance of Acquired Characters
- States that all changes acquired by an organism during its lifetime are inherited by its offsprings.
- Eg. long necks of giraffes evolved as an adaptation to reach leaves on tall trees. This trait was passed on to offsprings.

DARWINISM

- Charles Darwin was on a voyage on the ship HMS Beagle
- During his voyage he stayed at Galapagas islands
  He noticed that birds in the island resembled the birds on the mainland
- He concluded that these birds descended from a common ancestor and then adapted to different environments. (adaptive radiation)
- Key concepts of his theory of evolution

1. Branching descent
   Evolutionary process where species diverge from a common ancestor into distinct lineages, forming a branching pattern of evolutionary history

2. Natural selection
   Process by which organisms with traits better suited to their environment are more like to exist for longer durations.

- Thomas R Malthus - wrote an essay on 'Principles of Population'
  He highlighted the consequences of reproductive potential
  His work influenced Darwin
- Sir Alfred Wallace - working in Malay Archipelago came to the same consequences as Darwin regarding natural selection.

Survival of the fittest

- Nature favours the organisms that are fit to survive.
- According to Darwin, fitness refers to reproductive fitness
- Organisms better suited to enviroment ⟶ leave more progeny ⟶ survive more ⟶ selected by nature.

NEET SYNAPSE

The rate of appearance of new forms is related to the life span of the organism – organisms with shorter life spans undergo faster genetic changes.

MUTATION THEORY

- Given by Hugo de Vries
- States that new species arise due to saltatory variations - jerky, discontinuous.
- These were called mutations
- Mutations - large & sudden changes in DNA
  - heritable and are subjected to natural selection.
  - directionless, can be useful or harmful.
  - Useful mutations are usually selected by nature, while harmful ones are rejected.

MECHANISMS OF EVOLUTION

Speciation - formation of new species due to accumulation of changes in a population over time

Mechanism of speciation

1. Mutation - sudden heritable changes in an organism.
   Considered ultimate source of variations
   for mutation to be heritable, it must occur in gametes.
   mutation can also change the frequency of existing alleles.
2. Recombination - occurs as a result of independent assortment and crossing over
   - results from exchange of genetic material between homologous chromosomes during meiosis.
   - it can occur b/w genes or within genes resulting in formation of new alleles.
3. Gene Flow - (Gene Migration) movement of genes into and out of a population
   members of 2 different populations may exchange their genetic materials.
4. Genetic Drift - (Seawall Wright Effect) random fluctuation in allele frequencies in a small population due to chance events.

Founder's effect	Bottle neck effect
When small group of individuals establishes a new population, carrying only limited genetic diversity from original population. It leads to differences in allele frequencies compared to original population.	Occurs when a population is drastically reduced in size due to a catastrophic event. It results in loss of genetic diversity. Surviving population may have altered allele frequencies.

5. Natural Selection

- Some genetic arrangements make organisms better adapted to environment.
- This set of alleles is selected by nature (as it helps in survival & reproduction)

Conditions for Natural Selection

- Variations must exist among individuals in a population
- Variations must be passed to the offsprings

NEET SYNAPSE

Genetically identical individuals may be phenotypically different due to different environments – however it does not lead to any evolutionary change.

Types of Natural Selection

Frequency

Normal distribution

1. **Stabilising or Normalising selection**
   It favours the individuals that possess intermediate forms of a trait.
   Does not promote evolutionary change, but tends to maintain phentotypic stability

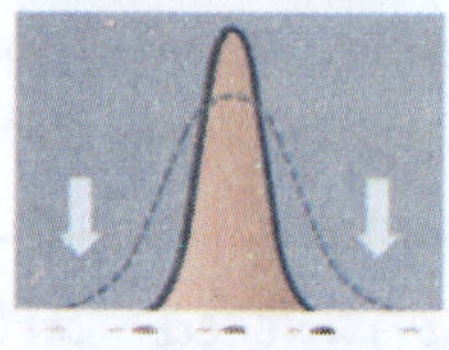

Eg.
human birth weight
human height
human skin colour

2. **Directional selection**
   Produces changes in favour of one extreme while reducing/eliminating the other extreme

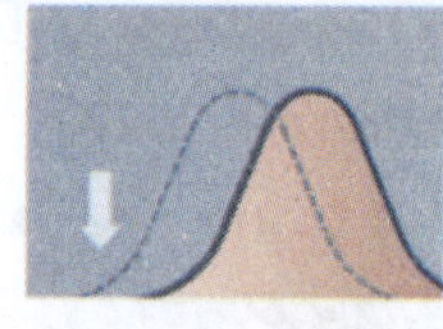

Eg.
Industrial melanism
Antibiotic resistance in bacteria

3. **Disruptive / Diverging selection**
   Results in decline of average individuals in a population and increase the population of extreme types.

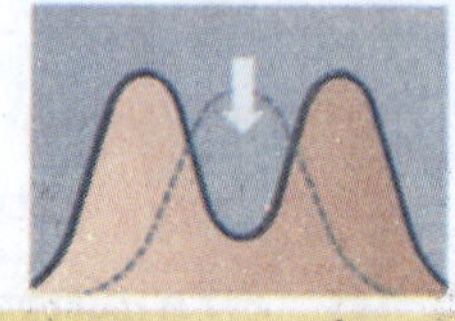

Eg.
Beak size in Darwin's finches

Hardy Weinberg Eqb doesn't exist in reality as variations are always taking place.

HARDY WEINBERG EQUILIBRIUM

- States that genes and genotypic frequencies in a Mendelian population remain constant generation after generation.

Conditions for equilibrium (eqb)

1. Absence of mutations – mutation can lead to variation hence disruption of eqb.
2. Absence of genetic drift – the population should be large, so any changes may be insignificant
3. Absence of gene flow – addition or deletion of genes may cause variations.
4. Absence of natural selection – some traits may be favoured leading to disruption of eqb.
5. Presence of random mating – Pairing occurs by chance → maintains eqb.

Mathematical Expression

$$p^2 + 2pq + q^2 = 1 \quad \text{or} \quad (p+q)^2 = 1$$

p = frequency of dominant allele	p^2 = % homozygous dominant (AA) individuals
q = frequency of recessive allele	q^2 = % homozygous recessive (aa) individuals
pq = heterozygous individual (Aa)	2pq = % heterozygous (Aa) individuals.

Sum total of all allelic frequencies of a gene is 1.
Any change in gene frequencies indicates evolution.

BRIEF ACCOUNT OF EVOLUTION

ORIGIN AND EVOLUTION OF PLANTS

- First cellular life forms originated about 2 bya
- Early cells were anoxygenic
- Some cells developed ability to release O_2
- It was released as a byproduct of photosynthesis.
- This lead to accumulation of O_2 in atmosphere
- These cells were similar to blue-green algae
- They became ancestors of first eukaryotic plant cells (chlorophyte ancestors)
- Initial plants were under water
- Eventually, after evolution they invaded land
- Gradual evolution occured in the sequence- algae ⟶ bryophyta ⟶ pteridophyta ⟶ gymnosperms ⟶ angiosperms.

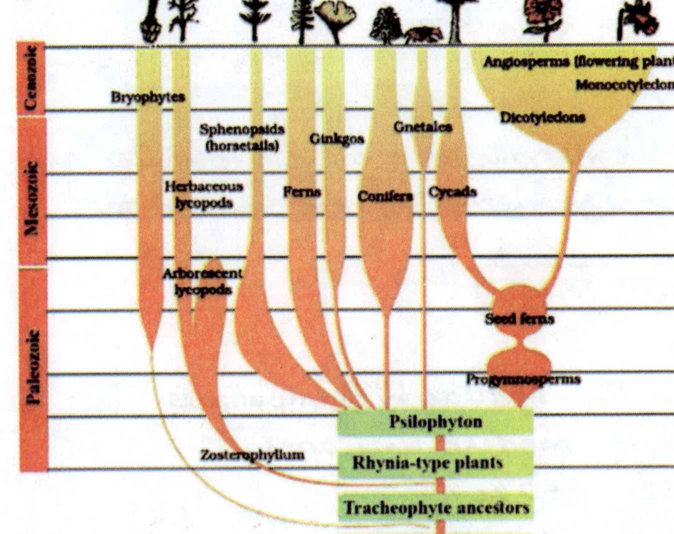

NEET SYNAPSE

- Bryophytes diverged from chlorophyte ancestors in carboniferous period.
- Zosterophyllum is a genus of vascular land plants.
  ↳ They originated in Silurian period
- Lycopods are oldest living land plants.
- Arborescent lycopods were dominant during Palaeozoic era
- Rhynia is also a genus of vascular land plants.
- Modern ferns and seed plants evolved from Psilophyton.
- Cycads are connecting links between gymnosperms and angiosperms.
- Angiosperms- dicots and monocots are dominating land plants in the present era.

Palaeozoic era- age of ferns
Mesozoic era- age of gymnosperms
Present time- age of angiosperms

ORIGIN AND EVOLUTION OF ANIMALS

- Invertebrates & lower animals - about 500 million years ago.
- Evolution of fish
- Jawless fish evolved around 350 mya
- Fish with stout and strong fins - 320 mya
  ↳ These could move on land & return to water.
  ↳ They were called lobefins.
- In 1938, a coelocanth (lobefin) - previously thought to be extinct was caught in South Africa ∴ it is considered as a living fossil.

Evolution of amphibians

- Lobefins are believed to have evolved into first amphibians.
- Earliest amphibians are extinct - they gave rise to modern day amphibians

Evolution of reptiles

- Amphibians evolved into reptiles.
- They lay thick-shelled eggs (do not dry in sun) - unlike those of amphibians.
- Some land reptiles went back to water, evolving into fish like reptiles.
- Eg. Ichthyosaurus - around 200 mya.
- These land reptiles were dinosaurs.

Tyrannosaurus rex - largest dinosaur - 20ft tall, dagger like teeth.

- About 65 mya, dinosaurs became extinct
- Reptiles evolved into birds

Evolution of mammals

- First mammals were small sized - shrews (rat like)
- Mammals were viviparous
- They exhibited greater intelligence.
- NEET SYNAPSE
  Continental drift - Earlier, all continents were one single mass
  Geological changes lead to their separation

ORIGIN AND EVOLUTION OF MAN

PRIOR TO APE MAN

1. Dryopithecus - Hairy, walked like gorillas & chimpanzees.
   Direct ancestor of modern day apes.
   Cranial capacity - 450 cc.

2. Ramapithecus - more man-like than Dryopithecus.
Its fossils were discovered from Shivalik Hills of India

APE MEN

1. Australopithecus - First ape man; connecting link b/w apes & man
Fossil was discovered from Tuang in Africa.
↳ It was the skull of a baby - hence Tuang baby.
Hunted with stone weapons but essentially ate fruits.
Cranial capacity - 500 cc

Ape like features - ape like brain, brow ridges projected over eyes, no chin
Man like features - bipedal, erect posture, omnivorous diet, human like teeth.

2. Homo habilis - Skillful man / Handy man / Tool man
- first human like being - Hominid
- cranial capacity - 650-800 cc
- capable of making tools, lead community life.

3. Homo erectus - probably ate meat; hunted aggressively, used fire.
protruding jaws, projecting brow ridges & small canines & large molar teeth.

TRUE MEN / MODERN LIVING MAN

1. Neanderthal Man (Homo sapiens neanderthalensis)
Prognathous face; walked upright; much bulkier than us.
Cranial capacity - 1300-1600 cc.
Most numerous about 10000 years ago
Became extinct about 30000 years ago
Adapted to cold environment
He was a hunter and predator; used animal skin as clothing.
Buried his dead with flowers and tools.

2. Living Modern Man (Homo sapiens sapiens)
Evolution of culture took place ; cranial capacity - 1450 cc
Appeared about 25000 years ago
Started spreading over Earth about 10000 years ago.
Arose during ice age - 75000 - 10000 years ago.

NEET SYNAPSE
Cave paintings by prehistoric humans were seen in Bhimbetka Rock Shelter in Raisen district of Madhya Pradesh

26. Human Health and Diseases

- Health- a state of complete physical, mental and social well being.
- Health is affected by-
  - Genetic disorders
  - Infections
  - Lifestyle
- Disease - adverse functioning of one or more organs of body characterised by various signs and symptoms

Diseases can be
- Congenital (present since birth)
- Acquired
  - Infectious - AIDS
  - Non infectious - Cancer

NEET SYNAPSE

Disease causing organisms are called pathogens. (Pathos -disease)

COMMON DISEASES IN HUMANS

BACTERIAL DISEASES

- Include Typhoid, Pneumonia, Dysentry, Diphtheria, Plague etc.

	TYPHOID	PNEUMONIA
Causative agent	*Salmonella typhi*	*Streptococcus pneumoniae* *Haemophilus influenzae*
Transmitted by	• Contaminated food and water	• Aerosol / Droplet inhalation
Organs affected	• Small intestine	• Alveoli of lungs
Symptoms	• Sustained high fever • Constipation, • loss of appetite, • Stomachache • Headache	• Fever, chills, cough, • Rapid shallow breathing • Blood mixed with sputum • Headache • Respiratory problems
Severe cases	- • Intestinal perforation	• Finger nails turn gray to bluish.
Diagnosis	Widal Test	Bacterial culture.

Typhoid Mary - Mary Mallon was a typhoid carrier who continued to spread typhoid for several years through the food she cooked

HELMINTHIC DISEASES

	ASCARIASIS	FILARIASIS / ELEPHANTIASIS
Causative agent	• *Ascaris lumbricoides*	• *Wuchereria bancrofti* *Wuchereria malayi*
Transmitted by	• Contaminated food and water.	• Bite of female *Culex* mosquito
Organs affected	• Intestines	• Lymphatic vessels of lower limbs.
Symptoms	• Internal bleeding • Muscular pain • Fever, Anaemia • Blockage of intestinal passage.	• Chronic inflammation of lymphatic vessels of lower limbs. • Gross deformities of genital organs.

NEET SYNAPSE - Eggs of adult *Ascaris* pass out through faeces of infected person in soil etc. These eggs when consumed cause ascariasis

FUNGAL DISEASES / VIRAL DISEASES

	RINGWORM	COMMON COLD
Causative agent	• *Microsporum* • *Tricophyton* • *Epidermophyton*	• Rhinovirus
Transmitted by	• Using towels or clothes of infected individuals.	Droplet / aerosol • contamination or inhalation
Organs affected	• Dry scaly lesions on skin, nails & scalp	• Infects nose & respiratory passage but not lunge
Symptoms	• Intense itching b/w toes & in groin region	• Nasal congestion & discharge Sore throat, headache, cough.

PROTOZOAN DISEASES

	AMOEBIASIS	MALARIA
Causative agent	• *Entamoeba histolytica*	• *Plasmodium* – *vivax*, *malariae*, *falciparum*
Transmitted by	• Oro faecal route	• Bite of female *Anopheles*
Organs affected	• large intestine	• Liver, blood, brain
Symptoms	• Constipation, abdominal pain, stools with mucus & blood.	• Fever with chills, repetition after every 3-4 days.

LIFE CYCLE OF MALARIAL PARASITE

Mosquito bites
↓
sporozoites of Plasmodium enters human body
↓
Sporozoites enter liver cells
↓
Asexual reproduction occurs in liver
↓
Merozoites are released in blood
↓
They enter RBC where asexual reproduction occurs
↓
trophozoites are formed
↓
trophozoites grow into schizont.
↓
RBC's rupture → merozoites are released into blood.
Rupture of RBC's is associated with the release of haemozoin - responsible for chills & fever.
↓
Some merozoites develop into male & female gametocytes
↓
Gametocytes are picked by mosquito
↓
Fertilisation occurs
↓
development of zygote occurs in gut of mosquito
↓
sporozoites escape from intestine & move to salivary glands.

They are stored in salivary glands and are released during bite.

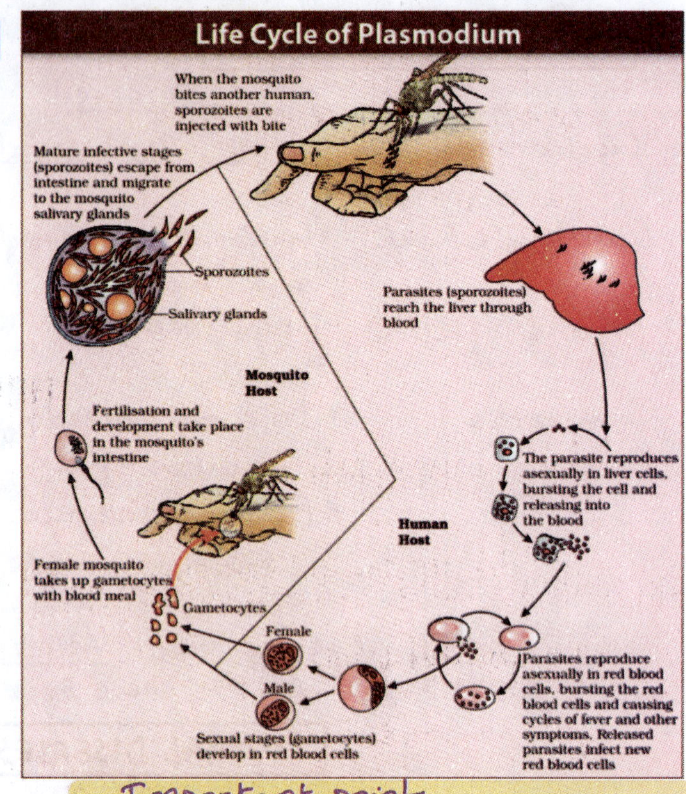

Important points

- Plasmodium is digenetic - requires 2 hosts to complete its life cycle
- Hosts [1° - Mosquito, 2° - Human
- Mosquito is called definitive host as sexual reproduction takes place there.
- P. falciparum causes cerebral / malignant malaria.
- It affects the brain & can be fatal.

NEET SYNAPSE

Diseases that spread through insect vectors
1. Dengue - Aedes mosquito
2. Chikungunya - Aedes mosquito
3. Malaria - Anopheles mosquito
4. Filariasis - Culex mosquito

IMMUNITY

INNATE IMMUNITY

- Non specific – does not differentiate b/w different pathogens.
- Present since birth.

Barriers of Innate Immunity

Physical	Physiological	Cellular	Cytokine
• Skin, • mucous membrane lining of GIT, urinogenital & respiratory tract • It traps microbes entering body	• Acid in stomach • Saliva in mouth • Tears in eyes • Cerumen in ears • Prevent the growth of microbes.	• Neutrophils (PMNL) • Monocytes • NK cells (Natural killer cells) • Carry out phagocytosis & destruction of microbes	• Interferons - proteins secreted by virus infected cells • Protect other cells from infection

PMNL – Poly Morpho Nuclear Leucocyte
Monocytes are of macrophagic origin

NEET SYNAPSE
Inflammatory barrier of innate immunity occurs due to presence of inflammatory mediators like histamine, heparin, serotonin.

ACQUIRED IMMUNITY

- Acquired during lifetime of an individual due to exposure to various pathogens.
- Also called adaptive or specific immunity.
- Present in vertebrates only.
- It is characterised by

Specificity - ability to distinguish b/w different types of pathogens.
Diversity - can recognise large vareity of foreign molecules.
Discrimination b/w self and non self - it can recognise & respond to non-self molecules & avoid response to self molecules.
Memory - the ability to remember a certain pathogen.
- this feature forms the basis of concept of vaccination.

Immune response

Primary	Secondary / Anamnestic
• It is generated when the body encounters a pathogen for the first time	• It is generated when the body encounters the same pathogen for second time
• It is of low intensity	• It is of high intensity
• It is mediated by IgM	• It is mediated by IgG

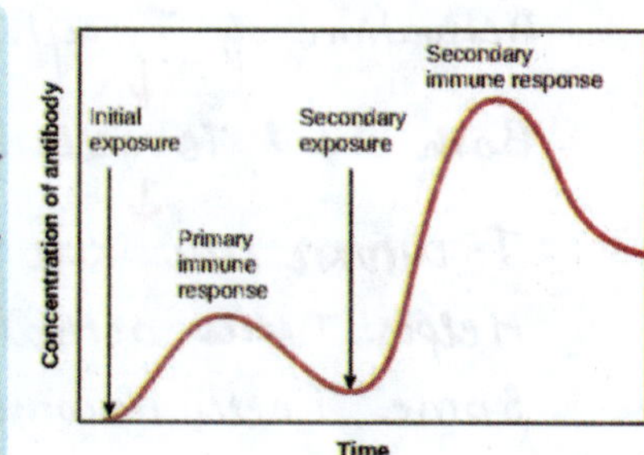

CELLS INVOLVED IN IMMUNE RESPONSE

	T-lymphocytes	B-lymphocytes
Origin	Bone marrow	Bone marrow
Maturation	Thymus	Bone marrow
Function	Cell mediated immunity	Humoral immunity

- B-lymphocytes differentiate to form plasma cells.
- These plasma cells secrete antibodies which are responsible for humoral immunity
- Undifferentiated B-cells remain as memory B cells.

HUMORAL IMMUNITY

- It is carried out by antibodies (Ab) / immunoglobulins (Ig's)
- Antibody - Y-shaped ; protein molecule
  - It has 2 halves ; each half contains –
    - A heavy chain (H)
    - A light chain (L)
  - It is represented as H_2L_2

Structure of an antibody

- Types of antibodies

IgA Present in body secretions - called secretory Ab
IgD B cell receptor. Present on surface of membranes
IgG Smallest & most numerous Ab
can cross placenta
IgE mediates allergic and antihelminthic responses
IgM pentamer ; largest Ab

- Function of Ab - interact with circulating antigens & clears them by forming complexes.

CELL MEDIATED IMMUNITY (CMI)

- It is mediated by T-cytotoxic cells (T_8 cell)
- Steps of CMI

Antigen Presenting Cells (APCs) present antigen to T cells
↓
Activation of T-helper (T_4/CD_4) takes place
↓
Activation of T-cytoxic cells takes place
↓
Both T_4 & T_8 cells undergo clonal expansion
↓
T-cytoxic cells kill the infected cells
Helper T cells activate other cells
Some T cells become memory cells.

NEET SYNAPSE

- APCs are macrophages, dendritic cells & B-cells
- Cytotoxic cells kill by releasing chemicals called perforins on infected cells. They cause perforation in cell membrane causing swelling & lysis.

TYPES OF ACQUIRED IMMUNITY

Active	Passive
◆ Involves active functioning of a person's immune system	◆ Does not involve active functioning of a person's immune system
◆ Synthesis of antibodies takes place in the body in response to a foreign antigen.	◆ Antibodies are readymade, they are injected into the body of an individual.
◆ It is a slower process	◆ It gives immediate protection

Active – Natural	Active – Artificial	Passive – Natural	Passive – Artificial
In case of disease or infection by a pathogen	Immunity is generated through vaccines	Mother ↓ IgG → Foetus; Mother ↓ IgA (colostrum) → Child	Antibodies from one individual are injected in another individual of same species.

VACCINATION AND IMMUNISATION

◆ **Vaccination** - introduction of antigenic proteins / inactivated or attenuated (weakened) pathogen in the body.
- It works on the principle of memory.
- Primary & secondary immune responses are generated.

◆ **Immunisation** - process by which body produces antibodies against antigens & neutralises them
- Serum is used for obtaining antibodies.

PASSIVE IMMUNISATION

◆ In case of snake bite or <u>Clostridium tetani</u> infection - pre formed antibodies are given to patients to neutralise toxins immediately. (antitoxins)

◆ They are called anti snake venom antibodies and anti tetanus serum (ATS injection) respectively.

RECOMBINANT DNA VACCINE

◆ Creation of antigenic polypeptide of pathogen using DNA sequence.

◆ Host used is either bacteria or yeast.

◆ This allows mass production of antigenic protein → availability of vaccine increases

◆ Eg. Hepatitis B vaccine produced from yeast.

NEET SYNAPSE

First generation vaccine - whole pathogen vaccine, eg BCG (weakened), Typhoid (killed)
Second generation vaccine - subunit vaccines (using only antigen), eg: Tetanus & herpes
Third generation vaccine - DNA vaccines.

IMMUNE SYSTEM IN THE BODY

Primary lymphoid Organs

- Site of formation & maturation of lymphocytes
  - Bone marrow & Thymus
  - ↳ Site of formation of all blood cells
- Thymus - Release thymosins → help in maturation of T cells.

Secondary Lymphoid Organs

- Site of differentiation of lymphocytes into effector cells.
- Once mature, lymphocytes move out of 2° lymphoid organs.
- Comprise - Lymph nodes, MALT, Spleen (Graveyard of RBC's)

NEET SYNAPSE

MALT - Mucosa Associated lymphoid Tissue
- Accounts for 50% of lymphoid tissue in human body.

ALLERGY / HYPERSENSITIVITY

- Exaggerated response of immune system to certain substances.
- Allergens - substances causing allergy.
- Antibodies involved - IgE
- Chemical Mediators involved - histamine and serotonin
- Treatment - antihistamines, adrenaline & steroids (reduce inflammation)

AUTO IMMUNE DISEASES

- When immune system fails to differentiate b/w self and non self.
- It starts attacking its own cells.
- Autoimmunity may cause chronic & serious diseases
- Eg: Rheumatoid arthritis, multiple sclerosis, insulin dependent diabetes.

ORGAN TRANSPLANTATION

- An organ is removed from the body of donor & placed in recipient's body.

GRAFT REJECTION

- Cell mediated immunity is responsible for graft rejection.
- Cells of body may have many antigens, which can lead to rejection.
- Prevention of Graft Rejection
  - Tissue matching - antigens of tissues should be matched.
    - maximum matches are seen among close relatives.
  - Immunosuppression - immune response is depressed using immunosuppresive drugs like steroids.

AIDS - ACQUIRED IMMUNO DEFICIENCY SYNDROME

- Syndrome - group of diseases
- AIDS caused by HIV (Human Immunodeficiency virus)
- Transmission occurs through
  1. unprotected sexual intercourse
  2. blood transfusion
  3. infected needles
  4. mother to baby

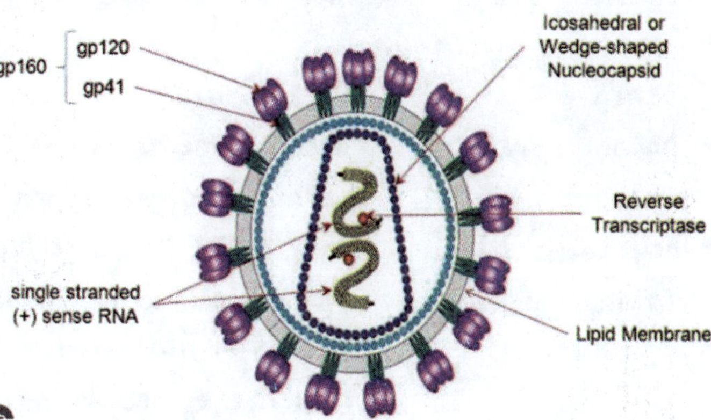

- Replication of HIV in body

Virus enters macrophages
↓
RNA genome —Reverse Transcriptase→ viral DNA
↓
Viral DNA integrates with host cell DNA
↓
Produces more virus particles (Macrophages - HIV factory)

Simultaneously,
HIV enters T-helper (T4/CD4) cells
↓
Replicate to produce more virus particles
↓
Reduction in the number of T-helper cells.

Opportunistic infections
They occur in immunocompromised state.
Organisms causing such infections- Toxoplasma, Mycobacterium, viruses, fungi etc.

Diagnosis
ELISA, PCR

Treatment - HAART
Acyclovir, Azidothymidine (AZT)

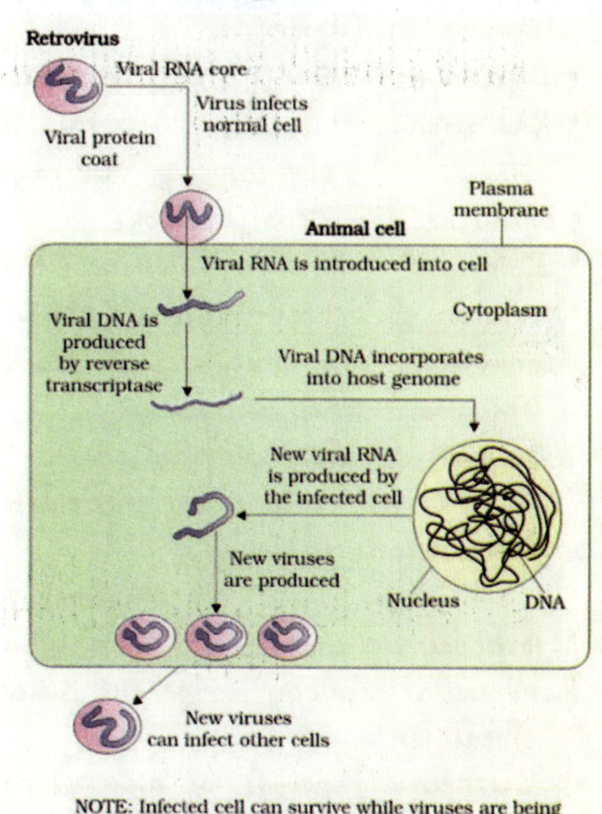

Figure 8.6 Replication of retrovirus

NEET SYNAPSE
AIDS is not a congenital disease.
HIV infection can be congenital.

CANCER

- Uncontrolled division of cells
- Breakdown of inhibitory mechanism of cell growth and differentiation.
- Loss of contact inhibition (uncontrolled growth of cells is inhibited by contact with other cells)
- Tumour- mass of tissue formed due to over proliferation of cells.
- Types of tumours

Benign	Malignant
• Do not spread to other organs	• Exhibit metastasis - spread to other organs
• They cause little damage to body	• They cause immense harm
	• They compete with normal cells for nutrition
	• Presence of neoplastic cells.

Classification of malignant tumours
1. Carcinoma - epithelial tissue
2. Sarcoma - connective tissue
3. Leukaemia - blood cells.

Normal and Cancer Cells

Causes of Cancer

- Carcinogens - agents that can induce cancer
- Radiations
  - Ionising - X rays, γ rays
  - Non ionising - UV rays
- Chemicals - tobacco smoke
- Biological - oncogenic virus (they have viral oncogenes)
- Mutation of proto oncogenes (present in all organisms) → conversion into oncogenes to cause cancer.

Detection and Diagnosis

1. Biopsy - histopathological study - tissue is taken & observed under the microscope for neoplastic transformation.
2. Radiography / CT / MRI
   X- rays ↳ Magnetic field
3. Antibody detection - formation of antibodies against cancer specific antigen.
4. Molecular biology for genetic susceptibility.

Treatment

1. Surgery - removal of affected part / tumour
2. Radiation therapy - X rays / γ rays used to destroy cancerous cells.
3. Chemotherapy - drugs that inhibit spindle formation, hence inhibit cell division - Eg. vinblastin, vincristin.
4. Immunotherapy - activation of immune system to target cancer cells. α interferons are used.

DRUG ABUSE

Drugs

- **Psychotropic**
  - Sedative/Hypnotic
    - Barbiturates
    - Benzodiazepenes (BZD)
  - Opioid Narcotics
    - Morphine
    - Heroine
  - Stimulants
    - Cocaine
    - Caffeine
- **Psychedelic** → Hallucinogens
  - Cannabinoids, LSD (Lysergic Acid Diethylamide)

OPIOID NARCOTICS

- Obtained from latex of Papaver somniferum
- Binds to opioid receptors present in CNS & GIT
- Have analgesic action; generally depressants of CNS
- Can be snorted or injected.

opium Poppy

Morphine

Types –

Natural	Semi Synthetic	Synthetic
Morphine used for pain relief	Heroine (smack or brown sugar) formed by acetylation of morphine White, bitter crystalline compound	Methadone Pethidine

CANNABINOIDS

- Products of Cannabis sativa
- Bind with cannabinoid receptors present in brain and affect CVS
- Mostly abused by sports persons
- Can be inhaled or ingested
- Include Bhang, Ganja, Charas, Marijuana, Hashish.
- Atropa belladona, datura, high dosage of coke

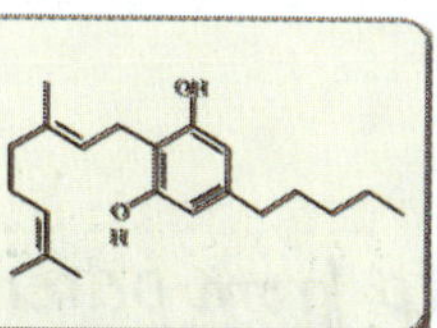

Cannabinoid

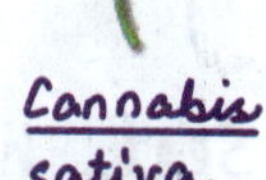

Cannabis sativa

COCAINE / COCA ALKALOIDS

- Obtained from Erythroxylum coca
- Also known as coke / crack / sniff etc.
- Interferes with transport of dopamine
- Has stimulating action on CNS

Clinical uses

1. Amphetamines - stimulant
2. Barbiturates - sedative
3. Benzodiazepenes - anti anxiety
4. Morphine - Analgesic

Datura

SMOKING

- Tobacco – smoked, chewed, snuffed
  – contains nicotine
- Nicotine causes adrenaline release
  ↓
  High BP, High Heart Rate (HR)
- Increased risk of cancer – lungs, oral cavity, urinary bladder, throat
- Can cause bronchitis, emphysema, heart disease etc.
- Smoking increases CO content & reduces HbO_2.
- It causes O_2 deficiency in the body.

ADDICTION AND DEPENDENCE

- Addiction – Psychological attachment to euphoria & temporary well being
- Repeated usage leads to increase in tolerance level of the receptors.
- Receptors respond to high doses leads to addiction.

Withdrawal syndrome

- Abrupt discontinuation of drugs
- Causes unpleasant symptoms
- Symptoms – anxiety, nausea shakiness, sweating
- Can be relieved if drug is resumed again
- Can be fatal also.

PREVENTION AND CONTROL

1. Avoid undue peer pressure – don't push a child to perform beyond his / her limits.
2. Education & Counselling – Face problems and stresses
   Accept disappointments and faliure
   Pursue hobbies
3. Seek help from parents & peers – vent out feelings of anxiety & guilt
4. Looking for danger signs – friends should inform parents about any abnormal activity
   proper remedial measures to be taken
5. Seeking professional medical help – specialised psychologists, psychyatrist, deaddiction and rehabilitation centres should be visited.

EFFECTS OF DRUG ABUSE

Immediate effects

- Reckless behaviour
- Vandalism
- Violence

- Excessive doses may lead to coma, death (resp failure, heart failure or cerebral haemorrhage)

Warning signs

- Drop in academic performance
- Unexplained absence from class
- Reduced personal hygiene
- Withdrawal & isolation
- Depression & fatigue
- Aggressive & rebellious behaviour
- Poor relationships
- Loss of interest in hobbies
- Change in eating & sleeping habits
- Weight fluctuations.

Adverse effects

- Deterioration in health
- Family's mental & financial distress
- Susceptibility to acquire serious infections like AIDS and Hepatitis B

ALCOHOL ABUSE

- Heavy drinking in adulthood
- Leads to cirrhosis (Liver damage)

Adverse affect on foetus.

MISUSE BY SPORTSPERSONS

- Misuse of narcotic analgesics, anabolic steroids, diuretics & certain hormones
- Purpose – ↑ muscle strength
  - ↑ bulk of body
  - ↑ aggressiveness
  - ↑ atheletic performance

Side effects in females

- Masculinisation
- Increased aggressiveness
- Mood swings
- Depression
- Abnormal menstrual cycles
- Excessive hair on face & body
- Enlargement of clitoris
- Deepening of voice

Side effects in males

- Acne
- Increased aggressiveness
- Mood swings
- Depression
- Reduction in size of testicles
- Decreased sperm production
- Breast enlargement
- Kidney & liver dysfunction
- Premature baldness
- Enlargement of prostate
- gland.

Common side effects (♂ & ♀)

- Severe body & face acne
- Stunted growth, premature closure of growth centres.

27. Microbes in Human Welfare

HABITAT

- Microbes are omnipresent (present everywhere)
  - In soil, air, water
  - Inside animal bodies
  - Inside plants.
  - Microbes are also present in
    - thermal vents (geysers)
    - deep in the soil
    - under several layers of snow
    - in highly acidic env.

- Microbes can be
  - Protozoa
  - Bacteria
  - Fungi
  - Microscopic plant & animal viruses
  - viroids
  - Prions - proteinaceous infectious agents.

Microbes in household products

- Production of curd from milk
  - LAB - produce acids which coagulate & partially digest milk proteins.
  - Inoculum is added (millions of bacteria)

Curd - ↑ B12

LAB - check disease causing microbes in stomach.

- Production of fermented dough

Sacchromyces cerevisae

- CO_2 creates puffed up appearance

- Production of toddy
  - produced from fermenta"n of sap from palms.

- Production of cheese

Swizz cheese

Propionibacterium shermanii

Roquefort cheese

Penicillium roqueforti (fungus)

Microbes in Industrial products

- Beverages & antibiotics
- Microbes grown in large vessels called fermentors

- Fermented beverages

Saccharomyces cerevisae (brewer's yeast)

- ferments malted cereals & fruit juices - ethanol

- Production of bread
  - Saccharomyces cerevisae (Baker's yeast)

- Alcoholic beverages

Distilled	Undistilled
Whiskey	Wine
Brandy	Beer.

ANTIBIOTICS

- chemical subs produced by some microbes & can kill or retard the growth of other microbes.
- Penicillin - first antibiotic
  Source - Penicillium notatum
- Flemming, Chain & Florey were awarded noble prize for its discovery
- Antibiotics can be used for treating
  - Plague - Yersinia pestis
  - Whooping cough - Bordetella pertussis
  - Diptheria - Corynebacterium diphtheriae
  - Leprosy - Mycobacterium leprae

CHEMICALS, ENZYMES, BIOACTIVE MOLECULES

- Citric acid - Aspergillus niger [F]
- Acetic acid - Acetobacter aceti [B]
- Butyric acid - Clostridium butylicum [B]
- Lactic acid - Lactobacillus [B]
- Ethanol - Saccharomyces cerevisae [F]
- Streptokinase (clot buster) - Streptococcus [B]
- Cyclosporin A (Immunosuppressant) - Trichoderma polysporum [F]
- Statins (Blood cholesterol lowering agent) - Monascus purpureus [F]
- Lipases - detergents - removes oily stains
- Pectinases & proteases - clearing bottled fruit juices.

MICROBES IN SEWAGE TREATMENT

- Municipal water waste is also called sewage
- Mainly consists of human excreta

Primary treatment

- Physical removal of large and small particles from excreta.
- Filtration & sedimentation

Floating debris removed by sequential filtration	Soil & small pebbles (grit) removed by sedimentation

NEET SYNAPSE
All solids that settle form primary sludge, supernatant forms effluent

Effluent goes for secondary treatment

Secondary / Biological treatment

- Primary effluent passed to aeration tanks
- Air pumped in aeration tank & mixture is agitated
- Growth of aerobic microbes takes place to form flocs
- Flocs - masses of bacteria associated with fungal elements in mesh like network.
- Aerobic microbes during growth consume organic matter.
- As a result BOD of effluent reduces
- BOD – Biochemical O_2 Demand

BOD - It is the amount of O_2 that would be consumed if all the organic matter in 1 litre of water is oxidised by bacteria.

NEET SYNAPSE
"BOD is a measure of organic matter present in water.
Greater BOD = more polluted H_2O.

- After BOD reduces, effluent is passed to settling tank.
- Flocs settle down
- This is called activated sludge
  - Small part sent back to aeration tank as inoculum
  - Large part sent to anaerobic sludge digesters
    ↓
    Anaerobic bacteria digest bacteria & fungi in sludge.
    ↓
    Anaerobic bacteria produce CH_4, CO_2, H_2S — BIOGAS
- Effluent from secondary treatment is released in water bodies.

Ganga Action Plan
Yamuna Action Plan

- Large no. of STP to be built so that only treated sewage is discharged in the rivers.

Microbes in production of Biogas

- Bacteria that grow anaerobically on cellulose produce large amount of CH_4 along with CO_2 & H_2
- These bacteria are called methanogens
  eg. Methanobacterium
- Methanogens are present in anaerobic sludge
- Also present in rumen of cattle
- Excreta of cattle used for generation of biogas (gobar gas)

Biogas plant

- Concrete tank (10-15 m deep) slurry of dung is fed this tank
- Floating lid
  - rises as gas accumulates
- Outlet 1 - supply biogas to nearby houses
- Outlet 2 - removal of spent slurry

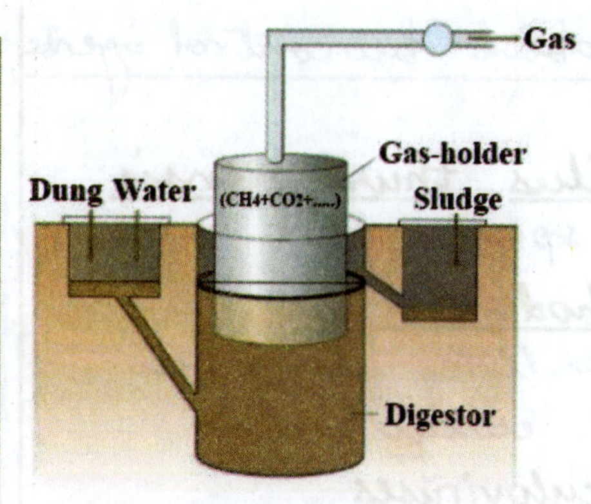

Biogas plant

- Concrete tank (10-15 m deep)
- Floating lid
- Outlet 1 - gas ; Outlet 2 - sludge

- Biogas plant technology was developed by –
  - IARI Indian Agricultural Research Institute
  - KVIC Khadi and Village Industries Commission

Microbes as bio control agents

- Biocontrol – use of biological methods for controlling plant diseases & pests.

Biological control of pests & diseases

- Natural predation
- Biodiversity improves ecological balance.
- Pests dont have to be eradicated, rather controlled.
- Chemical methods kill harmful as well as useful life forms.
- Lady bird controls aphids
- Dragonflies - control mosquitoes.

Microbial biocontrol agents

- **Bacillus thuringiensis**
  kills specific insect larvae
- **Trichoderma**
  - a free living fungi in root ecosystems.
- **Baculoviruses**
  Genus Nucleopolyhedrovirus
  species specific, narrow spectrum insecticides.

IPM
Integrated Pest Management

- conserving beneficial insects, killing only harmful insects.

Microbes as biofertilisers

- **Biofertilisers**
  organisms that enrich the nutrient quality of soil.
- Main sources
  - Bacteria, fungi, cyanobacteria.

• **Bacteria**

Rhizobium
roots of leguminous plants
fix atmospheric N_2.

Azospirillum, Azotobacter
free living N_2 fixing bacteria.

• **Fungi**

Glomus mycorrhiza

NEET SYNAPSE
Mycorrhiza - symbiotic association of fungi with plants.

Fungi

- absorbs phosphorous
- resistance to root
- borne pathogens
- Tolerance to salinity & draught
- Increase in plant growth & development.

Cyanobacteria

- Anabaena, Nostoc
  Oscillatoria
- fix atmospheric N_2.
- In paddy fields, cyanobacteria are imp biofertilisers
- Biofertilisers
  replenish soil nutrients
  reduce dependence on chemical fertilisers.

28. Biotechnology : Principles & Processes

■ EFB definition

The integration of natural science and organisms, cells, parts thereof and molecular analogues for products and services

Principles of Biotechnology

i) Genetic engineering
ii) Bioprocess engineering

Disadvantage of traditional hybridisation

- Leads to inclusion and multiplication of undesirable genes along with desired genes.

Techniques of genetic engineering include

- Formation of rDNA
- Gene cloning
- Gene transfer.

Advantage - only desirable genes can be chosen & cloned.

NEET SYNAPSE

- Alien DNA is linked with ORI (Origin of Replication) in order to replicate & multiply itself in host organism.

Clones - identical copies of template DNA.

First recombinant DNA

- Cohen & Boyer in 1972
- A piece of DNA was cut from a plasmid conferring antibiotic resistance using Restriction endonucleases - "Molecular Scissors"
- Cut DNA was linked with plasmid DNA [vector]
- Linking enzyme - Ligase, it linked vector DNA + alien DNA, Recombinant DNA
- Plasmid delivered this DNA to host organism - E.coli
- E.coli carried out cloning of alien gene & showed resistance to antibiotic.

First rDNA - gene encoding antibiotic resistance was linked with native plasmid of Salmonella typhimurium.

STEPS IN MAKING GENETICALLY MODIFIED ORGANISMS

1. Identification of desirable gene
2. Introduction of identified DNA into host
3. Transfer of this DNA to progeny of host.

Characteristics of plasmid

- Extra chromosomal
- Double stranded, circular
- self replicating DNA

TOOLS OF RDT

RE, polymerase enzymes, ligases vectors & host.

Restriction enzymes

- Restrict the growth of bacteriophages in bacteria.

1. Methylase - adds methyl grp to DNA (prevents digestion)
2. Restriction endonucleases - cleave phage DNA

First RE - Hind II

- RE cut DNA at specific base sequence c/a recognition sequence (palindromic seq) - specific for each RE (cleaves S-P bond)

NOMENCLATURE [EcoRI]

- 1st letter - Genus - Escherichia
- 2nd & 3rd letter - species - coli
- 4th letter - strain - RY13
- Roman numeral - sequence of [I] isolation of RE from that strain

- 900 REs have been isolated so far from 230 bacterial strains

Nucleases
- → Exonucleases - Removes nucleotides from ends
- → Endonucleases - cut at specific positions within DNA

Steps in formation of rDNA using EcoRI

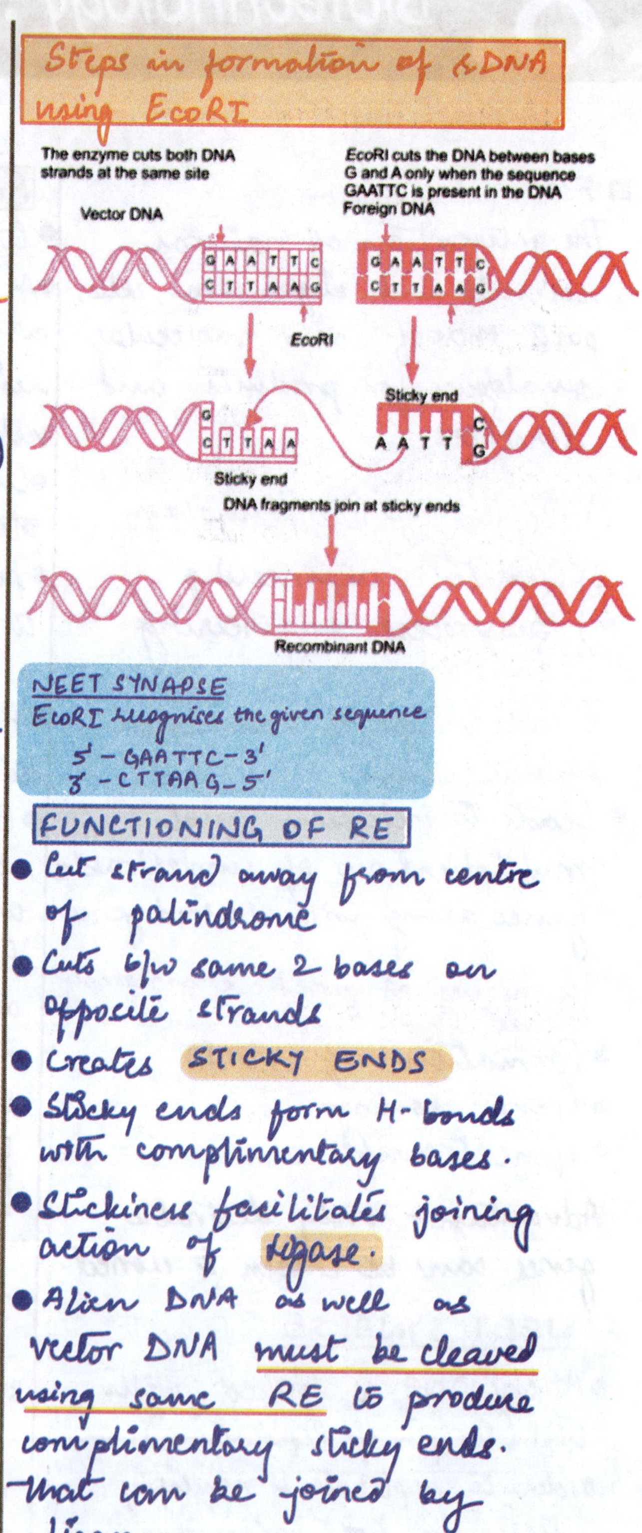

NEET SYNAPSE
EcoRI recognises the given sequence
5' - GAATTC - 3'
3' - CTTAAG - 5'

FUNCTIONING OF RE

- Cut strand away from centre of palindrome
- Cuts b/w same 2 bases on opposite strands
- Creates STICKY ENDS
- Sticky ends form H-bonds with complimentary bases.
- Stickiness facilitates joining action of ligase.
- Alien DNA as well as vector DNA must be cleaved using same RE to produce complimentary sticky ends. That can be joined by ligase.

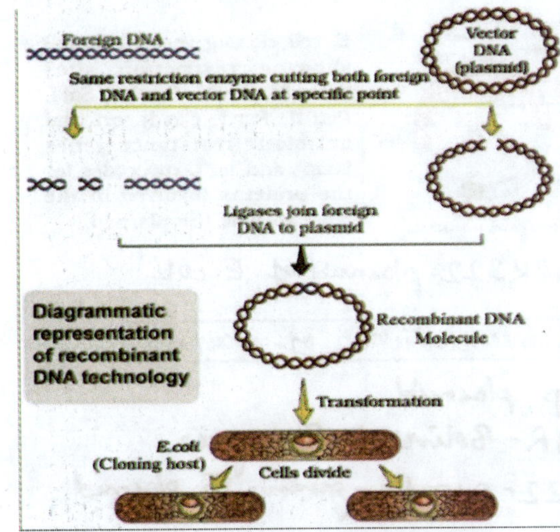

Separation and isolation of DNA fragments.

- Action of RE creates DNA fragments
- Gel electrophoresis separates them

Principle

- DNA fragments are negatively charged, hence can be separated under electric field when placed in porous matrix
- Fragments tend to move towards positive terminal (anode)

Matrix used - Agarose gel (extracted from red sea weeds)

Process - upon application of electric current, DNA fragments start moving towards anode.

- separated according to their size due to sieving effect of matrix

Visualisation - Stain with EtBr view under UV rays; Orange bands appear

Elution - Cutting and separation of DNA fragments from matrix.

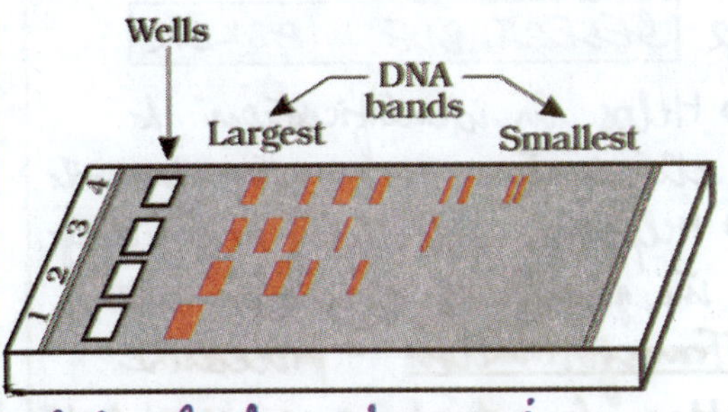

Gel electrophoresis

CLONING VECTORS

- Replicate within host cells independent of control of chromosomal DNA

Plasmids Copy number varies from 1-2 per cell to 15-100 per cell.

Bacteriophages Have very high copy number of their genome in bacterial cell.

NEET SYNAPSE

An alien piece of DNA when linked with a cloning vector, multiplies according to its copy number in the host body.

What facilitates cloning in a vector?

1. **ORI (Origin of replication)**

- Sequence from where replication starts
- Responsible for controlling copy number of linked alien DNA.
- High copy number is desirable in a vector.

2. SELECTABLE MARKER

- Helps in identification & elimination of non transformants
- Helps in selectively permitting the growth of transformants.
- Transformation – procedure through which a piece of DNA is introduced into host bacterium.
- Eg: For E.coli – antibiotic resistance genes providing resistance to antibiotics like ampicillin, chloramphenicol, kanamycin or tetracycline, are used as selectable markers.

NEET SYNAPSE
Native E.coli do not have antibiotic resistance genes.

3. CLONING SITES

Concept of MCS / Polylinker

- Multiple Cloning Sites
  A region of DNA that has recognition sites of many restriction enzymes.

(So any restriction enzyme can be chosen to cleave DNA)

- Each restriction enzyme should preferably have one recognition site in vector, so that only one fragment is created

EcoRI single site for EcoRI so that EcoRI cuts only at one place.

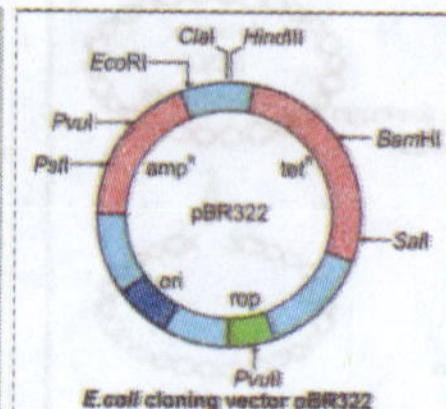

E. coli cloning vector pBR322 showing restriction sites (*Hind* III, *EcoR* I, *BamH* I, *Sal* I, *Pvu* II, *Pst* I, *Cla* I), ori and antibiotic resistance genes (amp^R and tet^R). rop codes for the proteins involved in the replication of the plasmid.

pBR322 - plasmid of E.coli

Nomenclature of plasmid

p - plasmid
BR - Bolivar & Rodriguez
322 - number given to plasmid

- pBR322 contains 2 antibiotic resistance genes.
  - amp^R – contains restriction site for Pst I, Pvu I
  - tet^R – contains restriction site for Bam HI, Sal I

Insertional inactivation in pBR322

- Alien DNA ligated at BamI
- Tet^R gene inactivated
- Resistance to tetracycline lost
- Recombinants can grow on ampicillin medium but will die in tetracycline medium

Amp med – Recombinants + Non Recomb survive
Tet med – Recombinants die; only Non Recomb survive
Recombinants – propagated further

Replica plating experiment

- Selective growth of only recombinants can be done

Insertional inactivation of lac z

Hindlll SphI PstI SalI XbaI BamHI SmaI KpnI SacI EcoRI
Polylinker
lacZ'
ampR
2.7 kb
ori
lac promoter
pUC18 vector

Lac z gene codes for β-galactosidase
↓
It splits X-gal (chromogenic subs) into an insoluble blue product.
↓
When foreign gene is inserted into lac z gene, it is disrupted.
↓
Disruption stops its activity
↓
X-gal is not broken down due to inactive lac z gene
↓
Blue colour not produced.
↓
Colonies appear white.

This is called blue white screening

NEET SYNAPSE
Recombinant colonies appear white while non recombinant colonies appear blue.

4. Vectors for cloning genes in plants & animals.

PLANTS -

Agrobacterium Tumefaciens

- pathogen of dicot plants contain Ti plasmid
- Ti plasmid contains T DNA
- T DNA transforms normal plant cells into tumour cells.
- Tumour cells produce chemicals required by pathogen.
- Ti plasmid is disarmed and used for transferring desired genes into host plant.

ANIMALS

- Retroviruses can tranform normal animal cells into cancerous cells.
- Retroviruses are also disarmed and used to deliver desirable genes into animal cells.

COMPETENT HOST

- Bacterial cells are made competent to be able to take up plasmid DNA

How to make bacteria competent?

- Treat bacteria with divalent cation (Ca^{2+}, Mg^{2+}) - it causes precipitation of DNA on surface → facilitates DNA entry in the cell.

Bacterial culture with plasmids

- Bacterial cells now exposed to
  - Ice
  - Heat shock (42°C)
  - Ice

  } Creates pores in membrane
- Bacteria now take up rDNA

- **Electroporation** — low intensity
- Electric current applied to cell membrane to create temporary pores.
- Pores facilitate DNA entry

- **Microinjection**

r DNA directly injected into nucleus of animal cell

- **Biolistics / Gene gun**
- Suitable for plants
- High velocity microparticles of Gold or Tungsten are coated with DNA and are made to bombard plant cells.

- **Disarmed pathogen**
- Disarmed pathogen is allowed to infect cell & transfer rDNA into host

PROCESSES OF RDT

Isolation of Genetic material

- DNA isolation requires
- Breakage of cells
  - Bacterial - lysozyme
  - Plant - cellulase
  - Fungus - chitinase
- Removal of proteins (histones)
  - Proteases
- Removal of RNA
  - Ribonucleases
- Purified DNA precipitates after addition of chilled ethanol - SPOOLING

Cutting DNA at specific locations

- DNA incubated with RE.
- Gel electrophoresis done
- Fragments of alien DNA and vector DNA are joined by ligases to obtain rDNA

Amplification of gene of interest

PCR - Polymerase chain reaction

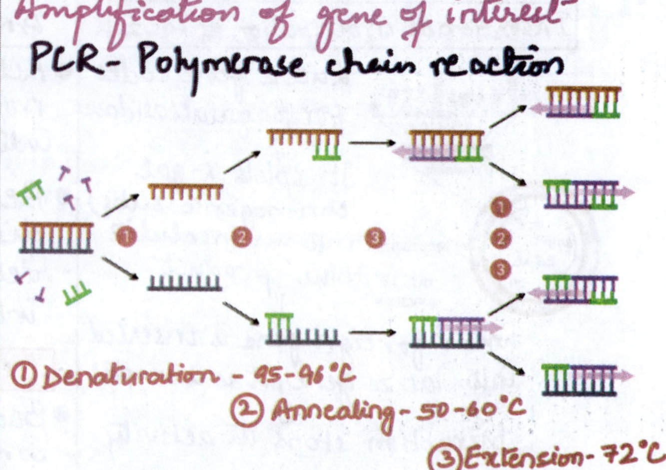

- Multiple copies of DNA synthesised in vitro
- Requirements
  - Two sets of primers
  - Nucleotides
  - DNA polymerase

NEET SYNAPSE
Thermostable DNA polymerase called Taq polymerase obtained from Thermus aquaticus

STEPS

1. Denaturation - breaking H-bonds ds DNA ⟶ ss DNA ; 92-94°C
2. Annealing - Addition of primers - 54°C
3. Extension - extending primers using Taq polymerase to form new DNA strand. Temp - 72-74°C

- DNA segment can be amplified to a billion copies
- Amplified DNA can be ligated with vector

Insertion of rDNA into host

- rDNA can be introduced into host cells by

Direct method	Indirect method
• Electroporation	• Agrobacterium mediated
• Biolistics	• Virus mediated
• Microinjection	
• PEG mediated	
• Heat shock; divalent cation	

- Selectable markers help in selection & propagation of transformants.

Obtaining the foreign gene product

Recombinant protein

- Protein obtained by a protein encoding gene in heterologous host
- Recombinant proteins can be obtained in large quantities by culturing bacteria in bioreactors.

BIOSYNTHETIC PHASE

- Synthesis of specific products, enzymes etc from raw materials under optimum cond. provided in a bioreactor.
- Bioreactor – large vessels – (100-1000 L)
- **Continuous culture** – used medium drained out from one side while fresh medium is added from other side
- Maintains maximum activity of bacterial cells – Log / Exponential phase.

Advantages

- Larger biomass
- Higher yield of protein

Disadvantages

- chances of contamination are high as it is open culture.

- **Batch culture**
- Microorganisms & nutrient medium added once and lid is closed
- Nothing is added during the process of fermentation.

Adv – chances of contamination are minimum.

Disadv – low productivity

- **Fed-batch culture**
- Nutrients are added to medium discontinuously during the fermentation process
- Semi open type of culture

Adv – Growth rate more as compared to batch culture

Disadv – Requires sophisticated equipment to control & monitor progress of fermentation.

Bioreactor

It possesses
- Agitator system
- Oxygen delivery system
- Foam control system
- Temperature control system
- pH control system
- Sampling ports – for periodic withdrawal of culture.

– It ensures optimum growth conditions (temp, pH, substrate, salts, vitamins, oxygen)

Commonly used bioreactors

Stirred tank bioreactor

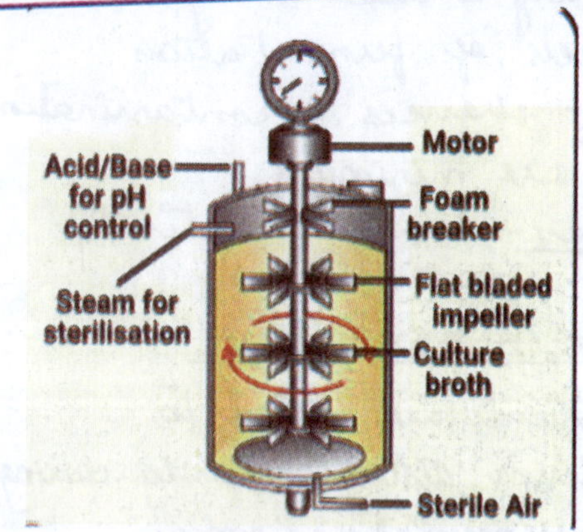

- Curved base for proper mixing
- Stirrer – for even mixing & Oxygen availability.

Sparged tank bioreactor

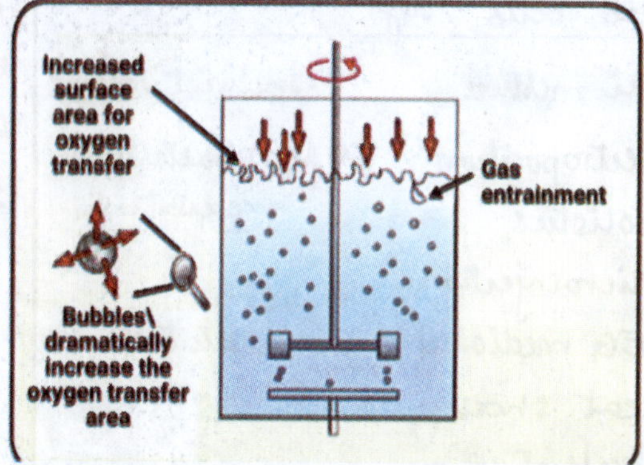

Air is bubbled through the bioreactor.

DOWNSTREAM PROCESSING

- Series of processes that a product is subjected to, before marketing.
- Steps

Separation
↓
Purification
↓
Addition of preservatives
↓
Clinical trials (drugs)
↓
Quality control testing
↓
Product is now ready for marketing.

29. Biotechnology and its Applications

- Critical research areas of biotechnology are
- To provide pure organism or enzyme
- To create optimal conditions for the process
- Downstream processing

APPLICATIONS IN AGRICULTURE

- Food production can be increased by
- Agrochemical based agriculture
- Organic agriculture
- Genetically engineered crop based agriculture

GREEN REVOLUTION

- Increased agricultural yield due to-
- Improved crop varieties
- Better management practices
- Use of agrochemicals

NEET SYNAPSE
Somatic hybrids are formed by fusion of protoplasts of two different plants.
Eg: Pomato = Potato + Tomato

GENETICALLY MODIFIED ORGANISMS

- Plants, bacteria, fungi, animals whose genes have been altered by manipulation.
- Advantages of GM crops
- Increased tolerance to abiotic stresses
- Reduced reliance on chemical pesticides
- Reduction in post harvest losses
- Increased mineral usage efficiency by plants.
- Enhanced nutritional value of food - Golden rice
- Tailor made plants can be created to produe starches, fuels, pharmaceuticals etc.

Examples of GMO's
Bt Cotton, Golden rice etc.

Bt COTTON

- Bacillus thuringiensis (Bt) can produce proteins against
- Lepidopterans (Tobacco budworm, Armyworm)
- Dipterans (Mosquitoes & flies)
- Coleopterans (Beetles)
- Bt forms protein crystals during spore formation
- Crystals contain toxic insecticidal protein
- In Bt protein is inactive protoxin, hence does not cause harm.
- When protoxin is consumed by insect, its crystals solubilise in alkaline pH of gut.
- Protoxin gets activated in alkaline pH
- Toxin binds to midgut epithelial cells of insect ⟶ creates pores ⟶ causes cell swelling & lysis.
- This causes death of insect.
- Bt toxins are insect group specific

[cry I Ac, cry II Ab] cotton bollworm] [cry I Ab - corn borer.]

GOLDEN RICE

- Variety of Oryza sativa, produced by genetic engineering.
- Biofortification of rice is done with β-carotenoid (precursor of Vitamin A)
- Gene for β-carotene was taken from daffodil.

PEST RESISTANT PLANTS

- Meloidogyne incognita infects roots of tobacco plants.
- RNA interference was done to prevent damage.

PRINCIPLE

- Silencing of a specific mRNA due to complementary ds RNA that binds to and prevents translation of mRNA (silencing)

Source of complimentary RNA

- Infection by RNA viruses
- Transposons that replicate via an RNA intermediate.

PROCESS

Nematode specific gene is isolated
↓
Introduced in vector *Agrobacterium tumefaciens*
↓
It infects host plant
↓
Sense and Anti sense RNA (dsRNA) produced in host plant
↓
ds RNA consumed by parasite (that attacks plant)
↓
ds RNA goes to parasite gut cells & gets cleaved to form si RNA (small interfering RNA)
↓
si RNA binds with RISC (RNA Induced Silencing Complex)
↓
In association with RISC - one strand undergoes cleavage and is destroyed.
↓
Other strand starts RNAi

It binds to mRNA sequence and stops translation of mRNA, thus the gene is stopped from expression (silenced)
↓
Thus parasite cannot survive & the host is protected from parasite.

APPLICATION IN MEDICINE

- 30 recombinant therapeutics have been approved worldwide.
- In India, 12 of these are marketed.
  Eg. Genetically engineered insulin.

NEET SYNAPSE

Insulin cannot be taken orally as it is digested upon by proteases in the stomach, hence it is injected.

GENETICALLY ENGINEERED INSULIN

Insulin consists of two polypeptides - Chain A and chain B linked by disulphide bonds.

- Insulin prohormone called proinsulin contains - A chain, B chain and an extra C chain.
- C peptide must be removed for conversion of proinsulin to insulin
- Eli Lily, an American company prepared DNA sequence for A chain and B chain separately.
- Then introduced them into plasmid of E. coli
- Thus A and B chains are produced separately & later joined by creating bonds.
- They were combined by disulphide bonds.
- Thus HUMULIN was produced.

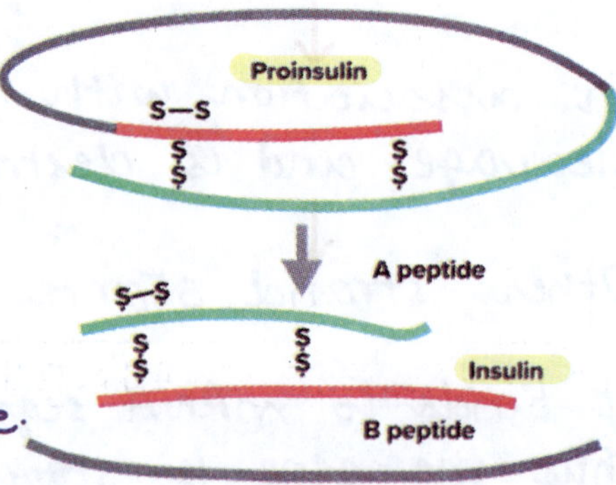

GENE THERAPY

- Correction of a genetic defect by replacing a faulty gene by a normal gene.
- This is done to restore the function of gene.

First clinical gene therapy - Done in 1990
In a 4 year old girl
Suffering from ADA deficiency
(ADA - Adenosine Deaminase)

ADA deficiency causes SCID (Severe Combined Immunodeficiency Disease)

NEET SYNAPSE

Humulin making procedure was improved in 1990 - Yeast was used instead of E. coli to make insulin chains A & B

TREATMENT MODALITIES

1. Enzyme Replacement Therapy
   Functional ADA is given to patient by injection.
2. Bone Marrow Transplant
   Bone marrow from healthy person is transplanted.
   Both of the above are not completely curative
3. Gene therapy
   Faulty gene is replaced by normal gene.

Process of Gene Therapy

Lymphocytes from blood of patient are grown in culture

↓

Functional ADA cDNA is introduced into these lymphocytes.

[Functional gene is incorporated in retrovirus genome → Retrovirus infects lymphocytes and induces the formation of cDNA (for ADA gene)]

↓

Thus, defective lymphocytes now have ADA gene and are called genetically engineered lymphocytes.

↓

These lymphocytes are introduced back into the patient.

Lymphocytes are mortal hence it is not a permanent cure. If gene isolate from marrow cells is introduced at early embryonic stages, it could be a permanent cure.

MOLECULAR DIAGNOSIS

Early diagnosis of a disease can be done by –

- RDT – Recombinant DNA Technology
- ELISA – Enzyme Linked Immuno Sorbent Assay
- PCR – Polymerase Chain Reaction.
  - ↳ very low concentration of virus or bacteria can be detected by amplification of their genetic material.

- Probe – a single stranded DNA or RNA tagged with a radioactive molecule.
  - used in molecular imaging for early diagnosis.

PROCESS OF USING A PROBE

DNA or RNA probes are capable of hybridisation with the sample DNAs

The radioactive labelled DNA/RNA probe would hybridise with its complimentary sequence in sample DNA

↓

If sample DNA has a mutation, then this hybridisation would not take place as desired.

↓

Thus mutation can be identified in places where no hybridisation takes place.

↓

This is done by autoradiography.

AUTORADIOGRAPHY

- A technique or photographic method that is used to detect radioactive materials.

ELISA

- Based on the principle of Antigen-Antibody interaction.
- Infection can be detected by the
  - presence of pathogens
  - presence of antibodies generated against pathogens.

TRANSGENIC ANIMALS

- Animals whose DNA has been manipulated to express a foreign gene.
- Over 95% of transgenic animals are mice.

USES OF TRANSGENIC ANIMALS

- Normal physiology and development
- Understanding the regulation and expression of gene
- Study of growth factors
- Studying the effects and results of such factors.
- Study of disease
  - understanding how genes contribute to development of disease
  - helps in developing new treatment modalities for disease
  - Transgenic animals are being used to study diseases like Alzheimer's, Rheumatoid Arthritis, Cancer, Cystic fibrosis.

BIOLOGICAL PRODUCTS

- Transgenic animals can produce useful biological products by introduction of foreign DNA sequences
- α-1 antitrypsin - to treat emphysema
- Human α lactalbumin - Human protein enriched milk produced by transgenic cow Rosie.
  This milk has high protein content (2.4%)
- Vaccine safety
  Transgenic mice are being used to test the safety of vaccines.
- Chemical safety testing
  Transgenic animals are more sensitive to toxic substances, ∴ they are good models for toxicity testing.

ETHICAL ISSUES

- Genetic modification of organisms can have unpredictable effects on the ecosystem.
- GEAC - Genetic Engineering Approval Committee
  - It makes decisions regarding the validity and safety of introducing GMO for public.

Patent - An exclusive right granted for an invention.
The inventor gets exclusive rights for the product / process.

- Developed countries and big companies are being granted patents for things that are indigenous to other people / places.

Eg. Rice - 200000 varieties of rice are present in India.
27 varieties of Basmati are found.

- An American company got patent rights on Basmati through US patent and trademark office.
- Indian Basmati was crossed with semi-dwarf varieties and was projected as novelty.
- Turmeric, Neem etc. are also being exploited for patent by western countries.

BIOPIRACY

- Use of bioresources by multinational companies without proper authorisation from countries and people without compensatory payments.
- Industrialised nations – Rich financially
  Poor in biodiversity
- Injustice, inadequate compensation and benefit sharing between developed and developing countries is growing in recent times.
- Exploitation of bio resources and traditional knowledge is taking place.
- Indian Parliament has cleared second amendment of Indian Patents Bill that deals with –
  - Patent terms emergency provisions
  - Research and development initiative.

30. Organisms and Population

POPULATION

- Group of organisms of the same species living in a particular area at a given time.

Community	Population
Group of individuals of different species living in an area.	Group of individuals of same species living in an area.
Interbreeding absent	Interbreeding present
Members are morphologically & behaviourally different	Members are morphologically and behaviourally similar
It is a large unit	It is a small unit
There is relationship of predation & prey.	No relationship of predation and prey.

POPULATION ATTRIBUTES

POPULATION DENSITY

- Number of individuals per unit area
- Represented as $D = \frac{N}{S}$ $\frac{\text{(Total no. of individuals)}}{\text{(Space / Area)}}$

NATALITY – Birth Rate

- Rate of production of new individuals per unit of population per unit time.
- Represented as $\frac{\Delta Nn}{\Delta t}$] N = Original no. of organisms, n = New individuals, t = time

MORTALITY

- Loss of individuals per unit time due to death.
- Calculated as $\frac{\Delta N}{N \Delta t}$

POPULATION DISPERSAL

- Emigration - outward movement of individuals. Decreases population
- Immigration - inward movement of individuals. Increases population

SEX RATIO

- Number of males & females in a population. Expressed as percentage.

NEET SYNAPSE

- Sometimes percentage covers or biomass is more meaningful than population size.
- Eg. Bacteria growing in a petridish.
- Sometimes relative density is a better measure to determine population density than measuring absolute density.
- Eg: no. of specific fish in a river. It is difficult to determine the exact number, hence a sample size is considered for determining the fish population.

AGE DISTRIBUTION

AGE PYRAMID

	Triangular	Bell shaped	Urn shaped
Pre reproductive	very large	equal number	lower
Reproductive	moderate	equal number	higher
Post reproductive	fewer	fewer	lower
	Growing population	Stable population	Declining population.

Post-reproductive
Reproductive
Pre-reproductive

POPULATION GROWTH

◆ Number of individuals added per unit population per unit time.

$N_t = N_0 + [(B+I) - (D+E)]$

N_t - Population at time t

N_0 - Initial population

B - Births ; I - Immigration

D - Deaths ; E - Emigration

Population increase $B+I > D+E$

Population decrease $B+I < D+E$

NEET SYNAPSE

In a newly settling population, immigration has more impact than birth rate

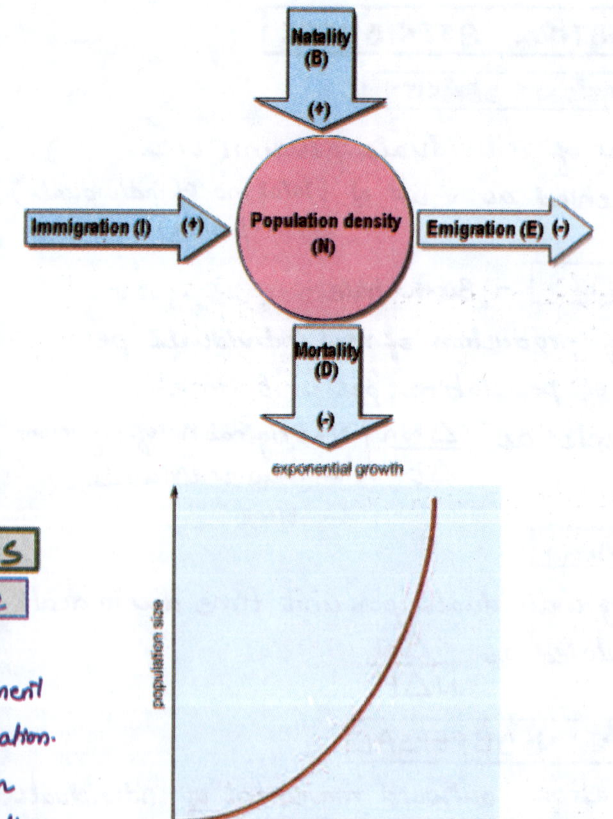

POPULATION GROWTH MODELS

J shaped / Exponential Growth Curve

◆ Shows unlimited resources

◆ Lag phase - organism adapts to environment
- no significant increase in population.

◆ Exponential phase - rapid reproduction
- Significant increase in population.

$\frac{dN}{dt} = rN$

N- Population size

t - Time

r- Intrinsic rate of natural increase

($r = b-d$)

Exponential growth equation

$N_t = N_0 e^{rt}$

N_t = Population density after time t

N_0 = Initial population

r = Intrinsic rate of natural increase

t = Time

e = base of natural logarithms.

S shaped / Sigmoid Growth Curve

- Limited resources
- Logistic Growth Curve
  Verhulst Pearl logistic growth.
- Lag phase - no significant increase in population.
- Acceleration phase - rapid increase in population. Attains full potential of growth.
- Deceleration phase - population begins to slow down as it approaches carrying capacity of the environment.
- Asymptote - population is stabilised
  Limited resources limit further increase in population.

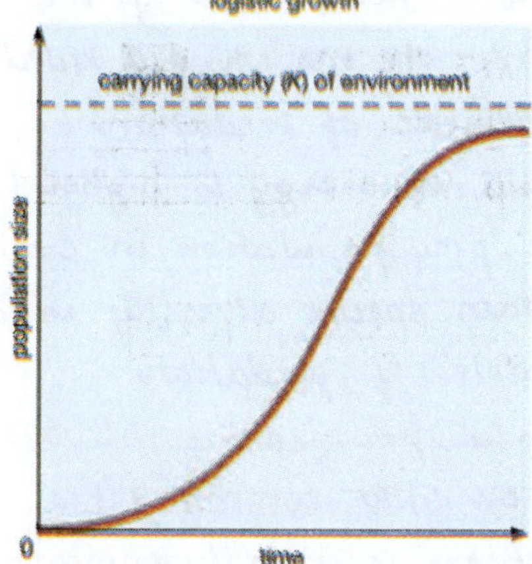

Logistic growth model is a more realistic growth model.

Carrying capacity (K) - maximum number of individuals that can be supported in the given environment with available resources. Beyond K, population starts to decline.

$\frac{dN}{dt} = rN\left[\frac{K-N}{K}\right]$ - N - Population size ; t = Time
K = Carrying capacity.

NEET SYNAPSE

Asymptote is achieved when K = N

LIFE HISTORY VARIATION

- Darwinian model - reproductive fitness (r) should be maximum
- Organisms breeding once in life ⟶ Pacific salmon fish, Bamboo
- Organisms breeding many times in life ⟶ most mammals & birds
- Organisms producing small size offsprings ⟶ Oysters, pelagic fish
- Organisms producing large size offsprings ⟶ Birds, mammals.

POPULATION INTERACTIONS

Negative interactions	Positive interactions	Neutral interactions.
◆ Predation	◆ Mutualism	◆ Commensalism.
◆ Competition		
◆ Parasitism		
◆ Amensalism		

NEET SYNAPSE
Interspecific (b/w species) interactions are based on Mode of obtaining food and habitat

PREDATION

- ◆ Predator - kills & eats up the prey
- ◆ Prey - the one who gets killed and eaten.
- ◆ Importance of predation
  - Conduits of energy to higher trophic levels.
  - Keeps prey population in control.
  - Maintain species diversity in a community.

Animal predator - carnivore
Plant predator - herbivore

PREDATORS MUST BE PRUDENT IN NATURE - If predators do not remain careful & exhaust the prey population, they may die of starvation in the absence of prey.

- ◆ Examples of predation
  - Prickly pear cactus introduced in Australia - became invasive weed. It was later controlled by introducing Cactoblastis (moth - predator of Cactus)
  - In rocky intertidal communities of American Pacific Coast, starfish Pisaster is a predator - when all starfish were removed, prey species (invertebrates) became extinct due to increased interspecific competition.

Prey adaptations to reduce predation

1. Camouflage - blend with the surroundings
   - evade detection by predators.
2. Mimicry
   - one organism (mimic) resembles another (model)
   - mimic behaves like someone who is disliked by predator.
   - Viceroy butterfly mimics monarch butterfly (acquires distasteful chemicals during larval stage.
3. Chemical defence - Prey secretes poisonous substances that keep predators away.

Defence adaptations in plants -

1. Thorns - in Acacia, Cactus - keep predators away.
2. Chemical substances - nicotine, caffiene, quinine etc keep predators away.
   - Calotropis produces highly poisonous cardiac glycosides to reduce the impact of predators.

COMPETITION

- Closely related species compete for same resources.
- Totally unrelated species can also compete for same resources
  Eg: Visiting flamingoes and resident fishes compete for zooplanktons in South American lakes.
- Interference competition
  Resources are abundant; competition occurs due to interference (feeding efficiency)
  Eg: Abingdon tortoise in Galapagos islands became extinct within a decade of goat introduction in the habitat.

NEET SYNAPSE

Competition is a process in which the fitness of one species (r) is lower in the presence of another species. (r - intrinsic rate of natural increase)
It may lead to death of some individuals of weaker species.

- Competitive release
  Weaker species expands its distribution range upon removal of competitively superior species.
  Eg: Connel's Field Experiment
  In rocky sea coast of Scotland, Balanus (superior barnacle) dominates the intertidal area and excludes Chathamalus (small barnacle).
- Gause's competitive exclusion principle
  Applicable only when resources are limited.
  States that - two closely related species competing for the same resources cannot co-exist indefinitely.
- Resource partitioning
  If two species compete for the same resource, they can avoid competition by partly dividing their resources.
  Eg: Mac Arthur showed 5 closely related species of warblers co-exist due to difference in foraging activities.

• Carnivorous animals like lions & leopards occupy the same niche, but lions predate mostly on larger animals while leopards mostly prey on smaller animals.

PARASITISM

- Parasite gets benefitted at the expense of host.
- Ectoparasites
  live on external surface
  Eg: lice on humans, ticks on dogs
  copepods on marine fish
  Cuscuta on hedge plant.
- Endoparasites
  Live within host's body
  Life cycles are more complex due to high specialisation.
- Brood parasitism
  Parasitic bird lays eggs in host's nest & lets the host incubate them.
  Parasitic bird's eggs look like host's eggs to avoid detection.
  Cuckoo (koel) lays its eggs in crow's nest (host) and the crow incubates them.

NEET SYNAPSE
Co-evolution of parasites- Host specific parasites must evolve in accordance of evolution of host in order to avoid rejection or resistance by host.

- Adaptations of parasites
  1. Loss of unnecessary sense organs
  2. Presence of suckers or hooks
  3. Loss of digestive system
  4. High reproductive capacity
  5. Thick integument (to avoid digestion)
  6. Life cycle may have 1 or 2 hosts.
     Monogenetic - one host eg: Ascaris
     Digenetic - two hosts eg: Plasmodium (requires vector for completing lifecycle)
     ↳ Primary & Intermediate
     Fasciola hepatica - snail & fish (intermediate hosts)

Obligate parasites
Live entirely as parasites- eg. Plasmodium.

Facultative parasites
Can live parasitic as well as free living stages.

- Effect of parasite on host
  Parasite reduces the host's
  Survival, Growth, Reproductive capacity, Population density.

AMENSALISM

- One member is harmed, another member is not affected.
  Eg: Penicillium releases penicillin which harms bacteria & their growth whereas Penicillium remains unaffected.

COMMENSALISM

- One species is benefitted, another is neutral.
- Orchid (+) growing as epiphyte on mango tree (0)
- Barnacles (+) growing on back of whale (0)
- Cattle (0) and egret (+) - egret eats insects which cattle walk.
- Sea anemone (0) and clown fish (+) - fish is protected from predation

MUTUALISM

- Both species are benefitted from their association.
- Lichens - algae + fungi
  - main body is formed of fungus (mycobiont) - provides fixation, water, minerals & shelter to algae.
  - Phycobiont (algae) - makes food (PS)
- Mycorrhizae - association of fungi with roots of higher plants.
- Plants & animals - animals - disperse seeds
  - carry out pollination

  plants - provide 'nectar' & food.

Pollen robbers - Animals that steal nectar without aiding pollination.

NEET SYNAPSE

Coevolution of flower & pollinator (species specific)

Eg. Fig & wasp

Female wasp uses fig for [oviposition
nutrition from seeds & fruits for larvae.

In return wasp pollinates fig inflorescence.

Sexual deceit

- Ophrys & bee - One petal of Ophrys resembles female bee.
  - Male is attracted to it & carries out pseudocopulation.
  - During the process, it transfers pollen.
  - Hence pollinates the flower.

Co-evolution - If female bee changes its pattern & colour, pollination will be reduced, thus Ophrys will have to co-evolve to look like female bee to ensure pollination.

31. Ecosystem

TYPES OF ECOSYSTEM

- Ecosystem = biotic community + physical environment.

1. Natural ecosystem – they operate and maintain themselves without any human interference. They can be –

Terrestrial	Aquatic
Land ecosystems. Includes forest, grassland, desert etc.	Includes freshwater (rivers, lakes) and marine ecosystems (sea, ocean)

2. Artificial ecosystem – maintained by humans for different purposes.
   – Include crop lands & artificial lakes.

COMPONENTS OF ECOSYSTEM

1. Abiotic components – Non living components.
   Include water, minerals, gases, salts, temperature etc.
   Edaphic – inorganic & organic nutrients in soil.
   Topographic – Latitude & altitude.

2. Biotic components – Include living organisms. They can be –

Producers (Autotrophs)	Consumers (Heterotrophs)	Decomposers
Make their own food Convert solar radiation into chemical energy Aquatic ecosystem Rooted & floating plants and phytoplanktons	Depend on plants & other animals for food. They can be primary, secondary & tertiary. Aquatic ecosystem Zooplanktons, small & large fishes.	Feed on dead & decaying matter. They bring about cyclic exchange of materials b/w biotic & abiotic components.

NEET SYNAPSE

Stratification – vertical distribution of species at different levels in ecosystem.
Eg. trees occupy top strata followed by shrubs, herbs and grasses.

FUNCTIONS OF ECOSYSTEM

1. Productivity
2. Decomposition
3. Energy flow

PRODUCTIVITY

- Primary production
  Amount of organic matter accumulated per unit area over a period of time by plants during photosynthesis.
  Expressed in terms of weight (gm^{-2}) or energy ($kcal\ m^{-2}$)

- Productivity — Rate of biomass production.
  Expressed as $gm^{-2}yr^{-1}$ or $kcal\ m^{-2}yr^{-1}$

Primary productivity
- Rate at which solar energy is stored in the form of chemical energy in plants.
- It varies in different plants in different habitats.

Secondary Productivity
- Rate of formation of new organic matter by consumers
- They utilise the food taken from producers to make their own organic matter.

Gross Primary Productivity (GPP)
- Rate of production of organic matter during photosynthesis
- A part of GPP is used for maintenance of plants i.e. respiration.

Considerable GPP is utilised during respiration.

Net Primary Productivity (NPP)
- Gross Primary Productivity minus Respiration losses.
  GPP − R = NPP
- Represents the biomass available for consumption by consumers.

Important points
- Primary productivity depends upon –
  - photosynthetic activity of plants.
  - availability of nutrients
  - environmental factors.

All ecosystems exhibit homeostasis – self regulatory mechanisms to maintain balance.

NEET SYNAPSE
- Annual NPP of whole biosphere = 170 billion tons (dry wt.) organic matter.
- Productivity of ocean = 55 billion tons (though oceans occupy 70% of earth's surface)
- Land productivity = 115 billion tons

DECOMPOSITION

- Physical & chemical breakdown of complex organic matter.
- Decomposers - bacteria & fungi.

PROCESS OF DECOMPOSITION

Fragmentation - Detritivores (eg. earthworm) feed on detritus and break it into smaller particles.

Leaching - Water soluble inorganic nutrients go down in the soil and precipitate as unavailable salts.

Catabolism - breakdown of detritus into simpler inorganic substances

Humification - Decomposition of organic matter form a dark, amorphous substance called humus. It doesn't breakdown easily. It releases nutrients over a period of time.

Mineralisation - Release of inorganic matter during the process of decomposition makes the soil mineral rich. Hence, it is called mineralisation.

NEET SYNAPSE

Mycorrhiza - Fungal association with roots of higher plants. Can enhance decomposition by stimulating saprotrophic microbes.

FACTORS AFFECTING DECOMPOSITION

1. Chemical nature of detritus -
   Slow Decomposition - detritus contains lignin, chitin, tannins or cellulose
   Rapid Decomposition - detritus contains more nitrogenous compounds eg. proteins, nucleic acids, carbohydrates etc.
2. Temperature - Maximum decomposition - 25°C
   decomposers are most active at this temp.
   Decomposition is slow at lower temp
   Enzymes of decomposers are most active at 25°C, hence rapid decomposition occurs. Enzymes are inactive at lower temp.
3. Moisture - Optimum humidity favours decomposition.
4. Aeration - Oxygen is needed for the activity of decomposers. Hence aeration is an important factor.

ENERGY FLOW

- Flow of energy in an ecosystem is unidirectional.
- Ultimate source of energy - Sun
- Photosynthetically Active Radiation (PAR) - The solar energy that is available to plants for photosynthesis. - less than 50% of incident sunlight
- 2-10% of PAR is utilised by plants for photosynthesis.

NEET SYNAPSE

Solar energy ⟶ falls on land ⟶ less than 50% available for PS (PAR) ⟶ utilise only 2-10% for production (rest is lost through radiation, absorption etc.)

FOOD CHAIN

- Transfer of food or energy through a set of organisms.

Producers ⟶ Herbivores ⟶ Carnivores [a simple food chain]

Eg. Pond ecosystem,
Producers - phytoplankton, consumers - herbivores etc.

TYPES OF FOOD CHAIN

Grazing Food Chain (GFC)

- Major conduit of energy flow in aquatic food chains.
- Starts from green plants and ends at carnivore.
- Also called predator food chain.

Detritus Food Chain (DFC)

- Major conduit of energy flow in terrestrial food chains.
- It begins from dead organic matter.
- Microbes like bacteria & yeast degrade the dead organic matter.
- These microbes are called saprotrophs or decomposers.

FOOD WEB

- Various food chains that intersect and interact with each other for a food web.
- The same organism may operate at more than one trophic level.
- The same organism may be eaten by several organisms of higher trophic level.
- Food chains are generally short; food webs are elaborate.

TROPHIC LEVELS

- Each level in food chain is a trophic level.

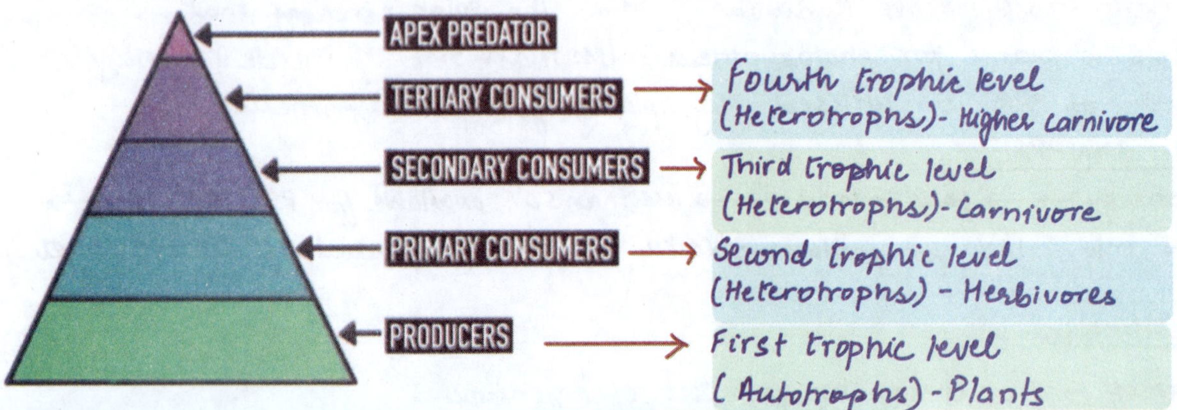

- TERTIARY CONSUMERS → Fourth trophic level (Heterotrophs) - Higher carnivore
- SECONDARY CONSUMERS → Third trophic level (Heterotrophs) - Carnivore
- PRIMARY CONSUMERS → Second trophic level (Heterotrophs) - Herbivores
- PRODUCERS → First trophic level (Autotrophs) - Plants

NEET SYNAPSE

Interpretations
- Primary consumers feed upon primary producers.
- Primary carnivores are secondary consumers
- Primary carnivores feed upon herbivores.
- Herbivores are primary consumers.

Number of trophic levels is equal to the number of steps in food chain.

Standing crop – Each trophic level contains certain mass of living matter (biomass) at a particular time. It is called standing crop.

10% LAW OF ENERGY TRANSFER

- Only 10% of energy is transferred to each upper trophic level from the lower trophic level.

- The rest 90% of energy is lost in the environment as heat or is consumed for respiration, digestion etc.

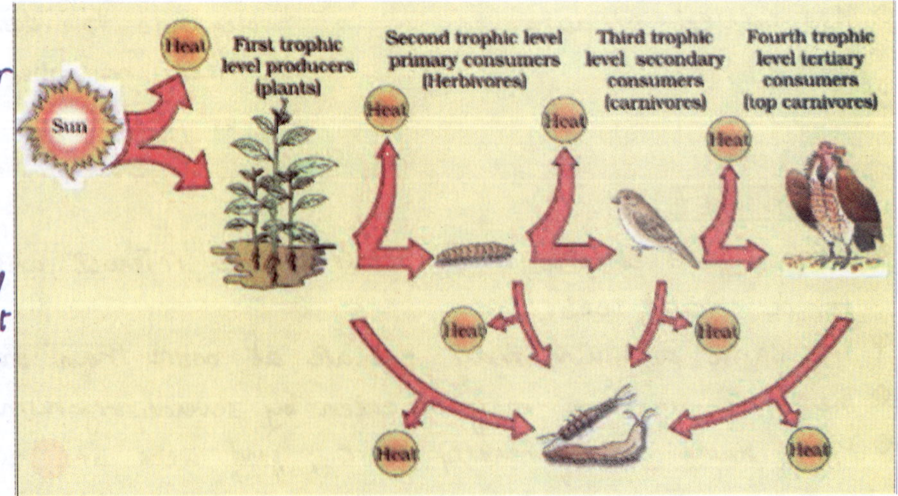

ECOLOGICAL PYRAMIDS

Concept of pyramids was given by Charles Elton.

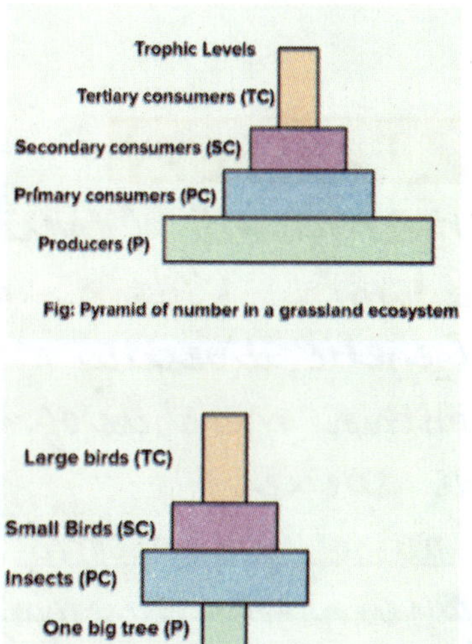

Fig: Pyramid of number in a grassland ecosystem

Fig: Pyramid of number on a tree ecosystem

PYRAMID OF NUMBER

Deals with number of producers & consumers.

1. Upright pyramid - most common.
   - no. of producers > no. of consumers.
2. Inverted pyramid - seen in tree ecosystem
   - 1 large size tree (producer)
   - many birds (consumers) feed on it
   - ectoparasites are more than birds.

   ∴ no. of consumers > no. of producers.

PYRAMID OF BIOMASS

Amount of living matter present in an ecosystem.

1. Upright pyramid - tree supporting large no. of birds.
2. Inverted pyramid - in a pond ecosystem large fish (consumer) eats large no. of phytoplanktons.

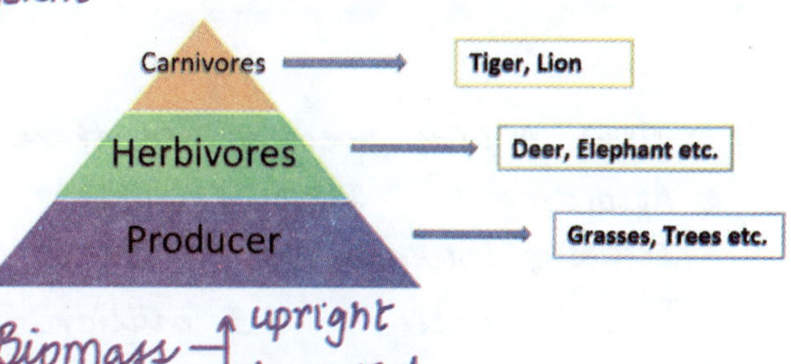

Biomass — upright / inverted

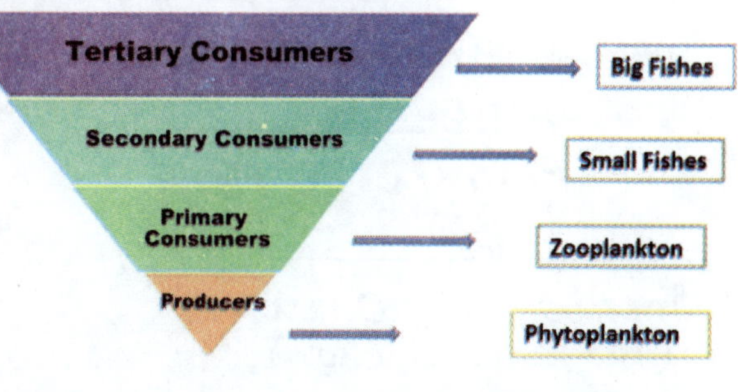

PYRAMID OF ENERGY

Always upright

Follows the 10% law of energy transfer.

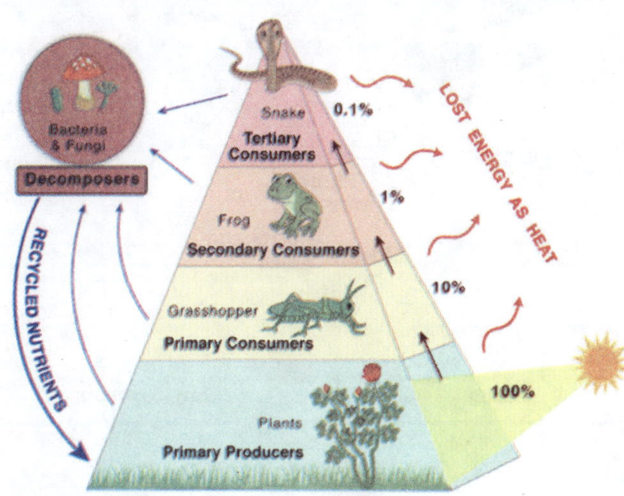

NEET SYNAPSE

Decomposers are not given any space in the ecological pyramids, despite playing major role in returning nutrients back to the environment.

32. Biodiversity and Conservation

BIODIVERSITY

- Heterogeneity (diversity) exists at all levels of organisation.
- Edward Wilson described biodiversity at various levels.

Genetic diversity
Within members of a species
Rauwolfia vomitoria - different varieties may have different concentrations of Reserpine.

Species diversity
At the level of species of a genus
Amphibian species diversity is more in the Western Ghats than Eastern Ghats.

Ecological diversity
At the level of biomes
Desert, rain forests, mangroves, coral reefs, wetlands, estuaries etc.
India has more ecosystem diversity than Norway.

How many species are there on Earth?

- According to IUCN (2004)
[IUCN - International Union of Conservation of Nature and Natural Resources]
- Total species - 1.5 million
- Robert May estimates global species diversity at 7 million.

Species
- Animals (70%)
  - Insects (70%)
  - Others (30%)
- Plants (22%)

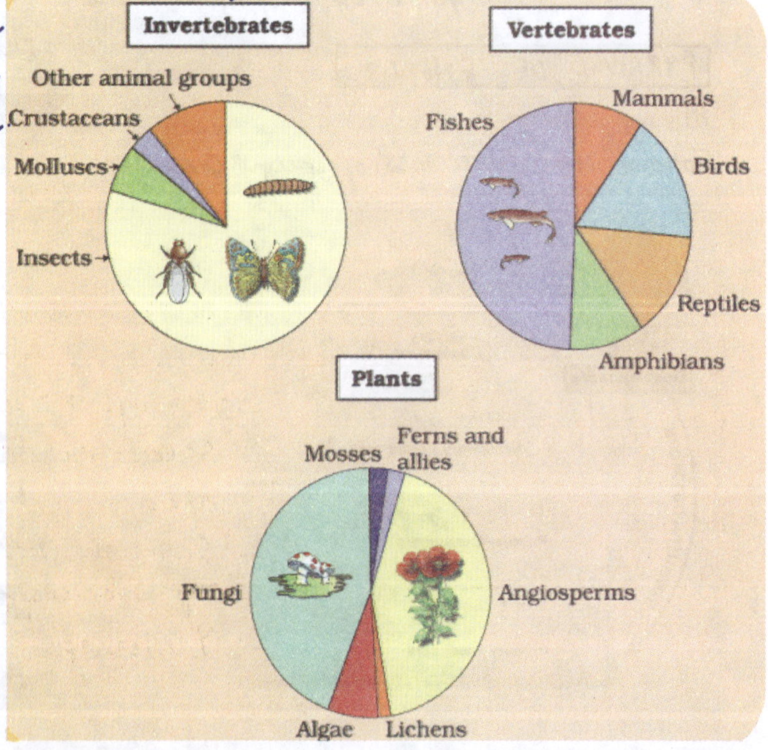

NEET SYNAPSE
- Plants include fungi, algae, bryophytes, gymnosperms and angiosperms.
- Microbes have not been included.

DIVERSITY IN INDIA

- Land area occupied by India - 2.4% of world's land area
- India's contribution to global species biodiversity - 8.1%
- 45000 plants species are present in India
- 90000 animal species are present in India

Nature's library is buring even before we catalogued the titles of all books stored there - large number of these species face the threat of becoming extinct even before discovery.

PATTERNS OF BIODIVERSITY

1. LATITUDINAL GRADIENT

- Species diversity decreases as we move from equator to poles.
- Amazonian rain forest has the greatest biodiversity on Earth.

Why species diversity is maximum at the tropics?

a) Speciation is a function of time - tropical latitudes have been undisturbed for millions of years, thus had more time for species diversification & evolution.

b) Tropical environment is less seasonal - climate remains constant which promotes niche specialisation → leads to greater biodiversity.

c) More solar energy - leads to higher productivity → greater diversity.

2. SPECIES AREA RELATIONSHIP

- Alexander Von Humboldt observed - within a region, species richness increased with increasing explored area but only upto a limit.

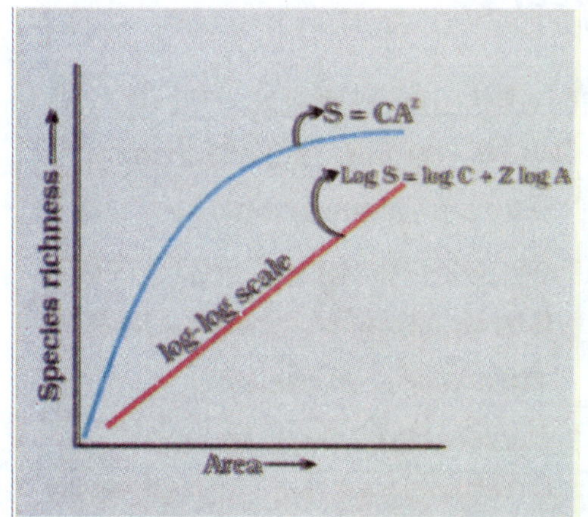

$S = CA^z$

On a log scale line this relation is -

$\log S = \log C + Z \log A$

S - Species richness

A - Area

Z - Slope of line (regression coefficient)

C - Y intercept

Relationship between species richness & area is Rectangular Hyperbola

NEET SYNAPSE

Value of Z → 0.1 - 0.2

Value of Z over large continents → 0.6 - 1.2 (steep slope)

Value of Z for animals in tropical forests → 1.15

In tropical regions, it is more likely that more species are present in lesser area, thus steeper slopes are observed.

IMPORTANCE OF SPECIES DIVERSITY IN ECOSYSTEM

- Communities with more species tend to be more stable than those with less species.
- Stable community
  - no variation in productivity from year to year.
  - resistant to invasion by alien species.
  - resilient to man made & natural disturbances.
- David Tilman's experimental observations-
  - Plots with more species showed less year to year variations in total biomass
  - Increased diversity contributed to higher productivity.

Paul Ehrlich - Rivet Popper Hypothesis

- Airplane = Ecosystem
- Rivets = Species

In an airplane all parts are joined by rivets.

- Removing rivets (species) from airplane (ecosystem) might not affect its stability initially but will affect dangerously in long run.
- Loss of rivets from crucial areas like wings (key species that drive ecosystem) will be a serious threat to airplane (ecosystem)

LOSS OF BIODIVERSITY

IUCN Red list documents extinction.

Some recent extinctions

Dodo- Mauritius
Quagga- Africa
Thylacine- Australia
Stellar's Sea Cow- Russia
Bali, Javan, Caspian (Tiger subspecies)

5 episodes of mass extinction have occurred in last 3 billion years.

Loss of biodiversity may lead to

- Decline in plant production
- Lowered resistance to environmental disturbances like drought, floods etc.
- Increased variability in plant productivity water use and pest & disease cycles

NEET SYNAPSE

Sixth mass extinction-
- Is in progress
- Is occuring at 100-1000 times faster than pre human times
- Occurring due to anthropogenic activities.

THE EVIL QUARTET

1. HABITAT LOSS AND FRAGMENTATION

Habitat loss

- Amazon rain forest (lungs of the planet) are being cut and cleared to grow soyabeans or conservation of grasslands for raising beef cattle.
- Degradation of many habitats by pollution also threatens the survival of many species.

Fragmentation

- Human activities ⟶ break up large habitats (fragmentation) ⟶ adversly affects mammals & birds requiring large territories ⟶ leads to decline in population.

2. OVER EXPLOITATION

- Over usage of some animals for human benefits has led to their extinction.
- Eg. Stellar's sea cow, Passenger pigeon
- Some marine fish are at the verge of extinction.

3. ALIEN SPECIES INVASION

- Alien species when introduced in a new habitat can turn invasive.
- This can cause harm to native species leading to their extinction.
- Eg. Nile perch introduced into Lake Victoria caused extinction of 200 species of cichlid fish in the lake

Carrot grass (Parthenium), Lantana, Eicchornia (water hyacinth) } posed a threat to our native species.

NEET SYNAPSE

Clarias gariepinus (African catfish) posing a threat to indigenous catfish in our rivers.

4. CO-EXTINCTION

- Species in obligate association with each other tend to become extinct if one of them evolves.
- Eg. Co-evolved plant pollinator relationships.
  Fish and parasite relationships.

BIODIVERSITY CONSERVATION

NARROWLY UTILITARIAN

- Conservation of biodiversity for human economic benefits.
- For food, wood, fibre, construction material, industrial products & medicines.
- More products of human benefit are yet to be discovered.

Bioprospecting - exploring molecular, genetic and species level diversity for products of economic importance.

BROADLY UTILITARIAN

- Biodiversity should be protected for intangible benefits like-
  - O_2 from plants (Amazon rainforest produces 20% of total O_2 of Earth's atmosphere)
  - Pollination - necessary for producing fruits & seeds.

NEET SYNAPSE - Bees, bumblebees, birds & bats are important pollinators.

  - Aesthetic pleasure } pleasant experiences.
  - Bird's chirping } pleasant experiences.
- These are all non economical benefits.

ETHICAL REASONS

- Ethically all animals and plants should be conserved.
- All living organisms share common habitats - we share common habitat with plants, other animals and microbes.
- Every species has an intrinsic value - even if it is not economical

HOW TO CONSERVE BIODIVERSITY?

IN SITU CONSERVATION

- On site conservation
- Save the entire forest to save the tiger
- Maximum protection to be given to 'biodiversity hotspots'.

Biodiversity hotspots - regions with high species richness and high degree of endemism

NEET SYNAPSE

Total number of biodiversity hotspots in the world - 34

- Biodiversity hotspots in Indian Subcontinent
  - Western Ghats
  - Sri Lanka , Indo-Burma
  - Himalayas

- In situ Conservation areas
  - Biosphere reserves → 14
  - National parks → 90
  - Sanctuaries → 448

	INDIA
Biosphere reserves	14
National parks	90
Sanctuaries	448

- Sacred grooves - Religious and culturally important areas that are given protection.
  - Eg: • Khasi & Jaintia hills, Meghalaya
    - Aravalli hills of Rajasthan
    - Western Ghats of Maharashtra & Karnataka
    - Sargiya , Chandar & Bastar of MP.

EX SITU CONSERVATION

- Off site conservation

Desirable when an organism is facing very high risk of extinction.
Threatened animals & plants are taken out from their natural habitat & placed in protected special setting.

- Ex situ Conservation areas
  - Zoological parks
  - Botanical gardens
  - Wildlife safari

Advantages
- Animals and plants can be preserved
- Gametes can be preserved in viable and fertile condition through cryopreservation.
- Eggs can be fertilised in vitro
- Plants can be propagated through tissue culture methods.
- Seeds can be preserved in seed banks.

Earth Summit - held in Rio de Janeiro (1992) - Various nations pledged
Appropriate measures for conservation of biodiversity.
Sustainable utilisation of its benefits.
World Summit on Sustainable Development - held in Johannesberg (2002)
190 countries pledged to achieve a significant reduction in the rate of biodiversity loss at global, regional & local levels.

NOTES

NOTES

NOTES

NOTES

NOTES